DRAWING THE LINE

DRAWING THE LINE

The Korean War, 1950–1953

RICHARD WHELAN

LITTLE, BROWN AND COMPANY

BOSTON   TORONTO   LONDON

FIRST EDITION

The maps appearing on pages x and xi are drawn
by George W. Ward, d'Art Studio.

The maps appearing on pages 102, 187, 244, and 309 by Raphael Palacios
are from *The Korean War* by Matthew B. Ridgway, copyright © 1967 by Matthew B. Ridgway,
and are used by permission of Doubleday, a division of Bantam, Doubleday, Dell Publishing
Group, Inc.

Excerpts from *Memoirs* by Harry S. Truman, published by Doubleday & Co., Inc., 1955, are
used by permission of Margaret Truman Daniel.

Excerpts from *Memoirs, 1925-1950* by George F. Kennan, copyright © 1967
by George F. Kennan, are used by permission of Little, Brown and Company.

Library of Congress Cataloging-in-Publication Data
Whelan, Richard.
    Drawing the line : the Korean War, 1950-1953 / Richard Whelan. —
1st ed.
        p.   cm.
Includes bibliographical references.
ISBN 0-316-93403-8
1. Korean War, 1950-1953. I. Title.
DS918.W46 1990
951.904'2 — dc20   89-13559
                                                              CIP

10   9   8   7   6   5   4   3   2   1

RRD-VA

Published simultaneously in Canada
by Little, Brown & Company (Canada) Limited

PRINTED IN THE UNITED STATES OF AMERICA

Dedicated
to the memory of my great-uncle,

John T. Reardon,

who for many years was
chairman of the History Department
at the Taft School, Watertown, Connecticut,
and who first inspired in me a love of history.

Contents

Illustrations follow page 174 and page 302.

Maps appear on the following pages: The Far East During the Korean War, page x; Korea, page xi; North Korean People's Army Invasion Routes, page 102; Landing at Inchon, page 187; Chinese Communist Intervention, page 244; Stalemate, page 309.

Acknowledgments

FROM AMONG THE MANY PEOPLE who have contributed to this book in one way or another, there are five to whom I must give special thanks: Melanie Jackson, my agent, without whose expertise, encouragement, and fine critical judgment I would be lost; Ray Roberts, my editor, who guided, coaxed, nurtured, and stood by me through thick and thin; Deborah Jacobs, whose superb copyediting greatly strengthened my manuscript; and Evan Cornog and Ann Goldstein, my landlords and friends, in whose house — full of light, good spirits, good food, and good books — I wrote this book.

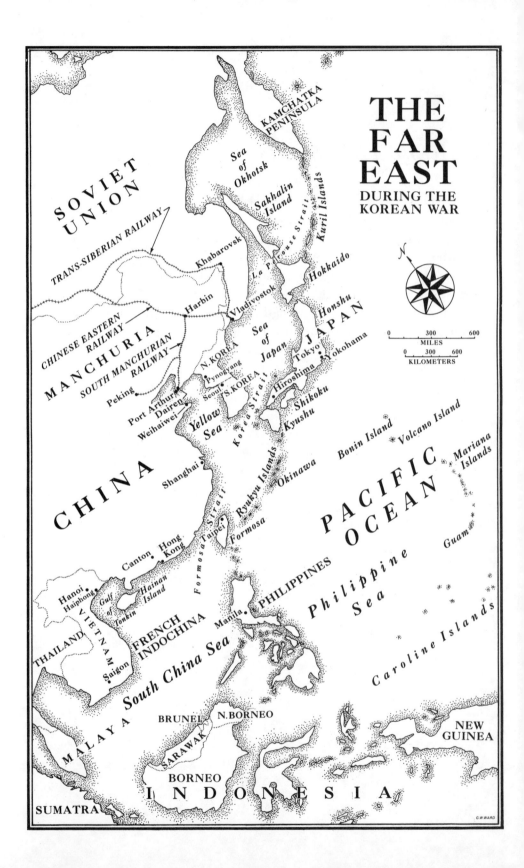

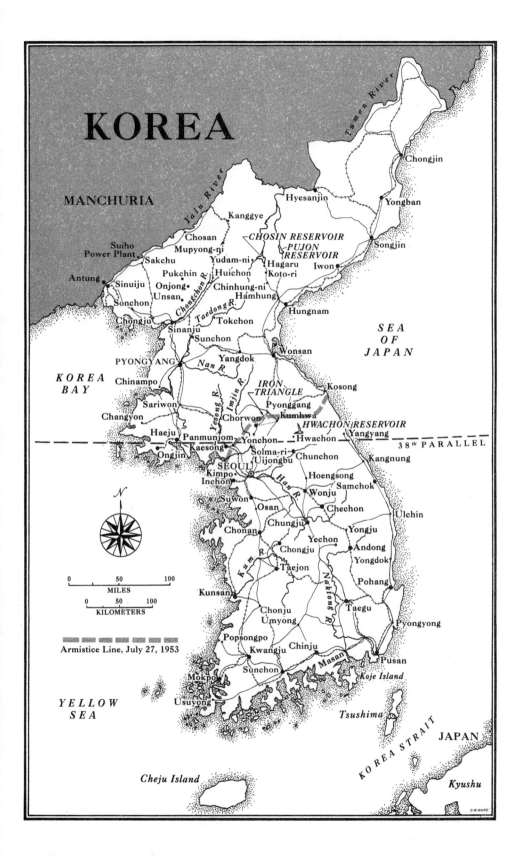

KOREA

MANCHURIA

Tumen River

Chongjin

Hyesanjin

Yongban

Kanggye

Songjin

CHOSIN RESERVOIR
PUJON
RESERVOIR

Chosan

Suiho
Power Plant

Mupyong-ni

Sakchu

Yudam-ni

Hagaru

Iwon

Antung

Pukchin

Huichon

Koto-ri

Sinuiju

Onjong

Chinhung-ni

Sonchon

Unsan

Hamhung

Chongju

Sinanju

Tokchon

Hungnam

Sunchon

SEA
OF
JAPAN

PYONGYANG

Yangdok

Wonsan

KOREA
BAY

Chinampo

Nan R.

IRON
TRIANGLE

Kosong

Sariwon

Pyonggang

Changyon

Chorwon

Kumhwa

HWACHON RESERVOIR

Haeju

Panmunjom

Yonchon

Hwachon

Yangyang

Ongjin

Kaesong

Solma-ri

38th PARALLEL

Uijongbu

Chunchon

Kangnung

SEOUL

Kimpo

Hoengsong

Inchon

Wonju

Samchok

Suwon

Osan

Chechon

Ulchin

Chungju

Yongju

Chonan

Yechon

Andong

Chongju

Yongdok

Taejon

Pohang

Kunsan

Chonju

Taegu

Umyong

Pyongyong

Popsongpo

Kwangju

Chinju

Masan

Pusan

Sunchon

Koje Island

Mokpo

Usuyong

Tsushima

YELLOW
SEA

KOREA STRAIT

JAPAN

Kyushu

Cheju Island

0   50   100
MILES

0   50   100
KILOMETERS

Armistice Line, July 27, 1953

G.W.WARD

Yalu River
Chongchon R.
Taedong R.
Yesong R.
Imjin R.
Han R.
Kum R.
Naktong R.

Introduction

ON JUNE 25, 1950, when the armed forces of Soviet-dominated North Korea invaded American-sponsored South Korea, most Americans hardly even knew Korea's location. Korea might as well have been an Asian Ruritania for all they knew or cared. But as reservists found themselves called up to fight again only five years after the end of World War II, and as families pored over maps in the daily papers in an effort to pinpoint where their sons and daughters, spouses, and parents were serving, Americans soon learned more than they had ever wanted to know about Korean geography.

Yet most Americans never really understood why the United States was fighting in Korea — why more than 5.7 million Americans served in the armed forces there between 1950 and 1953 or why some 33,000 of them died there from combat wounds or in captivity. They understood, of course, that the United States was determined to halt the spread of Communism. However, that truism didn't go very far toward answering the fundamental question, Why Korea? or its corollaries: Why did the Truman administration decide to intervene militarily in small and remote Korea after having done nothing more than protest as all of Eastern Europe and all of China fell under Communist domination? (In point of fact, Korea is neither very small nor especially remote. A unified Korea, though it would still be dwarfed by its neighbor China, would have an area only slightly smaller than the combined total of England, Scotland, and Wales. As for its remoteness, Korea occupies a central position between Japan and northern China.) Why was the U.S. government willing to go to the brink of World War III in order to save the repressive and only nominally democratic South Korean regime of Syngman Rhee? And why did the United States, the most powerful nation in the world after World War II, limit its strategy during the Korean War in such a way as to preclude the kind of total, resounding victory that the American public had come to expect as a result of the two world wars?

Those are among the questions that this book attempts to answer.

In doing so, it will focus more on the political than on the purely military aspects of the war and will examine "the Korean conflict," as it was officially designated by Washington, within the context of the global Cold War.

No one likes to dwell on his own failures, and the American public — most of which has since December 1950 wrongly perceived the Korean War as a failure — is no exception. Americans tend to regard the Korean War as an embarrassment best forgotten, as "the first war we lost." Even General Mark W. Clark, the American commander in the Far East in July 1953, added to that sense by lamenting that he "had gained the unenviable distinction of being the first United States Army commander in history to sign an armistice without victory." And yet the United States had accomplished what it originally set out to do: it prevented a Communist conquest of South Korea. Was that not a victory, even though the United States had failed in its misguided attempt to unify Korea under an anti-Communist government? Nevertheless, lacking a constituency as effectively militant as that of Vietnam veterans, the Americans who died in the Korean War still have no monument in Washington to commemorate them.

It is doubly unfortunate that so much of the American public and military establishment regarded Korea as a failure, for that judgment had much to do with the inception and conduct of the Vietnam War. To a great extent Vietnam began as an attempt to restore American military pride, as an effort to recoup the prestige that had been lost in Korea. And when things began to go wrong in Vietnam, memories of Korea perversely made American military leaders all the more determined to continue, certain that they could profit from their earlier mistakes and thus do things right the second time around. Tragically, the Korean War failed to teach the United States the vital lessons — about Asian nationalism as distinct from international Communism, about the impossibility of fighting a "moral" war against guerrillas, and about the futility of technological warfare against an enemy largely independent of mechanized transport — that might have spared the nation the fiasco of Vietnam.

Although the vast majority of Americans now know little more about the Korean War than what they have gleaned from the immensely popular television series *M★A★S★H*, the war was by no means a minor episode in American history, no mere "police action," as President Harry Truman described it at the outset (to his later regret). The Korean War was, rather, a turning point in postwar history, with momentous repercussions worldwide. It provided the stimulus that transformed NATO from a paper alliance into a powerful force for the defense of Western Europe. It gave the United States undisputed leadership of the United Nations and damaged that organization's usefulness as an international ombudsman by making it (temporarily at least) a virtual tool that America could manipulate while pretending to be its obedient servant. The war gave the Truman administration the justification it needed for quadrupling the American military budget within two years, thereby triggering the endless and exorbitant arms race. And it led the administration to reverse its earlier repudiation of Chiang Kai-shek's regime on Formosa, thereby exacerbating the tensions between the United States and Communist China, which developed into a bitter, twenty-year hatred once Peking had intervened in Korea, in the fall of 1950.

The Korean War greatly strengthened the special relationship between the United States and Britain. It brought to an end two decades of Democratic monopoly on the White House. It fostered the integration of white and black troops within the American army. And, as the first major military conflict of the Cold War, it demonstrated that the United States could, after all, oppose localized Communist aggression without having that response escalate uncontrollably into a nuclear world war.

From the perspective of global affairs, the Korean War had far less to do with Korea than with Japan and Germany. Joseph Stalin certainly authorized the North Koreans to invade the south because he wanted to counterbalance the steps that the United States was then taking to rehabilitate and to rearm Japan and West Germany. The Korean invasion proved to be one of the Soviet leader's most serious mistakes. For one thing, the fears of further Communist aggression that were intensified by that invasion contributed more than any other single factor to the speeding up of the very processes that had disturbed Stalin; the Korean War consolidated the international anti-Communist coalition. For another, the military aid that circumstances forced the Soviet Union to give to Communist China during the war did much to transform the latter into a major military power, to the Soviets' eventual chagrin when, in the mid-1950s, the Chinese felt strong enough to challenge their former patrons for leadership of the international Communist movement.

In a sense, the Korean War was a world war in miniature, in which military forces from seventeen anti-Communist nations (including South Korea) faced the North Koreans and the Chinese Communists. The figure rises if we discard the then-convenient fiction of Soviet noninvolvement and also count those UN members who sent medical units to Korea. In addition, we must take into account those non-belligerent nations, such as Japan, West Germany, and the Republic of China on Formosa, whose fates were profoundly affected by the war. It is as a world war, in this sense, that this book will consider the Korean War.

General Bradley said that we must draw the line [against Communist expansion] somewhere.

The President stated he agreed on that.

General Bradley said that Russia is not yet ready for war. The Korean situation offered as good an occasion for action in drawing the line as anywhere else.

— From the official minutes of
President Harry S. Truman's meeting
with his top military and foreign-
policy advisers at the Blair House
on the evening of June 25, 1950

DRAWING
THE LINE

CHAPTER 1

Korea and Yalta

THE SOVIET UNION was at war with Japan for only the last week of World War II. An atomic bomb was dropped on Hiroshima on August 6, 1945. Two days later Stalin declared war on Japan. Nagasaki was bombed the next day, and on the tenth the Japanese offered to surrender on the condition that the emperor be allowed to remain in power. The Allied reply, drafted in Washington, was intentionally ambiguous, for President Truman was prepared to agree to that condition but could not do so explicitly, since the American public would be satisfied with nothing less than unconditional surrender — and a majority of Americans wanted the emperor to be deposed and tried as a war criminal. But Hirohito read between the lines, as he was meant to do, and decided to accept the terms of the reply. Japan announced its surrender on the fifteenth.*

The war was over, but the role in Far Eastern affairs to which Stalin's declaration of war had entitled him — and which the hasty occupation of Manchuria and northern Korea by his troops guaranteed that he would play to the hilt — would lead, in less than five years, to the Korean War.

Stalin's policy in regard to entering the war against the Japanese was very simple: he had been determined all along to declare war upon Japan so that he would be able to claim a share of the victors' spoils, but he was also determined to wait until the last possible moment so that he could achieve maximum gains with minimal expenditure. Washington, however, was eager for the Soviets to enter the war in Asia as soon as possible. The question of Soviet involvement in the Far East forced Franklin Delano Roosevelt to play political poker against Stalin, and it happened that the latter was both lucky and an

---

* Because of the time difference and the international date line, it was still August 14 in Washington. Such discrepancies confuse all chronologies of Western dealings with the Far East.

expert bluffer. When he finally laid his cards on the table, in August 1945, the Americans were furious that he had taken the pot with such a poor hand.

When Roosevelt, Winston Churchill, and Stalin met at Yalta, on the Crimean coast of the Black Sea, in February 1945, the atomic bomb was far from ready to be tested, and although the directors of the Manhattan Project felt reasonably certain that a successful test could be made that summer, there was neither any guarantee that the bomb would work nor a consensus about how quickly the war could be brought to an end even once a stockpile of bombs became available for use. (For one thing, there was much disagreement over how powerful the bomb would prove to be.) The simple fact was that Allied military planners couldn't afford to base their strategy on an untried weapon. They had to be prepared for the worst-possible-case scenario, which predicted that Germany might hold out until the end of the year and that Japan might be able to fight on for as much as another year and a half after Germany's defeat — until the middle of 1947. The Allied plan called for a primarily American force to undertake an amphibious invasion of the Japanese home islands, beginning early in November 1945. Since the fanaticism with which the Japanese defended barren Pacific islands of little worth would surely be surpassed by that with which they would defend their home, estimates of probable Allied casualties ranged as high as one million.

The Allied planners' worst fear was that the Japanese Kwantung Army, which was occupying Manchuria, might be transferred to the defense of the home islands. American intelligence believed that this army, officered by archmilitaristic fanatics, numbered upward of seven hundred thousand crack troops and was extremely well equipped. As early as November 1944 the American Joint Chiefs of Staff had prepared a report stating that to prevent such a transfer the Soviet Union must engage the Kwantung Army in Manchuria at least three months before the Allied invasion of Japan was scheduled to begin.[1] That meant that the Russians would have to declare war on Japan and launch their attack on Manchuria early in August. At Yalta, Stalin promised Roosevelt no more than that the Soviets would enter the war in Asia within three months after Germany's surrender. (At the Tehran Conference, in late November 1943, Stalin had given FDR a general promise that the Russians would fight the Japanese after the Germans had been defeated; now that promise was reaffirmed and made more specific.)

Despite his strenuous later denials, in February 1945 even General Douglas MacArthur himself felt that it was absolutely essential to get the Russians to promise to take on the Kwantung Army. On February 13, two days after the end of the Yalta Conference, a War Department representative observing the campaign in the Philippines wrote a letter to General George C. Marshall, the army chief of staff, in which he summarized an hour-and-a-half conversation that he had had with MacArthur, who

> stressed the potency of the Japanese army and stated that when we entered Japan we must be prepared to reckon with the Japanese army in far greater strength than is there now. He was apprehensive as to the possibility of the movement of the bulk of the Manchurian Army and other Japanese forces from China to the defense of the homeland. He emphatically stated that we must not invade Japan proper unless the Russian army is previously committed to action in Manchuria. . . . He said that it was only necessary for action to commence in Manchuria to contain that force of Japanese in order to make possible our invasion of Japan and the rapid conclusion of the war. *He understands Russia's aims; they would want all of Manchuria, Korea, and possibly part of northern China. This seizure of territory was inevitable;* but the US must insist that Russia pay her way by invading Manchuria at the earliest possible date after the defeat of Germany [emphasis added].[2]

MacArthur was thus willing to see Russia rewarded for its services with far more than Roosevelt had just promised Stalin at Yalta. He was even willing to let the Russians have Korea.

In their November 1944 report the Joint Chiefs of Staff had observed that self-interest would "inevitably bring the Soviet Union into the war [in Asia] sooner or later" if Japan didn't attack it first.[3] There could be little doubt in any quarter that Stalin wanted very badly the advantages in the Far East that only a declaration of war against Japan could win for him. But there were considerable grounds for wondering whether even such an absolute dictator had the power to rally his devastated and exhausted nation to take on the Japanese. Perhaps as many as twenty million Russian soldiers and civilians had died in the war against Germany; thousands of Russian towns and villages had been completely obliterated by the ebb and flow of battle; and the nation's agricultural and industrial productivity had been decimated.

It was, however, precisely the ruination of European Russia that made Stalin so determined to develop Soviet power in Asia. Manchuria and Korea constituted one of the world's greatest industrial, agricultural, and transportation complexes — and this fantastically valuable region was already connected to Siberia and western Russia by the Trans-Siberian Railway and its branch lines. Stalin's dream was to incorporate Siberia, Manchuria, and Korea into a single great economic system that could sustain the Soviet Union while its western areas recovered from the war.

The five-year plans of the 1930s had done much to plant the seeds of heavy industry in western Siberia and all along the route of the railway. Fearing Hitler, Stalin had ordered thousands of factories in western Russia to be disassembled, transported in pieces across the Urals, and there reassembled, out of reach of a German invasion. A few major centers of industry, such as Novosibirsk, often called the Chicago of the Soviet Union, began to flourish. But Siberia remained a largely undeveloped frontier whose stupendous mineral resources could be effectively exploited after the war only if the Soviets had unlimited access to the factories, the food supplies, and the ice-free ports of southern Manchuria and Korea, which the Japanese had developed into a highly integrated system.

As a concentration of industry and agriculture, Manchuria mirrored the prewar Ukraine, the richest area of western Russia, which the "scorched earth" policies of successive Soviet and German retreats had destroyed. The value of the Ukraine, with its ports on the Black Sea, had in any case always been limited by Britain's success in ensuring that Russia would never gain control of the straits that connect that sea with the Mediterranean — a policy that Churchill continued to advocate passionately throughout World War II and after. The British feared that if the Russians gained a foothold in the eastern Mediterranean, they might soon become rivals for control of the Suez Canal, of Middle Eastern oil supplies, and even of India. Throughout the nineteenth century, every British victory over Russian expansionism in southeastern Europe forced the strangled giant to search elsewhere for outlets to the sea. As both a European and an Asian nation, Russia turned invariably to the Far East, and especially to Manchuria and Korea, which the Russians had come to view as the Pacific counterpart of the Ukraine-Balkan–Black Sea complex. (There are obvious geo-economic parallels between the mountainous Korean peninsula and the mountainous Balkan peninsula.)

Russian foreign policy from the midnineteenth century onward — indeed, up to the present day — has been shaped largely by an endless struggle to gain absolute control over at least one of those two complexes. Thwarted in the West, Russia would turn its attention to the East, and vice versa. Thus it was that, with his country having suffered so grievously in the West during World War II, Stalin set his sights on the East for the resurrection of the prostrated Soviet nation. But he could make the necessary gains in the East only if the Soviet Union contributed to the defeat of Japan.

Russia's horrendous suffering put Stalin in an excellent position for bargaining with his allies at Yalta. He was, in fact, able to insist on being enticed to do what nothing could have stopped him from doing. Among other factors, it was essential for the Americans and the British to be on good terms with the Soviets so that once Germany was defeated the United States could safely withdraw its troops from Europe and transfer them to the Pacific, without fearing that the Russians would move into the vacuum and occupy all of Europe. Concessions to the Soviet Union in the Far East would not only help to maintain a friendly relationship among the Allies but would also, of course, induce Stalin to transfer a substantial number of his own divisions to Asia, thereby reducing the potential Soviet military threat in the West.

At Yalta, Stalin promised that the Soviet Union would enter the war against Japan in return for four major concessions: (1) Outer Mongolia would remain a Soviet satellite, independent of China; (2) sovereignty over the Kuril Islands and the southern half of Sakhalin Island (both lying north of Japan and offshore from Siberia, Sakhalin having been divided between Russia and Japan since 1905) would be transferred from Japan to the Soviet Union; (3) a joint Sino-Soviet company would be formed to manage the Manchurian railways; and (4) the commercial port of Dairen, the terminus of the South Manchurian branch of the Trans-Siberian Railway, would be internationalized, and the Soviet Union would be permitted to lease neighboring Port Arthur as a naval base from China.[4]

Although many historians and politicians have expressed outrage over Roosevelt's having "sold China down the river" at Yalta, the greatest problem with the Yalta agreement was not that FDR had given Stalin so much but that Stalin had asked for so little. Roosevelt was pleased because he felt that the agreement formally and clearly limited the Soviet Union to a minor role in Asia while promising to spare the United States hundreds of thousands of casualties. The agreement was unusual in that both Roosevelt and Stalin were genuinely satisfied with it (since each put his own, quite different interpretation on it). The very ease of the negotiations misled FDR into concluding that American and Soviet goals in the Far East were not incompatible.

Not only did Stalin tacitly endorse the Open Door policy by agreeing that the Soviet Union would recognize and respect China's full sovereignty over Manchuria, but he also agreed to sign a pact of friendship and alliance with Chiang Kai-shek's government. That meant that Stalin implicitly acknowledged Chiang as the legitimate ruler of China and repudiated the Chinese Communists.

Unfortunately, Stalin had a more realistic view of Chiang than did Roosevelt. FDR thought that a China securely ruled by Chiang would emerge from the war as a strong, united, democratic, and pro-American nation. But Stalin saw that Soviet support of Chiang would guarantee a weak and strife-torn China unable to make excessive demands in return for Russia's economic paramountcy in Manchuria. His ideal was a China in which a pliant Chiang, grateful for Soviet endorsement, remained seriously threatened by the Chinese Communists. If necessary, Stalin would even secretly give enough aid to the Communists to ensure that Chiang would not be able to eliminate them. The Soviets could then play each side against the other to gain concessions. It was the old principle of divide and rule.

Both Roosevelt and Stalin wanted Chiang to be strong enough to block any Japanese attempts at resurgence. But while Stalin wanted Chiang to be weak enough to be manipulated, Roosevelt wanted him to be strong enough to resist manipulation by the Soviets. Korea figured into the president's plan to that end. It would serve as a bridge between northern China and Japan, just as it had served under the Japanese for decades, but now the profits would flow to China, not to Japan. The natural resources, the hydroelectric power, the railroads, and the ports of northern Korea would continue to serve the industry of Manchuria, which (with the help of lucrative American investments and trade) would become the cornerstone of China's new wealth and power. Korea itself would provide markets for China, and Korea's surplus rice would help to feed China's millions.

By the time of the Potsdam Conference, in mid-July 1945, the United States found itself in an awkward position regarding the Soviet Union's entry into the war in Asia. Roosevelt had died in April, to be succeeded in office by his vice president, Harry S. Truman. Disillusioned by Soviet actions in Poland, the Americans had realized that Russian troops would impose pro-Soviet governments in all the areas they occupied. Consequently, Washington assumed that if the Soviets occupied Manchuria, they would violate the Yalta agreement and turn the region into a satellite. That would weaken China and strengthen the Soviet Union to an unacceptable degree. Within days of becoming president, Truman had adopted a "get tough" attitude, but that had apparently led Stalin to worry that he would have to deal with an antagonistic America after the war. That fear prompted him to try to grab all the more so that the Soviet Union would be in the strongest possible position from which to hold its own against the Americans. Stalin's actions caused Truman to get all the angrier and tougher, and so on to extreme polarization.

The opening of the Potsdam Conference coincided with the successful testing of the first atomic bomb, at Alamogordo, New Mexico, but even then no one could be absolutely certain that the use of such a weapon against Japan would bring about an immediate and unconditional surrender. The Americans ardently hoped that it would do so before Stalin had had a chance to declare war against Japan. The Yalta agreement would then become null and void, and Stalin would have no legal claim to any gains at all in the Far East. The war would be over before the Soviet troops could even begin to occupy Manchuria.

But Truman hedged his bet. If the atomic bomb failed to bring a swift Japanese surrender, and if the Americans were going to have to invade Japan after all, they would want the Russians to deal with the Kwantung Army. Therefore, Truman assured Stalin that he was still counting on Soviet help in Manchuria. The Russians confirmed that they were planning to declare war on Japan on or about August 8, exactly three months after Germany's surrender. Hence the Americans frantically rushed to drop an atomic bomb on Japan before that date. The bombing of Hiroshima was thus almost as much anti-Soviet as it was anti-Japanese.

On August 8 Soviet foreign minister Vyacheslav Molotov informed the Japanese ambassador in Moscow that as of the following day the Soviet Union would be at war with Japan. The Japanese government was absolutely thunderstruck by the news, for the Russo-Japanese neutrality pact was not due to expire until April 1946. Japan was every bit as shocked by the blow as the United States had been by Pearl Harbor or as the Soviet Union had been by Germany's invasion in 1941. The fact that the Japanese surrender offer did not immediately follow the bombing of Hiroshima, but came only after the Soviet declaration of war, gave Stalin grounds for claiming that fear of Russia rather than fear of the atomic bomb had been the decisive factor in prompting the capitulation.

The atomic bomb was the ultimate extremist weapon, designed to relieve the United States of the need to negotiate. The American government hoped and expected that with the bomb in its pocket it would be able to dictate terms both to Japan and to the Soviet Union. The fear and resentment that it fostered among the Soviets, as well as the arrogance and unwillingness to compromise that it fostered among the Americans, did more than anything else to create the extreme polarization that led to the Korean War.

The central paradox of American foreign policy is that the vast majority of Americans generally tend to be extremist only in their hatred of, and in their reaction to, extremism. (Extremism is here defined as an unwillingness to compromise and a willingness to resort to violence in order to achieve the complete realization of one's radical goals.) Americans have an extreme hatred of extremism because it forces them to take extreme measures, and such measures are un-American and indeed subversive of all that America stands for. Reasonableness, compromise, moderation, and fair play are the prerequisites of democracy — for democracy requires prosperity, which in turn requires a level of stability that permits the long-range planning on which average businesses thrive. Extremists jeopardize stability by weakening or eliminating the center, thus giving rise to polarization. (The story of the Russian Revolution is largely that of Lenin's unrelenting and successful efforts to discredit and to break up the moderate and liberal coalition that took over when the czar abdicated. By polarizing the Russian people into extreme leftist and extreme rightist camps, Lenin removed all possibility of compromise or cooperation so that violent confrontation would be inevitable.)

The tragic irony is that the usual American response to extremism is itself extremist, even though such a response automatically puts the United States at a disadvantage by exacerbating the very polarization that it seeks to eliminate. An extremist response attempts not to remedy the conditions or to resolve the underlying conflict that led to the antagonist's extremism in the first place, but rather to teach the enemy a lesson that he will never forget and to render him incapable of making any further trouble. In American eyes, war (the ultimate form of extremism) is a regrettable measure to which the United States can be driven only by outrageous provocation on the part of foreign extremists. It must always be a crusade of innocent Good (the United States) against perversely aggressive Evil. Its purpose is not merely to thwart the enemy's designs but to demonstrate that trouble-making extremism is doomed, and that the American way — the way of strength and prosperity, of democracy, negotiation, and cooperation — is best and will triumph, always and everywhere, through the use of extreme violence if necessary.

The extremist American response to Japanese extremism led the American public to demand Japan's unconditional surrender, which prolonged the war until the Soviets were ready to enter, and it led to the use of the atomic bomb, which ushered in the Cold War. Extremism divided Korea. And the extremist American response to North Korean extremism led in the fall of 1950 to the counterinvasion of North Korea and thus to Chinese Communist intervention in the Korean War. The lesson seems to be that extremism must be met not with more extremism but rather with self-protective firmness tempered by understanding and a willingness to negotiate. Extremism is irrational; the difficulty is in responding to it rationally.

CHAPTER 2

The Russo-Japanese Rivalry in Northeast Asia

BY THE YEAR 1890 competition for control of Korea had spawned a deep and lasting enmity between Russia and Japan. Throughout the nineteenth century Russia had pursued its own version of Manifest Destiny by expanding eastward into Central Asia and the Far East, and Russian pioneers had begun to settle the frontiers of relatively hospitable southern Siberia, just as their American counterparts were claiming and populating the Far West. In Korea, Russia's eastward imperialist expansion collided directly with Japan's westward expansion onto the continent of Asia.

In Russia, as in America, railway construction played a vital role in colonization. Begun in 1891, the Trans-Siberian Railway would connect western Russia with the czar's principal Pacific port of Vladivostok, founded thirty years earlier. (It is revealing of Russian intentions that the city's name means "ruler of the East.") But if the railway was to parallel the Russo-Chinese border, its route would be circuitous — adding years to the construction time and days to the journey between Moscow and Vladivostok. The most direct route ran straight through the middle of Manchuria. In 1896 the representatives of Czar Nicholas II were able to persuade the beleaguered Chinese government to lease the right-of-way to Russia, and in 1903 the Chinese Eastern branch of the Trans-Siberian was completed. That same year the Russians also completed the South Manchurian line, which connected the Chinese Eastern with the Russian-leased Chinese ports of Dairen and Port Arthur. Thus was fulfilled at long last the Russian dream of unrestricted and profitable access to ice-free ports (Vladivostok was icebound for at least four months a year) giving quite directly (with no closable straits) onto major intercontinental trade routes. There were no such ports in European Russia.

The railways had provided both the excuse and the means for the Russians to take over Manchuria. Russian railway officials and merchants had established themselves around depots and had begun to transform their settlements into booming cities, in which Russian interests naturally had to be protected by Russian guards. During the construction of the railways, Russian entrepreneurs had obtained concessions to timber rights in order to supply needs ranging from roadbed ties to housing for the growing Russian population. And since Manchuria is rich in coal, it was only natural that the Russian railways should purchase mining rights to provide fuel for their locomotives.

In 1900, attacks upon Russian enterprises in Manchuria by the violently antiforeign Boxer movement gave the czar a pretext for sending in troops to occupy the region. By refusing to remove them even after the uprising had been put down, he incurred the wrath of the Americans and the Japanese, for both nations viewed Manchuria as a potentially lucrative market and area for investment. American secretary of state John Hay's 1899–1900 declarations of the Open Door policy had been specifically directed against Russian hegemony over Manchuria, for he felt that only so long as the decrepit Chinese Empire retained its sway over the region would the door remain open for American business. Yet, as the historian A. Whitney Griswold wrote, after the Boxer Rebellion even Secretary Hay himself was forced to accept "the fact that Manchuria was no longer an integral part of the Chinese Empire, but rather a Russian province."[1]

The Japanese feared that the next step would be for Korea to become a Russian province. In the Sino-Japanese War of 1894–95, Japan had succeeded in eliminating the last vestiges of the suzerainty that China had held over Korea for centuries. But when Japan then moved rapidly and ruthlessly to assert its own suzerainty — going so far as to murder Korea's powerful and anti-Japanese queen in October 1895 — the ineffective Korean king turned to Russia for help. For nearly a decade, until early in 1904, the Korean government would remain strongly pro-Russian, and Russian protection against Japan would afford Korea a period of liberalization and progress.

Barred from political dominance, the Japanese nonetheless managed to dominate the Korean economy during that period. In 1903, wishing both to extend its economic penetration into Manchuria and to remove the military threat to its investments in Korea, Japan demanded (with American and British support) that the Russians evacuate their troops from Manchuria, that they promise to respect

Chinese sovereignty over that region, and that they recognize Korea as Japan's exclusive sphere of influence and interest. This was more than even vulnerable Russia, with its shaky government and shaky economy, could agree to. The czar counterproposed that Japan recognize Manchuria as a Russian protectorate in return for Russian recognition of Japan's similarly imperialistic ascendancy in Korea. Or else, if Russia were to evacuate its troops from Manchuria and to acknowledge the region once again as an integral part of China in which Russian predominance would be purely economic, then it would want to be rewarded with the extension of its Manchurian sphere of economic influence. The enlarged sphere Russia demanded would have included all of Korea north of the 39th parallel of latitude (approximately sixty miles north of the present border between North and South Korea).[2] The failure to resolve this dispute led directly to the outbreak of the Russo-Japanese War, in February 1904.

Around the turn of the century the British government had decided to back Japan in order to keep Russia so embroiled in Northeast Asia — in Manchuria and Korea — that the czar would have neither opportunity nor resources to meddle in southeastern Europe or the Middle East. Accordingly, in January 1902, Great Britain concluded a treaty of alliance with Japan, the first such treaty on equal terms ever negotiated between a great Western power and a non-Western nation. The British intended the treaty to make the Japanese feel strong enough (and proud enough) to confront Russia with large and forceful demands. Britain was obligated to go to Japan's aid only if the Russians struck first, which they were quite certain not to do as long as the result would be war with an Anglo-Japanese coalition. The idea was not to help Japan gain predominance in Northeast Asia but rather to create a delicately balanced situation in which Japan and Russia would become mired in endless wrangling and hostilities. Neither of them would be in any position to challenge British interests elsewhere.

The Americans, too, hoped that Japan would do their dirty work for them. Secretary of State Hay observed to President Theodore Roosevelt in April 1903, "I take it for granted that Russia knows as we do that we will not fight over Manchuria, for the simple reason that we cannot. . . . If our rights and interests in opposition to Russia in the Far East were as clear as noonday, we could never get a treaty through the Senate, the object of which was to check Russian aggression."[3] How splendidly convenient it would then be if Japan could be induced to drive the Russians out of Manchuria — assuming, of course, that having done so with generous American encouragement, Japan would feel bound to return the region to Chinese sovereignty, thereby throwing open its doors to American business.

The Americans and the British thus had different reasons for supporting Japan, but their tactics were very similar. The key in both cases was to give Japan implicit permission to use Korea as a mainland base of operations against Russia. At the beginning of January 1904 the American ambassador to Korea informed the State Department that although he was "no pro-Japanese enthusiast," he thought that "Korea should belong to Japan by right of ancient conquest and tradition. I think our Government will make a mistake if it tries to have Japan simply continue this fiction of independence."[4] The department's leading expert on China agreed. He considered the annexation of Korea to be "absolutely indicated as the one great and final step westward of the Japanese Empire," and he felt that it would be "better for the Korean people and also for the peace of the Far East" once Japan was firmly in control of the peninsula.[5] President Roosevelt wasn't yet prepared to go quite that far, but in March he remarked to the Japanese ambassador that he saw no reason that Japan shouldn't have with Korea a relationship "just like we have with Cuba," which in 1902 had been established as a nominally independent republic under American "protection" and completely in thrall to American investments.[6]

By the middle of 1905 Japanese military successes against Russia had changed Roosevelt's thinking. His fear was now that Japan, intoxicated with confidence, might come to aspire to hegemony over a great Pacific empire. He was especially worried about the Philippines, over which the United States had recently established control in order to use the islands as a staging area for greatly expanded trade with China. Thus, when Secretary of War William Howard Taft visited Tokyo in July 1905 to work out the preliminaries for Roosevelt's mediation of the Russo-Japanese War, he negotiated an agreement with Prime Minister Taro Katsura whereby the United States acknowledged Japan's "suzerainty over" Korea in return for assurances that Japan would not challenge America's position in the Philippines.[7]

The terms of the Treaty of Portsmouth (September 1905), which ended the Russo-Japanese War, awarded Japan the right to establish a protectorate over Korea and transferred to Japan the Russian leases to the South Manchurian Railway and to Dairen and Port Arthur. The settlement, which had been reached with President Roosevelt's intercession, made Japan the dominant power in Northeast Asia, so much so that had it not been for TR's championing of the Open Door principle of China's territorial integrity, Japan would have claimed political sovereignty over southern Manchuria at once, rather than settling for merely economic and strategic dominance. Because the Japanese had been forced to relinquish some of what they believed they had legitimately won — including the right to annex southern Manchuria and the right to demand a large indemnity from the czar to put their war-exhausted economy back on its feet — many of them felt that Roosevelt had betrayed Japan and favored Russia. Huge anti-American riots broke out in many Japanese cities. Although Roosevelt won a Nobel Peace Prize for his role in the negotiations, he had planted the first seeds of the Japanese-American animosity that would lead directly to World War II in the Pacific.

The Japanese proceeded to declare a protectorate over Korea in 1905, and five years later they formally annexed it as a colony, justifying the move by claiming that the insufficiently advantageous terms of the Treaty of Portsmouth left them no choice if their economy was to recover from the recent war. Over the succeeding years Japanese investments developed the tremendous industrial and agricultural potential of Korea and Manchuria to serve Japan's needs.

Korea was an overwhelmingly agrarian nation whose principal crop was rice. This the colonial authorities shipped in ever more extortionate quantities to Japan, where it fed the rapidly growing number of industrial workers, whom Japan's own severely limited agricultural capacity could not support. So much rice was exported from Korea that huge numbers of Korean farmers had none left for themselves; they had to buy such cheaper and (to the Koreans and the Japanese) unpalatable grains as millet, barley, and corn, grown on the rich black soil of the great Manchurian plain, which also produced most of the soybeans so vital to the Japanese diet.

But by no means were Manchuria and Korea important to Japan only as sources of food. Of all the major industrial nations, Japan is the poorest in deposits of coal and iron ore. Manchuria happens to be especially rich in both and is thus naturally suited to be a center of the steel and heavy manufacturing industries. To get some sense of Manchuria's extraordinary value as it was developed by the Japanese, we might imagine the agricultural capacity (as well as the climate, terrain, and approximate size) of the Dakotas, Nebraska, and Minnesota, combined with something like the industrial potential of the region between Pittsburgh and Detroit and the shipping capacity of the Chesapeake Bay area, all connected by an excellent railway network.

To this industrial complex, northern Korea contributed not only substantial mineral deposits but also vast amounts of hydroelectric power. In addition, besides being a breadbasket for Japan, Korea was the natural bridge between Japan and Manchuria. The superb harbor of Pusan, in the extreme south of the Korean peninsula, is just one hundred miles from Japan. Once the Manchurian railways had been extended throughout Korea, only a ferryable gap interrupted direct rail service between the Japanese home islands and Japanese holdings on the mainland of Asia. Several harbors on the northeastern coast of Korea, only a short rail hop from the Manchurian centers of industry, are hundreds of sea miles closer to ports in central and northern Japan than are Dairen and Port Arthur. Korea provided the vital link in the growing Japanese Empire.

The Russians had begun the development of Manchuria in earnest, but it was the Japanese who brought it to fruition. By the late 1920s they had invested billions of yen in the region, building factories, exploiting natural resources, extending the railways, and greatly intensifying agriculture. Furthermore, nearly a million Japanese subjects, many of them Koreans who had been evicted from their ancestral farms by Japanese officials and speculators, had settled in relatively sparsely populated Manchuria.

Protecting Japanese interests in Manchuria was the Kwantung Army, which had developed from the small force first stationed in southern Manchuria in 1906 to guard the ports and the railway lines that Japan had won in the war against Russia. The army became a much enlarged and quite independent command in 1919, in the wake of the concessions that Japan, one of the victorious Allied powers, extorted from China during World War I. From that time onward, the Kwantung Army's officers became more and more convinced that Japanese sovereignty over Manchuria was the key to Japan's future strength and prosperity.

Especially in the light of the developments of the 1920s, these officers felt that only total political and military control of the region could guarantee the security of Japanese investments. The first of these developments was the attempt by the Japanese, taking advantage of the anarchy and civil war in the years that followed the Russian Revolution of 1917, to seize a huge chunk of territory in eastern Siberia. The invasion failed, largely because of American pressure on Japan to observe the Wilsonian injunction against annexations by any of the Allied powers. The Japanese accomplished nothing more than to ensure that the Soviet government would hate and fear them as much as the czarist regime had. Moreover, when Lenin's hopes for proletarian revolution throughout Europe were disappointed, he came to feel that the best immediate prospects for Communism, and thus for the Soviet Union, lay in the East.[8] The emergence and consolidation of a Bolshevik Russia meant that Japan, with its burgeoning and discontented proletariat, felt particularly vulnerable to ideological penetration, while the enormous Japanese investments in Manchuria appeared — above all in the eyes of the Kwantung Army's officers — to be endangered by the very real possibility of direct Soviet aggression.

It was bad enough for Japan to face a renewed threat from Russia, but added to that was the success of Chiang Kai-shek's nationalist Kuomintang movement, which posed new dangers from China itself. On the principle that "my enemy's enemy is my friend," Chiang and Stalin struck up an alliance against the Japanese. Chiang had no intention of provoking a full-scale war with Japan, or at least not until he had more fully consolidated his control over China, much of which was still ruled by rival warlords. He needed Russian help in order to gain sufficient power to take on Japan, but he understood that if he were to succeed in driving the Japanese out of Manchuria, thus removing the Japanese threat to the Soviet Union, then Russia — which wanted to regain the power in southern Manchuria that it had lost in 1905 — would cease to support him and would become his main antagonist. Stalin put it nicely when he said in 1927 of Chiang and the Kuomintang: "They have to be utilized to the end, squeezed out like a lemon, and then thrown away."[9]

By 1930 Chiang had become strong enough that he believed he could force the Japanese to accept a compromise. He would give them considerable leeway to develop Manchuria as long as a sizable share of the profits would find its way into his coffers, thereby enabling him to pay the armies and to buy the armaments that he needed to bring the rest of China firmly under his control. Of course, once Chiang was at the head of a united and strengthened China, he would feel ready to drive the Japanese out of Manchuria altogether. A unified and modernized China able to draw fully upon the newly developed wealth of Manchuria would be able to hold its own even against a coalition of Japan and Russia.

As the officers of the Kwantung Army — and many other Japanese as well — saw matters, Japan had essentially bought Manchuria with the lives of the hundred thousand Japanese soldiers who had died in the 1904–1905 war and with the enormous investments the nation had made in the development of the region's industrial and agricultural potential. China had done almost nothing to develop Manchuria and so, felt the Japanese, had no legitimate claim to reap the benefits. Finally, feeling that it was imperative to act before Chiang became too strong, the Kwantung officers took matters into their own hands in 1931. They dynamited a section of railway track, blamed the Kuomintang, and proceeded, on that excuse, to occupy most of Manchuria by force, against the wishes of the Japanese government. The civilian government of Japan was by then so intimidated by the ruthlessness of the military faction — which did not hesitate to assassinate uncooperative politicians — that it reluctantly accepted the fait accompli. In 1932 the Kwantung Army set up the Japanese puppet state of Manchukuo under Pu Yi, the last emperor of China, himself a Manchu, who had been deposed in 1912. The real power, however, remained with the officers, who themselves held many of the key posts in the administration of the new state. They also took over control of the railways and organized a giant holding company, the Manchurian Heavy Industry Company, to finance and coordinate the steel, manufacturing, and chemical industries, as well as mining, electrical power, transportation, and communications. Manchuria was then well on its way to becoming the greatest concentration of industry in Asia outside Japan itself.

This flagrant violation of the Open Door policy outraged the United States, both on principle and because the monopolies established by the Japanese excluded American business from Manchuria. As a direct response to the Japanese takeover, President Roosevelt in 1933 gave formal diplomatic recognition to the Soviet Union in the hope that the prospect of a Soviet-American alliance might force the Japanese to back down. More than any other factors, the American determination to return Manchuria to Chinese sovereignty and the equally strong Japanese determination to hold on to that region led to World War II in the Pacific.

One of the Soviet Union's principal anti-Japanese tactics was the support of Korean nationalism, for if Korea would revolt, Japan's dominance of Manchuria would be seriously weakened and the Russians could then move back in. Just as Napoleon had opportunistically championed Polish nationalism in his effort to weaken the great empires that had divided Poland among themselves, so had Lenin during World War I endorsed the liberation of subjugated peoples as a means of destabilizing both the czarist empire and the principal powers — the German, Austrian, and Turkish empires — against which Russia was fighting. Once it became clear to him that Europe was not ripe for revolution, he turned his sights eastward, where his major enemies were the British and the Japanese empires. The Soviets therefore took up the cause of Asian nationalism — Korean, Chinese, Mongolian, and Indian — in an attempt to manipulate the balance of power in the East for their own benefit.[10]

As the most passionately anti-Japanese people in the East, the thousands of Koreans active in the resistance movement, both within Korea and in exile in Manchuria and in eastern Siberia, were natural allies for the Soviets. To cement the bond, many of them were quite willing to call themselves Communists. Once Japan had signed the Anti-Comintern Pact with Germany, in 1936 — and even more so once the Soviet Union began the following year to aid the Chinese in their fight against the invading Japanese — to be militantly anti-Japanese and to be Communist came to be pretty much one and the same in the minds of many Koreans. The Soviets gave aid to exiled

Koreans who formed guerrilla bands along the Manchurian and Siberian borders of Korea and made forays into their native country to harass the Japanese. From the 1920s until 1945 increasingly large numbers of Korean exiles served in the Soviet army or received special training in such fields as guerrilla tactics and political indoctrination at Moscow's University of the Toilers of the East. Hence within the Soviet Union there developed a large cadre of grateful and Russophile Koreans that would be fully prepared to establish, at the first opportunity, a Communist government in Korea.

Japan treated Korea very much the way czarist Russia had treated Poland. (The parallels between Korea and Poland are striking. Both are or have been surrounded by Russia and two of her imperial rivals. Both have been fatally weakened by intensely factional domestic politics, and both have endured long periods of partition.) Especially once Japan went to war with China in 1937, the Japanese did everything in their power to stamp out Korean nationalism, to suppress the Korean language, to abolish the Korean press, to eradicate both Christianity and native Korean religious sects, to use the educational system for pro-Japanese indoctrination, and, in general, to force the Koreans to come to think of themselves as Japanese in every way. Late in the 1930s laws were even passed ordering Koreans to adopt the Japanese state religion, Shinto, with its emphasis on emperor worship, and — most absurd and humiliating of all — to replace their Korean surnames with Japanese ones. Such extreme measures could not help but provoke extreme resentment and defiance, strengthening the very nationalism that they were meant to destroy.

From 1910 onward, tens of thousands of Japanese settled in Korea. Many of the immigrants were businessmen — merchants, manufacturers, bankers, and moneylenders — and they included both individual entrepreneurs and representatives of Japanese firms. They exploited Korea's natural resources, built factories, and bought up huge tracts of farmland at bargain prices. Hundreds of thousands of Koreans were evicted from their ancestral lands or reduced to destitute tenancy, while Japanese farmers moved in on advantageous terms. Before long the Koreans were largely excluded from reaping the profits of their nation's economy. Except for a relatively small number of wealthy Korean landlords whose friendship the Japanese found it expedient to cultivate, the Korean people constituted a labor pool, a service class, to be exploited and oppressed by their Japanese masters. Although industrialization and the expansion of the governmental bureaucracy created many new jobs, those given to Koreans were mostly menial or clerical; managerial and administrative positions were reserved for the Japanese.

As the Japanese war effort became increasingly desperate, Japan's exploitation of Korea became increasingly extreme. More than 3 million Koreans were conscripted for forced labor in mines and munitions factories and on military construction projects in Korea and elsewhere in the Japanese Empire. (Some estimates hold that as many as 25,000 of the approximately 100,000 people who died in the atomic bombing of Hiroshima were Korean forced laborers.[11]) Such exploitation naturally led to heightened resistance, which forced Japan to station growing numbers of troops in its restless colony. In 1941 there were 46,000 Japanese soldiers in Korea; by the end of the war the number had risen to 300,000, in addition to which thousands of sociopathic Koreans were recruited to serve in the ranks of the repressive police. Korea became a slave-labor camp under armed guard.

A great many Koreans dreamed, throughout the thirty-five years of Japanese rule over their country, that liberation would bring about not only the complete independence of Korea as a sovereign nation but also a drastic and sweeping repudiation of everything in any way associated with the hated Japanese domination. In the realm of human affairs, as in physics, for every action there is an opposite and equal reaction. As the Japanese oppressed and exploited the Koreans more and more rapaciously, so did it inevitably follow that many Koreans came increasingly to think of their eventual liberation as the coming of the millennium — as the end to all their suffering and as the solution to all their problems. Liberation would entail a radical transformation of Korean politics, of Korean society, and of the Korean economy — in short, a revolution.

While the polarization between the oppressed and exploited Koreans and their Japanese oppressors and exploiters became ever more extreme, the ideological appeal of Communism became greater — for Marxism-Leninism is essentially a philosophy of polarization. The vast majority of those people around the world who have called themselves Communists have longed neither for a life under a totalitarian dictatorship nor for the domination of their country by the Soviet Union. They have simply longed for deliverance from conditions that have made them desperately unhappy. They have longed for swift and radical change. Their misery has made them desperate, and their desperation has made them extremist. They have felt that they have earned the right not to have to compromise. And Marxism-Leninism has assured them that they will not have to. The forces of history, they are told, are on their side, and their victory will be as complete as it is inevitable.

For such people — and they have constituted the great mass of ardent Communists — *the primary content of Communism has been its extremism.* They have been drawn to Communism by its message that radical polarization will irrevocably lead to radical change, to a complete and final liberation. The downtrodden are instructed to take courage from the observation that the more miserable they become, and the more highly polarized the society in which they live, the sooner the revolution will come. Compromise is to be eschewed, for it can only delay the revolution.

In June 1946, after more than ten months of Russian occupation of northern Korea — and despite the fact that Russian soldiers had done enough raping and looting to earn themselves considerable hatred — Edwin W. Pauley, Truman's roving ambassador investigating reparations (and one of the very few Americans to be allowed to travel in the Russian zone), observed in a letter to the president, "Communism in Korea could get off to a better start than practically anywhere else in the world."[12] Nationwide democratic elections with universal suffrage, could they have been held in Korea in 1945, would most probably have led to the creation of a government friendly enough toward the Soviet Union to satisfy Stalin. This was, of course, precisely the opposite of the irresolvable dilemma in Poland, where the free elections that the Americans were demanding could never have yielded anything but an anti-Soviet government totally unacceptable to Stalin. That was so because the Russians had subjugated and oppressed the Poles for two hundred years. It was Japan, however, that had subjugated and oppressed Korea, while the Russians had championed Korean nationalism. The problem was that the Americans could not believe that any nation could be naturally pro-Soviet, nor could they tolerate a Communist Korea.

CHAPTER 3

The Division of Korea

PRESIDENT FRANKLIN ROOSEVELT'S VISION of the postwar world was apparently shaped largely by his own experience of bipartisan cooperation in American politics. The Republicans, blamed for the Depression and unable to bring it to an end, had by 1932 lost the national majority that had maintained their monopoly on the White House and their domination of Congress throughout the 1920s, during which period the Democratic party had been gravely weakened by urban-rural and regional rivalries. Roosevelt's masterstroke, made possible by nearly universal agreement that it was time for radical action to end the Depression and to alleviate its miseries, was to forge all the squabbling Democratic factions into a strong and united party. In 1932 Roosevelt emerged from his first presidential campaign not only with victory but also with such a substantial congressional majority that he was able virtually to dictate policy with the assurance that it would become law. Throughout his more than twelve years in office, and especially after Pearl Harbor, he continued to enjoy a high degree of cooperation from many Republicans. Their party seemingly reduced to the status of a permanent minority, progressive Republicans realized that they could get ahead only if they behaved more or less like Democrats.

During World War II, Roosevelt acted as though he regarded the democratic nations of the world — including the United States, Great Britain, France, and (stretching the point) China — as analogous to the factions of the Democratic party. Under his benevolent leadership, which promised benefits to all of them, they would coalesce into a harmonious unity. Since the United States was the only one of the great powers that had been economically strengthened rather than ruined by the war, all the other powers would recognize that it was in their vital interest to cooperate with America. The very fact that the United States would emerge from the war as the world's strongest power would demonstrate to all, including the Russians, the superiority of the American way and establish America's right to dominate the "party" of liberal democracy — and thus to lead the world. As a coherent voting bloc in the international organization that Roosevelt advocated, the democratic powers — with the nuclear monopoly, economic strength, and sheer numbers on their side — would be unassailable. As for the Russians, they would be like the Republicans, the perpetual minority, the permanent opposition, who could hope for favors and benefits only if they were prepared to cooperate with the Democrats. If the Soviets embraced democratic liberalism and free trade, they could do business with the United States and prosper. Otherwise, they could starve.

Roosevelt and Stalin discussed the Korean question only briefly and informally at Yalta. FDR made the point that because Korea had been under Japanese rule for so long, the Koreans had very little political experience (none of self-government) and would need a period of tutelage. This should be supplied by a trusteeship government composed of representatives of the Great Powers. This government would acquaint the Korean people with the principles and procedures of democracy and would train Korean politicians and administrators, who, as they gained experience, would gradually assume more and more responsibility. Roosevelt cited as his paradigm the American "tutelage" of the Philippines, which had lasted nearly fifty years, since the Spanish-American War. (After almost forty years of American colonial rule, the Philippines had been allowed to set up a republic, in 1935, with the understanding that the new government would remain under close American supervision for another ten years; at the end of this time the nation would be granted full independence.) Since the Koreans were somewhat more advanced than the Filipinos had been in 1898, the trusteeship over Korea would not have to last as long — say, twenty to thirty years.[1]

According to Ambassador Averell Harriman, Stalin replied that in his opinion the period of trusteeship should be as brief as possible. Indeed, he said, he really didn't see any need for a trusteeship at all, since the Koreans would be perfectly capable of governing themselves once their nation had been liberated from the Japanese. Harriman took this to mean that Stalin assumed the Koreans, left on their own, would form a Communist government friendly to the Soviet Union.[2]

That was precisely what Roosevelt wanted to prevent. His conception of trusteeship for Korea was based on the assumption that the United States, supported by Britain and China, would dominate the arrangement and would thus be in a position to dictate Korean policy until such time as the Koreans themselves had adopted American ways and could be trusted to act consistently in a manner optimally favorable to American interests, which would in turn greatly benefit Korea. He recognized that the Soviet Union had legitimate concerns about a nation with which it shared a border near the strategically vital port of Vladivostok, and he understood that Stalin would not tolerate a Korean government hostile to Soviet interests. But the catch was that, as FDR envisioned it, the friendship of Korea toward the Soviet Union was not to be spontaneous, arising from any fundamental sympathy of the Korean people for the ideals of Communism or from long-standing ties with Russia in the struggle against Japan; it was, rather, to be a gift bestowed, at the direction of the United States, in return for Soviet cooperation — which is to say, as a reward for Soviet acknowledgment of the superiority of the American way at home and abroad. As long as the Russians behaved themselves in Korea and didn't try to achieve dominance of the peninsula, the Americans would see to it that the Soviet Union had unrestricted access to Korea's ports and natural resources, on the same generous terms that other nations would enjoy.

Korea had hardly figured in the Allies' military planning before the 1945 Potsdam Conference, for Washington expected that the Soviets would be faced with a long, hard fight in Manchuria, while the Americans would have their hands full in Japan proper. In such a scenario, it would be months before either Soviet or American forces were in any position to enter Korea. Planning for such an eventuality could therefore be postponed. At Potsdam, American military leaders informed their Soviet counterparts that the United States had no plans to conduct operations in Korea or to occupy that nation. But that was not entirely true. On August 10, in response to the Russian declaration of war two days earlier, Harriman cabled President Truman from Moscow:

[W]hile at Potsdam, General Marshall and Admiral King told me of the proposed landings in Korea and Dairen if the Japanese gave in prior to Soviet troops occupying those areas. . . . I recommend that these landings be made to accept the surrender of the Japanese troops at least on the Kwantung Peninsula and in Korea. I cannot see that we are under any obligation to the Soviets to respect any zone of Soviet military operation.[3]

The trouble was that the Russians had clearly demonstrated in Eastern Europe that in areas occupied by their troops they could not be trusted to adhere to their contractual obligations, let alone defer to American wishes. Once the Soviets had occupied Korea, they would never allow a four-power trusteeship to be set up. Korea would, instead, become yet another Soviet satellite. The American goal, then, was to keep the Russians out of Korea — or at least out of as much of it as possible.

Unfortunately, American troops were so exhausted and depleted, and so dispersed over vast areas of the Pacific, that no substantial force could possibly be hastily dispatched to Korea. Indeed, the Joint Chiefs of Staff, confronted in mid-August with the task of receiving the Japanese surrender not only within Japan itself but also on dozens of widely scattered islands, estimated that it might be the end of September — more than six weeks away — before they could send any troops at all to occupy even part of Korea.

The U.S. government would probably have been happiest if Korea simply had not existed. Although the army had trained some two thousand civil-affairs officers to set up a military government in Japan, it had not made the slightest effort to prepare any personnel to direct an occupation of Korea. No group of officers had been taught the Korean language or been versed in Korean history, culture, and customs. No Korean-Americans had been recruited to man or to lead occupation units. And none of the leading Korean patriots in exile had been groomed to serve as a figurehead through whom the military could temporarily govern. Nor had the United States had any intention whatsoever of fighting the Japanese in Korea. Washington had hoped only that once Japan had surrendered, American troops could swiftly occupy all of Korea before the Russians had had a chance to move in. Once the United States was firmly in control, then perhaps the Russians could safely be allowed to assume their subsidiary role in the four-power trusteeship. The United States was in the position of the dog in the manger: it didn't really want anything to do with Korea except to prevent the Russians from occupying the peninsula and installing a Communist puppet government — as they had been carefully preparing for decades to do.

The United States was not wrong in wanting to prevent Korea from becoming a Soviet satellite. But if that aim was really so important, then the Americans were foolish indeed to postpone action until the very last minute and to approach the issue in such a confused and haphazard manner — a manner that could hardly have more effectively antagonized both the Koreans and the Russians if it had been explicitly designed to do so.

The Japanese surrender offer, on August 10, and the entry of the first Russian troops into northern Korea on the same day, made the problem urgent: what, in the absence of American troops to block the way, was to stop the Soviets from occupying the entire Korean peninsula? The irony is that, as we shall see shortly, a simple communication from the U.S. government (MacArthur's General Order Number One) was all that it took. This is ironic because the Soviet Union was to be excluded from as much of Korea as possible precisely because the Americans had come to believe that the Russians could not be trusted to cooperate or to abide by their agreements unless they were confronted directly by an American military presence.

How odd it was, then, for Washington to hit upon the expedient of suddenly and unilaterally announcing, without any prior consultation, that it intended after all to claim half of Korea, even though it would not for some time yet be able to dispatch any forces to carry out that mission. The purpose of the move was blatantly anti-Soviet, and yet the Americans hoped that the Soviets, who were such hard bargainers, would simply accept the proposal — as they, in fact, did.

The precedent for the demarcation line had been set at Potsdam, where agreement had been reached that in Indochina the British would accept the surrender of the Japanese troops below the 16th parallel and the Chinese would do so above that line. But no such arrangement had been made in regard to Korea.

In Washington on the evening of August 10, just hours after the receipt of the Japanese surrender offer, the State-War-Navy Coordinating Committee — the liaison between the diplomatic and the military branches of the U.S. government — convened an all-night meeting to discuss the problem of assigning Allied commanders to accept the surrender of Japanese forces in various regions of Asia and the Pacific. Among those present was Dean Rusk, a thirty-six-year-old colonel on the War Department General Staff who had recently returned from serving under General Joseph Stilwell in China and who would later serve as secretary of state under Presidents John F. Kennedy and Lyndon B. Johnson. Around midnight, as Rusk later recalled, he and Colonel Charles H. Bonesteel III (who had known each other as Rhodes scholars at Oxford in the 1930s) were asked by Assistant Secretary of War John J. McCloy "to retire to an adjoining room and come up with a proposal which would harmonize the political desire to have the U.S. forces receive the surrender [in Korea] as far north as possible and the obvious limitations on the ability of the U.S. forces to reach the area."[4]

The paramount concern was to reserve for the United States the prestige of having the Korean capital within its zone and thus of receiving the surrender of the Japanese colonial governor-general. American military forces could then take over the centralized administrative apparatus and the communications system of the entire nation. American occupation of Seoul would both symbolize and make possible American domination of the trusteeship.

Rusk and Bonesteel wanted to follow provincial boundary lines, but there was no time for such niceties. They settled instead on the line of latitude 38 degrees north because it had the great virtue of already being on most maps of Korea. The line, approximately halfway up the peninsula, divided Korea into a northern sector of 48,000 square miles and a southern of 37,000. It was intended to be no more than a temporary and facilitative demarcation line, simply for the purpose of accepting the surrender of Japanese troops, and not in any sense a political boundary.[5]

Washington hoped that the Russians would be willing to trade exclusive domination of northern Korea for shared access to the entire peninsula. What concerned the Soviets most, however, was in the north: railway lines and a number of warm-water ports as well as mineral resources and hydroelectric power vital to Manchurian industry. Furthermore, as they apparently saw matters, exclusive control of a North Korean buffer was greatly preferable to any arrangement that would bring an American presence right up to the Soviet border near Vladivostok.

The proposal to divide Korea into two temporary occupation zones was included nonchalantly in the middle of the lengthy text prepared in Washington to be issued as General MacArthur's post–V-J Day General Order Number One, specifying responsibilities for accepting the Japanese surrender in areas throughout the Far East and the Pacific.[6] On August 15 Ambassador Harriman received the text of the order in Moscow and submitted it to Stalin for his approval. In his reply the next day Stalin agreed to the terms, not even singling out Korea for any special comment. But he had two requests, which were surely meant as tacit exchanges for his acceptance of the division of Korea, all of which was then more or less his for the taking. First, he wanted Soviet troops to accept the Japanese surrender in the Kuril Islands, which were to become Soviet territory in accordance with the Yalta agreement. Second, and more important, he wanted Soviet forces to occupy the northern half of Hokkaido, the northernmost of the four major Japanese home islands.[7]

There can be little doubt that Stalin wanted to annex northern Hokkaido, dividing the island with Japan as Sakhalin Island had been divided from 1905 to 1945. That really was not such an unreasonable request, since it would have surrounded the Sea of Okhotsk completely with Soviet territory, giving the Soviet Union legitimately deserved control of the La Pérouse Strait, between the northwestern tip of Hokkaido and Sakhalin, through which shipping from Vladivostok to the east coast of Sakhalin and to the Kurils had to pass. Truman said yes to the Kurils but no to Hokkaido. Japan was not to be divided into occupation zones, though Stalin would be welcome to send a small contingent of troops to serve under MacArthur in carrying out occupation duties.[8] Stalin declined.

Even after Stalin had approved General Order Number One, there was no certainty that Soviet forces would actually halt when they reached the 38th parallel and encountered no American troops to block their advance southward. Korea would provide an interesting and important test of Soviet willingness to cooperate and to abide by agreements — which was, after all, the fundamental issue that was precipitating the Cold War. It must constantly be borne in mind that the emergence of the Cold War was not sudden and decisive. It was, instead, like the long and agonizing breakup of a marriage, with angry scenes and hopeful reconciliations, with reluctance to think that what has been lost is irrecoverable, with uncertainty as to whether toughness or generosity will be more effective in restoring amity, and with a growing burden of rage and recrimination that makes a return to harmony increasingly difficult.

If the Russians didn't stop voluntarily, there would be very little else to stop them. They had assembled 1.6 million men along the Manchurian and Korean borders for their invasion. Such a force would have been necessary to subdue the full-strength Kwantung Army, but it turned out that that army, which American planners had so feared, had been greatly depleted and was now badly equipped. Several hundred thousand of its men had been transferred from Manchuria to the Marianas, Leyte, Okinawa, and the Japanese home islands; they had been only partially replaced by relatively untrained ethnic Manchurian and Korean troops. The Russians had from the outset overwhelming superiority of force, with more than twice as many men and five times as many tanks as the Japanese. The Soviet forces would encounter some fanatic resistance, but the Kwantung Army simply couldn't hold in the face of such might.

Both the Japanese and the Americans feared that the Russians would keep right on going until they reached Pusan, in the extreme south of Korea. But once the Soviet troops had reached the 38th parallel, on August 28, Stalin had all that he really needed — all, that is, except northern Hokkaido, and that he still hoped to win by halting his forces at the appointed line in Korea, thereby demonstrating how cooperative he was prepared to be.

To preserve order until the American and Russian troops arrived, the Japanese colonial government in mid-August gave its support to a group of Koreans who soon proclaimed their interim administration of the government of the Korean People's Republic. This group began as a very broad coalition, with adherents across the entire political spectrum, from rightists through moderate leftists to avowed and militant Communists. They all agreed on only one issue: that Korea must achieve immediate and complete independence. Beyond that, all was confusion, controversy, factional rivalry, personal opportunism, and out-and-out hatred.

Although the KPR remained a coalition, it soon came to be dominated by leftists — some of them quite moderate, some of them Communists, and some radical nationalists — at which point the most conservative rightists deserted to form their own opposition group. The KPR then encouraged peasants throughout Korea to seize Japanese landholdings, advocated the takeover of Japanese factories by their workers, and set up local governments (the People's Committees) to assume police duties and to supervise such essential services as food distribution. Because such policies found a tremendous amount of popular support, the KPR quickly became a very extensive nationwide organization, with 145 branches in cities and in the countryside, both above and below the 38th parallel.

The significant difference between the northern and southern zones was that the Russians, unlike the Americans, chose to recognize the People's Committees as legitimate local governments. The policies of the KPR were, after all, in keeping with those that the Soviets were instituting in the countries they had occupied in Eastern Europe. The People's Committees dealt harshly with the Japanese and with collaborators, executing or imprisoning many, impounding their wealth, and confiscating their holdings of land and industry. Land reform and the nationalization of industry were throughout the growing Russian empire the cornerstones of the policy designed to win the loyalty of the masses.

Within their occupation zone the Russians did away at once with the Japanese colonial bureaucracy, turning the Japanese out of office and scrapping the old structure altogether. In marked contrast to what the Americans would do in the south, the Russians did not set up a military government but instead operated by insinuating their Korean protégés into the People's Committees and into their central executive committee in Pyongyang, which became the de facto government of the Russian-occupied zone. This was terribly important, for what the Koreans wanted more than anything else was independence — and although the Soviets certainly did not grant them that, they managed to create an illusion of independence that the great mass of unsophisticated Koreans found persuasive and satisfactory. For the most part the Russians remained relatively inconspicuous and operated skillfully behind the scenes, moving cautiously but persistently to remove their political rivals.

As was pointed out by George McCune, the Korea expert of the U.S. State Department's Japan Affairs Division at the time, the situation was paradoxical: because the power in northern Korea was in the hands of genuinely pro-Soviet Koreans, there was "considerable evidence to indicate that the Russians actually did permit the Koreans of their choice to exercise real authority, whereas in the American zone, the Korean employees of the Military Government were allowed little power and no authority."[9]

To head the pro-Soviet government the Russians installed the thirty-three-year-old Kim Il-sung, who throughout the 1930s had been the leader — the "general" — of a band of several hundred Korean guerrillas whose forays from their bases in Manchuria into northern Korea had been so vexatious to the Japanese that the colonial government had organized a special squad to hunt Kim down. In the early 1940s he and his men had sought refuge in southeastern Siberia from the intensive Japanese crackdown against Manchurian guerrillas. He then evinced his loyalty to the Soviet Union and to the Communist cause in the hope of enlisting Russian aid in the fight against Japan. Realizing that Kim could be very useful to them in Korea, the Russians groomed him for leadership.

Kim's politics were as apparently self-contradictory as Tito's. Kim was a genuine nationalist and a genuine Socialist who was pro-Soviet because he was counting on Soviet support in establishing a nation that the Russians would allow to be independent precisely because it was dependably pro-Soviet. Like Tito, Kim put the interests of his own nation before those of the Soviet Union. But unlike Tito's, Kim's goals did not conflict with Stalin's.

The fact is undisputable that Kim and the Soviets established a totalitarian police state in northern Korea. The more fully Kim consolidated his power, the more ruthless he became in suppressing both the Communist and the non-Communist factions that opposed him or that questioned his policies. Tens of thousands of officials and bureaucrats at all levels of government, from the Communist party headquarters in Pyongyang to the People's Committees in the countryside, were removed from office. Some were killed, but most were imprisoned or else simply excluded from participation in politics. All in all, the regime was (and still remains) a civil libertarian's nightmare. But the great majority of ordinary North Koreans evidently found it highly preferable to the Japanese occupation. In the Soviet zone — at least to all appearances — the Koreans were governed by Koreans whose socializing reforms did much to alleviate the exploitative conditions that had been imposed by the Japanese.

The tragedy was that American good intentions and anti-Communism would lead to the establishment of a regime in the south nearly as repressive as that in the north, only its brutality would not be balanced by economic reform.

CHAPTER 4

The United States and the Establishment of South Korea

THE LEADERS of the Korean People's Republic made it clear that they would welcome American troops south of the 38th parallel to help with the repatriation of Japanese soldiers and colonists. But the Koreans would regard the Americans as guests rather than as occupiers and would expect them to depart as soon as their task had been completed. This was not an unreasonable expectation, since the Koreans still had not been informed about the trusteeship plan. Indeed, on September 13, 1945, the U.S. State Department was embarrassed to discover that the British government was not aware of any such scheme in which it was expected to participate.[1]

Set on the establishment of a four-power trusteeship, the Americans refused to deal with any group that claimed to have a mandate to rule Korea. When the KPR would not agree to stop calling itself the government and to reorganize as just one more political party, the Americans denounced it as a Communist organization and set out to destroy it. By eliminating the only force that could legitimately claim to represent a coalition spanning both sides of the political center, the Americans exacerbated the radical polarization that was already under way by the time they arrived on the scene.

XXIV Corps, under Lieutenant General John Reed Hodge, was chosen for occupation duty in Korea not because of any special qualifications but rather because it was the corps closest to Korea at the time of the Japanese surrender. Having exhausted itself in the terrible fight for Okinawa, which had ended on June 21, the outfit was still on that island in August; it had suffered very heavy casualties and was being reinforced with recruits hastily sent over as soon as they had completed basic training. In mid-August, Washington estimated that it would be the end of September before either of the corps's divisions, the 7th and the 96th, would be in any shape to move into

Korea, but mounting fears of a Communist takeover there led the landing date to be pushed up to September 8, regardless of readiness. Even when that date arrived, the corps still had no civil-affairs officers who spoke Korean or who had any special knowledge of Korea beyond that provided by State Department briefing manuals.

The timing couldn't have been worse. The rush meant that XXIV Corps went dangerously unprepared into a highly volatile situation, while the lapse of three weeks between the Japanese surrender and the American arrival seemed to justify the Russian taunt that "the American command preferred to land troops in Korea only after the end of all fighting without incurring any risk and with purely imperialist aims."[2] General Hodge himself admitted that the Russians were at a great advantage because the Koreans had seen them "come in here and fight."[3]

Even once XXIV Corps had arrived in Seoul, on September 8, and had received the surrender of the Japanese governor-general the next day, Hodge felt that he had no choice but to retain Japanese officials at their posts in the bureaucracy so as to prevent a nationwide breakdown of administration and services. After all, as George McCune reported, "more than 80 percent of the highest ranking officials, 60 percent of intermediate rank, and about 50 percent of the clerks, secretaries, and minor ranks were Japanese."[4] To have turned them all out of office before Koreans had been trained to replace them would have invited anarchy. But cries of outrage came from the Koreans, who began to accuse the Americans of being pro-Japanese. Upon receiving urgent orders from MacArthur to remove all the top Japanese officials at once, Hodge stripped them of their titles. But he kept most of them behind the scenes as "advisers" to the American Military Government, which he set up and headed.

What Hodge felt he desperately needed was a number of Koreans with whom he could work comfortably — preferably men who spoke English and who would be as cooperative, orderly, and docile as the Japanese. He soon found them. Wealthy businessmen and landowners, most of them were graduates of the American Protestant missionary schools that had flourished in Korea before 1910. Unfortunately, many of them were also archconservatives who had collaborated with the Japanese.[5] These men were especially anxious to enlist American support against the socialistic and retributive actions of the KPR. As if Hodge were not already sufficiently opposed to the KPR on account of its disruptiveness and its resistance to American paternalism, the conservatives further prejudiced him by insisting that the KPR was completely dominated by Communists and that their own organization, the Korean Democratic Party, had a monopoly on American-style democratic ideals.

In the late summer and fall of 1945, Korea, the Land of the Morning Calm, was about as calm as the national convention of a major American political party during nominations for the presidency. General Hodge, unprepared to deal with this unanticipated tumult, commented that the Koreans were the "most politically minded people" he had ever seen; "every move, every word, every act is interpreted and evaluated politically."[6] Korea simply seethed with political parties, factions, and organizations, all of them diligently campaigning and propagandizing.

Hodge was a down-to-earth and forthright midwesterner who had been raised on a farm in Golconda, Illinois, and who had worked his way up through the ranks. "A soldier's soldier" he was, when it came to fighting, a man to send in to get the job done. Brave and unpretentious, he was liked and admired by his men. For his highly effective leadership on Guadalcanal, on Leyte, and on Okinawa, he had been awarded the Legion of Merit and the Distinguished Service Medal. He was, in short, a thoroughly military man, a man for whom discipline, order, fairness, candor, and dignity counted for much. But he was by no means cut out to be a statesman, especially in the arena of anarchic, opportunistic, and extremist Korean politics.

Hodge and his associates understood that their primary task was to ensure that Korea did not come under Communist control. They earnestly tried to forge a coalition with the moderate left, but they expected the leftists to do most of the compromising and to acknowledge the reasonableness of the American position. The fundamental problem was that the leaders of the American Military Government assumed that the true goals of the Korean people must naturally be identical to those that Washington had set for Korea. Any opposition could therefore be due only to subversive and anti-Korean influences from the Soviet Union. Thus it was that the AMG came to rely increasingly on the obsequious conservatives to maintain order and to suppress all opposition.

The rightward drift of the AMG must be attributed less to malice than to despair in the face of debilitating confusion. Washington sent Hodge mixed signals and expected him to do the impossible: to create a broad political coalition loyal to a military government that was almost universally resented, to win the support of Korean nationalists for a trusteeship plan that would postpone the independence that they craved above all else, and to establish democratic stability in a nation that was profoundly disrupted — politically and economically — by its liberation after thirty-five years of harsh Japanese rule and by its division into two hostile parts.

Both Hodge and Washington came to feel that what the AMG needed was a figurehead who was dependably conservative, English-speaking, and pro-American — and who was at the same time a respected Korean nationalist who could persuade the majority of the Korean people to support the Americans. The most obvious candidate for the role was the seventy-year-old Syngman Rhee, who had gone on from a Methodist missionary school in Seoul to study theology at George Washington University, in Washington, D.C., graduating with a B.A. in 1907. He had then earned a master's degree in history and political science from Harvard and a Ph.D. in the latter subject from Princeton. He returned to Korea in 1910 but two years later went into what would turn out to be a thirty-three-year-long exile. Rhee, who had maintained an unswerving anti-Japanese position since the 1890s, was the most prominent of the living patriarchs of the resistance. His prestige was so great that when the Korean People's Republic was founded, in August 1945, its leaders had immediately offered him the post of cabinet chairman. He declined the offer.

From 1919 until the fall of 1945, Rhee had spent much of his time, in vain, lobbying in Washington for the cause of Korean independence. Incredibly tenacious, he weathered rebuffs and insults that would have driven most men to silence and despair. But Rhee was not merely obstinate and persevering; he was messianic and monomaniacal. His unshakable belief that it was his destiny to lead a united Korea to independence sustained him on an unwavering course.

The Washington officials whom he pestered relentlessly regarded him as a tiresome but basically harmless crank, and in the fall of 1945 they came to feel that gratitude for American support would make this old man a docile and cooperative figurehead. But they failed to understand that Rhee's advancing age only heightened his sense of urgency. (He called the party that he founded upon his return to Korea the Central Committee for the *Rapid* Realization of Korean Independence.) Furthermore, he was self-righteous as only a person with a sense of having a divinely ordained mission can be. Despite his Christianity, he was Machiavellian; in his eyes the end of fulfilling his task of leading Korea to independence justified any means, however ruthless. Docile was something that Syngman Rhee was incapable of being.

In October the State Department granted permission for Rhee and a number of other prominent exiles to return to Korea, as long as they did so (at least ostensibly) as individuals and not in any presumed official capacity or with overt sponsorship by the AMG. They would have to declare themselves representatives of a political party, not of a provisional government.

Rhee was the first to return. On his way to Korea he stopped in Tokyo for secret meetings with Generals MacArthur and Hodge, and then he was delivered to Seoul in a U.S. Army plane. This was all done clandestinely so that Rhee would appear to have returned to Korea spontaneously and to have endorsed the AMG because he thought it was a good thing. So bad was the military government's reputation by that time that any suggestion that it was sponsoring Rhee could have diminished even that venerable nationalist's prestige. When Rhee made his first dramatic public appearance, at a huge rally in Seoul on October 20, General Hodge was beside him on the platform. But the point that the AMG wanted to make was that Rhee was endorsing the AMG, not the other way around.

Hodge was hoping that Rhee would be a figurehead who would win Korean sympathy for the AMG and enable the Americans to govern effectively until a four-power trusteeship had been set up. But he was to be very disappointed. Rhee was not cut out to be a figurehead. He was an extremist, and once he returned to divided Korea he wanted only one thing: to establish a secure base for himself as the leader of an independent South Korea with strong U.S. backing so that he could take over North Korea by force. He opposed all negotiations with the Soviets to unify his nation, for he felt that any settlement that would be acceptable to the Russians would inevitably open the way for them to achieve dominance over the entire peninsula. Instead, his way (ironically enough) was that which had worked so well for Lenin: to destroy all possibility of compromise or coalition and by thus radically exacerbating polarization to make violent confrontation inevitable.

To this end Rhee was so aggressively and flamboyantly anti-Communist in his statements that he embarrassed even General Hodge, who was no slacker in such matters. Indeed, Hodge eventually had to insist that Rhee submit his speeches to the American censors so that the most provocative anti-Soviet remarks could be deleted before delivery. But Rhee was not to be so easily deterred. His idée fixe was to stir up Soviet-American relations to the point where no reconciliation would be possible. He would at the same time do his utmost to convince the Americans that only an independent South Korea under his leadership would have the internal strength and popular support needed to withstand Communist incursions from the north. He would heighten American fears of a Communist takeover of southern Korea, and he would present himself as the one unshakable bulwark against Communism in the south. The Americans would have to support him diplomatically, economically, and militarily whether they liked him or not.

That was pretty much the way things actually worked out. Within a few months of Rhee's return to Seoul, Hodge had come to dislike the Korean quite intensely, for Rhee did everything in his power to discredit both the military government and the trusteeship plan that he had been brought in to champion. Hodge would have liked nothing more than to abandon Rhee, but as fears of Communism mounted, Rhee showed himself to be the one Korean leader able and willing to take the extremist measures that seemed increasingly necessary to preserve "law and order," and as such he made himself indispensable.

Having established themselves securely in their respective zones of Korea, neither the United States nor the Soviet Union had any intention of giving up what it already had except for more — for a united Korea that it would effectively dominate. Both obviously viewed a divided Korea as far preferable to a potentially hostile one; each advocated unification mainly in order to retain the loyalty of Korean nationalists and to make it appear that the other's intransigence was entirely responsible for the division. Although there were moderate rightists and moderate leftists who were eager to form a coalition government friendly to both superpowers, their voices were drowned out by those of the extremists, whose interests were best served by polarization.

Korea's situation can most instructively be compared with that of Austria, another liberated (rather than defeated) nation that was divided into occupation zones (American, British, French, and Russian) and that finally, in 1955, emerged independent and unified. The difference was that in Austria the dominant parties of the left and the right were moderate enough to be able to form a stable coalition. In Austria the most powerful political forces were centripetal, in Korea centrifugal.

Austria's fate was in part determined by the facts that the country had relatively little strategic or industrial value and that it did not border on the Soviet Union. Furthermore, the Russians were anxious to foster a strong sense of Austrian nationalism to ensure that the country would never again consider unification with Germany. But the decisive factor was the nation's stability under a sequence of moderate left-right coalitions, which demonstrated to the Russians that the Austrian government could be counted on not to run to extremes and that it could be trusted to maintain the strict and perpetual military neutrality that was the principal condition for Soviet withdrawal.

Political rivalries in the American occupation zone could have been rendered more moderate only if the majority of Koreans south of the 38th parallel had enjoyed a reasonable level of prosperity. From an economic point of view, however, South Korea was a disaster area. For one thing, in a misguided attempt to bestow the blessings of American-style free enterprise upon the Korean people, the AMG instituted a free market for rice in the fall of 1945. With all price controls removed, unscrupulous speculators thrived, paying farmers low prices for the abundant harvest and then hoarding immense quantities of rice to drive up prices. Famine reached epidemic proportions in the south. The AMG desperately needed large amounts of rice to send to the north in exchange for the coal without which South Korean industry and transportation could not function, but none was available. The Soviets, unable to comprehend how the AMG could fail to take the ironfisted measures necessary to remedy the situation at once, suspected a deliberate attempt to starve the north.

More than any other single factor, it was the arbitrary division of Korea that wreaked economic havoc. The Japanese had developed the northern and southern regions of the peninsula to be complementary and mutually dependent. The north had most of the natural resources and heavy industry, and both had been thoroughly integrated with the resources and industry of Manchuria. The temperate south, with just over two thirds of Korea's thirty million people, was heavily agricultural and grew most of the rice that, once the Japanese occupation was ended, should have fed the harsher, industrial north. In return, the south needed raw and crudely processed materials from the north for the light processing and consumer goods industries that increasingly supplemented its agricultural economy.

Beginning in the fall of 1945, the south was flooded with between one and two million refugees from the north and with hundreds of thousands of Koreans demobilized from the Japanese army and from forced-labor brigades. Meanwhile, the division of the nation meant grave shortages of synthetic fertilizer from the north for increased food production, of coal for power, and of such materials as steel, aluminum, magnesium, copper, lead, zinc, carbide, glycerin, absolute alcohol, and rayon pulp, without which South Korean factories — which had, in any case, lost most of their managers and highly trained technicians with the departure of the Japanese — simply could not operate.[7] With a drastically swollen labor force and hundreds of closed factories, unemployment became rampant in South Korea. Furthermore, a glutted labor market meant low wages, while the rice shortage inflated prices to absurd levels. Industrial and rural discontent began to erupt in outbreaks of violence. The AMG, wanting to avoid direct clashes between American troops and the Korean population, and certain that the incidents were fomented by Communist agents who had infiltrated from the north, suppressed the disorders with the only Korean forces that were well trained and disciplined, highly experienced, and dependably anti-Communist: the extreme rightist paramilitary forces, which were largely manned and led by former employees of the Japanese colonial police (80 percent of the officers had worked for the Japanese). In December 1945 General MacArthur gave Hodge permission to begin arming these men as a national police force, a full-fledged constabulary. By the summer of 1946 the force had grown to some twenty-five thousand men, twice the number the Japanese had maintained in southern Korea.

By no means was Hodge's aim to create a fascist police state under Rhee. He simply wanted to preserve law and order until a quiet, moderate, and stable democracy could be set up. The right provided the only force that could keep the lid on securely for the time being, but that only made things worse in the long run, since hatred of the national police force and of the AMG that sponsored it was driving huge numbers of Koreans further to the left.

By mid-1947 Washington had finally grasped that fact. It was time for the United States to cut its losses and get out of Korea. During his visit to the American capital early that year, Rhee had convinced many congressmen that the AMG was doing a bad job and that money spent to support it was money wasted. This was a powerful argument in the view of the parsimonious, Republican-dominated Eightieth Congress, which convened in January 1947 determined to slash defense spending. The $400 million that Truman scared Congress into granting to Greece and Turkey in March only meant less to spend elsewhere. Korea seemed like a good place to cut back.

In September 1947 the Joint Chiefs of Staff provided the line of reasoning that opened the way to withdrawal. Convinced that the Soviet Union was just waiting for the right opportunity to invade Western Europe — an opportunity that might well be provided by the Communist electoral victories that seemed imminent in both France and Italy — they believed that the United States might soon have to fight World War III in Europe, with Asia as a secondary theater of operations. Depriving the Soviet Union of the strategic advantages it would gain by controlling the entire Korean peninsula was still an important objective, but the Joint Chiefs now felt that the "neutralization" of Soviet air and naval forces based in Korea "by air action would be more feasible and less costly than large-scale ground operations."[8] Given that this was still the period of the American atomic monopoly, we must assume that that bland statement implied the liberal use of atomic bombs in Korea, such as would be unthinkable in Europe, where ground troops would have to be relied upon.

The Joint Chiefs outlined their thinking on Korea in a memorandum, dated September 25, stating that from the standpoint of military security, the United States has little strategic interest in maintaining the present troops and bases in Korea. . . .

In the light of the present severe shortage of military manpower, the corps of two divisions, totalling some 45,000 men, now maintained in south Korea, could well be used elsewhere. . . .

Authoritative reports from Korea indicate that continued lack of progress toward a free and independent Korea, unless offset by an elaborate program of economic, political and cultural rehabilitation, in all probability will result in such conditions, including violent disorder, as to make the position of United States occupation forces untenable. A precipitate withdrawal of our forces under such circumstances would lower the military prestige of the United States, quite possibly to the extent of adversely affecting cooperation in other areas more vital to the security of the United States.[9]

Late in the summer of 1945 American forces had rushed into Korea to keep the entire peninsula from falling into Soviet hands. Now they had to withdraw from Korea to accomplish that same end — only they had to do so in such a way as to save face.

It was obvious what had to be done. The problem had to be turned over to the United Nations. Perhaps the organization would be able to create a united and pro-American Korea. At worst, the UN would give its sanction to an independent South Korea, so that, even once American troops were withdrawn, the Communists would not dare to attack it. Instead of paying for an expensive and unpopular military occupation that alienated the Korean people, the United States would supply aid that would win Korean friendship, strengthen the Korean economy, and create a strong base for democracy in the south that would irresistibly draw the oppressed masses of the north into its orbit.

If the United States were to place the Korean issue before the UN Security Council, the Soviets would surely block any action. The only solution, therefore, was to bring the question before the General Assembly, in which the Soviets did not have a veto and the majority of members were friendly to American interests. Accordingly, on October 17, 1947, John Foster Dulles, then one of the

American delegates to the assembly, submitted a draft resolution calling for legislative elections throughout the Korean peninsula by March 31, 1948.[10] The occupying power in each zone would conduct its own elections, but UN observers would see to it that the elections were fair and democratic. Representation in the new legislature would be proportionate to population, meaning that two thirds of the representatives would be from the south. Pro-American delegates might therefore outnumber pro-Soviet ones by as much as two to one.

The Soviets vehemently denounced the American action and counterproposed the simultaneous withdrawal of all Soviet and American troops from Korea by January 1, 1948, leaving the Koreans to settle matters for themselves — in all probability with a civil war leading to the establishment of a leftist government. Nevertheless, on November 14 the General Assembly passed a slightly revised version of the American resolution, the only significant change being that the elections were to be held nationally under UN auspices rather than zonally.

The Russians had made it perfectly clear that they considered the American submission of the Korean question to the UN an illegal move. Hence it should have been no surprise to anyone that when the members of the UN Temporary Commission on Korea arrived in Seoul in January 1948 and then set out to inspect conditions in the north, they were stopped by North Korean guards at the 38th parallel and turned back. Their letters to the authorities in Pyongyang received no reply.

Finally, on February 26, the UN General Assembly authorized UNTCOK to proceed with preparations for elections in South Korea alone. The elections would, however, fill only 200 of the total of 300 seats in the new National Assembly. The 100 vacant seats would be reserved for representatives from the north in the hope that the Russians, recognizing the folly of their uncooperativeness and embarrassed by world opinion, would eventually permit elections and reunification. But political leaders throughout Korea were not taken in; they understood very well that the holding of elections in South Korea would put an end to all reasonable hopes for peaceful unification.

American optimism regarding the elections was groundless. The AMG hoped that somehow the extreme right — out of gratitude for American support — would become moderate and liberal while remaining firmly anti-Communist, and that the left would finally recognize the obvious virtues and advantages of pro-Americanism. The Korean people could then happily proceed to the polls and cast their ballots for a moderate coalition that would imbue the nation with democracy, stability, prosperity — and an unwavering determination to resist Communist encroachments. Motivated by such utterly unfounded hopes, General Hodge launched an ambitious registration campaign and by the middle of April claimed the enrollment of 91.7 percent of enfranchised citizens. In meetings with local officials and police chiefs throughout the south, he stressed the need to ensure that the elections would be fair and calm. To win the sympathy of the left, he even pardoned more than three thousand Koreans who had been imprisoned for minor political offenses.

But it was all in vain. The left, as well as those elements of the moderate right that still hoped for the peaceful reunification of Korea, condemned the elections and called upon their followers to do all they could to obstruct them. Rhee's youth gangs and the police retaliated with their habitual savagery. Over the course of the ten days before the election, 323 people were killed in riots or police raids, and more than 10,000, most of them leftists, were arrested. As if these mass arrests wouldn't bar enough leftists from casting protest votes, the AMG decreed that persons with a police record — which meant tens of thousands more of real or suspected leftists — would not be allowed to vote.

Election Day, May 10, 1948, was relatively calm by Korean standards. Only 44 people were killed, and the State Department reported an excellent voter turnout. After some heated controversy among its members, UNTCOK decided that it was satisfied that the election had been "a valid expression of the free will of the electorate" of southern Korea.[11] But the fact that the overwhelming majority of seats in the National Assembly were won either by Rhee's avowed followers or by extreme rightists who called themselves independents makes it clear that violence and repression rather than democratic freedom had determined the outcome, for even AMG reports to the State

Department had been warning for some time that Rhee's constituency was quite small.

The National Assembly met for the first time at the end of May and, as was inevitable, proceeded to elect Rhee its chairman. The first major order of business was the drafting of a constitution, for which a special committee was organized. The document that it formulated was ratified by the legislature in mid-July, and shortly thereafter the assembly elected Rhee the first president of the Republic of Korea. On August 15, the third anniversary of the Japanese surrender, formal inauguration ceremonies took place in Seoul, during which General MacArthur delivered a speech that greatly pleased Rhee. "An artificial barrier has divided your land," said the general. "This barrier must and shall be torn down. Nothing shall prevent the ultimate unity of your people as free men of a free nation."[12] Although an objective listener would recognize these statements as the high-flown but basically empty rhetoric appropriate to such occasions, anyone looking for a sign of official American encouragement of Rhee's belligerent ambitions would quite naturally have read it into Mac-Arthur's words.

The response of the north to the elections and their aftermath was swift and decisive. The first step was, on May 14, to cut off the flow of electricity to the south, whose already shaky economy then had to limp along on its own meager resources of hydroelectric and coal-generated power until the United States could begin large and regular shipments of coal, as well as the construction of new power plants (most of this paid for by American taxes). Then, in July 1948, the North Korean People's Assembly announced that an election would be held on August 25 for representatives to a Supreme People's Assembly. Shortly after the election, in one of its boldest and most imaginative propaganda moves, the north announced that more than 75 percent of the more than 8 million eligible voters in the south had secretly participated in the balloting — quite a feat of clandestine organization, if it had been true. (Rhee took the claim seriously enough to have some 1,300 people arrested on suspicion of having taken part.) When the assembly convened at the beginning of September, 360 of the 572 delegates in attendance were said to represent the south. The assembly thus purported to be truly national, unlike that in the south, in which the seats reserved for the north remained vacant. On September 9 the Democratic People's Republic of Korea was proclaimed, with Kim Il-sung as premier. Korea was thus divided into two hostile states — not really by American design, but by confusion, drift, misunderstanding, resentment, expedience, incompetence, good intentions, intransigence, failed bluffs, dashed hopes, and fear.

CHAPTER 5

The Korean War and the Cold War in Europe: The Legacy of Appeasement

AT ABOUT 6:00 A.M. on the rainy morning of Sunday, June 25, 1950, the North Korean People's Army launched an all-out, blitzkrieg-style invasion of South Korea. After a heavy artillery barrage that began about 4:00 A.M. and that served as their declaration of war, seven North Korean divisions — some ninety thousand men and about 150 Russian-made tanks — surged southward across the 38th parallel. Most of them advanced along the main roads to Seoul, fifty miles to the south, while others struck key towns on the east and west coasts of the Korean peninsula. The strategy for the attack, devised by Soviet military advisers, was carefully coordinated and deadly. The lightly equipped and poorly trained South Korean army was no match for the formidable force from the north. Despite the determined, and occasionally even effective, opposition mounted by scattered South Korean units, some of the invaders were able to advance as much as ten to fifteen miles the first day.

At 11:00 that morning Pyongyang radio announced that North Korea had declared war on the Republic of Korea in response to a massive invasion from the south. This was a lie, one that called for some fancy footwork if it were to be believed, even by those who were predisposed to accept it as the truth. As Kim Il-sung's official North Korean biographer conceded, "It is almost unprecedented in the history of war of the world" for an army to be able to "counterattack at once, when taken by surprise by the enemy. Looking back on past wars, we see that a country which suffered a full-scale invasion would be thrown more or less into confusion and compelled to retreat, and would initiate its counterattack after holding the front and preparing its strength for some time."[1] How, then, were the Communists to account for the fact — obvious to all observers — that there was not the slightest element of confusion in the operations of the North

Korean army as it began its resolute thrust southward immediately after the outbreak of fighting?

This presented no problem to Kim's biographer, echoing statements made by North Korean propagandists at the beginning of the war. If the course of events seemed incredible, he argued, that only testified to the extraordinary genius of Kim. "The strategy of immediate counterattack devised by Comrade Kim Il-sung was a powerful demonstration of the great vitality . . . [of the] working class who had seized political power [and] had prepared for the imperialists and their war," anticipating what action would have "to be taken to meet the attack of the aggressors."[2]

Washington had had no comparable foresight. Indeed, the Pentagon had not prepared any war plan at all to counter with force a simple, straightforward North Korean invasion of the south. This was largely because two conflicting views regarding Korea prevailed in the capital.

The "there's nothing we'll be able to do about it" school of thought was best represented by Senator Tom Connally (Democrat, Texas), who had been, except for a hiatus of two years, chairman of the Senate Foreign Relations Committee since 1941. In an interview published in *U.S. News & World Report* on May 5, 1950 — less than two months before the invasion — Senator Connally was asked, "Do you think the suggestion that we abandon South Korea is going to be seriously considered?" The senator, who apparently believed that the terms "Russians" and "Communists" were totally interchangeable, replied,

> I am afraid it is going to be seriously considered because I'm afraid it's going to happen, whether we want it to or not. I'm for Korea. We're trying to help her — we're appropriating money now to help her. But South Korea is cut right across by this line — north of it are the Communists, with access to the mainland — and Russia is over there on the mainland. So that whenever she takes a notion she can just overrun Korea just like she will probably overrun Formosa when she gets ready to do it. I hope not, of course.

Such a statement about Korea in a publication that was carefully studied in Moscow (*Pravda* occasionally commented on its articles) did everything but put out the welcome mat for Kim's army.

The other school of thought in Washington held that Kim was Stalin's puppet and that consequently a North Korean invasion of the south could occur only on Stalin's initiative, presumably as an opening or diversionary move in a coordinated Soviet plan to conquer the world. The Americans assumed (and assumed that Stalin assumed) that because an invasion of South Korea would quickly escalate into World War III, the Russian leader would not issue orders to Kim until the Soviet Union was ready for world war — which is to say, until it had developed nuclear capability and had manufactured a large stockpile of atomic bombs.

The United States had been profoundly shaken in September 1949 by the news that the Soviet Union had successfully tested an atomic bomb, three years earlier than the most pessimistic American predictions. (Some optimists had believed that the American atomic monopoly would last ten years or more.) But by mid-1950 the Russians could as yet have produced only a few bombs. Therefore, many U.S. leaders — both in government and in the military — still discounted the possibility that Stalin would order the North Koreans to invade the south. The buildup of troops and equipment on the northern side of the 38th parallel that American intelligence reported in the spring of 1950 was taken to be simply defensive, or else a bluff intended to intimidate.

But even if the intelligence reports had been interpreted correctly, those who believed that an invasion of South Korea could only be the overture to World War III would have demanded that the few American military and civilian advisers in Korea be hastily evacuated in accordance with the Pentagon's global war plan. Although that plan had been revised early in 1949, it still adhered to the concept that the Joint Chiefs of Staff had developed in the fall of 1947, calling for the destruction of enemy bases and forces throughout Korea by means of atomic bombs. American ground troops would have no role in Korea in the event of a world war.

Once the North Korean invasion was actually under way, however, the Pentagon's grand strategy was quickly shelved, and Washington's indecision, if not its confusion, was rapidly dispelled. A consensus suddenly emerged that the United States had to go to South Korea's rescue. Now the rationale was that to fail to do so would be "appeasement" of the Soviet Union, which would lead inexorably to yet more audacious Soviet moves, precipitating World War III.

If Washington was caught off guard by the invasion, the North Koreans were no less surprised by, and unprepared for, America's swift and massive intervention in the conflict. Indeed, most historians of the war agree that if either Stalin or Kim had had any inkling of such a response, the invasion would never have been launched in the first place. All signs had seemed to indicate that the United States would be both unwilling and unable to save Syngman Rhee's government. (Again a striking parallel with Poland — in 1939 Adolf Hitler had been staggered by what he viewed as Britain's irrational decision to honor its guarantee of Polish security.)

What the North Koreans and the Russians failed to understand was that although the United States still did not care much about the welfare of Korea as such, let alone about the well-being of Rhee, American and international politics had recently placed the Truman administration in the position of *having* to oppose militarily, anywhere in the world, what was perceived as overt Soviet aggression.

American intervention in Korea was primarily *symbolic* in intention; it was meant to demonstrate to the world America's willingness and ability to aid friends and allies in their struggle to resist Soviet domination. It was a matter of credibility and prestige. It was a matter of timing in relation to events elsewhere. And it was a matter of Truman's demonstrating to the nation and to the world that he was as determined to halt the spread of Communism as was any Republican.

In order to understand the Korean War, we must recognize that — as far as the Americans and the Russians were concerned, if not the North and South Koreans — it had far more to do with Germany, Japan, and China than with Korea as such. Thus, before we look at the course of the war itself, we must consider the international situation in which it erupted.

Perhaps the single most important and unfortunate fact in the history of the first half of the twentieth century is that, at least in Europe, World War II paralleled so closely, and followed so soon after, World War I. Allowing somewhat for oversimplification, we may say that in both wars Germany and Austria were allied against Great Britain,

France, Russia, and the United States. Given that that was so, and that the military situation at the end of World War I had led to a draconian and unworkable peace settlement that had in turn made World War II inevitable, military and political leaders of the principal combatant nations in the second war were constantly looking back over their shoulders, resolved to avoid repeating the mistakes of the previous conflict. They came to regard World War I as a dress rehearsal for World War II. And they believed that the second time around, with the benefit of hindsight, they could conduct the war and arrange the peace in such a way as to achieve all the exalted goals for which World War I ostensibly had been fought.

As disappointments and fears increased after 1945, however, many top American and British leaders became convinced that the dreadful cycle was beginning all over again, and that if wise and decisive action weren't taken to stop it, the familiar course of events would soon lead to World War III. Even before the end of World War II Truman and Churchill felt that Stalin was beginning to behave the way Hitler had in the 1930s. With Germany and Japan eliminated as anti-Soviet powers by their defeat, with the nations of Eastern Europe occupied by Soviet troops, and with China succumbing to Communism, the United States and Western Europe would have to face alone a Soviet Union bent on world conquest. As for Stalin, he watched during the late 1940s as the West worked for the recovery of Germany and Japan. What he saw apparently led him to fear a revival of the Anti-Comintern Pact — this time including the United States, Britain, and France — encircling the Soviet Union to prepare for an effort to destroy Communism once and for all.

And there was the bomb. Many people believed that the atomic bomb had rendered conventional warfare obsolete. In the Atomic Age, so it was thought, any serious breach of the peace between the superpowers would escalate uncontrollably into a world war. The bomb was an extremist weapon, and it seemed to have eliminated the option of limited, localized war. In this view, global relations were made all the more dangerous by the polarization of the world into two hostile camps, each under the aegis of one of the superpowers. The consolidation of these camps in the late 1940s was fostering the perception that an attack by any member of one camp upon any member of the other was to be considered an attack by one superpower upon the other.

Although Franklin Roosevelt and Winston Churchill worked quite well together during World War II, they looked at the war from somewhat different perspectives, the outlook of each determined by his own personal and/or national experience in the previous war. Churchill, who was rather vain about his abilities as a military strategist, had been first lord of the Admiralty in 1915 and had championed the plan of an ambitious landing at Gallipoli, on the Dardanelles. The war in France had already settled down into the murderous stalemate of trench warfare, and Churchill believed that an attack on the enemy's rear, his "soft underbelly" in the eastern Mediterranean, would break the stalemate. In particular, a successful landing would have knocked Germany's ally Turkey out of the war, thus freeing up the Allied troops who were defending Britain's Middle Eastern interests against the Turks. It would also have given the Allies access to the mouth of the Danube, up which the Royal Navy could then have penetrated into the heart of the Central Powers' home territory. And it would probably have brought the neutral and opportunistic Balkan nations of Greece, Romania, and Bulgaria (all of which wanted to end up on the winning side) into the Allied camp.[3]

The landing failed disastrously, not because the underlying strategy was wrong, but rather because (as he later lamented in his World War II memoirs) Churchill had not been in a position powerful enough to allow him to give orders to all the various squabbling factions upon whose cooperation the success of the venture depended.[4] The British government and public blamed the failure entirely on him. The uproar cost him his cabinet post, jeopardized his political career, and drove him to the brink of a nervous breakdown. Determined to continue fighting the Germans, but with no hope of government office, Churchill thereafter served as an officer in France, where he was appalled by the massive and senseless slaughter he witnessed in the hellish trenches and in the desperate Battle of the Somme.

Roosevelt and Churchill were greatly worried throughout World War II that Stalin would conclude a separate peace with Hitler (as Lenin had with the kaiser), bringing about a repetition of the calamitous scenario of the last months of the previous war. Aware of these fears, Stalin played upon them to extract concessions from his allies. From January 1942 until June 1944 his most insistent demand was for the Americans and the British to undertake an amphibious invasion of northern France that would draw a sizable number of German divisions away from the Russian front. Roosevelt was glad to promise the prompt opening of such a second front, for America's experience in France during World War I had been relatively encouraging. The Americans had swept in and, together with their allies, had defeated the Germans in fairly short order. Churchill's position, however, was very different. He was determined that the British and the Americans would not invade France until their troops were so numerous, so well equipped, so battle-hardened, and so confident of their ability to crush the Germans that there would be no possibility of another trench-bound stalemate.

To understand Churchill's reluctance, we might draw a rough parallel. If at any time after the end of the Vietnam War the United States had found itself called upon to invade mainland China, the last invasion route that any American president in his right mind would have considered was that through Vietnam, so great would have been the public outcry at home. British memories of the French trenches, where a generation had been decimated, were even more painful than would be later American memories of the Southeast Asian jungles.

And so, while Stalin clamored for a cross-Channel invasion of France, Churchill advocated operations all around the Mediterranean. There were several reasons for this. One was to maintain access to the Suez Canal route connecting the British with the Pacific theater of operations as well as with their colonies and Commonwealth partners, upon whose men and economic resources they were so dependent. Another was to gain practice in amphibious landings against the weaker Axis nation, Italy, before taking on the Germans in France. But there also seems to have been a third reason. Churchill was determined to vindicate himself in regard to his sponsorship of the 1915 Dardanelles landing. Between the wars a number of British military historians and German generals alike had called the strategy brilliant and had written that if the plan had been properly executed, it would probably have changed the course of the war dramatically in favor of the Allies.[5] Now that Churchill was prime minister, he was finally in a position to coordinate such a plan successfully. Thus his obsession with amphibious landings on the Mediterranean coasts of Europe and Africa.

Stalin, of course, didn't give a damn about Churchill's reasons. All he knew was that the Russians were fighting at times as many as 240 of the toughest divisions fielded by Germany and its allies, while in North Africa, Sicily, and Italy the Americans and the British were fighting only a dozen or so divisions of Germans and Italians, many of the latter so sick of battle by the spring of 1943 that they began to surrender by the tens of thousands. As the war dragged on, Stalin became more and more convinced that Churchill's preoccupation with the Mediterranean and the Balkans was more anti-Soviet than anti-German; he believed that the prime minister wanted British troops in place to prevent the expansion of Soviet influence into the Balkan region, and he suspected that Churchill was happy to see the Germans bleeding the Russians to death. Stalin began to think about making a separate peace.

If Churchill was primarily concerned with profiting from the military lessons of World War I and with vindicating himself for Gallipoli, Roosevelt's outlook was equally shaped by past mistakes, in his case by American guilt over not having joined the League of Nations. Many Americans and Europeans believed that if the United States had joined the league, that organization would have been strong enough to oppose successfully the German, Italian, and Japanese moves that, unchecked until too late, led to World War II. Roosevelt was determined that this time around the American people would not retreat once again into isolationism. They would, however, endorse internationalism only if they believed that it would create a world of peace and prosperity, of free trade and justice. The president was, therefore, particularly concerned with preserving Allied harmony, so that it would carry over into the postwar period and provide the basis for the effective functioning of the UN. Americans would support the organization only if they felt certain that it would not drag them into more wars. (They had stayed aloof from the league because they had believed that the terms of the Treaty of Versailles would cause another war with Germany and that membership in the league would oblige the United States to fight.) If, after bringing the Axis nations to utter defeat, the Allies could remain friends, peace would be guaranteed. And so it was that Roosevelt devoted so much energy to maintaining friendly relations with Stalin. If he sometimes made efforts to seem more pro-Soviet than pro-British (as he really was not), it was because he wanted to keep the Soviet Union in the European war, to get Russian help in Asia, and to assure the success of the UN.

Stalin's goals were quite simple. First and foremost, he wanted to ensure that Germany would never again be able to invade the Soviet Union. That was the grand obsession that determined all his wartime and postwar European policies and moves. To that end, he favored the fatal weakening of Germany by permanent division. Although he seems to have entertained the possibility of a united Germany completely under ruthless Soviet domination, he evidently feared that an intact Germany would somehow revive itself (as it had done, despite harsh measures and extreme adversity, after World War I) and that German resentment in such a situation would be directed primarily toward the Russians. He therefore apparently decided that a divided Germany would ultimately best serve his purposes, as long as a large segment was Communist and the rest punitively occupied by, and split into three separate and uncooperative parts among, the other Allies, whose dissensions were to be exacerbated by the Soviets in order to prevent the fusing of their zones.

A splintered Germany would remain economically weak and would pose no threat to Russia. Agricultural eastern Germany could feed itself and contribute to the Soviet economy, but the industrial western zones — their industries disrupted and dormant, and their populations swollen by millions of refugees from the east who had to be fed — would place onerous burdens on the economies of their occupiers. Financial depression and political strife within the Western camp would offset the Anglo-American atomic monopoly.

The final stroke of Stalin's plan for Germany was to try to win the friendship of all Germans, eastern and western, by posing as the champion of German unification while doing everything possible to oppose it. The Western powers were to bear the blame for a divided Germany, and German resentment was to be directed westward.

The second major aspect of Stalin's grand design for Europe was the political and economic domination of all the nations along Russia's western border. They were to constitute a fortress wall against the possibility of an eventually resurgent and aggressive Germany, and they were to contribute to the reconstruction of Russia's devastated economy. Until the early stages of the Marshall Plan, Stalin was content to tolerate coalition governments in these nations, as long as they were decidedly friendly toward the Soviet Union. But he seems to have believed that since Soviet troops had borne the brunt of fighting in Europe and could thus claim primary credit for the defeat of Germany, the Soviet Union had a moral right to impose its will on those of its neighbors who failed to see the justice of Russia's claims. The nations of Eastern Europe had joined together after World War I to prevent the westward spread of Bolshevism; many had allied themselves with Nazi Germany or had offered little resistance to German invasion; they had provided Germany with invasion routes to Russia; Hungarian and Romanian troops had participated in the German invasion of the Soviet Union; and Eastern Europe had been liberated from German rule by Russian troops. Now — preferably with Western acquiescence and tractable coalition governments, but without those luxuries if need be — they were to be firmly under Soviet control.

By early 1945 the United States was very disturbed by developments in Eastern Europe, but there seemed to be little it could do about them as long as it wanted Russian help against Japan. By the time the Soviet Union entered the war in Asia, the United States had moved most of its troops from Europe to the Pacific and hence couldn't very well threaten to use force to oppose Russian moves in Eastern Europe. And once the war was over, America disarmed rapidly. As General Albert C. Wedemeyer said, "America fought the war like a football game, after which the winner leaves the field and celebrates."[6] At the time of the victory over Japan, the U.S. Army, which then still included the air force, numbered about 8.2 million men. Within a year, in response to a tremendous public demand to "bring home the boys," that number had shrunk to about 1.5 million, and Truman had ordered further cuts that would bring the number down to 1 million. The defense budget had shriveled from $82 billion in 1945 to a low of about $10 billion for fiscal year 1946–47. And although all these cuts were supposedly justified by American possession of the atomic bomb, Soviet leaders seemed to understand as well as did Western ones that the climate of public opinion in the postwar world of the UN made the bomb unusable. Despite the bomb, the United

States was in the position of speaking loudly and carrying a small stick.

The American government protested vehemently against Soviet moves in Eastern Europe, but even Truman's toughest talk was meant to restore an atmosphere of cooperation ("Cooperate, or else"), not to heighten antagonism. One of Britain's major postwar tasks, therefore, was to convince the Americans that hopes of renewed harmony with Russia were futile. The British were determined to demonstrate to the United States that the Soviets posed a grave danger that could be countered only with threats backed up with powerful armed forces and alliances. The British had been through it all after World War I — disarmament, belief in the power of the League of Nations to prevent war, appeasement necessitated by military weakness — and now they saw the United States repeating the pattern. Moreover, Britain desperately needed both massive American economic aid and an Anglo-American military alliance that would allow a grievously weakened England to divert moneys from domestic and international defense to economic recovery. The only way to get such commitments out of the Americans in their postwar mood of penny-pinching, fence straddling, and neo-isolationism was to exaggerate the Soviet menace — just as Truman had to do in order to get congressional backing for his programs of economic aid to Europe.

In November 1918, one week after the end of World War I, Churchill had submitted a memorandum entitled "The Unfinished Task" to the British cabinet. In it he asserted that "it is ridiculous to suppose that the war is over because the fighting between the armies has stopped. . . . We have got to make just as great an effort in the next six months as we should have made if the war had been going on at full blast: indeed in some ways we have got to make a greater effort." The reason for this (as he wrote soon thereafter) was that he did "not believe there will be any real peace in the world as long as the Bolshevik tyranny endures."[7]

As World War II drew to a close, Churchill remained true to form. On May 12, 1945, only four days after the German surrender, he sent a cable to Truman saying that if Communist expansionism "is handled firmly before our strength is dispersed, Europe may be saved from another blood-bath. Otherwise the whole fruits of our victory may be cast away and none of the purposes of World Organization [i.e., the UN] to prevent territorial aggression and future wars will be attained."[8] That same day, in another cable, he warned Truman that if American forces were withdrawn from Europe too hastily, "it would be open to the Russians in a very short time to advance if they chose to the waters of the North Sea and the Atlantic."[9] Truman was a good audience for this. On May 11, in a cable to Churchill, he had complained that the Communists were engaging in "uncontrolled landgrabbing [and] tactics which are all too reminiscent of those of Hitler and Japan."[10]

The unconditional surrender of the Axis nations, the establishment of the UN, and American possession of the bomb were supposed to put a permanent end to such behavior. If Stalin was going to pursue an expansionist program in the face of these developments, he must — so went the prevalent reasoning — be both ruthless and desperate. The model most conveniently at hand to explain such behavior, and to predict its course, was that provided by Hitler. According to the dangerous logic of the relentless cycle of world wars, Stalin was assumed to have taken up Hitler's failed project of world conquest.

Both in and out of office, Churchill did much to encourage this line of thought — though he maintained that Stalin's position in the early postwar period was like Hitler's before his 1936 move into the Rhineland and not yet like that of the 1939 Hitler eager for war. In his "Iron Curtain" speech, in Fulton, Missouri, on March 5, 1946, Churchill said, "I repulse the idea that a new war is inevitable, still more that it is imminent. . . . I do not believe that Soviet Russia desires war. What they desire is the fruits of war and the indefinite expansion of their power and doctrines."[11] Nor did Churchill desire war, but he desired the fruits of the threat of Soviet domination of Western Europe.

All through the 1930s, when he was out of the cabinet and his views were out of fashion, Churchill had railed against British disarmament and against the appeasement of Germany, which were two sides of the same coin. The British feared war because they were unprepared for war. In March 1936, when Hitler boldly marched thirty-five thousand troops into the Rhineland, which the Treaty of

Versailles had declared a permanently demilitarized zone, the British and the French did nothing but protest. The French were strong enough to have stopped him alone, but they were still, less than twenty years after the armistice, terrified of Germany. The British wouldn't join them in a show of force, because they were afraid that they might be pulled into another disastrous war. For Hitler the occupation of the Rhineland was a great victory, since all his generals had advised him that the move was too dangerous. In his World War II memoirs Churchill wrote, "Undoubtedly Hitler's prestige and authority in the supreme circle of German power was sufficiently enhanced by this episode to encourage and enable him to march forward to greater tests."[12] Of France he wrote that by remaining "completely inert and paralyzed," it "lost irretrievably the last chance of arresting Hitler's ambitions without a serious war."[13]

That last observation provides the key to Churchill's postwar position. He suggested in his memoirs that World War II should be called "The Unnecessary War," and he maintained that never in history had there been a war that could more easily have been prevented.[14] Prevented, that is, if Churchill had been listened to at the time. The frustration he felt as a result of having been ignored exceeded even the frustration he felt in regard to Gallipoli. The second time around, after World War II, he was determined to be heard and to be heeded. And he was.

The publication of the first volume of Churchill's World War II memoirs, in the spring of 1948, was surely one of the most important events in the early days of the Cold War. In his preface Churchill wrote that

> the human tragedy reaches its climax in the fact that after all the exertions and sacrifices of hundreds of millions of people and of the victories of the Righteous Cause, we still have not found Peace or Security, and that *we lie in the grip of even worse perils than those we have surmounted* [emphasis added]. It is my earnest hope that pondering upon the past may give guidance in days to come.[15]

He stated in the first chapter that it was his purpose "to show how easily the tragedy of the Second World War could have been prevented; how the malice of the wicked was reinforced by the weakness of the virtuous; . . . how the middle course adopted from desires for safety and a quiet life may be found to lead direct to the bull's-eye of disaster."[16]

The book was, in effect, an appeal for a buildup of American military strength and for an Anglo-American alliance against the Soviet Union. It was an impassioned and eloquent — though oblique — argument against Western appeasement of Stalin. This time Churchill's views were not ignored. His book was serialized in both *Life* magazine and the *New York Times* during April and May 1948, and it was a selection of the Book-of-the-Month Club. Reviews and editorials hammered home the parallels between the events that Churchill described and those that were currently taking place in Europe. The book's impact was tremendous. Appearing between the Czech coup of February 1948 and the Berlin blockade in June, Churchill's volume was certainly partially responsible for the decisive and effective handling of the second crisis, in contrast to the anguished but evasive response to the first. It also had considerable influence both upon the formation of NATO and upon the American decision to intervene in Korea in June 1950.

Furthermore, although Churchill was out of office, it happened that his views were not out of fashion in Britain. Ernest Bevin, the foreign secretary of Clement Attlee's Labour government, had held a post in Churchill's coalition cabinet during the war and was as determined to win the commitment of a militarily strong America to the defense of Europe as was Churchill himself.

CHAPTER 6

The Korean War and the Cold War in Europe: To the Brink of War

EAST-WEST TENSIONS were dramatically heightened in the summer of 1947 by the announcement of the Marshall Plan and by the preliminary conferences to organize its realization. The Marshall Plan was instituted because of widespread fears that poverty in Europe was breeding political discontent that would win millions of new converts to Communism and make all of Europe vulnerable to attack or infiltration. A strong Europe was needed to resist Russian threats and intimidation, to prevent or to repulse a Russian invasion, and to stop the spread of Communism. Thriving European economies were also vital to American trade, and the revival of Europe was viewed in Washington as essential to preventing a recurrence of the Great Depression, which had been so powerful a factor in bringing about World War II. However, by exacerbating the polarization of the nations of Europe into two hostile camps, each feeling so insecure that it failed to understand how greatly the other feared its strength and intentions, the Marshall Plan did much to intensify the Cold War. In effect, this plan for the economic rehabilitation of Western Europe was directly responsible for removing whatever lingering possibility there might have been for a unified Korea.

The catch in the Marshall Plan was that Europe could not regain its economic health unless the German economy was resuscitated. Thus, although the western zones of Germany were not formally represented at the exploratory conference in Paris in July 1947, their needs and their ability to contribute were considered. The Western powers viewed the revival of Germany as purely defensive, as a measure forced upon them by threats of Communist encroachments and Soviet conquest. Germany was to be made strong — and its resources to be made available to the other nations of Western Europe — because otherwise the West would be vulnerable.

Implicit in the Marshall Plan's treatment of Germany were both the formation of a united West Germany and the rearmament of that nation. As European economic recovery reduced the possibility of Communist electoral victories, Stalin would find himself increasingly forced to resort to military intimidation or outright invasion if he wished to gain ascendancy over Western Europe. In such circumstances, Europe would be able to resist only if it could call upon the resources of a strong western Germany — not only upon its industry for armaments but also upon its population for soldiers. The West took a long time (until 1950) to acknowledge this, let alone to accept it, but the Soviets understood at once the implications of the Marshall Plan, which they accordingly denounced as "the Martial Plan."

Long experience had made Stalin unable to conceive of a prosperous and armed Germany as anything but aggressive, especially toward Russia — and now, in 1947, the West's motivation for strengthening Germany was specifically and explicitly anti-Soviet. No matter that the West declared its actions purely defensive. Stalin simply couldn't believe such claims. His fears of a resurgent Germany were genuine and great.

Here we come to an absolutely basic fact of the Cold War that neither side understood at the time: the Russians and the West were equally afraid of each other. Each side viewed its own ever more drastic moves as defensive responses to specific increased threats posed by the other. Because this was so, each side regarded the countermoves of the other as unprovoked and unjustified acts of aggression, rather than as natural moves of defense. As Americans tended to see matters, the Russians acted arbitrarily, and the Americans were forced to react; the Soviet Union aggressed, and the United States defended. This lack of understanding and communication led to a sequence of escalating crises and tensions much like that which characterized Japanese-American relations before World War II.

The most obvious and immediate Soviet response to the initial stages of the Marshall Plan was the organization of the Communist Information Bureau (Cominform) in September 1947. (Soviet foreign minister Vyacheslav Molotov announced the plan to establish it four days after he walked out of the Paris conference.) Its purpose was twofold: first, to put pressure on the strong Communist parties of France and Italy to make the complete failure of the Marshall Plan their primary goal; second, to weaken nationalism in the nations of Central and Eastern Europe in favor of Communist (i.e., pro-Russian) unity. It was Yugoslavian unwillingness to submit to this second dictate that led to Tito's split with the Kremlin, early in 1948.

As Stalin apparently viewed the situation, the announcement of the Marshall Plan meant that Europe was to be divided irrevocably into two hostile camps. He tended, in the best of circumstances, to have a siege mentality, but now it became obsessive. He would consolidate his empire, raise the drawbridges, institute martial law, and strive to make his empire self-sufficient in order to withstand a long blockade. "In unity is strength" became his guiding principle; the nationalistic impulses of the nations within his bloc, and the political diversity that still existed within those nations, posed serious threats to the pro-Russian Communist unity in which lay the greatest possible strength. Unity is, always and everywhere, the primary goal of absolutism. Stalin set out to achieve *absolute* unity.

This goal had a direct counterpart in the West, formulated in reponse to fears of a consolidated Soviet empire. The Marshall Plan was intended to promote not only economic recovery but also European cooperation and unity. In fact, many American congressmen wanted to make Marshall aid contingent upon the integration of the nations of Western Europe into a United States of Europe.[1] Here, too, was the idea that in unity is strength.

The year following the establishment of the Cominform saw the Soviet-ordained removal of all non-Communists (as well as of Communists who were insufficiently pro-Russian) from the governments of Poland, Hungary, Romania, and Czechoslovakia, all of which border on the Soviet Union. The Soviets even put pressures on their neighbors Finland and Norway. For several reasons, the February 1948 Communist seizure of the Czech government evoked a particularly strong reaction in the West. It especially concerns us because it parallels in a most revealing way the situation in Korea in 1950.

Eduard Beneš, who had been president of Czechoslovakia before the war and who, during the war, headed the nation's provisional government in exile in London, went to Moscow in 1943 to assure Stalin of his friendship. The Western sacrifice of their nation to Hitler at Munich in 1938 had, in any case, made the Czechs bitter toward the West and inclined to look eastward for security. Therefore, when the Red Army liberated Czechoslovakia, in the spring of 1945, Beneš was allowed to return to Prague and to form a coalition government, in which the Communists (who received 38 percent of the vote in the democratic parliamentary elections of 1946, the largest total of any party) held only eight of the twenty-five ministries. Moreover, the Communist ministers seemed to be, relatively speaking, both humane and cooperative.

Czechoslovakia was all that both Stalin and the West had hoped Poland might be: democratic, friendly enough toward the Soviet Union to satisfy Stalin, and yet also friendly toward the West. Truman called it "the stronghold of democracy in central Europe."[2] As for Beneš, he felt that Czechoslovakia was ideally suited, and ideally situated, to be an intermediary between East and West, maintaining its independence through a skillful balancing act.

Were it not for its geographical situation, Czechoslovakia might well have gone the way of Austria. But it had the misfortune to border on both western Germany and the Soviet Union. It could, so Stalin must have reckoned, serve as a corridor through which a rearmed Germany could invade Russia. Therefore, it would have to be brought under rigid Russian control. Soviet pressures on Czechoslovakia began in the summer of 1947, almost immediately after Molotov walked out of the Marshall Plan conference.

The timing of the Czech coup is highly significant. In November and December 1947, the foreign ministers of the four Allied nations occupying Germany met in London to make yet one more attempt to conclude a peace treaty with Germany and to settle on terms for the nation's reunification. By this time, of course, the Marshall Plan had made the Soviets more determined than ever to block any settlement. Their obstructive behavior at the conference was so offensive that it led the United States, Britain, and France to decide to exclude the Soviets from future conferences; the three Western powers would make their own arrangements for uniting their zones. The Russians denounced this decision as illegal and incited the French Communist party to agitate against France's participation in any conference to which the Soviets were not invited. Nevertheless, the first tripartite conference on Germany opened in London on February 23, 1948. The Czech coup took place two days later.

The Communist takeover of Czechoslovakia, which the West

viewed as an unprovoked act of aggression, was thus a direct and considered response by the Soviets to fears that western Germany — over which the Kremlin would have no control, and in whose occupation councils it would have no say — would soon be united, rearmed, and allied with the West. The most interesting fact for our purposes is that the Korean peninsula occupies a geographical position between the Soviet Union and Japan that is (except for the intercession of the Korea Strait) roughly analogous to that of Czechoslovakia between the Soviet Union and West Germany. It would appear (as George Kennan observed at the time) not coincidental that the North Korean invasion of the south followed closely on the news, which began to circulate in the winter of 1949–50, that the United States was ready to proceed with a Japanese peace treaty over which the Soviets would have no veto.[3] Japan, so it seemed, was to become to the American defense system in the East what Germany would be to Western European defenses: an outpost for military bases, a great industrial workshop, and a valuable ally. Like Germany (so Stalin was led to believe), Japan was to be rearmed, and its role was to be specifically anti-Soviet. Stalin could no more imagine a purely defensive rearmed Japan than he could imagine such a Germany. Like Czechoslovakia, Korea provided a potential route for an invasion of the Soviet Union. Both of these small nations were drawbridges leading into Russia, and both had to be raised.

The intensity of the Western reaction to the Czech coup in February 1948 was at least partly due to the fact that Czechoslovakia had been the victim of the Munich Pact of September 1938. The British and the French had hoped that if they appeased Hitler by giving in to his demands at Munich, they would avoid war, they would win his friendship, and they would encourage him to direct his aggression against the Soviet Union. But the cowardly British and French abandonment of their Czech allies made Hitler confident that if he could reach an agreement with Stalin, he could launch an invasion of Poland with impunity.

Because of the obviousness of the parallel with the past, the 1948 Czech coup induced in the West an almost hysterical certainty that unless decisive action were taken to prevent Stalin from making any further moves, the Soviet Union would soon have all of Western

Europe under its control. A map of Europe on the front page of the *Washington Post* showed the area already under Soviet control and asked, "Where next?" Arrows indicated France, Italy, Austria, and Finland as possible targets. At the end of March, a National Security Council position paper stated that "the U.S.S.R. is attempting to gain world domination by subversion . . . but might ultimately resort to war if necessary to gain its ends."[4]

A fundamental axiom of the so-called Truman Doctrine held that subversion could best be countered by economic rather than by military means. Communism appealed to many people in Europe because they were miserable and thus desired radical change. Prosperity would make them content, moderate, democratic, and cooperative. Prosperity would thus foster both political stability and international anti-Communist unity.

Therefore, the first American response to the Czech coup was economic. On March 14 the Senate, which had been stalling for months, voted 69–17 to approve the Marshall Plan and to appropriate some $17 billion for aid to be distributed over the course of the next four years. Twelve days later the House followed suit, 329–74.

Things moved quickly after the Czech coup, which finally convinced the French that the Russians posed far greater and far more immediate dangers to them than would a unified and revived western Germany. On March 6, 1948, the United States, Britain, and France issued a joint communiqué stating that they had decided to integrate western Germany fully into the economic reconstruction of Europe, and in Brussels on March 17 Britain, France, and the Benelux nations signed a mutual-defense treaty that was clearly directed against the Soviet Union. Addressing a joint session of Congress that same day, Truman declared that the Brussels Treaty "deserves our full support." He went on to say, "I am sure that the determination of the free countries of Europe to protect themselves will be matched by an equal determination on our part to help them protect themselves."[5] Thus was planted the seed that grew, within a little more than a year, into the North Atlantic Treaty Organization.

By June 1, 1948, the tripartite talks had reached a general agreement to unify the western zones of Germany under an independent government, and on June 18 the three Western powers announced their intention to issue a new currency to be used throughout their zones in an effort to put an end to crippling and demoralizing inflation — which the Soviets had exacerbated by flooding the western zones with worthless bank notes. On June 24 the Russians halted all surface traffic between Berlin and the three western zones.

Stalin had clearly decided to present the Western powers with a difficult choice: they could either unite their zones into a West German nation or they could stay in Berlin, but not both. The abandonment of Berlin would have entailed such a loss of prestige for the West — and would so have destroyed German confidence in the West's ability to provide security — that it would have negated much that the Marshall Plan was intended to achieve. The West Germans would probably have come to feel that they might suffer serious consequences if they went along with Western plans for unification against Russian wishes.

The Berlin airlift, which Truman authorized on June 26, was the Western solution. Since the Soviets didn't dare to close the air lanes from the three western zones to Berlin (surface traffic could be stopped by roadblocks, but air traffic could be stopped only by shooting), American, British, and French planes were able to supply their zones of the city with thousands of tons of supplies a day for 324 days. It was a heroic accomplishment, but it gave the Soviets a mixed message: yes, the United States was now ready to block Soviet moves directly and effectively; but no, it was not ready to respond militarily to a Soviet challenge.

If the Czech coup pushed through the Marshall Plan, the Berlin blockade was the decisive factor in the formation of NATO. Stalin's audacity in Berlin convinced the people and the governments of the West that his next planned move might be an invasion of Western Europe. It was, therefore, essential to create the strongest possible military deterrent, emphasizing Western unity as much as actual buildups of troops and arms. Such a deterrent would give Europe the confidence in its security that it needed in order to flourish and to resist Soviet intimidation. (It was also essential as a counterbalance to German revival; a strong and united West could keep Germany from getting out of hand.) But the British and the French felt that they could not enjoy such confidence unless a heavily armed

America would give them a binding commitment to respond, immediately and militarily, to a Soviet invasion. In both world wars the United States had entered relatively late, after much damage had been done. The barrier to such an American commitment was the Constitution's prohibition against the signing of any treaty that would obligate the United States to declare war automatically under any given circumstances. Any declaration of war had to be approved by Congress.

A compromise was finally reached. Article 5 of the NATO pact, signed on April 4, 1949, stated that an attack upon any of the signatories would be viewed as an attack upon all of them. All were bound to take "such actions as each deems necessary" to restore and maintain peace and security. The result was what one reporter called a "moral obligation as distinct from specific, written-out obligation to use armed force."[6] The NATO pact was less a treaty of alliance than a pledge of unity intended to give the nations of Western Europe the confidence they needed to thrive and to maintain a firm stance against Communism.

By the spring of 1949 the Soviets had been forced to acknowledge that their moves to counter Western moves were only making matters worse, hastening the very developments that they wished to prevent. It was time for them to relax the tensions in Europe and to alter their global strategy. Early in May, Stalin ended the Berlin blockade, and the Soviets shifted to propaganda efforts aimed at persuading Western Europeans to oppose their governments' military buildups. The party line called for agitation against NATO as a manifestation of American imperialism and warmongering. At the same time — thwarted in Europe by the Marshall Plan and by the formation of NATO — the Soviets did what Russian governments since the midnineteenth century had always done when they found their European initiatives blocked: they shifted their attention to the Far East. Under the terms of the NATO pact, any further Russian attempts to move into Western Europe entailed the risk of precipitating a world war; in the Far East, however, postwar anti-Western nationalism and anticolonialism opened up a number of tempting areas, for the defense of which the United States was certainly not prepared to embark upon an all-out war. Moreover, with Mao Tse-tung's victory in China now virtually inevitable, it was essential to increase Russian influence in the East, lest Mao eclipse Stalin as the great leader of international Communism in that region.

The progress of the anti-Communist cause in Europe continued unabated through the summer of 1949. In August, Konrad Adenauer was elected the first chancellor of the Federal Republic of Germany. That same month the Greek civil war more or less came to an end. Because the Soviet economic blockade of Yugoslavia had forced Tito to look to the West for trade partners and for economic assistance, he had stopped allowing the Greek Communists to use southern Yugoslavia as a safe refuge and supply base. Confined to Greek soil and cut off from their principal source of supplies, the Communist guerrillas were rapidly weakened, checked, and destroyed.

It looked as though the West were winning the struggle to contain Communism. Marshall aid was beginning to revive Europe. NATO provided a greatly heightened sense of security. The French and Italian Communist parties were in decline. Yugoslavia was being detached from the Soviet bloc. Greece had been saved. And a democratic West Germany had been brought into being.

But then, in September 1949, came a profoundly disturbing revelation. Although the United States didn't expect the Soviets to develop an atomic bomb until at least 1952, the U.S. Air Force put its Long-Range Detection System into operation early in 1949 to monitor the atmosphere all around the Soviet Union for evidence of a nuclear explosion. On September 3, 1949, one of the reconnaissance planes recorded an exceptionally high radioactive count at 18,000 feet over the North Pacific. The USAF and the Royal Air Force tracked the cloud, and a panel of eminent scientists was assembled to analyze the samples and the data collected. Their conclusion was that the Soviets had successfully tested an atomic bomb late in August. At 11:00 A.M. on September 23, Truman issued a press release, somewhat hedging in its avoidance of the word "bomb," stating that "we have evidence that within recent weeks an atomic explosion occurred in the U.S.S.R."

The Soviet breaking of the atomic monopoly was crucial in bringing about a change in American military planning, though the need for that change had already been implicit in the NATO pact and the change was not actually adopted as official policy until after the outbreak of the Korean War. In short, the imminent neutralization of the American nuclear threat (once the Soviets had had time to manufacture a stockpile of bombs) meant that the United States would have to redevelop its conventional military forces if it hoped to confront the Russians with anything less than a war of mutual annihilation. America could no longer afford to maintain its extremist all-or-nothing attitude toward war. It was time to take the concept of limited war out of mothballs.

The American development of the atomic bomb, coupled with rapid demobilization and the country's budget-conscious mood after V-J Day, had left the air force the branch of the service on which the United States placed its greatest reliance. The air force — the deliverer of atomic bombs — seemed to be the military service of the future, rendering both the army and the navy to a great extent obsolete. Furthermore, the air force seemed to offer the most cost-effective deterrent to the huge Soviet army; it gave far more bang for the buck than did expensive-to-maintain ground troops.

This thinking was very clearly reflected in the defensive war plan that the Joint Chiefs of Staff drew up in March 1948, two weeks after the Czech coup. If the Soviets invaded Western Europe, the air force would bomb the Soviet Union, while the U.S. Army and Navy would play relatively minor supporting roles. The JCS war plan called for the expansion of the air force from 45 groups to 70 (a total of approximately 7,000 planes, counting both bombers and fighters).[7] In the eyes of a large congressional bloc of air-power zealots, the building of a 70-group air force became a matter of do or die.

It was not immediately recognized, except by a few sophisticated planners in the State and Defense departments, that the Soviet bomb would change all that. Indeed, Truman's first response was simply to make a bigger bomb. At the end of January 1950 he announced a program to develop the hydrogen bomb, but, of course, it would be at least a couple of years before the bomb was ready. Therefore, he simultaneously called for a high-level review of the policies and strategies that the United States should pursue in the meantime.

The State Department's Policy Planning Staff, headed by Paul Nitze, worked for several months on its report, which, when it was adopted by the National Security Council, became known as NSC-

68. The paper departed most radically from prevalent analyses of Soviet behavior in its postulate that, rather than preparing to launch World War III, the Russians were hoping to eat away gradually at the free world through an endless series of limited and localized offensives, both subversive and military, to which the United States was dangerously unprepared to respond proportionately. "The U.S. will therefore," warned the report, "be confronted more frequently with the dilemma of reacting totally to a limited expansion of Soviet control or of not reacting at all (except with ineffectual protest and half measures)."[8] It was imperative that America embark on a crash program to build up its conventional military forces, especially infantry and armored divisions, so that it could respond effectively and appropriately to Soviet moves anywhere in the world. "The assault on free institutions is world-wide now, and in the context of the present polarization of power a defeat of free institutions *anywhere* is a defeat *everywhere*" (emphasis added).[9]

The necessary buildup of conventional forces would be very expensive, but Nitze believed that the United States could easily afford to devote what was then the staggeringly vast sum of $50 billion — some 20 percent of the gross national product — to its military budget. That figure was, however, so far in excess of the $14 billion ceiling on military expenditures that Truman adamantly enforced that Secretary of State Dean Acheson, one of the report's most enthusiastic and dedicated supporters, asked Nitze not to mention any specific figures in the report, lest it be rejected out of hand on that basis alone.

Truman approved NSC-68 on April 25, 1950, which is to say that he acknowledged the soundness of the principles embodied in the report. He declined to order its implementation, however, until further study could be made of the costs entailed. In other words, he rejected the report's recommendations as too expensive.

The PPS had intended all along that NSC-68 would be made public and had accordingly overstated its case in order to sell it to Congress and to put the Russians on notice. But Acheson insisted that the paper be classified as top secret until he had, through personal influence and persuasion, won over a decisive number of supporters in the highest echelons of the government. Only then, once he could be sure of its quick ratification, would the report be presented to Congress. Until that time, the secrecy was designed to protect the report from tax-obsessed congressmen, not to keep the Russians in the dark. But if Stalin had been aware of the recommendations of NSC-68, he would almost certainly have forbidden Kim Il-sung to invade South Korea, for the invasion bore out the predictions of the report and would smooth the way for its implementation. As one of Acheson's aides later recalled, "We were sweating over NSC-68, and then, thank God, Korea came along."[10]

CHAPTER 7

Cold War Developments in Asia

THE AMERICAN PUBLIC was just beginning to assess the blow that the announcement of the Soviet bomb dealt to its complacency when, eight days later, on October 1, 1949, the news came from Peking that Mao Tse-tung had formally proclaimed the establishment of the People's Republic of China.

Early in August, in an attempt to prepare the American people for this climax, the U.S. State Department had published a thousand-page collection of documents relating to American efforts to aid Chiang Kai-shek and to bring about some sort of compromise with the Chinese Communists. In his introductory letter Secretary of State Acheson wrote that

> it has been argued that relatively small amounts of additional aid — military and economic — to the National Government would have enabled it to destroy communism in China. The most trustworthy military, economic, and political information available to our Government does not bear out this view.
>
> A realistic appraisal of conditions in China, past and present, leads to the conclusion that the only alternative open to the United States was full-scale intervention in behalf of a Government which had lost the confidence of its own troops and its own people. Such intervention would have required the expenditure of even greater sums than have been fruitlessly spent thus far, the command of the Nationalist armies by American officers, and the probable participation of American armed forces — land, sea, and air — in the resulting war. Intervention of such a scope and magnitude would have been resented by the mass of the Chinese people, would have diametrically reversed our historic policy, and would have been condemned by the American people.[1]

As many Americans viewed the situation, however, a relatively small number of Chinese malcontents and troublemakers had somehow, incredibly, succeeded in imposing atheistic, totalitarian, and anti-Western Communism on all of China. They had done so (assumed the Americans) against the supposedly indomitable will of the Chinese people, who revered the United States for having championed the Open Door policy and for having defeated Japan, who were profoundly grateful for all the educational and medical assistance that American missionaries had given them, and who had been rapidly embracing democracy and Christianity. Those Americans simply could not comprehend why the United States, the strongest nation in the world, would, as they saw it, stand aside and allow such a loyal and valuable friend as China to succumb to Communism — unless, of course, the Far Eastern policy of the United States had been formulated by Communist sympathizers. The view thus arose that FDR and his socialistic New Deal advisers had deliberately "sold out" China at the Yalta Conference, and that Communist sympathizers and agents in the State Department — both officials in Washington and foreign-service officers in China — had encouraged President Truman to repudiate Chiang. Thus was laid the foundation for McCarthyism, and thus was Truman placed in the position of having to oppose with force the North Korean invasion — to demonstrate that his administration was not at all sympathetic to Communist expansion.

At least since late in the summer of 1947 the Truman administration had seen a Communist victory in China as more or less inevitable. In July of that year Truman had sent General Albert Wedemeyer, who had succeeded Joseph Stilwell as the Allied commander in China in 1944, to make an inspection tour of China, to report on the military situation in the Chinese civil war, and to evaluate what could be done to help Chiang against the Communists. What he found provided little basis for optimism. In the statement Wedemeyer made on August 24, at the end of his tour, he remarked that "it is discouraging to note the abject defeatism of many Chinese" regarding the possibility of a complete Communist takeover. "To regain and maintain the confidence of the people," he said, Chiang's government "will have to effect immediately drastic, far-reaching political and economic reforms. Promises will no longer suffice. Performance is absolutely necessary. *It should be accepted that military force in itself will not eliminate Communism*" (emphasis added).[2]

In China, as in Europe, only an increased level of general prosperity could halt the spread of Communism. But China's desperate situation did not lend itself to the Marshall Plan solution, for the corruption of Chiang's government, coupled with his determination to inflict a military defeat on the Communists, meant that very little of any aid given to China would be used to improve the welfare of the Chinese people. Wedemeyer did, however, recommend a program of American aid "in specified economic and military fields," as long as the use of that aid was rigorously supervised by American advisers.[3] The United States, he said, would have to give Chiang an ultimatum: no reforms, no aid.

Drastic measures indeed would be called for if the current trends were to be reversed. "Under the impact of civil strife and inflation, the Chinese economy is disintegrating," wrote Wedemeyer in his official report to Truman, dated September 19, 1947.

> The most probable outcome of present trends would be, not sudden collapse, but a continued and creeping paralysis and consequent decline in the authority and power of the National Government. . . . With the disruption of transportation facilities and the loss of much of North China and Manchuria, important resources of those areas are no longer available for the rehabilitation and support of China's economy.[4]

Although Wedemeyer believed that military force alone could not eliminate Communism, he also recognized that the military and economic situations in China were closely interrelated. Grave as the economic outlook was, Chiang's military prospects were even bleaker. "The overall military position of the National Government has deteriorated in the past several months and the current military situation favors Communist forces," reported the general.[5] In particular, he wrote, "the situation in Manchuria has deteriorated to such a degree that prompt action is necessary to prevent that area from becoming a Soviet satellite. The Chinese Communists may soon gain military control of Manchuria and announce the establishment of a government" in that region. Soviet relations with such a government could "ultimately . . . lead to a Communist-dominated China."[6] Wedemeyer suggested that Chiang ask the UN to establish a five-power

(Chinese, American, Soviet, British, and French) "guardianship" over Manchuria.[7] The Truman administration feared, however, that Chiang might find such a suggestion so insulting — and that the Chinese people might find its implications regarding Chiang's weakness so demoralizing — that it might make Chiang less amenable than ever to American demands for reforms, and that it might only advance the Communist cause within China.[8]

Although Wedemeyer's report was not made public until August 1949, it had considerable immediate impact within the State Department. Since China was likely to be taken over by the Communists, Japan would have to be strengthened and securely allied with the United States to offset that development, just as a strong Germany was needed to balance Soviet gains in Eastern Europe. In his memoirs George Kennan recounted that late in the summer of 1947, after urgent preliminaries for the Marshall Plan had been completed, the State Department's Policy Planning Staff, which he then headed, attempted "to take stock of America's world position as a whole." He concluded that

> the theaters of our greatest dangers, our greatest responsibilities, and our greatest possibilities at that moment were the two occupied areas of Western Germany and Japan. These places were the centers, respectively, of the two greatest industrial complexes of East and West. Their recovery was essential to the restoration of stability in Europe and East Asia. It was essential, if any sort of tolerable balance of power was to be established in the postwar world, that they be kept out of Communist hands and that their great resources be utilized to the full for constructive purposes.[9]

That is to say, utilized in the struggle against Communism. Kennan was especially worried about Japan, which, he wrote,

> had no effective means of combatting the Communist penetration and political pressure that was already vigorously asserting itself under the occupation and could be depended upon to increase greatly if the occupation was removed and American forces withdrawn. In the face of this situation the nature of the occupational policies pursued up to that time by General MacArthur's headquarters seemed on cursory examination to be such that if they

had been devised for the specific purpose of rendering Japanese society vulnerable to Communist political pressures and paving the way for a Communist takeover, they could scarcely have been other than what they were. [10]

Under the occupation, not only leading militarists but also several hundred thousand persons who had served the wartime regime — willingly or unwillingly — had been purged from the government and from positions of responsibility in Japanese society. In May 1947 General MacArthur had given Japan a democratic and liberal constitution that guaranteed freedom of speech even to Communists, thousands of whom had been released from Japanese prisons in 1945. Large deliveries of Japanese industrial equipment had been made to the Allied nations as reparations. Japan was demilitarized and disarmed, and its national police force had been decentralized. Land reform, the breaking up of the great financial-industrial cartels (the *zaibatsu*), and the organization of labor had all been undertaken with great zeal. All this has led Edwin O. Reischauer, one of the most eminent American historians of Japan and the U.S. ambassador to that nation from 1961 to 1966, to call MacArthur "the most radical, one might even say socialistic, leader the United States ever produced, and also one of the most successful." [11]

By early 1947, however, Communists had largely succeeded in taking over the Japanese labor unions and were using them as forums from which to denounce the American occupation. The radical but far from completed land reform had created what Kennan called "a situation of great confusion and instability in the relationships of agricultural land ownership." [12] The "indiscriminate purging of whole categories of individuals" [13] was depriving Japan of the services of a large portion of its most highly educated and competent bureaucrats, managers, and teachers. And zaibatsu-baiting, as the occupiers called it, had reduced Japanese industry to a state of chaos.

Furthermore, the Japanese people were beginning to resent the American occupation troops, whose role was becoming less constructive and more parasitical. Enthusiastically embracing their new constitution and their demilitarized society, the Japanese were coming to feel that authoritarian American military occupation was no longer necessary or appropriate. What's more, the costs of the occupation were absorbing approximately one third of the Japanese national budget, thus presenting a serious obstacle to economic recovery.

On February 26, 1948, the day after the beginning of the Czech coup, Kennan left for Tokyo to confer with General MacArthur. "The regime of control by SCAP [the Supreme Commander for the Allied Powers] over the Japanese government should," he recommended,

> be relaxed. The Japanese should be encouraged to develop independent responsibility. *No further reform legislation should be pressed. The emphasis should shift from reform to economic recovery.* The purges should be tempered, tapered off, and terminated at an early date. An effort should be made to reduce occupation costs. Reparations should be generally halted, *the opposition of other Far Eastern Commission powers notwithstanding* [emphasis added].[14]

MacArthur was quite ready to put Kennan's proposals into practice. As early as February 1947, when Communist labor leaders had threatened a general strike to back up their political demands, the general had begun to take action to curb the unions; he then realized that it was time to end the punitive and reforming stage of the occupation and to shift to the revival of Japanese industry and economic strength. On March 17, 1947, he startled the world by announcing that, since the major antimilitaristic and antifeudal reforms had been carried out or were well under way, Japan was ready for a conciliatory peace treaty.[15] The U.S. State Department supported this initiative, but the Soviet Union and the Nationalist Chinese government were dead set against it. MacArthur, though essentially an autocrat, felt himself sufficiently bound by the wishes of the Allies, as represented on the Far Eastern Commission, that he did not dare to undertake a 180-degree reversal of established occupation policy solely on his own authority. Throughout the remainder of 1947 the reforms continued under their own momentum, and as late as December of that year some twelve hundred industrial combines were marked for possible breakup during 1948.

The most significant aspect of Kennan's visit to Tokyo early in 1948 was that he presented MacArthur with a highly legalistic loophole in the interpretation of the FEC's authority, which would permit the general to foster Japanese economic recovery despite the opposition of the other Allies.[16] The clear implication of this, of course, was that the United States was now prepared to dispense with the inconvenient fiction of Allied unity in governing Japan. (Kennan's visit coincided with the first conference on German recovery and unification that excluded the Soviets.)

General MacArthur was pleased, and he proceeded at once to reorient the occupation from reform to economic recovery. After Kennan's visit very few firms were forced to divest, and over the course of the next several years the occupation relinquished much of its direct control over Japanese affairs; many restrictions were removed from Japanese industry; the labor unions were reorganized and their activities curtailed; many victims of the purges were restored to their former positions; and a new purge was begun, this one directed against Communists.

MacArthur believed that if the United States took the lead in sponsoring a conciliatory peace treaty — bullying the vindictive Allies to accept one, however reluctantly they might do so — then the Japanese government, out of gratitude, would allow the United States to retain military bases in Japan. But the Joint Chiefs of Staff felt that this approach was too risky. They feared that Japan might emerge from a peace conference neutralized and stripped of all defenses, whether its own or American. This would be completely unacceptable, for Japan was the keystone of American defenses in the Pacific. Not only did the JCS want American bases in Japan from which they could bomb the Soviet Union in the event of a world war, but they also feared that a neutral Japan might soon fall to Communist subversion and/or attack.[17]

In order to grasp fully the importance of Japan in the view of the JCS, we must consider the official concept of the American "defense perimeter" in the Pacific. Its most candid public definition was written by MacArthur himself, in August 1950. After World War II, said MacArthur,

> our strategic frontier . . . shifted to embrace the entire Pacific Ocean, which has become a vast moat to protect us as long as we hold it.
>
> Indeed, it acts as a protective shield to all of the Americas and all free lands of the Pacific Ocean area we control to the shores of Asia by a chain of islands extending in an arc from the Aleutians to the Marianas held by us and our free Allies. From this island

chain we can dominate with air power every Asiatic port from
Vladivostok to Singapore and prevent any hostile movement into
the Pacific.

Any predatory attack from Asia must be an amphibious effort.
No amphibious force can be successful with our control of the sea
lanes and the air over these lanes in its avenue of advance.[18]

The loss of this island chain to a potential enemy would, MacArthur
averred, "shift any future battle area 5,000 miles eastward to the coasts
of the American continents, our own home coast."[19]

Early in 1949 the JCS drafted a revised defensive war plan for
World War III, which they assumed would center on a Soviet invasion
of Western Europe. As in World War II, the United States would
initially throw its greatest resources into the task of rescuing Europe,
giving secondary status to Asia. No positions on the continent of Asia
were considered tenable or worth trying to hold. But Japan and Okinawa were to be held at all costs, with the Philippines playing a role
of only somewhat lesser importance. Japan, as the island group of the
American defense perimeter closest to the Soviet Union, would be
essential in performing three tasks: (1) preventing any Soviet moves
across the Pacific toward the United States; (2) serving, in effect, as
a group of huge, unsinkable, and easily defensible aircraft carriers
from which to bomb Siberia, Manchuria, and Soviet-occupied Korea;
and (3) forcing the Soviets to divert some of their strength from Europe
in order to defend the Far East. If a peace treaty deprived the United
States of its Japanese bases, the entire American strategy for World
War III would fall apart.

By the end of 1949, pressured by the Communist victory in China,
the State and Defense departments had tentatively worked out a
compromise. The U.S. government would sponsor a lenient and conciliatory peace treaty guaranteeing a strong, economically healthy,
and anti-Communist Japan that would allow the United States to
retain its military bases. The treaty itself would not authorize American retention of base rights, but a separate agreement to be negotiated
at the same time would do so.

Such a treaty would obviously be totally unacceptable to the Soviets, who were demanding a punitive, Versailles-type treaty that
would prevent their perennial Asian enemy from regaining its strength

and ever again posing a threat to Russian interests in the Far East. And, of course, the Soviets would do everything in their power to oppose American retention of military bases in Japan. A Soviet-American compromise was as impossible in Japan as it was in Germany or Korea — or anywhere else. The United States would proceed on its own toward a "separate" Japanese peace treaty (i.e., one over which the Soviets would have no veto). By this time Western moves in Germany could leave Stalin in no doubt that the United States would carry out its intentions in Japan despite Russian protests, warnings, and obstructions. Stalin must have hoped, however, that the British, who were anxious to protect Hong Kong and eager to rebuild their trade with mainland China, might oppose a separate Western treaty on the grounds that it would hopelessly antagonize the Chinese Communists.

Late in 1949 Japanese legislators were debating whether it would be a violation of their new constitution to grant military base rights to the United States in the event of a separate treaty. In his New Year's message of January 1, 1950, General MacArthur assured the Japanese that it would be legal, and he asserted that with Japan's progress in economic recovery and the relaxation of occupation controls during 1949, Japan and the United States had "virtually arrived at a *de facto* peace."[20] Hardly any clearer notification of American intentions could have been given to the Kremlin.

And then, as if intentionally to confirm Stalin's worst suspicions and fears, the four members of the JCS (General Omar N. Bradley, chairman; General J. Lawton Collins, army chief of staff; Admiral Forrest P. Sherman, chief of naval operations; and General Hoyt S. Vandenberg, air force chief of staff and nephew of the influential Republican senator Arthur Vandenberg) arrived in Tokyo at the end of January for discussions with MacArthur, principally concerning a Japanese peace treaty and the retention of American bases. Nor was either the visit or its purpose a well-kept secret. On February 4, according to George Kennan, "the Soviet papers carried . . . a Tokyo story on the visit of the Joint Chiefs, specifically citing, as an example of the significance of the visit, the statement of Admiral Decker, commander of the Yokosuka base, to the effect that the US Navy would require that base permanently."[21] On February 15, a few days after the Joint Chiefs had left Tokyo, the *New York Times* stated that MacArthur's political adviser, William J. Sebald, was reported to have outlined to a Bangkok conference of American diplomats a plan to go ahead with a separate Japanese peace treaty. And in its issue of February 17, *U.S. News & World Report* ran a two-page spread on the recent JCS visit to MacArthur; the layout even included a map of the proposed permanent U.S. military bases in Japan.

In December 1949 Mao Tse-tung had arrived in Moscow; he would remain there until mid-February 1950, engaged in negotiating with Stalin a Treaty of Friendship and Alliance as well as an agreement for Soviet economic aid to China. The prospect of a revived and probably rearmed Japan in alliance with the United States, quite possibly serving as the cornerstone of a Pacific version of NATO directed against both Communist China and the Soviet Union, clearly had an impact of the greatest magnitude on the negotiations. Since Stalin and Mao were both genuinely and more or less equally afraid of a resurgent Japan, the American moves served to force the two old enemies into a bond, if not of true friendship, then at least of co-operation. (Reactionary Stalin much preferred the cynical and manipulable Chiang to the idealistic and sincerely revolutionary Mao, and Mao bitterly resented all the help that Stalin had given Chiang since the 1920s.) The crucial point was that the threat of an American-Japanese alliance led Stalin to abandon his wish for a weak and divided China. He now wanted a united and grateful, and thus subordinate, China that would be a strong ally — strong, but not *too* strong — against Japan.

The news that Mao was in Moscow gave great urgency to American efforts to convince the Chinese Communist leader that the Soviet Union posed a much greater threat to Chinese nationalism than did the United States. Mao should (so Washington insisted) view the Russians as his real enemies, and the Americans as his real friends. Secretary of State Acheson, in particular, had high hopes that Mao would turn out to be another Tito, who by the end of 1949 was well on the way to demonstrating that it was possible for a nation to call itself Communist and to pursue an ambitious domestic program of Socialism while at the same time defying Moscow and enjoying friendly economic and diplomatic relations with the West. Russian moves to suppress Yugoslav nationalism had led to Tito's break with the Kremlin, and Acheson was fervently hoping that the pattern would repeat itself in China. The Americans felt it was vital, on the one hand, to convince Mao that Stalin wanted to detach Manchuria from China and make it a Soviet satellite, while, on the other hand, making it clear that the United States had no designs on any Chinese territory and was even ready to acquiesce in a Communist takeover of Formosa, to which Chiang's government had fled early in December and which the Communists had said they would invade as soon as possible.

In August Acheson had written, "It is abundantly clear that we must face the situation as it exists in fact. We will not help the Chinese or ourselves by basing our policy on wishful thinking."[22] The Communists were in control of China. That was an inescapable fact, and an extremely important one. The best would have to be made of the situation. And the best that could be hoped for was a rift between the Chinese Communists and the Russians.

By abandoning Chiang, the United States would show that it bore Mao's government no ill will. With Chiang finally out of the way, the American people would have to accept the fait accompli of a Communist-controlled China. The way would then be clear to give official recognition to the Communist regime and to establish friendly economic and commercial relations with it — relations that would benefit both China and the United States and that would gradually wean China away from Communism. To that end, on December 23, 1949, the U.S. State Department sent a memorandum to all American embassies and consulates around the world, informing them that a Communist takeover of Formosa was to be expected in the very near future and that such a development was not to be either opposed or denounced by the U.S. government. A Communist victory on Formosa, continued the memo, would pose absolutely no threat to American security.[23]

On January 3 a copy of the memo was leaked to the United Press, which promptly distributed the text, causing a great flap in Washington. Two days later Truman was forced to make an official announcement that America would "not provide military aid or advice to Chinese forces" on Formosa.[24] Acheson elaborated that Chiang had enough money to buy all the military equipment he needed. What his troops lacked, the secretary pointedly implied, was not matériel but the "will to resist."[25]

One week later, on January 12, Acheson delivered a major speech on U.S. Far Eastern policy to the National Press Club, in Washington.[26] The speech is routinely cited as one of the factors contributing to the North Korean decision to invade the south, since Acheson made it quite clear that South Korea did not constitute an element in the American defense perimeter in the Pacific. At the time of the North Korean invasion, many commentators said that the speech had given the green light to the Communists, and since then many historians have concurred. They have maintained that Acheson was stating as clearly as he possibly could that the United States would not go to South Korea's rescue. In fact, however, he was saying something a great deal more subtle and sophisticated.

The main point of Acheson's speech was that nationalism — a passionate desire for independence and for an end to the foreign exploitation that had condemned the Asian peoples to poverty — had become the dominant ideology in the East. The trouble was, however, that many Asians had been misled into believing that the Russian brand of Communism endorsed Asian nationalism, when actually, Acheson declared, "Communism . . . is really the spearhead of Russian imperialism." Specifically, he contended,

> the Soviet Union is detaching the northern provinces of China from China and is attaching them to the Soviet Union. This process is complete in Outer Mongolia. It is nearly complete in Manchuria, and I am sure that in Inner Mongolia and in Sinkiang there are very happy reports coming from Soviet agents to Moscow. . . . I should like to suggest . . . that this fact that the Soviet Union is taking the four northern provinces of China is *the single most significant, most important fact in the relation of any foreign power with Asia* [emphasis added].[27]

Perhaps that would have been true if the United States hadn't at that very time been so obviously moving toward a Japanese peace treaty to which the Russians and the Chinese Communists could not possibly give their assent. By January 1950 *that* had become the single most significant fact in the relation of any foreign power with Asia.

It was so significant that it forced Stalin to promise Mao, as formally stated in their treaty, that the Soviet Union would return complete control of the Manchurian ports and railways to China by the end of 1952. The Soviets were going to have to respect Chinese nationalism after all.

The preamble of the treaty that Stalin and Mao signed on February 14, 1950, specifically stated that their alliance was directed against "the revival of Japanese imperialism and the resumption of aggression on the part of Japan or any other state [i.e., the United States] that may collaborate in any way with Japan in acts of aggression."[28] Lest we dismiss Russian and Chinese fears of a renewal of Japanese imperialism as completely insincere and calculated, it is worth noting that so astute and objective an observer as George McCune, the State Department's expert in Korea, wrote early in 1950 that "fear of a possible re-enactment of invasion from a resurgent Japan is at present an obsession of Koreans, both north and south. They see in the present U.S. policy of the creation of a strong Japan, a terrifying resemblance to the events of 1902–04, which resulted in a Russian-Japanese war and their own loss of statehood."[29]

When Acheson outlined America's Pacific defense perimeter in his speech, his point was certainly not to announce that the United States would turn its back on South Korea if that nation were attacked. His point was that Formosa was not included in the perimeter. Indeed, he implied, the United States — unlike the Soviet Union — had no designs whatsoever on the continent of Asia. The United States was quite content to see the Chinese Communists establish and maintain control not only over Formosa but over all of China's traditional territories. America would, in other words, extend the Open Door policy to the Communist regime in return for Peking's friendship and for its recognition that the Soviet Union was China's enemy.

As for South Korea, Acheson's message was that because the United States was the champion of Asian nationalism, it was committed to helping South Korea to help itself. A new day had dawned in Asia, said Acheson, "in which the Asian peoples are on their own, and know it, and intend to continue on their own." The old relationships of exploitation and paternalism were over, and the "relation of east and west must now be in the Far East one of mutual respect and mutual helpfulness." American policy would be to help South Korea to develop the self-respect that would follow as it became confident it could defend itself; the necessary strength would arise naturally from economic prosperity and political stability. The United States, strongly committed to that policy, had already given South Korea much help in getting itself established. "We are asking the Congress to continue that help until it is firmly established," Acheson went on to say, "and that legislation is now pending before the Congress. *The idea that we should scrap all of that, that we should stop half way through the achievement of the establishment of this country, seems to me to be the most utter defeatism and utter madness in our interests in Asia"* (emphasis added).[30] Under the circumstances, he could hardly have made a clearer or more forceful statement of the American commitment to South Korea.

Acheson was evidently hoping that with Communist China friendly to the United States, and with the United States able to draw upon the resources of a strong Japan, the Soviets would not dare to invade, or to authorize the North Koreans to invade, South Korea. But that plan began to fall apart just two days after the secretary of state made his speech. On January 14 Chinese Communists seized the American consulate in Peking. American pro-Chiang congressmen immediately insisted that this move demonstrated the complete failure of Acheson's China policy, and they demanded his resignation. Bowing to the pressures of this most embarrassing situation, Acheson told a press conference on the eighteenth that the seizure of the consulate forced him to conclude that the Chinese Communists did not want U.S. recognition, but he said nothing about resuming aid to Chiang.[31] China had indeed, as Mao put it, "leaned to one side," but the United States would continue to straddle the fence as long as it could.

CHAPTER 8

Setting the Stage

AS SECRETARY OF STATE ACHESON mentioned in his National Press Club speech in January 1950, legislation authorizing a new installment of economic aid to South Korea was then pending before the House. Seven months earlier, on June 7, 1949, a few weeks before the United States was to withdraw the last of its occupation troops from Korea, President Truman had requested a grant of $150 million for South Korea, most of it to be used to develop alternative supplies of resources — including coal and other minerals, electric power, and chemical fertilizer — that had before 1945 been obtained from northern Korea.[1]

Acheson testified before the House Foreign Affairs Committee that South Korea would fall to the Communists within two or three months if the bill wasn't passed quickly,[2] but that alarmist line was turned against the administration by such critics as military correspondent Hanson W. Baldwin, who wrote in the *New York Times* on June 11, 1949:

> Southern Korea has been — strategically — indefensible since the Communist conquest of Manchuria. We have never been able to guarantee a free and independent Korea, and should never have made such a promise; the Yalta terms, exclusive of other factors, made the keeping of such a promise impossible.
>
> The presence of United States troops in Southern Korea has been the real major deterrent to domination by the north. With the departure of the last of those troops by July 1, there will remain only the relatively weak military and police forces of the Southern Korea government, forces which are none too reliable politically. The appropriation of $150,000,000, therefore, for Economic Recovery Administration aid to Korea in the coming year could well mean money down the drain.

Nevertheless, the Senate approved the aid bill (48–13) on October 12, but the House took no action on it during the remainder of 1949 except to reduce the stipulated appropriation to $60 million, less than half of what Truman had requested. (The administration was able to give piecemeal aid of about $60 million to South Korea during the interim.)

By the end of 1949 there was a growing conviction, in Washington and in Tokyo alike, that South Korea's days were numbered, and that very little could or would be done about it. Around the turn of the year, as one *Time* correspondent later put it, "South Korea, bedeviled by guerrilla raids, galloping inflation and the daily threat of invasion from the north, looked like a candidate for the same mortuary as Nationalist China."[3] Upon being stationed in Tokyo in November 1949 as a captain in the Military History Section attached to Mac-Arthur's headquarters, James F. Schnabel (who has since written one volume of the official history of the U.S. Army in the Korean War) attended an intelligence briefing for newly arrived officers. "Discussing the military situation in the Far East at the time," he relates in a footnote, "the briefing officer . . . quite frankly stated that the feeling in [the intelligence section] was that the North Koreans would attack and conquer South Korea in the coming summer. The point was not emphasized particularly and the fact seemed to be accepted as regrettable but inevitable."[4]

The United States was handicapped by its usual mix of uncertain goals, confused intentions, and contradictory plans regarding Korea. The central problem was that Syngman Rhee seemed to be another Chiang Kai-shek, obsessed with inflicting a military defeat upon his enemies and unable or unwilling to concentrate on creating a stable, democratic, and prosperous society within the area under his control.

The Truman administration wanted to see an unbelligerent and economically healthy South Korea that was armed just strongly enough to deter the North Koreans from invading. The United States was willing to go to considerable lengths to nurture such a South Korea, but it wanted to make absolutely certain that nothing it did in Korea would either lead to war or constitute what could be construed as a commitment to send American troops to rescue Rhee's regime. In May 1949, just a month after the signing of the NATO pact and in the midst of discussions concerning the withdrawal of the last American occupation troops (in an effort to prevent which Rhee had "moved heaven and earth," as Washington's ambassador to Seoul, John J. Muccio, put it[5]), Rhee announced that the South Korean government wanted to know whether the United States would regard a Communist invasion of the south as "tantamount to an attack on the American people."[6] Rhee wasn't fussy about what form Washington's commitment would assume. He would have been satisfied, he said, by a Pacific pact modeled on NATO, by an alliance between the United States and South Korea for mutual defense against "aggressor nations," or even by an unequivocal official announcement from Washington that it would defend South Korea. But such arrangements were precisely what America wanted to avoid. It was determined to help South Korea economically without allowing itself to be dragged into a war.

Rhee was a bellicose man who made no secret of his eagerness to invade and conquer North Korea. So frequently and candidly did he express this eagerness — as well as his confidence of success — that the U.S. government had to remind him from time to time that any such move would mean an immediate and complete end to all forms of American aid. But Rhee's threats arose out of frustration and political bluster rather than out of any concrete intentions. Knowing that it was impossible for him to do what he and many of his countrymen wanted very badly to do, he and they had to settle for the compensatory satisfaction of repeated announcements of his readiness to unify Korea by force. To stay in power, Rhee had to show himself the militant Korean nationalist that he genuinely was.

Be that as it may, Rhee's bellicosity led American military and political leaders to ask not how much military aid South Korea would need in order to defend itself adequately, but rather how much aid it was safe to give Rhee without creating the danger of his invading the north. In March 1949 MacArthur went so far as to recommend that the South Korean army "be so organized as to indicate clearly its peaceful purpose and to provide no plausible basis for allegations of being a threat to North Korea."[7]

On June 8, 1949, the day after Truman made his request to Congress for $150 million to be given to South Korea, Undersecretary of State James Webb announced that when the U.S. troops left Korea at the end of the month, they would leave behind a large quantity of military equipment for the South Korean army and police.[8] The equipment had a 1949 replacement value of approximately $110 million and included 100,000 rifles, 50 million rounds of small-arms ammunition, 2,000 light bazookas, and several hundred light artillery pieces and mortars — but no combat aircraft, tanks, or even bazookas powerful enough to pierce the armor of the tanks with which the Soviet Union was supplying North Korea. In addition, the United States turned over about 2,000 jeeps and trucks, as well as several million dollars' worth of medical supplies. All this was enough to outfit a light defensive ground force of 50,000 men that would be sufficient to maintain internal order and to put down border skirmishes but not to repulse a full-scale invasion. To reorganize the South Korean army and to train its men to use the transferred matériel, the United States would also leave behind 500 officers and enlisted men, the Korean Military Advisory Group (KMAG, pronounced "kay-mag"), to be headed by Brigadier General William L. Roberts.

One of the clearest indications of the U.S. government's estimate of Korea's importance in the overall scheme of world affairs was provided by the sweeping military-aid bill that Truman signed on October 6, 1949. Out of a total appropriation of $1.3 billion, NATO members would receive $1 billion, and $211.3 million would be shared by Greece and Turkey, the original Truman Doctrine beneficiaries. Seventy-five million dollars was earmarked for use at the president's discretion in the "general area" of China, and the remaining $27.6 million was to be divided among Iran, Korea, and the Philippines.[9]

Eventually, though not until the following March, Congress authorized the payment to South Korea of its share, which was fixed at $10.9 million, considerably less than 1 percent of the total appropriation. Although both General Roberts of KMAG and Ambassador Muccio strongly recommended that a portion of the money allotted to the general area of China be used to bring the South Korean total up to $20 million, for the purchase of tanks and planes, Congress rejected that proposal. Much of the aid it approved was to be in the form of spare parts for the equipment that had already been given. Because of the U.S. Army's own need for such parts, together with the low priority assigned to Korea among the nations to receive American aid, only a few hundred dollars' worth of signal wire reached

Korea before the beginning of the North Korean invasion, although signal equipment costing $52,000 and spare parts worth $298,000 were then en route from San Francisco by sea.[10]

In mid-January 1950 the South Korean economic-aid bill that had been pending since the previous June was finally due to come before the House for debate. The timing was, alas, highly inauspicious. The Truman administration had very recently announced that it was abandoning Chiang to his probable fate, and there seemed to be no reason — especially given the way in which Acheson's speech of January 12 was widely interpreted — to believe that the U.S. government would act otherwise toward Rhee if things got rough in Korea, as they showed every sign of doing. Moreover, Chiang's failure to curb the rampant inflation that had so disastrously demoralized the Chinese people and rendered them susceptible to Communism (as if it were an infectious disease) had long been cited by the administration as one of the principal reasons it would have been futile to give further aid to the Nationalists. As it happened, just as the House was beginning its debate, Ambassador-at-Large Philip C. Jessup was in Seoul to chastise Rhee about his government's finances. On January 14 the *New York Times* reported that the Korean economic situation was described by American experts as "deteriorating in the face of unchecked deficit spending" and that inflation was becoming a very serious problem. During the first eight months of fiscal year 1949–50, government *deficit* expenditures had exceeded the entire budget for that year. The biggest spenders were the Ministry of National Defense and the Home Ministry, the latter's budget paying for a "police force of army proportions." The prime minister's office had spent more than three times its entire budget on intelligence activities alone. This extravagance was paid for by printing more money or by making overdrafts on the Bank of Korea. Throwing into question not only Rhee's competence but also his claim to head a regime more democratic than the one in the north, the *Times* article noted that the National Security Act, as recently amended at Rhee's direction, established "re-education camps" and eliminated the right to appeal in cases in which that law applied.

Given all these discouraging circumstances, it is hardly surprising that many congressmen — especially Republicans and southern

Democrats — were most reluctant to vote in favor of aid for Korea. John M. Vorys (Republican, Ohio), leader of the opposition to the bill, insisted that it made no sense to pour more money "down the Korean rat hole," as he so crudely put it.[11] Others argued that to continue to give aid to South Korea would only fatten the prize and make it all the more attractive to the Communists, perhaps even hastening an invasion or leading the North Koreans to step up their efforts to win control of the south through subversion. Vorys and his colleagues took the position that unless the United States was prepared to take decisive action throughout the Far East to stop the spread of Communism — and that meant helping Chiang — aid to Korea was money thrown away.

On January 19 the House defeated the Korean aid bill by one vote, 193–192, with 131 of the nays cast by Republicans. The next day the *New York Times* called the defeat "the first major setback for the Administration at the hands of Congress on a matter involving foreign affairs since the war's end." *Time* reported that "nobody was more embarrassed by the vote than Senate Republicans, who had been blaming Acheson for doing too little too late. Their anchor man, California's hefty, well tailored Bill Knowland, said tersely: 'Korea will get its help at this session.' "[12]

During the last days of January, Acheson went before House and Senate committees to work out a compromise, by the terms of which Korean aid was tied to a provision extending, from February 15 to June 30, the deadline for spending on Formosa some $104 million of previously appropriated economic aid.[13] On February 9, after two days of debate in which Republicans railed against the administration's "do-nothing" policy in Asia, the House voted 240–134 to pass the combined Korea-Formosa aid bill. The Senate passed the bill the next day after a debate lasting only seven minutes.[14] But the damage was irreparable. The House had shown the world that it was quite unenthusiastic about helping South Korea. And the administration's having to tie Korean aid to aid for Chiang set a most unfortunate precedent. At the time of the North Korean invasion, Truman believed that he would have to defend Formosa if he were going to win congressional support for his decision to defend South Korea.

*　　*　　*

The Sino-Soviet treaty of February 1950 bound both parties to take measures "for the purpose of *preventing* aggressive action on the part of Japan" (emphasis added). To that end, even before the treaty was concluded, the Russians launched a campaign of subversion designed to turn the Japanese against the United States and to make impossible a separate treaty. Early in January 1950 the official Cominform journal called upon the Japanese Communist party — which, in its professed effort to be "lovable," had maintained a reasonably cooperative stance in the Japanese Parliament and had refrained from denouncing the monarchy — to demonstrate in the streets, and to harangue in the press, against imperialism, militarism, and capitalism. In February the Soviet press alleged that the United States was planning to reorganize the Japanese police into an armed force of five hundred thousand men, increased its criticism of the pro-American Liberal government of Japanese prime minister Shigeru Yoshida, and demanded that Emperor Hirohito be tried as a war criminal. The Japanese Communist party had already, in the summer of 1949, lost much support and sympathy when it was widely held responsible for several acts of violence. The new orders and propaganda from Moscow only weakened the party further, led to the suppression of its newspaper and a purge of its leaders by the occupation, and made the great majority of Japanese more anti-Soviet and pro-American than ever.[15]

Throughout the early months of 1950, the United States worked diligently to smooth the way for a separate Japanese peace treaty. To keep abreast of the latest developments, the Russians needed only to monitor the *New York Times*, as they most certainly did. On March 30 the paper carried a story reporting that Secretary of State Acheson had said that America should draft and negotiate a treaty, and that he was seeking a Republican ambassador-at-large to help with the task — which is to say, to win bipartisan congressional support for the project. Let us note that during the following two months, April and May 1950, the Soviet Union made very large deliveries of military equipment to North Korea.

Stalin had not previously evinced any inordinate interest in controlling South Korea. As we have seen, the railroads and resources that had most urgently concerned him were located in the north, which also had several good warm-water ports to supplement Port Arthur and Dairen. Early in 1950, however, having reluctantly agreed to relinquish Soviet control of the Manchurian ports and railroads by the end of 1952, Stalin surely found himself all of a sudden much more keenly interested than he had been in the South Korean ports of Inchon and Pusan, the two finest and most developed harbors on the Korean peninsula. Nevertheless, acquisition of these two ports was hardly sufficient reason by itself to justify the risks entailed in a military invasion of South Korea.

As far as we can fathom the closely guarded mysteries of Soviet strategy, we may surmise that by authorizing and assisting the North Koreans to conquer the south, Stalin hoped to accomplish the following:

1. To readjust the balance of power in the Far East to compensate for the effects of the Japanese policy to which the United States seemed irrevocably committed. If the United States was going to take Japan all for itself, then the Soviet Union would take all of Korea for *itself*.

2. To eliminate the possibility that the United States, in alliance with Japan, might eventually use South Korea as a base from which to launch an invasion of the Soviet Union. If America was deprived of South Korea, then any invasion it might undertake would have to be amphibious and/or airborne and thus more precarious than an overland invasion would be.

3. To embarrass the United States in the Far East and to demoralize the Japanese. Until a peace treaty was signed, the Allies were technically still at war with Japan. Both the United States and Japan feared, therefore, that if the United States went ahead with a separate treaty, the Soviets might invoke the rights of belligerency and invade Hokkaido. If America and Japan were to become allies, then at least (as Stalin was assumed to view the matter) America would be allied to a weakened Japan and the Soviet position in the Far East would be greatly strengthened. A successful invasion of South Korea would lend point to the threat to Hokkaido and perhaps even convince the Japanese that they

didn't dare to form an alliance with the United States, for by so provoking the Soviets they would endanger the territorial integrity of their nation.

4. To inflict a major defeat on American prestige in the eyes of the entire world. A successful and unopposed invasion of South Korea would expose America as a cowardly friend and, by implication, as a potentially worthless ally, thereby undermining the security of NATO. An invasion would also enable Stalin to gauge what the American response might be to Soviet moves elsewhere, especially in Europe and the Middle East.

We might speculate that Stalin may have hoped that even if the United States responded to the North Korean invasion by hastening to strengthen its position in Japan, that would force the Chinese Communists to rely more heavily on the Soviets for defense and would reduce the possibility of Mao's becoming an Asian Tito.

We may also presume that Stalin had more local and limited motives, the foremost of which was surely to reinforce Kim Il-sung's prestige vis-à-vis his domestic rivals, some of whom were then embarrassing him with accusations that he was more pro-Russian than pro-Korean. If he were to lead a successful invasion of the south, his credentials as a Korean nationalist would become unassailable. As the patriot who succeeded in reunifying Korea (so, at least, he and Stalin must have hoped) he would be revered by the majority of Koreans. Firmly in control of the peninsula and profoundly grateful to the Soviets for their assistance, he would be one of the Soviet Union's staunchest and most valuable friends. Korea would be tied so closely to the Soviet Union that Stalin would feel safe in entrusting the nation with the highly strategic railroad he was planning to build between Vladivostok and Dairen, which he was still hoping he might be able to detach from China. Such a railroad would enable the Soviets to develop their interests in the Far East without being dependent on a potentially hostile China for transit rights through Manchuria. Furthermore, reunification of the two complementary halves of the Korean economy — the mineral-rich and heavy-industrial north with the agricultural and light-industrial south — would, so Kim is said to have assured Stalin, quickly transform Korea into one of the Soviet Union's most prosperous friends and most lucrative trading partners.[16]

Stalin was pleased that all his goals could be accomplished through what he could argue was strictly a civil war for which the Soviet Union bore no responsibility. (The Russians would give advice and arms to North Korea, but they would not participate overtly in the invasion. Russian advisers were to be kept so far behind the lines that there would be no danger of captures that would implicate the Kremlin.[17]) As Nikita Khrushchev put it in his presumptive memoirs, Stalin liked the idea that the forceful reunification of Korea would be "an internal matter which the Koreans would be settling among themselves."[18]

Khrushchev said he thought it was at the end of 1949 that Kim arrived in Moscow to ask Stalin for permission to invade South Korea.

> The North Koreans wanted to prod South Korea with the point of a bayonet [he recalled]. Kim Il-sung said that the first poke would touch off an internal explosion in South Korea and that the power of the people would prevail — that is, the power which ruled in North Korea. Naturally, Stalin couldn't oppose this idea. . . . [He] persuaded Kim Il-sung that he should think it over, make some calculations, and then come back with a concrete plan.[19]

It was evidently in late February or early March 1950 that Kim returned to Moscow with a plan to invade South Korea in June. The decisive factor in Kim's planning seems to have been his belief that there were as many as five hundred thousand Communist guerrillas and clandestine Communist party members in South Korea who would rally to help the invaders, and that millions of less militant South Koreans — including members of the armed forces — had come to hate Rhee enough that they would support the North Koreans after the invasion had been launched.*

According to Kim's plan, once the North Korean army had taken Seoul, the rest of the nation would easily be won over. Rhee's gov-

---

* In a radio broadcast on June 26, the day after the opening of the invasion, Kim confidently called upon South Korean guerrillas to attack Rhee's forces from the rear, to disrupt communications, and to destroy roads and bridges over which the South Korean army could retreat. He also incited all South Koreans to turn against their government: soldiers should defect to the ranks of the North Korean forces, workers should go on strike, farmers should give food to the Communist guerrillas, and intellectuals should foment a popular uprising.[20] Some heeded these calls, but accounts of Communist brutality turned the majority of South Koreans against the invaders.

ernment would be discredited if it fled, and control of the capital would mean control of the south's transportation and communications network. The invasion would be swift — so swift that the United States would not even have time to intervene. Kim apparently believed that if he invaded in late June, all of Korea would be united and sufficiently pacified by early August to permit nationwide legislative elections to be held. The new assembly would convene on August 15, the fifth anniversary of the liberation from Japan.

Meanwhile, the United States proceeded further toward a separate Japanese peace treaty. On April 25 the *New York Times* reported that the Japanese expected American troops to remain in Japan after the signing of a treaty with the Western powers, and on May 9 Prime Minister Yoshida was said to have declared that a de facto separate peace already existed between Japan and the United States; the current relationship needed only to be given a formal, legal basis. A story on May 16 held that the issue of a separate peace versus a treaty with all of the Allies was the main issue in the upcoming elections for the upper house of the Japanese Diet. The May 19 issue reported that Truman and Acheson had appointed the Republican John Foster Dulles, a rabid anti-Communist, to handle the preliminaries for a treaty, and on June 2 a statement by the Japanese minister of foreign affairs was said to indicate that Japan was ready to sign a separate treaty with the West. A major obstacle was cleared when Yoshida's Liberal party emerged from the June 4 elections with a plurality, though only by a slim margin and with dependence on a coalition whose cooperation could not be assumed on all issues.

In mid-June General Bradley returned to Tokyo for further talks with MacArthur, this time accompanied by Secretary of Defense Louis A. Johnson. Just in case there was any doubt in Moscow or Peking concerning the purpose of their visit, Dulles was to be in Tokyo at the same time. On June 23 the *Times* reported that Dulles had hinted Japan might be given a status similar to that of West Germany, with the removal of the military occupation government and the retention of Western defense forces. He was quoted as saying that the current talks in Tokyo were laying the basis for action. The North Korean invasion began two days later.

CHAPTER 9

The Real Thing?

THE PRINCIPAL STRATEGIC AIM of the North Korean invasion was to capture Seoul as quickly as possible. To that end, the four prongs of the central and most powerful thrust made by North Korean armored forces and infantry on the morning of Sunday, June 25, 1950, were directed along the converging highways and railroads that threaded their way through the widest valleys in the semimountainous terrain between the 38th parallel and the capital. Coordinated with the central thrust were attacks on the east and west coasts. In the east, an amphibious force landed at Kangnung, where the road that runs along the entire eastern coast intersects with a major east-west road, along which the North Koreans could approach Seoul from the southeast and cut off retreating South Korean troops.

The invasion caught the South Koreans completely off guard. The buildup of North Korean forces and equipment along the border had been observed and reported by intelligence, but it had been dismissed: by some as a defensive measure motivated by the Soviet Union's universal paranoia, by others as a stage in an annual rotation that had not in previous years led to an invasion, and by still others as a tactic of intimidation to give weight to recent North Korean calls for unification under Kim Il-sung's leadership. The rainy season was just beginning on June 25, and, since heavy rains would soon inhibit use of the tanks and planes that gave North Korea decisive military superiority over the south, no one expected that the north would choose such an apparently disadvantageous moment to invade — though, of course, the element of surprise to be gained by attacking at just such a time gave the north a greater advantage than ever.

Full of unwarranted confidence, the army of the Republic of Korea had prodigally issued weekend passes to officers, and the majority of the Korean Military Advisory Group's American officers were complacently spending the weekend in Seoul. What's more, the ROK army was badly deployed to meet the invasion. Three of its seven divisions were fighting guerrillas in the interior of South Korea, far from the border, and the remaining four divisions were strung out all along the parallel rather than concentrated to guard the key roads along which the North Koreans attacked. Relatively small units patrolled the area directly along the parallel, the divisions keeping most of their manpower in reserve anywhere from ten to thirty miles below the line. Finally, by attacking at 6:00 A.M. the North Koreans managed to catch most of the ROK army sound asleep. Startled by the sudden barrage of enemy fire, many of the poorly disciplined South Korean soldiers panicked and fled.

The North Koreans threw nearly all of their tanks into the central, four-pronged onslaught toward Seoul. Although the thirty-two-ton, Soviet-made T-34 was classed as only a medium tank, the ROK army had no weapons powerful enough to pierce its armor. Nor did the South Koreans have any tanks of their own with which to block the advance. The ROK minister of defense had repeatedly asked the U.S. government for tanks, but the requests had always been turned down on the grounds that Korea was not "good tank country."[1] Its terrain was considered too mountainous, its roads too primitive, and its bridges too flimsy for the efficient use of tanks — and since the Pentagon assumed that the Soviets would make the same evaluation, it didn't bother to supply South Korea with any heavy antitank bazookas. Unfortunately, the Russians judged Korea suitable for armored warfare and supplied their neighbor accordingly.

The invasion amply bore out their judgment. Even with the rain, the valley roads were not yet muddy enough to impede the armored advance, and the bridges held. Early in the invasion a few heroic South Korean soldiers girded themselves with explosives and threw themselves under tanks — the only available way to stop them. But volunteers for such suicide tactics were scarce, and most of the tanks smashed relentlessly through the impotent South Korean defenses. Indeed, the tanks proved to be the critical weapon that gave the invasion its early success. Their value was not only tactical but also psychological, for many of the South Korean soldiers had never seen a tank before; confronted with a column of these demonic behemoths, whole regiments quite understandably lost their courage and dispersed into the hills.

*   *   *

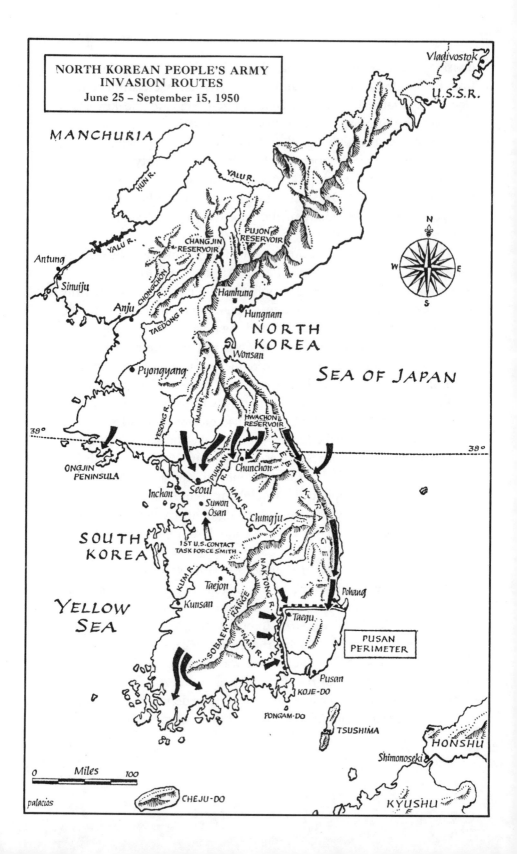

NORTH KOREAN PEOPLE'S ARMY
INVASION ROUTES
June 25 – September 15, 1950

Vladivostok

U.S.S.R.

MANCHURIA

HUN R.

YALU R.

YALU R.

Antung

Sinuiju

CHONGCHON R.

Anju

CHANGJIN RESERVOIR

PUJON RESERVOIR

Hamhung

Hungnam

TAEDONG R.

NORTH KOREA

Pyongyang

Wonsan

SEA OF JAPAN

YESONG R.

IMJIN R.

HWACHON RESERVOIR

38°

38°

ONGJIN PENINSULA

PUKHAN R.

Chunchon

Inchon

Seoul

HAN R.

T A E B A E K   R A N G E

Suwon

Osan

Chungju

1ST U.S. CONTACT
TASK FORCE SMITH

SOUTH KOREA

KUM R.

Taejon

NAKTONG R.

Pohang

YELLOW SEA

Kunsan

SOBAEK RANGE

NAM R.

Taegu

PUSAN PERIMETER

Pusan

KOJE-DO

PONGAM-DO

TSUSHIMA

HONSHU

Shimonoseki

0   Miles   100

palacias

CHEJU-DO

KYUSHU

Certainly the most urgent of the many questions asked, both at the front and in Seoul, in the confusion of that first morning was whether the North Koreans were really launching a full-scale invasion. There had been so many threats, so many border skirmishes instigated by both sides, so many conflicting intelligence reports, and so many false alarms — some of them, at least, apparently intended by Rhee's government to frighten the United States into providing the republic with more arms — that defenses were careless and responses slow when the real attack came. South Korea had cried wolf too many times.

Since the establishment of the two Korean regimes, in August and September 1948, there had been hundreds of minor clashes along the border, a few of which had escalated into serious battles involving artillery and hundreds of casualties, with localized fighting sometimes taking several weeks to die down.[2] On April 13, 1950, having just returned from a visit to South Korea, Ambassador-at-Large Philip Jessup told an American radio audience that the 38th parallel was "the front line in an actual shooting war." He continued, "There are very real battles, involving perhaps one or two thousand men. When you go to this boundary, as I did, you go very well protected. You see troop movements, fortifications, and prisoners of war. And you can feel the tension."[3] Just two weeks later, however, General William Roberts of KMAG told a reporter that the number of border raids from North Korea was down from sixty or seventy a month to only seven or eight. He assured his interviewer that it was as safe in Korea as it was in the United States: the Communists would not dare attempt to conquer the Republic of Korea.[4]

On December 30, 1949, Major General Charles Willoughby, the intelligence chief at MacArthur's headquarters in Tokyo, had sent to Washington several reports indicating that North Korea was planning to invade the south in March or April 1950. But Willoughby noted on the reports that in his own opinion an invasion at that time was "unlikely." A month and a half later he forwarded two more reports, which he also discredited, one stating that an invasion was scheduled for March, the other giving June as the target date. And on March 10 he received a report from South Korean intelligence affirming that the North Korean invasion had definitely been postponed from March to June. Like the majority of American military and political leaders, however, Willoughby remained set in the belief that Stalin would not authorize an invasion of South Korea until he was ready to fight World War III. Until then he would limit his minions to tactics of subversion. "The most probable course of North Korean action this spring and summer," Willoughby informed Washington, "is furtherance of attempts to overthrow the South Korean government by creation of chaotic conditions in the Republic of Korea through guerrillas and psychological warfare."[5]

It seemed indeed a promising time for subversion, since Rhee was acting as though he were bent on alienating all but his most fanatic supporters. Communist guerrilla activities throughout the winter had given substance to his warnings of infiltration and had made him more high-handed than ever — taking full advantage of his stringent and antilibertarian National Security Act. Whether genuinely frightened or simply glad for an excuse to deal harshly with ever more of his antagonists, he filled South Korea's jails with thousands of political prisoners and closed down newspapers that criticized his regime.

Rhee also appointed a few cabinet ministers of whom many National Assembly members disapproved. On February 8, 1950, amid charges of corruption in the executive branch, the dissident legislators proposed a constitutional amendment that would make appointments subject to approval by the assembly, to which the cabinet would become responsible. Three days later Rhee arrested thirteen members of the assembly and charged them with being Communists.[6]

As the mid-March vote on the amendment approached, many observers feared that the North Koreans might take advantage of the prevailing crisis atmosphere to stage a coup or to foment a popular insurrection. The situation became so tense that on March 11 a fist-fighting brawl broke out on the floor of the assembly when Rhee supporters tried to bring the debate on the proposed amendment to an end.[7] It was widely rumored that if the amendment passed, Rhee might use his huge security-police force to close down the assembly altogether. If he were to do so, popular resentment against him might well boil over.

In the end, however, the proposed amendment failed to win the necessary two-thirds majority. Its disappointed champions then turned their hopes toward the legislative elections that were scheduled for May 30. Anti-Rhee feelings were running so high that the new assembly might very well be able to pass the legislation.

Rhee's relations with the assembly were by no means his only problem. The inflation that had led the Truman administration to send Ambassador Jessup to Seoul in January was completely out of hand by mid-March. The rise in the price of rice had long since far outstripped wage increases, leading to hunger and anger, and greatly increasing popular susceptibility to Communist propaganda. Late in March Rhee received a reprimand about the inflation from the U.S. Economic Cooperation Administration, but he only turned around and used the message as an excuse to postpone elections until November, saying that the National Assembly had to pass a balanced budget for the coming fiscal year before elections could possibly be held.

On April 7 Secretary of State Dean Acheson sent Rhee a formal note stating that

> it is the judgment of this Government that the financial situation in Korea has already reached critical proportions, and that unless this progressive inflation is curbed in the none too distant future, it cannot but seriously impair Korea's ability to utilize effectively the economic assistance provided by the Economic Cooperation Administration.

If the Korean government did not soon begin to take "the drastic measures required to curb the growing inflation," warned Acheson, the United States would have "to re-examine, and perhaps to make adjustments in" its Korean aid program. "Of equal concern to this Government," continued the note, were Rhee's intentions of postponing legislative elections. "United States aid, both military and economic, to the Republic of Korea has been predicated upon the existence and growth of democratic institutions within the republic. Free, popular elections . . . are the foundation of those democratic institutions."[8] Rhee promptly rammed a balanced budget through the National Assembly and announced that elections would, after all, be held on May 30. He forced government departments to adopt, and adhere to, tight budgets, and he instituted price controls. By the end of April retail prices began to fall, and currency in circulation dropped from a high of 75 billion won (the basic Korean monetary unit) to 57.7 billion by mid-May.[9]

These improvements greatly displeased the North Korean government, which was hoping that Rhee's responsibility for political oppression and for economic chaos would motivate the southerners to rise against him once the north began its invasion in June. Toward the end of May, Kim's regime declared the upcoming elections illegal and threatened to bomb and strafe polling booths.[10] Although a few Communist agents attempted acts of sabotage, and despite two serious border attacks mounted by the north on Election Day to distract and intimidate voters, the balloting went ahead. The big winners were moderately conservative independent candidates, who ousted many of Rhee's party regulars.[11] The U.S. government was pleased with the results, for it seemed likely that the new assembly would force Rhee to become more moderate, more democratic, and more responsible. In an atmosphere of political moderation and stability, the economy would flourish and South Korea would become strong enough to stand on its own. Nor was the administration alone in believing that as conditions in Korea improved, so would Rhee. On June 20, after the new assembly had convened, the *New York Times* ran an editorial stating that "President Rhee's government is far from perfect (as most governments are) but it has done a good job considering the appalling conditions under which it has had to work."

On May 10, six weeks before the invasion, Captain Sihn Sung Mo, the South Korean minister of defense, held a press conference in Seoul at which he stated that the North Koreans had recently built up their forces along the 38th parallel to 185,000 men, 173 tanks, 32 naval vessels, and 197 planes. (The estimate of troops was more than double the size of the actual invasion force, but the figures for matériel were remarkably accurate.) He insisted it was impossible to avoid the conclusion that North Korea was planning to launch an invasion in the near future, and he closed with a plea to the United States for more arms with which to resist. General Roberts of KMAG replied that although he believed the reports of North Korean strength, he did not foresee an attack.[12] Here, once again, the problem was apparently that Americans placed so much confidence in their incorrect analysis of worldwide Soviet intentions that they failed to give anything like adequate weight to contradictory reports, in this case intelligence assessments of North Korea's capability of carrying out a localized and isolated military conquest.

In the spring of 1950 American intelligence officers, both in Tokyo and in Washington, predicted that the presence of the four U.S. divisions stationed in Japan made Communist aggression, if it were going to occur at all, more likely in Indochina — far removed from those troops — than in Korea.[13] The previous fall Ho Chi Minh had proposed a compromise to the French government: if France would recognize an independent and unified Vietnam under his leadership, Ho would keep Vietnam in the French Union. He also promised to keep Vietnam neutral in the Cold War. The French, however, ignored Ho's offer and continued to back Bao Dai, the pathetic playboy and former Japanese-supported figurehead-emperor behind whom they hoped to regain the full force of the colonial power they had lost during World War II.

On January 14, 1950, Ho proclaimed the establishment of the Democratic Republic of Vietnam as the nation's only legitimate government; it was soon given official recognition by both the Soviet Union and the People's Republic of China. Mao Tse-tung, whose conquest of China by that time extended to the Vietnamese border, began supplying weapons to the Viet Minh guerrillas for their struggle against the French. On May 8 — as the Chinese Communists were driving the last of Chiang Kai-shek's troops off Hainan Island, in the Gulf of Tonkin, less than two hundred miles from Haiphong — Secretary Acheson announced the U.S. decision to give the French in Indochina a large part of the $75 million that the current military-aid bill authorized the president to spend at his discretion in the China area. The first installment would come to about $23 million. Thus did America take a major step toward direct involvement in Vietnam.[14]

Early on the morning of June 25, despite all the reasons North Korea couldn't and wouldn't launch an invasion, the South Koreans and their American advisers were faced with the reality of a North Korean attack. By 9:30 A.M., after consultation with the South Korean high command, the levelheaded American ambassador, John Muccio, had come to believe that the simultaneous attacks at various points along the 38th parallel were *probably* the beginning of a full-scale invasion. In any case, the situation was clearly serious enough for him to notify Washington at once. Reflecting his lingering skepticism, his cable to the State Department began by pointing out that so far only some of the ROK army reports had been confirmed by KMAG officers in the field. (The lack of full confirmation was due to a compound of weekend passes and poor communications.) But he felt sufficiently certain to conclude his message: "It would appear from nature of attack and manner in which it was launched that it constitutes all out offensive against ROK."[15]

The question then was whether the South Korean army would be able to repulse the invaders. In the June 5 issue of *Time,* just three weeks before the invasion, correspondent Frank Gibney had reported that during the previous two years South Korea, with the help of KMAG, had "trained and equipped a first-rate ground army," which most observers rated "the best of its size in Asia." The obvious implication was that it was better than the roughly comparable-sized North Korean army. "No one now believes," continued Gibney, "that the Russian-trained North Korean army could pull off a quick, successful invasion without heavy reinforcements. . . . Only the lack of air power might tip the scales against the South." "Heavy reinforcements" was, of course, a euphemism for Soviet participation.

Unfortunately, evaluations of the Korean military situation tended to be influenced more by expediency and self-interest than by objectivity. When, for instance, an appraisal was offered in conjunction with an appeal for economic aid of a nonmilitary nature, the supplicant would most often vigorously emphasize South Korean strength, in order to dispel fears that the gift might ultimately benefit the enemy. Thus when William C. Foster, deputy administrator of the Economic Cooperation Administration, testified on June 13 before a congressional committee weighing an aid request, he asserted that "the rigorous training program [in South Korea] has built up a well-disciplined army of 100,000 soldiers, one that is prepared to meet any challenge by the North Korean forces and one that has cleaned out the guerrilla bands in South Korea in one area after another."[16] Indeed, the army's suppression of the guerrillas and its successes in opposing North Korean border raids had led to much unjustified confidence.

The most glowing reassurances on the eve of the invasion came from General Roberts of KMAG, who retired in mid-June and, on his way home to the States, stopped off in Tokyo for debriefing at MacArthur's headquarters. General Omar Bradley was there at the time for discussions concerning a Japanese peace treaty; on June 20 Roberts told him that he doubted an invasion was impending and that, even if an attack did come, the South Korean army could "meet any test the North Koreans imposed on it."[17] To another interlocutor he folksily and extravagantly averred that the ROK army was "the best doggoned shooting army outside the United States."[18] By no stretch of any unbiased imagination was it any such thing, but those were the parting words of a man who obviously wanted to believe, and wanted others to believe, that he had done a superb job of carrying out his last assignment.

The fact of the matter was that in June 1950 the South Korean army was inadequately equipped and only partially trained. Since January the ranks had swollen from 60,000 men to more than 95,000 (there was also a paramilitary police force of approximately 50,000), and by the time of the invasion many of the new recruits still had not completed basic training. Many of them had simply been handed a gun and sent to units engaged in rooting out guerrillas hiding in caves in the mountains; they had never come anywhere near the infantry training school, modeled on Fort Benning, Georgia, that KMAG had set up and that it continued to supervise. Even the men with basic training had never taken part in any maneuvers involving more than a battalion. On the whole, the army's communications and supply systems were primitive, its discipline and morale poor, and its mastery of the coordination necessary for battle nonexistent.[19]

Moreover, the ROK army had equipment for only about 65,000 men, and of that — as General Roberts informed all KMAG advisers on May 5 — 10 to 15 percent of the army's weapons and 30 to 35 percent of its vehicles were not in working order. Unless spare parts and additional equipment were received, the army could defend South Korea for no more than fifteen days.[20] Even that prediction was overly optimistic, for it failed to take into account the fact that the army had no tanks, no combat aircraft, and no antiaircraft batteries. Its heaviest artillery had a maximum range of about seven miles, in contrast to the north's 122-millimeter guns with a range of almost seventeen miles.[21] As for a navy, the Republic of Korea had just bought a few small surplus vessels from the United States, but at the time of the invasion they were still in Hawaii.[22]

The military situation was very different in the north. In June 1950 the North Korean People's Army consisted altogether of 135,000 men, perhaps as many as 30,000 of whom had acquired extensive battle experience while serving in the Chinese Communist army during World War II and the Chinese civil war. (In the fall of 1949, his victory achieved, Mao had begun to release his Korean troops to Kim's army, but even at the time of the invasion thousands more still remained in China.) Several thousand North Korean tank and air force officers had received three years of training in the Soviet Union, and the enlisted men were assiduously trained under the supervision of a Soviet military mission numbering about 3,000. Although Stalin had not at first been overly generous to Kim, during the spring of 1950 the Soviet Union thoroughly equipped the NKPA with automatic weapons, tanks, high-performance combat planes, and heavy artillery.[23] With such an arsenal the north could surely conquer the south — unless, of course, the United States intervened, as seemed unlikely.

When it came to the test, the performance of South Korean army units ran the gamut from disastrous to superb. Some units were simply massacred in the early hours of the invasion, while others stood and held, even in the face of far superior force. The most successful resistance was offered by the well-trained ROK 6th Division, whose senior American adviser, Lieutenant Colonel Thomas D. McPhail, had anticipated an attack and had persuaded the division commander to cancel all leaves for the weekend of June 24–25. For three days the division blocked the easternmost of the NKPA's four central lunges toward Seoul, but ultimately the flight of South Korean units on its flanks left it open to the danger of being surrounded and cut off, and so it was forced to retreat.[24]

During the course of the invasion's first day, reports from the front drifted piecemeal into Seoul, giving a highly fragmentary picture of the overall situation. Seizing, naturally enough, on the encouraging reports from the 6th Division, the South Korean high command and KMAG made unjustified extrapolations and on the afternoon of the first day declared that the invasion had been "virtually stopped."[25] Of course, the most badly routed units were in no position to send any messages at all to Seoul, and reports from some units in serious trouble were colored by the need to maintain morale and to save face. Under the circumstances, bluster was unavoidable, like that of the South Korean officer who declared: "By tomorrow morning we shall have defeated them completely. Our only cause for dissatisfaction is that there has been no order to advance into the North."[26]

CHAPTER 10

Washington's First Response

SINCE THE CLOCKS IN KOREA were thirteen hours ahead of Eastern Daylight Time, in Washington it was 5:00 in the afternoon on Saturday, June 24, when North Korean tanks and infantry began to cross the 38th parallel. The first word of the invasion didn't reach the capital until shortly after 9:00 that evening. Having just received an urgent cable from its correspondent in Seoul, the United Press called W. Bradley Connors, public affairs officer of the State Department's Bureau of Far Eastern Affairs, for confirmation. Connors thus became the first official in Washington to learn of the invasion. He could not confirm or deny the report, for Ambassador Muccio's cable, though filed for sending twenty minutes before the UP correspondent's, was delayed more than an hour by coding and decoding.

As soon as Connors got off the phone with the UP, he called Dean Rusk, assistant secretary of state for Far Eastern Affairs, finally reaching him at a dinner party at the Georgetown house of nationally syndicated columnist Joseph Alsop. Rusk left for the State Department at once, accompanied by Secretary of the Army Frank Pace, Jr. By the time they arrived, the text of Muccio's cable had become available. The ambassador was regarded as a circumspect and highly reliable observer; so alarming a message from him meant that the secretary of state had to be notified immediately.

It was about 10:30 when Rusk telephoned Dean Acheson, who was spending the weekend at his farm in Sandy Spring, Maryland. The secretary had been hoping for a chance to relax after an exhausting week in Washington, though it was difficult for him to unwind even at his beloved retreat ever since Joseph McCarthy's attacks on him had begun to generate so many crank-mail threats that it was felt necessary to post guards around his house, both in town and in the country, day and night. After a few hours of gardening and a good dinner, he was trying to read himself to sleep when the phone rang.

Through the rest of the night Harewood Farm would be a crisis center.

John D. Hickerson, the assistant secretary of state for UN Affairs, called Acheson about 10:45. Consistent with the plan that had been drawn up more than a year earlier for any such eventuality, they decided to alert UN Secretary-General Trygve Lie immediately to the probability that the United States would formally request an emergency meeting of the Security Council to be held the next day.

Only then did President Truman first learn of the invasion. Earlier that day he had flown home to Independence, Missouri, for a long weekend, scheduled to last until Monday, in order to take care of some family business. The clocks in Independence were two hours behind those in Washington, and Acheson's call found Truman sitting with his family in the library of their house after dinner. "Mr. President," announced Acheson, "I have very serious news. The North Koreans have invaded South Korea."[1] Truman's first impulse was to return to Washington at once, but the secretary dissuaded him, arguing that a hasty nighttime flight would be both dangerous and alarming. Besides, there was not yet sufficient information on which to base any serious decisions. Acheson said that for the moment the main thing was to initiate moves to bring the crisis before the UN. Truman agreed wholeheartedly.

The situation as it was understood in the United States on Sunday morning was well summed up by the *New York Times*, which gave the story only one column on its front page, without a banner headline. The cramped heading read:

WAR IS DECLARED
BY NORTH KOREANS;
FIGHTING ON BORDER

Communist Regime Attacks
South Republic, Uses Tanks
— Broadcasts Hostilities

FIRST DRIVE SEEN CURBED

United States, Holding Soviet
Responsible, Watches Event
— Plea to U.N. Likely

The big headline story that day was the crash of a Northwest Airlines plane in Lake Michigan. It was feared that all fifty-eight people aboard the plane, which had been downed by a storm, were dead, making the accident the worst disaster up to that time on a regularly scheduled commercial flight in the United States.

When Acheson called Truman on Sunday, it was late morning in Independence. The secretary informed the president that the Security Council was about to convene, and he read Truman the draft resolution that the American delegate would be presenting, charging the North Koreans with a "breach of the peace" and calling upon them to cease fighting. Truman gave his approval, but he agreed with Acheson that even if it were passed by the Security Council, the resolution would probably have little effect on events in Korea. That being so, as Truman recalled in his memoirs, "some decision would have to be made at once as to the degree of aid or encouragement which our government was willing to extend to the Republic of Korea."[2] He decided to return to Washington as soon as the presidential plane could be readied for takeoff.

Of one thing Truman felt certain right from the outset: if the North Koreans were invading South Korea, it was because Stalin had ordered them to do so. (Let us not forget, amid all the complexities, that this oversimplification was not so very far from the truth, in spirit if not in letter.) Truman's view would only have been reinforced by a report in the June 5 issue of *Time* that stated:

> North Korea is, for all practical purposes, a Russian colony. Even the Chinese Communists have no representatives in North Korea, and Mao's visage is conspicuous by its absence. Said a refugee North Korean major recently: "Russia, not Korea, is held up to us as the motherland. We don't even study Korean history in the schools there."

Truman was faced with a dilemma. It could be argued that the conflict in Korea was a civil war, the internal struggle of an intolerably divided nation to achieve unification, just as the American Civil War had been. But the U.S. government regarded the conflict as a case of thinly veiled aggression by the Soviet Union, through its North Korean proxy, upon the independent and sovereign Republic of

Korea, the establishment of which had been sponsored by both the United States and the UN. The United States wanted the UN to respond to the invasion as a full-scale act of international aggression, but the responsibility of the Soviet Union was not to be mentioned officially, and everything was to be done to avoid bringing about the overt participation of Russian forces in the fighting. At the very least, any direct accusations against the Soviet Union might bring its UN delegate, Iakov Malik, back to the Security Council, which he had been boycotting since January to protest the continued seating of the representative from Chiang Kai-shek's Nationalist Chinese government and the exclusion of the People's Republic of China. Were he to return, his veto could prevent the Security Council from taking any action whatsoever regarding the North Korean invasion.

The awkwardness of the situation forced Truman to adopt some carefully contrived language to enable him to make his meaning perfectly clear without actually saying what he meant. His instinct, however, was to say exactly what he meant. In his draft of the formal statement he was to issue on the morning of June 27, he wrote that the North Korean forces, "armed for this purpose by the Soviet Union with planes and tanks, have invaded the Republic of Korea."[3] But the British cabinet — to which he submitted his draft so as to be sure of British support in the UN — persuaded him to drop that phrase.[4] Hampered by diplomacy, Truman must have envied the uninhibited State Department official who was quoted by the *New York Times* on June 26 as having likened the relationship between the Soviet Union and North Korea to that between Walt Disney and Donald Duck.[5]

In his June 27 statement Truman said, "The attack upon Korea makes it plain beyond all doubt that Communism has passed beyond the use of subversion to conquer independent nations and will now use armed invasion and war."[6] (He had employed the term "centrally directed Communist Imperialism" in his draft, but London had found that wording "ham-fisted" and had urged him to substitute the milder "Communism."[7]) That single sentence, rich in implications, summed up Truman's view of the war at its beginning. In order to stress, albeit tacitly, that he held the Soviet Union directly responsible for the invasion, he spoke of Communism's attack upon Korea rather than of North Korea's attack upon South Korea. This was consistent with the fact that the United States didn't recognize Kim Il-sung's government and considered North Korea little more than a republic of the USSR. As far as Truman was concerned, the Seoul government was the only legitimate one on the Korean peninsula, and it was being attacked by troops who were first and foremost Communist — in other words, subject to Stalin's orders — and who were only quite incidentally from the northern part of Korea.

During his three-hour flight back to Washington on that first Sunday, Truman had time to reflect upon the situation. As he recounted in his memoirs, his thoughts at that time ran along the following lines:

> In my generation, this was not the first occasion when the strong had attacked the weak. I recalled some earlier instances: Manchuria, Ethiopia, Austria. I remembered how each time that the democracies failed to act it had encouraged the aggressors to keep going ahead. Communism was acting in Korea just as Hitler, Mussolini, and the Japanese had acted ten, fifteen, and twenty years earlier. I felt certain that if South Korea was allowed to fall, Communist leaders would be emboldened to override nations closer to our own shores. If the Communists were permitted to force their way into the Republic of Korea without opposition from the free world, no small nation would have the courage to resist threats and aggression by stronger Communist neighbors. If this was allowed to go unchallenged it would mean a third world war, just as similar incidents had brought on the second world war. It was also clear to me that the foundations and the principles of the United Nations were at stake unless this unprovoked attack on Korea could be stopped.[8]

This was the climax of all the talk about appeasement, the culmination of Churchill's repeated admonitions that if Hitler had been firmly opposed early on, World War II could have been prevented. Truman would now see to it that, one way or another, action was taken to stop Soviet expansion in Korea — and to prevent World War III.

Despite all the military planning and the theretofore predominant analysis of Soviet intentions, Washington did not jump to the conclusion that the invasion of South Korea was the beginning of World War III. A more restrained interpretation of events was formulated, primarily because the United States still had an overwhelming advantage over the Soviet Union in the size of its atomic arsenal. American intelligence estimated that the Soviets didn't yet have more than ten bombs, while the United States had several hundred. But that wasn't all. In the May 5 issue of *U.S. News & World Report* Senator Tom Connally was quoted as having observed that the Russians "are not ready now for war. They've got plenty of land troops, and . . . a good many submarines and a good many airplanes, I suppose. But in production, when you figure the industrial production necessary for war, they're way down. . . . They're having very serious difficulties."

During the course of the day on Sunday, June 25, a consensus quickly emerged at the highest political and military levels in Washington that although the Soviet Union was not yet strong enough to want to launch World War III, it was nonetheless prepared to make attempts to expand its empire by increasingly daring and ambitious acts of aggression. (This was, of course, the hypothesis underlying NSC-68.) The Korean invasion demonstrated that the Kremlin was now willing to take bigger risks than it had up until then. The Truman administration evaluated the invasion as a softening-up operation, the first move on a timetable of aggression that would, if not opposed, lead inevitably to World War III.

Most of Truman's advisers agreed that Stalin had ordered the invasion of South Korea in accordance with a global master plan of Soviet strategy, a schedule of acts of aggression to be launched in sequence around the world. The greatest danger was that perhaps Stalin, recklessly, was after all ready to adhere to his program of conquest even if it meant the outbreak of another world war. Secretary of State Acheson, in particular, feared that Stalin was hoping the United States would get bogged down in Korea to such an extent that it would be unable to respond with anything short of atomic bombs to Soviet moves in Europe — and the use of such weapons in the event of any crisis other than a full-scale Russian invasion of Western Europe would probably be precluded by American fears of retaliation.

At the time of the Korean invasion, Washington was especially worried about Yugoslavia. On June 25 the *New York Times* reported that Tito's government had formally protested the massing of Bulgarian troops along the Yugoslav border, and on the twenty-eighth Hanson Baldwin wrote that similar, though somewhat smaller, build-ups had been observed in regions of Hungary and Romania adjacent to Yugoslavia. There can be no doubt that Stalin would have liked to invade the nation whose defection from the Soviet bloc had so frightened, infuriated, and embarrassed him. But by mid-1950 Yugoslavia was well braced to counter an invasion, and Tito had won considerable sympathy in the West, which could not be expected to relinquish impassively the valuable precedent that the renegade Communist offered in exchange for economic aid.

Even more worrisome were the obvious parallels between Korea and divided Germany. Indeed, the first reports of the Korean invasion induced something close to panic in a disarmed and perfunctorily occupied West Germany. Twenty-seven Red Army divisions were stationed in East Germany, and during the previous year the Russians had greatly enlarged their satellite's constabulary. Might not an invasion from the east be next on Stalin's agenda if the invasion of South Korea were successful? On July 3 Chancellor Konrad Adenauer formally petitioned the Allied High Commission to augment his nation's defenses.[9] It happened that the Pentagon had already, in April, secretly approved a plan for the rearmament of West Germany.[10] Thus it was that in September 1950 the North Atlantic Council resolved to create an integrated European army under a centralized command; West Germany would be allowed to organize and arm ten divisions for this international force, but there would be no independent West German army. In the interim, until the European Defense Community could be brought into being, the United States would send several divisions of its rapidly expanding army to Europe and would devote to European defense a large part of the tripled military budget (as called for by NSC-68) that Congress approved in stages during the first months of the Korean War. This was as Truman wished; in January 1951 he told General MacArthur that one of the reasons the United States had originally intervened in Korea was "to lend point and urgency to the rapid buildup of the defense of the Western world."[11] Stalin, on the other hand, could hardly have been more displeased by these direct results of the Korean invasion. The plan for a European army fell through, but the advance toward West German rearmament was irreversible. In October 1954 the Western powers agreed to admit the Federal Republic of Germany to NATO as a sovereign and independently armed nation.

*   *   *

The working hypothesis adopted in Washington on Sunday, June 25, held that *the invasion of South Korea was a Soviet test of American willingness and ability to oppose further Communist expansion*. Truman assumed Stalin reasoned that if the United States took determined action in Korea, an area to the defense of which it was far less committed than to that of Europe, then it would not be safe for him to proceed with invasions elsewhere. Effective opposition to the Soviet move in Korea would, in other words, make it clear to the Russians that they could not get away with any further attempts to expand *anywhere*. If the United States allowed the North Korean invasion to succeed, not only would the Soviets be emboldened to take additional steps, but also nations that were prime Soviet targets would be demoralized and would not have the confidence they needed to stand up to Russia. On the other hand, a firm American response in Korea might very well prevent World War III — though it was a gamble, and a very serious one. American intervention might also start a world war. That, however, seemed by far the less likely of the two possibilities, especially if the United States had the UN on its side. It was a risk that Truman and his advisers felt that they had no choice but to take.

To overstate the case only slightly, had the United States not feared imminent Soviet moves in areas far more important to American interests than Korea, it would probably not have gone to South Korea's rescue. In fact, if it had been strictly a matter of foreign affairs, that would not be an overstatement at all. However, there was also the factor of domestic politics: criticism of the Truman administration's repudiation of Chiang had become so intense that the president's failure to oppose Communist aggression, *wherever* it might have occurred, could well have led to his impeachment and would almost certainly have led to Acheson's.

Truman wrote in his memoirs that once he had decided to intervene in Korea, America's allies and friends abroad were informed that "we considered the Korean situation vital *as a symbol* of the strength and determination of the West" (emphasis added).[12] In retrospect, we may say that the rescue of South Korea was not an end in itself. It was a means to an end, or rather to several ends: (1) to convince the Soviets that they didn't dare to make any further aggressive moves and (2) thus to prevent World War III; (3) to uphold America's prestige in the eyes of the entire world; (4) as Truman later put it, "to demonstrate to the world that the friendship of the United States is of inestimable value in time of adversity";[13] and (5) to squelch domestic, and specifically Republican, criticism of the Truman administration. To those ends must be added one more, which we shall soon consider in more detail: to demonstrate the ability of the UN to *halt* aggression (not merely to denounce it) and thus to bolster the Western system of collective security.

Although a vast amount has been written about Truman's extended decision-making process over the course of the first week of the war, leading to the commitment of American ground troops to the fighting in Korea (of which he later wrote, "This was the toughest decision I had to make as President"[14]), the essential point is that the president made his crucial decision — the political one — on Sunday, June 25. He has recorded in his memoirs that at the Blair House conference with his top military and State Department advisers immediately following his return to Washington that evening, there was "complete, almost unspoken [unquestioned?] acceptance on the part of everyone that *whatever had to be done to meet this aggression had to be done* [emphasis added]. There was no suggestion from anyone that either the United Nations or the United States could back away from it."[15] From then on, it was a question of what exactly had to be done to save South Korea, not a question of whether or not to do it.

Indeed, Truman wrote that at that very first meeting he had "asked General [J. Lawton] Collins how many divisions we had in Japan and how long it would take to move two or three of them to Korea."[16] Right from the beginning, Truman was prepared to commit American ground troops to Korea *if the military situation demanded that he do so.* His guiding aim was to do whatever was necessary — though no more than was absolutely necessary — to push the North Koreans back above the 38th parallel. If it became clear that that task could not be accomplished without the participation of American infantry, then he would not hesitate to order U.S. troops to Korea.

The main problem that first week of the war was the extreme difficulty of making anything like an accurate assessment of the military situation in Korea. Contradictory reports and conflicting evaluations of their implications — most of this information being channeled through General MacArthur's headquarters in Tokyo — flooded into Washington. As late as Thursday, June 29, Hanson Baldwin wrote in the *New York Times* that "the normal fog of war — greatly accentuated in the Korean campaign by the paucity of communications — has left Washington with insufficient information to determine with precision our future course."

One of the roots of the tragedy of the Korean War was Washington's dependence upon MacArthur's headquarters for information. This meant that once Truman had made his fundamental *political* decision, the subsequent *military* decisions were based almost entirely on MacArthur's reports, evaluations, recommendations — and demands.

It was fateful that General Douglas MacArthur was then the American commander in the Far East, for his personality and preoccupations were to have almost as much influence over the initial course of the Korean War as would Truman's. In MacArthur, Washington was getting a commander with very strong convictions about global strategy — convictions directly opposed to those held by Truman and his principal advisers. Above all else, MacArthur was obsessed by his view that Asia was of far greater importance to the United States than was Europe and that the Communist victory in China was therefore an unmitigated and inexcusable disaster. He assigned top priority to Asia largely because he had spent the past fifteen years in the Far East and in the South Pacific — and he tended to believe that wherever he found himself was the most important place on earth.

Various revisionist historians of the Cold War have charged that MacArthur conspired with Syngman Rhee deliberately to precipitate and to escalate the Korean War.[17] He is said to have done so as the first step toward forcing the United States to reopen the Chinese civil war; with American military support Chiang would reverse the Communist victory and Communism would be driven out of Asia once and for all. However, it seems preposterous to claim that MacArthur could have planned the course of events and that things went just as he had intended. There had been far too many indications that if the North Koreans invaded South Korea, the United States would do nothing but protest to the UN Security Council, where the Soviet veto would block any action. And even once American troops entered the fighting in Korea, it seemed quite possible that the Communists would push them right off the peninsula and into the sea — and that would be that. The revisionist accusation can thus be taken no more seriously than the claim advanced by some of the same scholars that Franklin Roosevelt purposely aggravated Japan into bombing Pearl Harbor so that he could lead a pacifistic and isolationist America into World War II in order to save Britain. In both cases the accusations are nevertheless disturbing because events proceeded in such a way that the charges might almost just as well be true.

When George Kennan went to Tokyo in February 1948 to advise MacArthur on the change of policy in Japan from political reform to economic rehabilitation, he found the general "so distant and full of mistrust" toward the Truman administration that his mission was "like nothing more than that of an envoy charged with opening up communications and arranging the establishment of diplomatic relations with a hostile and suspicious foreign government."[18] MacArthur's hostility toward Washington dated from World War II, when he had been outraged and frustrated by FDR's decision to give first priority in the allocation of army troops, transport, and equipment to the European theater of operations, while fighting the war against Japan primarily with the navy. The general seems never to have wavered in his belief that he could bring the world war to a swift end if only he were given unlimited authority and if all his demands for men and matériel were met. From his point of view, all limitations imposed by Washington were disastrously misguided.

MacArthur's egotism was only further developed by his rule over Japan. By 1950 the seventy-year-old general had grown accustomed to the exercise of nearly absolute power; he had long since fallen out of the habit of obeying orders. Revered by a large bloc of Republican congressmen who deplored Truman's emphasis on Europe and his abandonment of Chiang, MacArthur had begun to look toward the White House. He and his commander in chief were thus political adversaries — a sure formula for trouble.

Truman had long harbored a rather intense dislike of MacArthur. As early as 1945 the president had inveighed against the general in his private diary, calling him "Mr. Prima Donna," a "stuffed shirt," and "a play actor and a bunco man," not a real general or fighting man.[19] We can only wonder whether Truman knew that in the 1930s FDR had once remarked that Huey Long was "one of the two most dangerous men in the country." Asked the identity of the other, the president replied, "Douglas MacArthur."[20] During the final months of 1950 and the early months of 1951, MacArthur would amply bear out Roosevelt's judgment.

CHAPTER 11

The UN's First Response

THE SOVIETS MAINTAINED all along that the conflict in Korea was a civil war that had been started by a South Korean attack upon the north, to which the exasperated northern regime had justifiably responded with all the forces at its disposal. At first, the Soviet newspapers did very little more than voice that position and relegate news from Korea to the inside pages. A wait-and-see attitude prevailed.

But once the United States and the UN were fully committed to intervention, the Kremlin's propagandists went to work and produced a brilliant position paper to embarrass America in the eyes of the world. Drafted by Deputy Foreign Minister Andrei A. Gromyko and released for maximum effect on the Fourth of July, the text claimed that in Korea, just as in the American Civil War, the reactionary, agricultural south had attacked the progressive, industrial north. In both civil wars, motivated by the need not only to repulse the attack but also to crush the illegal southern government and to reunify the nation, the northerners had "transferred military operations to the territory of the Southern states, routed the troops of the planters and slaveowners, who did not enjoy the support of the people . . . and created the conditions for establishing national unity." It was most convenient for this line of propaganda that in the American Civil War the north had been the side of emancipation and reunification and that it had emerged victorious. The North Koreans, so the Russians argued, would also triumph, despite the fact that the United States was helping the South Korean government, just as Britain had futilely aided the Confederacy. The ultimate point of the Russian statement was that since the war in Korea was a civil war, the UN had no business getting involved.[1]

The United States and its allies dismissed the clever Russian analogy as preposterous — a case of the devil citing Scripture for his own purpose — but some highly responsible Americans, including George Kennan, insisted at the time that the conflict in Korea was indeed a civil war and that although America was right to intervene in order to protect its interests, it should not have sought UN sponsorship for its actions. "The term 'aggression' in the usual international sense was as misplaced here as it was to be later in the case of Vietnam," wrote Kennan in his memoirs. "The involvement of the United Nations . . . was thus in no way necessary or called for."[2]

In the language of diplomacy, the term "aggression" connotes an armed attack by one sovereign nation upon another. It was the most serious charge that could be made under the UN Charter, roughly equivalent to first-degree murder in criminal law. The United States would very much have liked the UN to categorize the North Korean invasion officially as an "act of aggression,"[3] but that would have implied either diplomatic recognition of the North Korean government or else a direct accusation against the Soviet Union. Neither implication was acceptable to the majority of UN members, or to the United States itself. So the American government would have to settle for the North Koreans' being charged with having committed a "breach of the peace," a lesser offense but one against which the UN was nevertheless empowered by its Charter to act as firmly as against an act of aggression. "Breach of the peace" had the advantage of being a vaguer term, which could be stretched to cover a civil war, even though, under ordinary circumstances, the UN had no authority to meddle in the internal affairs of nations.[4]

A day or two after the beginning of the North Korean invasion, Truman most revealingly referred to Korea as "the Greece of the Far East."[5] But the recent conflict in Greece, as no one disputed, had been a civil war. The UN had become involved only because in December 1946 the Greek government had complained to the Security Council that the Greek Communist guerrilla forces were receiving aid from Albania, Yugoslavia, and Bulgaria. The council established a commission to investigate the alleged border violations and to recommend what might be done to end them. The commission found Greece's northern Communist neighbors guilty as charged, and the Security Council ordered them to desist.

The role of the UN in the Greek civil war was, at least ostensibly, entirely a matter of trying to ensure that the conflict would remain strictly domestic — though everyone understood that if the guerrillas were deprived of aid from, and refuge in, the countries to the north, they would almost certainly be suppressed in fairly short order. The UN, however, had no jurisdiction to intervene directly in the civil war. Its sole avowed concern was to see to it that foreign governments were prevented from giving aid to guerrillas who sought to overthrow the legitimate Greek government, recognized by the UN, of which Greece was a member nation.

But early in 1947 the Truman administration felt that it was perfectly within its rights to give financial aid to the Greek government without first seeking UN permission — especially since the matter would have had to be presented to the Security Council, where the Soviet delegate would certainly have vetoed it. The failure to seek prior UN endorsement for the Truman Doctrine was a costly tactical error; the uproar occasioned by the administration's having "bypassed" the UN — thereby, said some, displaying contempt for the principles of the UN Charter and undermining the organization's chances for success — jeopardized congressional passage of the aid bill. Senator Arthur Vandenberg, the Republican champion of bipartisanship, stepped in and mollified his colleagues by adding some showy but meaningless clauses pretending to involve the UN. That did the trick. The episode taught Truman and his State Department a lesson that they would take to heart when they came to consider intervention in the Korean conflict: they could not afford to circumvent the UN.

To see that its financial aid was used effectively, the United States sent to Greece not only a delegation of civilian officials from the Economic Cooperation Administration but also, in February 1948, the military officers of the American Mission for Aid to Greece, headed by General James Van Fleet, who would in 1951 assume command of the Eighth U.S. Army in Korea. AMAG's role was purely advisory (though often peremptorily so), and America sent no troops to fight in Greece. As we have already seen, the Greek civil war ended in 1949 with a victory for the royal government largely because Tito stopped aiding the guerrillas.

The hope that a similar scenario would play itself out in Korea was a major factor contributing to the American decision of June 24–25 to appeal to the Security Council. Washington believed, on the basis of overestimates of South Korea's strength and underestimates of North Korea's, that the south could repulse the attack as long as neither the Russians nor the Chinese Communists became directly involved. Thus the original American draft resolution called upon all UN members to "refrain from giving assistance to the North Korean authorities."[6] Communist China was, of course, not a member of the UN, but the Americans hoped that the weight of world opinion would not only deter the Russians but would also lead them to order the Chinese to remain aloof.

That might have been the full extent of the UN's role in Korea had it not been for the fact that the North Korean attack was widely viewed as a direct challenge to the organization's authority, effectiveness, and prestige. When, late in the evening of June 24, State Department official John Hickerson telephoned UN Secretary-General Trygve Lie to inform him of the invasion, Lie exclaimed, "My God, Jack, that's war against the United Nations!"[7]

Although South Korea was not a member of the UN, it was a favorite nephew. The May 1948 elections had taken place under the auspices of the UN Temporary Commission on Korea, and in December of that year the report submitted by the commission asserted, in a somewhat ambiguous manner, that the government of the Republic of Korea was the only lawfully established government in Korea. The General Assembly, in which the Soviets had no veto, had then voted to accept the commission's report. But a nation could become a member of the UN only on the Security Council's recommendation to the General Assembly, and the Soviets persistently vetoed any such motion.

The commission's second assignment was to observe the withdrawal of all Russian and American occupation troops from Korea. The Russians announced in December 1948 that they had completed their evacuation, but the commission was never given an opportunity to verify that claim. With the departure of the last American troops at the end of June 1949, it seemed that UNCOK (from whose name the word "Temporary" had been dropped in December 1948) had accomplished all that it could reasonably hope to do within the foreseeable future. Late that summer it submitted an official report stating that it could not possibly carry out the final task with which it had been charged — the reunification of Korea — until and unless the

United States and the USSR settled their overall differences, thereby ending the Cold War. The report also criticized both the southern and the northern regimes, stated that civil war (that was the term employed) seemed likely, and suggested that the UN hand the problem of Korean unity back to America and the USSR.[8]

Secretary of State Dean Acheson strongly resisted that last proposal and called not only for an extension of the commission's term in Korea but also for an expansion of its responsibilities. The commission was to watch for any signs of impending civil war (Acheson carefully spoke of "military conflict" and avoided the former term) and to report such signs to the UN so that steps could be taken to avert hostilities or, if they broke out, to end them.[9]

Until June 1949 the presence of American troops had deterred an invasion from the north; now the certainty that an attack would elicit an immediate UN response was to serve that purpose. The North Koreans, however, had given fair warning that they would not be intimidated by the UN. On October 18, 1949, while the debate over the extension and expansion of UNCOK's responsibilities was under way in the General Assembly, the North Korean foreign minister sent a letter to the UN's leaders stating that if the organization continued to consider the Korean question without the participation of North Korea, "the Korean people will not abandon the struggle and will reserve for itself the right to continue by measures at its disposal the struggle for the immediate removal of the United Nations Commission from Korea and for the final unification of the country *by its own forces* into a unified democratic state" (emphasis added).[10] Such a threat only ensured the passage of the American resolution on October 22, despite vehement Soviet opposition.

Some observers believed that the Soviet delegate continued to boycott the Security Council on June 25 because the Kremlin wanted to demonstrate to the world that even without the obstruction of a Soviet veto, the UN would behave just as the League of Nations had done when confronted with the Manchurian and Abyssinian crises in the 1930s. Inept and cowardly, unable and unwilling to take any effective action, the UN would be exposed as a negligible force in international affairs. The Soviets had good reason for wanting to discredit the UN, once and for all, since the U.S.-dominated General Assembly was becoming a real nuisance. The Soviets had been embarrassed on numerous fronts during the assembly's session in the fall of 1949, even having to endure the supreme outrage of having their then archnemesis, Yugoslavia, elected to the Security Council.

Conversely, the Truman administration was eager to demonstrate the effectiveness of the UN, on which the militarily weak United States was still relying heavily for its security, especially outside the North Atlantic area. Acheson certainly wanted to vindicate himself for having said in his National Press Club speech six months earlier that Asian nations outside the American defense perimeter in the Pacific would, if attacked, have to rely first upon their own resources and "then upon the commitments of the entire civilized world under the Charter of the United Nations, which so far has not proved a weak reed to lean on."[11] It was time to show the Russians just how strong a force the UN could be.

These issues were highlighted by the coincidence that June 25 happened to be the fifth anniversary of the meeting in the San Francisco Opera House at which the delegates of all fifty nations represented had adopted by unanimous acclaim the Charter of the United Nations. On June 25, 1950, the very survival of the UN seemed to be at stake. The collapse of the League of Nations had, it was generally believed, opened the final chapter that had inexorably led to the outbreak of World War II. Once again the postwar world, or at least that part of it not under Stalin's sway, was determined to profit from the lessons learned, at such grievous cost, from the interwar period.

The first emergency session of the UN Security Council dealing with the Korean crisis convened at 2:20 on the afternoon of Sunday, June 25. Until the organization's Manhattan headquarters were ready for occupancy, in 1952, the UN leased the former Sperry Gyroscope plant in Lake Success, Long Island, only a few miles east of the limits of the New York City borough of Queens; it was in those bleak, industrial surroundings that the council met. Present were representatives of four of the five permanent members: France, Great Britain, Nationalist China, and the United States. Also present were delegates from the six temporary members: Cuba, Ecuador, Egypt, India,

Norway, and Yugoslavia. To the great relief of the Americans, the Soviet delegate did not attend.

The general sense of urgency had been heightened considerably by the receipt that morning of a cable from UNCOK, which stated that the fighting in Korea was "assuming the character of full-scale war and may endanger the maintenance of international peace and security."[12] Such a message from the UN's own observers gave weight to the American demands that they would not have had if they had been based solely on reports channeled through the U.S. State Department.

The draft resolution presented by the American delegate spoke of the "armed invasion of the Republic of Korea by armed forces from North Korea," and it called upon "the authorities in North Korea (a) To cease hostilities forthwith; and (b) To withdraw their armed forces to the 38th parallel."[13] After several hours of deliberation — complicated by the fact that, because it was Sunday and the meeting had been called on very short notice, some delegates had not been able to get instructions from their government — a very slightly revised version of the American resolution was adopted. The most significant change substituted "armed attack on" for "armed invasion of," the goals of the former potentially being less than complete conquest.

The resolution formally characterized the North Korean attack as a "breach of the peace," for the suppression of which its Charter authorized the UN to "take effective collective measures." Article 41 of the Charter invested the Security Council with the power to impose economic sanctions or blockades, or to call upon members to sever diplomatic relations with offending nations, in order "to give effect to its decision." Article 42 stated that "should the Security Council consider that measures provided for in Article 41 would be inadequate or have proved to be inadequate, it may take such action by air, sea or land forces as may be necessary to maintain or restore international peace and security."[14] But at this first meeting of the Security Council the United States did not call upon the UN to take any drastic action. Indeed, the first resolution did little more than fix the legal blame on the North Koreans. It was a court order to desist, issued by an organization with no standing police force to see that it was obeyed.

Shortly before 6:00 P.M. the amended resolution passed, 9–0, with

Yugoslavia abstaining. Because the UN Charter specified that in order to be adopted, resolutions on nonprocedural matters required seven affirmative votes, including the concurring votes of all five permanent members, the Soviet Union maintained that the vote was invalid. But during the Soviet boycott, the Security Council had adopted the principle that the Soviet failure to vote constituted an abstention, not a veto. In Friday's *New York Times* James Reston wrote:

> The legality of the "veto by walk-out" has never been tested, but the Soviet Union itself has agreed with the other major powers that if it abstains in a vote, that abstention does not prevent the Council from acting. . . . To accept the principle that one member of the United Nations should have the right to paralyze the operations of that organization unless Governments that it does not like are kicked out seems a fantastic proposition to officials here.[15]

What would have happened if the Soviet delegate had, after all, appeared? He would surely have prevented the adoption of the American resolution, but the American ambassador was prepared, in that case, to call for an emergency meeting of the General Assembly, which ordinarily met only in the autumn. Because of the rather complicated logistics involved, the UN Charter provided for a lengthy period of notification before a special session of the assembly could be convened, but the United States cavalierly maintained that the rule could be waived in this case; the Soviets could not block the move, since procedural questions were not subject to the veto. That would still leave a major problem. Although the General Assembly had it within its powers to adopt the relatively mild first American resolution, it had no authority to call for the use of economic sanctions or armed force. If such measures became necessary after the assembly's first vote, the United States was apparently planning to intervene in Korea as it saw fit, justifying its actions and calling upon the cooperation of its friends and allies on the basis of the first resolution, without specific Security Council orders. To ensure that such a quandary should never arise again, the United States introduced at that fall's General Assembly session a proposal (entitled "Uniting for Peace") enabling the assembly to meet on twenty-four hours' notice to deal with aggression and breaches of the peace, bypassing the Security Council, where a veto might stand in the way of effective action. Under such circumstances the assembly would have all the powers of the council.[16] The passage of that resolution, on November 3, was the final step in making the UN essentially an instrument of American foreign policy — as it would remain until the 1960s, when the influx of newly liberated African and Asian states would shift the balance in the General Assembly decisively away from U.S. influence.

CHAPTER 12

The First Blair House Meeting

UPON HIS ARRIVAL in Washington from Missouri on Sunday evening, Truman went straight to the Blair House, normally the vice president's residence, where he and his family were living while the White House was undergoing major structural repairs. From his plane he had radioed Secretary of State Dean Acheson, instructing him to summon the top military men as well as key officials from the State Department for a 7:30 dinner conference. The men at that meeting — five from State and eight from the Pentagon — would constitute the inner circle of Truman's advisers throughout the early days of the Korean War. A diverse group, they were:

Dean Acheson, fifty-seven, secretary of state. Educated at Groton, the elite New England prep school that Franklin D. Roosevelt and Averell Harriman had also attended, at Yale, and at Harvard Law School, Acheson was a patrician, Anglophile lawyer passionately devoted to the ideals of American democracy. Urbane and witty, he typically characterized the McCarthyite campaign of slander against him as "the attack of the primitives." Acheson, who was formidably intelligent, with a keen sense of his own abilities, suffered fools most reluctantly; unfortunately, his effectiveness as secretary of state was sometimes hampered by his making no secret of the fact that he placed into that category almost everyone who in any way resembled a congressman.

As assistant secretary of state during World War II and as undersecretary during the first two postwar years, Acheson was one of the principal architects and advocates of the doctrine that bore Truman's name and of the plan that bore Marshall's. In January 1949 President Truman, who had great admiration for Acheson and liked him personally, called upon him to serve as the nation's forty-ninth secretary of state. The president stood by him through all the vicious criticism, and Acheson retained his post until Truman left office, in 1953.

James E. Webb, forty-four, undersecretary of state. A lawyer and business executive, Webb had been director of the Bureau of the Budget from 1946 to 1949. Acheson called him "able and loyal" and admitted that Webb "knew more about administration than foreign policy."[1]

Philip Jessup, fifty-three, ambassador-at-large. Described by *Time* magazine as "a diplomat with a lawyer's incisive mind," Jessup was Hamilton Fish professor of international law and diplomacy at Columbia University. A brilliant and affable man, he was one of Acheson's closest personal friends. Taking time off from Columbia, he had represented the United States in various capacities at the UN. In the spring of 1949 his private conversations with the Soviet delegate to the Security Council, Iakov Malik, had been instrumental in ending the Berlin blockade. The Truman administration valued him as a statesmanlike emissary who could be dispatched to trouble spots anywhere in the world.

Dean Rusk, forty-one, assistant secretary of state for Far Eastern Affairs. One of the men who had chosen the 38th parallel as the dividing line between Russian and American operations in Korea in 1945, Rusk had gone on to become the State Department's key liaison with the UN. Fascinated by the Far East (he had been General Joseph Stilwell's deputy chief of staff in the China-Burma-India theater late in World War II) and disturbed by both the international and the domestic implications of Acheson's China policy, Rusk had volunteered in March 1950 for a step down from deputy undersecretary of state to the politically risky Far Eastern Affairs desk. Rusk later served as secretary of state under Presidents Kennedy and Johnson, and in that role he strongly advocated American military involvement in Vietnam.

John Hickerson, fifty-two, assistant secretary of state for UN Affairs. After having worked his way up through the ranks of the Foreign Service and the State Department bureaucracy, Hickerson, a quiet-spoken but strongly principled and firm Texan, was given the UN desk in 1949. Before the outbreak of the Korean War, he had been concerned mainly with the international control of atomic energy, the principal obstacle to which, he felt, was Soviet intransigence.

Louis Johnson, fifty-nine, secretary of defense. Johnson, a successful West Virginia lawyer whose firm had an office in Washington, had long been active in Democratic party politics. An infantry captain in France during World War I, he had been national commander of the American Legion in 1932–33 and had parlayed that position into an appointment as assistant secretary of war in 1937. Expecting to replace the isolationist Henry Woodring as secretary, Johnson was outraged when, in June 1940, FDR gave the position to the Republican and pro-Allied Henry L. Stimson. Johnson resigned and returned to his law practice.

A leading fund-raiser for Truman in the 1948 election campaign, Johnson asked for the job of secretary of defense, which replaced the old post of secretary of war in the postwar reorganization of the nation's military establishment, and, this time, his request was granted. But he was still not satisfied; he wanted to be president. A hulking man who frequently resorted to bluster and temper tantrums in order to get his way, Johnson employed the strategy of attacking his colleagues in the administration until (he hoped) he could emerge in the public eye as the only one who was competent and anti-Communist. Once Republican criticism of the Democrats' China policy began, Acheson made an especially easy target for Johnson's self-serving slanders. Johnson went so far as to cultivate friendships with Republicans hostile to the administration and to provide them with fuel for their attacks. Acheson was of the opinion that Johnson was mentally ill.

Johnson and Acheson wrangled not only over China but also over military spending. Johnson apparently hoped that if he impressed Congress and the electorate with his ability to hold the Pentagon to a tight budget, he would be catapulted into the White House. The implementation of NSC-68 would obviously interfere with these plans.

By the time the Korean War broke out, Truman had already decided to ask for Johnson's resignation at the first opportunity.

Frank Pace, Jr., thirty-eight, secretary of the army. A graduate of Princeton and of Harvard Law School, the lanky and independently wealthy Pace was the youngest high official in the Truman administration — a real comer. His military experience consisted solely of having held various legal and administrative posts in the U.S. Army Air Force's Air Transport Command during World War II. After his discharge, he served for two years as executive assistant to the postmaster general of the United States and in 1948 was made assistant director of the Bureau of the Budget, becoming its director in January 1949. He was appointed secretary of the army in April 1950, just three months before the North Korean invasion. His specialty was management; in each of his jobs his aims were to heighten efficiency, to streamline, and to cut costs.

Francis P. Matthews, sixty-three, secretary of the navy. A senior member of a prestigious Omaha law firm, Matthews had been chairman of the Nebraska delegation at the 1948 Democratic National Convention, where he swung the state's votes over to Truman. He subsequently contributed generously to Truman's campaign. The navy post was his reward. General Omar Bradley later wrote that "by his own public admission, Matthews, who had never served in the armed forces, knew nothing about the Navy or the military."[2]

A devout Roman Catholic, both of whose parents had been born in Ireland, Matthews was very active as a fundraiser, executive, and international emissary for Catholic charities. For his services, Pope Pius XII had awarded him the title of "Secret Papal Chamberlain with Cape and Sword."

Matthews subscribed to the Catholic Church's alarmist position regarding the dangers to American democracy posed by Communist aggression and infiltration; this attitude had been reflected in the reports he had issued in the late 1940s as chairman of the U.S. Chamber of Commerce's Committee on Socialism and Communism.

Matthews resigned as navy secretary in July 1951 to accept the post of U.S. ambassador to Ireland, a job for which he was perhaps better suited.

Thomas K. Finletter, fifty-six, secretary of the air force. A prosperous Wall Street lawyer, Finletter had served during World War II as an important government adviser on international economic affairs and had been a consultant to the U.S. delegation at the 1945 UN Charter conference, in San Francisco. In July 1947 Truman appointed him chairman of the President's Air Policy Commission, which six months later submitted a report — "Survival in the Air Age," also known simply as the Finletter report — that recommended expansion of the air force to seventy groups. After a one-year stint as chief of the Economic Cooperation Administration's mission to Britain, Finletter was made secretary of the air force early in 1950.

General Omar Bradley, fifty-seven, chairman of the Joint Chiefs of Staff. After his successful campaigns as commander of II Corps in North Africa and Sicily, Bradley was given command of all the American forces that would participate in the Normandy landings on D day. He then led the 12th Army Group brilliantly in France, the Ardennes, and Germany, proving himself to be one of the outstanding American generals in World War II. An intelligent, down-to-earth, and quiet man — the opposite of George Patton — he was well liked by his officers and men. After the war he served for two years as head of the Veterans Administration before being made army chief of staff and then, in 1949, the first permanent chairman of the Joint Chiefs. Bradley was promoted to the five-star rank of General of the Army in mid-September 1950.

General J. Lawton Collins, fifty-four, army chief of staff. Early in World War II, on the Pacific islands of Guadalcanal and New Georgia, Collins had shown himself to be an excellent commander. In 1943 General George Marshall recommended him for a corps command, but MacArthur said that the forty-seven-year-old Collins was too young. Marshall then transferred Collins to Europe and gave him command of VII Corps, which performed superbly in Normandy, in the Battle of the Bulge, and in Germany. Collins's drive earned him the nickname Lightning Joe. Considering him his finest corps commander, Bradley chose Collins to succeed him as army chief of staff in 1949. According to Bradley, Collins was "not a deep thinker or strategist"; he was a man of action and an able executive, though he could be impetuous.[3]

Admiral Forrest Sherman, fifty-three, chief of naval operations. After graduating from Annapolis in 1917, second out of a class of two hundred, Sherman trained to be a naval aviator. In 1942 he was given command of the aircraft carrier USS *Wasp*, which was sunk by Japanese torpedoes off Guadalcanal in September of that year. He ended the war as chief of staff to Admiral Chester W. Nimitz, commander in chief of the Pacific Fleet. After the war he served in Washington as deputy chief of naval operations and was involved with the reorganization of the armed forces. Appointed commander of the Mediterranean Fleet in January 1948, he was made chief of naval operations in November 1949. General Bradley called him "one of the most impressive military officers" that he had ever met "in any service" and characterized him as "urbane, intellectual, diplomatic, and smart as a whip."[4]

General Hoyt Vandenberg, fifty-one, air force chief of staff. Vandenberg graduated from West Point in 1923, during Mac-

Arthur's tenure as superintendent of the academy, and then climbed his way up through the ranks of the U.S. Army Air Force. As chief of staff for the Northwest African Strategic Air Force, he played an important role in the air campaigns over North Africa, Sicily, and Italy. In the spring of 1944, General Eisenhower appointed him commander of the American air forces that would take part in the Allied invasion of France. During 1946 and 1947, he headed first the War Department's military intelligence section and then the new Central Intelligence Group, immediate predecessor of the CIA. In April 1948 he was made air force chief of staff.

These men were already assembled when Truman arrived at the Blair House, and although the formal conference was not to begin until after dinner, discussion started at once. Its subject, rather surprisingly, was not Korea but Formosa. Secretary Johnson and General Bradley had returned the previous day from their Tokyo conference concerning the Japanese peace treaty, and they were still under the spell of MacArthur's rhetoric. The Far Eastern commander had been passionately opposed to Truman's decision at the turn of the year to withhold further aid from Chiang Kai-shek and thus to acquiesce in a Communist takeover of Formosa. MacArthur took advantage of this high-level visit from Washington to state his case. Bradley needed no convincing, for the JCS had felt all along that it would be dangerous to allow Formosa to fall into unfriendly hands. And Johnson was thrilled to have new ammunition for his feud with Acheson.

Waylaying Truman before the group could go in to dinner, Johnson got Bradley to read aloud the message regarding Formosa that they had brought from MacArthur, as well as the memorandum on that same subject that Bradley had written earlier in the day, which said in part:

> While Formosa is not essential as a base of U.S. troops, its occupation by an unfriendly power would seriously affect our position in Japan, Okinawa, and the Philippines. It has many prepared air fields which move any unfriendly combat planes sufficiently close to our positions and routes of communication to increase their effectiveness many fold. For example, our present fighter planes

have just enough range to permit their movement between the Philippines and Formosa. Any detour to avoid interference from Formosa makes this lateral movement impracticable or extremely hazardous.[5]

Johnson said that while they were in Tokyo, MacArthur's intelligence staff had reported a buildup in recent weeks of Chinese Communist forces along the coast opposite Formosa from 40,000 to about 156,000, obviously in preparation for an invasion. General Bradley believed that while South Korea could probably defend itself, Formosa "lay nearly bare, ripe for the plucking."[6] Now that the Communists had shown they were ready to resort to armed aggression against American interests in Asia, Formosa would be more vital than ever.

When dinner had been cleared away and the meeting began in earnest around the large mahogany dining table, Johnson insisted that consideration of Formosa be the first order of business. Truman firmly squelched that demand and gave the floor to Acheson and Korea.

Acheson opened the discussion by announcing that the Security Council had adopted a version of the American resolution, but Truman said that he didn't think the North Koreans would pay any attention to it. On the basis of some reports from the field, it appeared that the South Korean army might be able to repulse the invaders, although other reports were discouraging. If the ROK army collapsed, then the UN would have to resolve to use force against the North Koreans, and the United States would have to supply most of that force. General Vandenberg and Admiral Sherman thought that air and naval aid would probably suffice in that case, but General Collins argued that if the South Korean army was really being routed, the intervention of American ground forces would also be necessary. In order to be prepared for the worst, Truman ordered the service chiefs to take steps to ready all branches of the armed forces for the possibility of an eventual call.

The United States would do whatever it had to do. General Bradley seemed to speak for all present when he said that America would have to "draw the line somewhere" to stop Communist expansion, and Korea seemed as good a place as any to draw it.[7] So it seemed that first night, but at one point several months later Acheson would slam his fist down on his desk and exclaim, "If the best minds in the world had set out to find us the worst possible location to fight a war, the unanimous choice would have to have been Korea!"[8]

By the time the meeting broke up, at 11:00 P.M., Truman had made three important decisions and had given orders for them to be carried out:

1. American civilians (technical advisers and the families of KMAG officers and of the American diplomatic mission staff) were to be evacuated from Korea at once by air and by sea, but the men of KMAG were to remain with their Korean units. General MacArthur was ordered to use U.S. naval vessels to keep open the port of Inchon, adjacent to Seoul, while the evacuation was under way; they were also to escort the ships transporting the Americans to Japan. More significantly, he was instructed to use U.S. fighter planes to protect Seoul's Kimpo Airport and its vicinity until the evacuation was completed. Truman assumed that MacArthur would understand, though it was not explicitly stated in the intentionally vague orders dispatched to him, that American aircraft were not only to keep North Korean planes away from the area but also to attack the North Korean tanks in the vanguard of the lunge toward the capital. The orders emphasized, however, that under no circumstances were the U.S. planes to operate north of the 38th parallel.

   Although these actions were to be taken purely in the guise of protecting American citizens, they constituted intervention in the fighting — and were intended to slow the North Korean advance, to signal American willingness to make a larger commitment if necessary, and to boost South Korean morale.

2. MacArthur was to rush ammunition and supplies to the South Korean army — as much as possible by immediate airdrop — and he was to use American air and naval cover to ensure the safe delivery of this matériel. The next day the *New York Times* reported that the United States was sending arms that military leaders believed would be "sufficient to aid the Republic of Korea successfully to beat back the invasion from the north unless the Russians aid it militarily."

3. The Seventh U.S. Fleet — which included the aircraft carrier *Valley Forge*, a heavy cruiser, and eight destroyers — was to proceed at once from the Philippines toward the Formosa Strait. Here it would be in a position to prevent a Chinese Communist amphibious invasion of Formosa, but no orders were to be issued yet regarding that aspect of its mission. Such orders would represent an about-face on a major policy of the administration, and Truman didn't want to rush into it. His affirmative decision was, however, something of a foregone conclusion, for not only Johnson and Bradley but also Acheson himself now felt that it was essential to protect Formosa — and it was Acheson who suggested using the Seventh Fleet.

The Korean invasion had led the secretary of state earlier that day (with the encouragement of George Kennan, among others) to reverse the position that had brought him under such fierce attack during the past six months.[9] He did so not because of any change of heart regarding Chiang, but rather because it was necessary to consider the worst-case scenario: the loss of both Formosa and South Korea to the Communists would make the American position in Japan dangerously tenuous. Furthermore, following the precedent set by the economic-aid bill earlier in the year, congressional criticism of the administration's intervention in Korea might well be stifled if it were linked to protection of Chiang and Formosa. But Acheson was dead set against giving Chiang any more money that he could invest in American real estate for his personal gain rather than use for defense. Positioning the Seventh Fleet in the Formosa Strait seemed to be the perfect solution.

At about 11:00 the conferees slipped out a back door of the Blair House to avoid the reporters who were waiting in front. Truman had decided not to make any official announcement of the evening's decisions, and especially not to reveal that the administration was prepared to intervene militarily if the South Korean army proved unable to repulse the invasion. For the moment, it behooved the president to get a clearer picture of the situation in Korea before making any public commitment. Until then, trivialities would have to suffice. The next morning Truman issued a press release, which said: "Our concern for the lawless action taken by the forces from North Korea, and our sympathy for the people of Korea in this situation, are being demonstrated by the cooperative action of American personnel in Korea, as well as steps taken to expedite and augment assistance of the type being furnished under the Mutual Defense Assistance Program."[10]

CHAPTER 13

The Decision to Intervene

ON MONDAY, June 26, the news from Korea was bad and steadily worsening. Deep concern finally ignited into alarm early in the evening when the Pentagon received a cable from MacArthur in which he characterized the situation as "rapidly deteriorating." He said that North Korean tanks were already entering the northern suburbs of Seoul and that Syngman Rhee's government had fled southward. He concluded that because the ROK army lacked tanks, fighter planes, training, and the "will to fight," his estimate was that "a complete collapse is imminent."[1] John Foster Dulles's aide John M. Allison saw MacArthur shortly after the general had sent off his message (it was Tuesday morning in Tokyo); he later wrote that he had "never seen such a dejected, completely despondent man as General MacArthur was that . . . morning." MacArthur told him that all of Korea was lost and that "the only thing we can do is get our people safely out of the country."[2]

When Dean Acheson was informed of this cable, about 7:30 P.M., he immediately notified Truman, who called a meeting for 9:00 that evening. The group that gathered at the Blair House was the same as that of the previous night, except that navy secretary Frank Matthews was absent (but "not missed," recalled General Bradley) and Undersecretary of State Webb's place was taken by his deputy, H. Freeman Matthews.[3]

High officials from the State and Defense departments had met during the day and had resolved to propose to the president that American air and naval forces be ordered to provide cover and support for the South Korean ground troops, with authorization to strike all enemy targets south of the 38th parallel. They believed that the commitment of these forces would make all the difference. The invasion could then be repulsed and the border restored — those being at that time the U.S. government's maximum goals. They also believed that by limiting operations to below the 38th parallel (that is, by not taking either tactical or punitive action against North Korea on its own territory), Soviet and Chinese Communist participation could probably be avoided. On the basis of MacArthur's grim report and its obvious implication that the North Koreans intended to ignore the UN resolution, Truman did not hesitate to give his assent to the proposal. That was what the military situation seemed to call for, hence that was what had to be done. It was that simple.

Or at least nearly that simple. On June 28 the secretary of state would draft a top-secret policy statement acknowledging the grave dangers inherent in Truman's decision but precluding the automatic escalation of the conflict into a world war if the Soviets became overtly involved in Korea:

> The decision now made to commit United States air and naval forces to provide ground cover and support for South Korean troops does not *in itself* constitute a decision to engage in a major war with the Soviet Union if Soviet forces intervene in Korea. The decision regarding Korea, however, was taken in the full realization of a risk of war with the Soviet Union. If substantial Soviet forces actively oppose our present operations in Korea, United States forces should defend themselves, should take no action on the spot to aggravate the situation, and should report the situation to Washington.[4]

In other words, the decision of how to respond to Soviet intervention, if it should come, was not to be left up to MacArthur, to whom a version of this statement was sent the next day.

On June 27, in announcing his commitment of American air and naval forces to Korea, Truman would justify his move by citing the first Security Council resolution on Korea, which called upon "all Members to render every assistance to the United Nations" in bringing about both an end to the hostilities and the withdrawal of the North Korean forces to above the 38th parallel. By making such a claim, the president would rather brazenly distort the resolution's intended meaning, for what the council members had in mind when they adopted it was mediation, not military intervention. The majority of them, however, agreed with the Truman administration that *whatever* had to be done to save South Korea would have to be done. Therefore, Truman and Acheson felt certain all along that if the United States introduced a resolution specifically authorizing military intervention on behalf of the UN, the Security Council would pass it.

Accordingly, Acheson assured Truman at the June 26 meeting that such a resolution would be submitted to the council the next morning and that it would probably be passed by the time the president released his statement to the press, around noon. As it turned out, the Security Council meeting was delayed until that afternoon, because the Indian delegate was awaiting instructions from his government. Having already announced the time at which he would reveal his decisions, Truman was forced to resort to a bit of sleight of hand, hoping that no one would notice that the United States was doing something more than obediently following the UN's directives.

The Blair House meeting then turned to the issue of Formosa. Truman had made up his mind that the Seventh Fleet should neutralize the Formosa Strait, not only blocking any Communist invasion attempt but also putting an end to the air raids that the Nationalists were then carrying out against the mainland. (In his official statement the next day he said imperiously that "the Seventh Fleet will see that this is done.") He justified his decision by stating that "the occupation of Formosa by Communist forces would be a direct threat to the security of the Pacific area and to United States forces performing their lawful and necessary functions in that area."[5] He hoped that by curbing Chiang Kai-shek as well as Mao Tse-tung, he might assuage the wrath of the Chinese Communists. In fact, however, Peking was infuriated. Moreover, the neutralization of the Formosa Strait led the Communists to transfer a large force northward, from the coast opposite Formosa to Shantung. From that pivotal position, the troops could be moved quickly to reinforce the North Korean army, to defend Manchuria, to oppose any moves that Chiang might make against the mainland, or, if it became possible, to carry out their original mission of invading Formosa. Finally, Truman's reversal of so emphatically stated and firmly defended a policy as the abandonment of Chiang made the Chinese Communists unable to take very seriously any future American assurances of benign intentions.

The meeting next moved on to other possible danger spots in the Pacific region. The result was that toward the end of his statement the next day, Truman announced:

I have also directed that United States forces in the Philippines be strengthened and that military assistance to the Philippine Government be accelerated. I have similarly directed acceleration in the furnishing of military assistance to the forces of France and the associated states in Indochina and the dispatch of a military mission to provide close working relations with those forces.[6]

During the next four years the United States would underwrite the hopeless French cause in Indochina to the tune of nearly $3 billion, including an annual allowance of $4 million for Bao Dai's personal disposal. As for the military advisers charged with ensuring that American aid was put to effective use, the French found their presence insulting and fastidiously ostracized them. Nevertheless, once the United States had made such an enormous investment of money and prestige in Vietnam, it would from then on do whatever it had to do to protect that investment.

The Blair House conferees worked their way expeditiously through their lengthy agenda. Unanimity prevailed, and Truman resolutely gave his approval to one proposal after another in quick succession. The momentous meeting lasted only forty minutes.

Truman made one more extremely important decision that evening: he would not submit to a congressional vote the question of committing American air and naval forces to intervention in Korea. He was not, after all, declaring war; he was simply sending American planes and ships to help bring the invasion of South Korea to a speedy end — and he claimed to be doing so at the behest of the UN. His predecessors in the White House had on numerous occasions taken it upon themselves to dispatch American troops to pacify trouble spots, though mostly hitherto in Central America and the Caribbean, where the United States felt that the Monroe Doctrine gave it a perfect right to intervene at will.

Truman's reasons were quite simple. He believed that it was imperative to act at once, and he wanted *personal* credit for the decision to stand up to Communist aggression. It did, in fact, seem quite possible that a congressional debate would hold things up. The Senate Republican Policy Committee had met Monday afternoon and had announced to the press its resolution that America should aid South

Korea with as much matériel as possible but that the nation should not become directly involved in the fighting and risk getting itself dragged into another major war. The committee had, however, apparently adopted this position not so much out of conviction as out of resignation. The partisan dissension that had convulsed the government for months had to be suppressed in the face of a national emergency; the Republican senators generously, if unenthusiastically, advocated the course of action that they expected Truman to choose. That their announced policy did not reflect beliefs they were prepared to defend was demonstrated by the alacrity with which they discarded it once Truman had issued his statement the next day.

None of the major decisions that Truman had made in the Blair House meetings on June 25 and 26 was made public until Tuesday the twenty-seventh. A mood of depression pervaded the capital on Monday as reports from Korea grew more disheartening and as certainty increased that the Truman administration was not prepared to take any effective action. The statement issued by the president on Monday seemed to be a case of rhetoric "full of sound and fury, signifying nothing." It appeared likely that Truman would abandon Rhee, just as he had abandoned Chiang, when the going got tough. There was much talk of appeasement, of Munich, and of World War III. The outlook was bleak indeed. Washington dubbed Monday night the night of the big gloom, so complete was the blackout on information about what had transpired at the Blair House. It was almost as though, with a theatrical sense of timing, Truman were deliberately heightening the tension to prepare for his masterstroke.

Not until 11:30 A.M. on Tuesday, June 27, did Truman meet with fourteen leading members of the two houses of Congress (nine Democrats and five Republicans), including each party's senior members of the Senate Foreign Relations Committee, of the House Foreign Affairs Committee, and of both Armed Services committees. As he proceeded down the list of his decisions, the president received almost nothing but encouragement from the amazed and gratified legislators.

Having cleared that hurdle, Truman then released his formal statement accusing "Communism" of having attacked Korea and making public his decision to intervene. When the text was read in the House of Representatives, all the members except Communist sympathizer Vito Marcantonio of New York City sprang to their feet and cheered. The reception in the Senate was more restrained, some senators grumbling at first that Truman seemed to be "arrogating to himself the power to declare war." But then Senator William F. Knowland (Republican, California) — known as "the senator from Formosa" for his passionate support of Chiang — spoke out: "I believe that in this very important step which the President of the United States has taken in order to uphold the hands of the United Nations and the free peoples of the world, he should have the overwhelming support of all Americans regardless of their partisan affiliation."[7] Coming from such an ardent critic of the administration, these words meant nothing less than the restoration of the bipartisanship that had been so notably lacking for at least the previous six months.

On Tuesday evening, correspondent James Reston wrote in his article for the next day's *New York Times:*

> There is in Washington tonight a spirit of far greater cooperation than at any time in the last few years. Moreover, the somber spectacle of American planes engaged against a Communist aggressor 7,000 miles away from home, long before the United States is ready for a major war, has finally overwhelmed the atmosphere of McCarthyism that has pervaded this city for months.[8]

Perhaps a bit carried away, the *Christian Science Monitor*'s Washington correspondent, Joseph C. Harsch, gushed: "I have lived and worked in and out of this city for twenty years. Never before in that time have I felt such a sense of relief and unity pass through this city. . . . I have never seen such a large part of Washington so nearly satisfied with a decision of the government."[9]

The universal reaction to Truman's statement of June 27 — from Congress, from the American and European press, from foreign governments, and from the American public — was overwhelmingly favorable. The Gallup poll registered a great upward leap in Truman's popularity, and the deluge of mail received by the White House supported the president ten to one. Congressmen who had hitherto joined Senator McCarthy in muttering threats of impeachment against Truman suddenly had nothing but praise for the president (though McCarthy himself kept hammering away about the damage done by the administration's earlier abandonment of Chiang). Even New York governor Thomas E. Dewey, whom Truman had defeated in the 1948 presidential election and who was still nominal head of the Republican party, sent a telegram to the White House endorsing all of Truman's recent decisions: "I wholeheartedly agree with and support the difficult decision you have made today to extend American assistance to the Republic of Korea in combatting armed Communist aggression. Your action there, in Formosa, the Philippines and Indo China was necessary to the security of our country and the free world. It should be supported by a united America."[10]

The night of the big gloom was followed by immense relief, approval, and solidarity. The big step had been taken at last, and everyone was ready to do whatever it entailed. The long period of tension, frustration, and appeasement was over, or so it seemed; the time for action had arrived. The prevalent feeling might be compared with that among antifascists all over the world at the outbreak of the Spanish civil war. Now at last there was an opportunity to fight the enemy, to echo the defenders of Madrid, who had declared, "They shall not pass!"

CHAPTER 14

The UN Goes to War

AMERICA WAS NOW COMMITTED to armed intervention, but Truman feared that if the United States acted alone, the Soviet Union or Communist China might respond in kind. If, however, the United States could claim to be acting on behalf of the UN, with world opinion and the possibility of an international military force on its side, the great Communist powers would probably be deterred from overt involvement in Korea. And so it was that at 3:00 in the afternoon on Tuesday, June 27, the American delegate placed before the Security Council (this dramatic meeting of which was televised) a resolution calling upon the members of the UN to "furnish such assistance to the Republic of Korea as may be necessary to repel the armed attack and to restore international peace and security in the area."[1]

In other words, the United States was asking that, for the first time in history, an international peacekeeping organization resolve to use collective armed force to stop an act of aggression — which is what everyone considered the North Korean invasion, even if they called it a breach of the peace. The UN would do what the League of Nations had never dared to do. The league had denounced the Japanese aggression in Manchuria and the Italian invasion of Abyssinia, but it had taken no effective action to oppose them. It had collapsed because it had no armed force with which to enforce its decisions, and it lacked armed force because its members didn't dare to take action without the commitment of the United States. Now everything was to be different. The United States and the UN were to reinforce each other. As President Truman would later tell General MacArthur, one reason America was fighting in Korea was "to bring the United Nations through its first great effort in collective security and to produce a free world coalition of incalculable value to the national security interests of the United States."[2]

Indeed, one might say that the Korean War provided the impetus for the final step in transforming the UN into what was virtually, despite the Soviet Union's obstructive efforts, the free-world counterpart of the Cominform. Many Americans came to believe that the interests of the United States and those of the UN were identical. Senator William Knowland spoke for this constituency when he said, after the Soviet Union had announced that its delegate would return to the Security Council on August 1 to serve his scheduled turn as chairman, "To invite or permit Mr. Malik to gain the chairmanship by rotation is like permitting a member of the Capone crime syndicate to head the F.B.I."[3]

When the Korean War broke out, the end of the Soviet boycott was still more than a month away. Despite a personal invitation from Secretary-General Trygve Lie, Iakov Malik refused to attend the crucial June 27 meeting of the Security Council. Once it became clear that he was not going to show up, there was no doubt that the American resolution would pass; the only question was by how large a majority it would do so, the three possible dissenting votes being those of Egypt, India, and Yugoslavia.

The case for adopting the resolution was strongly reinforced by several UNCOK reports that had arrived since Sunday, unequivocally affixing blame to North Korea for the outbreak of hostilities. Nevertheless, the delegates from Egypt and India felt that they could not vote one way or the other on such a weighty matter — which might obligate their nations to send troops or aid to Korea — without specific instructions from their governments. At 11:00 P.M., after several recesses prompted by the vain hope that such instructions might finally arrive, the American delegate insisted on a vote, for the United States wanted the resolution passed that night to give legitimacy to Truman's claim that he was acting on behalf of the UN. By 11:45 the United States, Britain, France, Nationalist China, Cuba, Ecuador, and Norway had cast the seven affirmative votes that were the minimum needed to pass the resolution. Yugoslavia cast a negative vote, and Egypt and India abstained, though two days later the Indian government decided to change its vote retroactively to a yea. By the end of the week 33 of the UN's 59 member states had expressed their support of the resolution, and another 20 would eventually endorse it, but only 16 nations actually sent combat units to Korea.

Most of those who did so were members of NATO (the United

States, France, Belgium, the Netherlands, and Luxembourg), of the British Commonwealth (Australia, New Zealand, and the Union of South Africa), or of both (Great Britain and Canada). Three additional NATO states (Denmark, Italy, and Norway) sent medical units. Iceland and Portugal were the only two NATO members that did not send either military or medical units, the former because it maintained neither an army nor a navy, the latter because it did not join the UN until 1955.

Of the remaining six nations that sent combat units to Korea, Greece and Turkey (both of which would enter NATO in 1952) were obligated to the United States as recipients of aid under the Truman Doctrine and the Marshall Plan, and Thailand and the Philippines were eager for America to form a Pacific version of NATO. (Of the eventual members of the Southeast Asia Treaty Organization, established in 1954 — the United States, Great Britain, France, Australia, New Zealand, Pakistan, the Philippines, and Thailand — only Pakistan, which was then suffering from grave internal problems, did not contribute to the Korean War.) Ethiopia, which had been betrayed and abandoned by the League of Nations, sent troops as a gesture of support for the UN. And the one infantry battalion sent by Colombia was the token force from the United States' Latin American clients. (Bolivia, Costa Rica, Cuba, El Salvador, and Panama offered to send troops, but their offers were never taken up.) The UN force was thus by no means shaped simply by the determination of disinterested nations to uphold the sanctity of the UN Charter and its principles of international morality.

A total of about 40,000 non-U.S. troops from UN members was eventually sent to Korea, some 20,000 of them from the British Commonwealth (consolidated into a single division in 1951), 6,000 from Turkey (the Turks proved to be some of the toughest fighters of all), 5,000 from the Philippines, and 4,000 from Thailand. Other contingents represented contributions that were more symbolic than substantial; most consisted of one infantry battalion or even just one infantry company, a few naval vessels, or a small squadron of combat or transport aircraft with crews.

These forces were minuscule in comparison with the total of 5,720,000 Americans who would eventually participate in the Korean War: 2,834,000 army troops, 1,177,000 navy men, 424,000 Marines, and 1,285,000 air force personnel.* It cannot be denied that the non-U.S. troops made a real contribution, sometimes demonstrating a valor and tenacity in key battles that gave their roles significance out of all proportion to their small numbers, but their presence occasionally seemed to the Americans more a burden than a blessing. This was especially the case regarding supplies, for which the United States bore nearly all the responsibility. General Matthew B. Ridgway later wrote that

> catering to all the particular preferences, in food, in clothing, in religious observances — gave our service and supply forces a thousand petty headaches. The Dutch wanted milk where the French wanted wine. The Moslems wanted no pork and the Hindus, no beef. The Orientals wanted more rice and the Europeans more bread. Shoes had to be extra wide to fit the Turks. They had to be extra narrow and short to fit the men from Thailand and the Philippines. . . . Only the Canadians and Scandinavians adjusted easily to United States rations and clothes.[4]

One permanent member of the UN Security Council whose offer of troops was turned down — by the United States, not the UN — was Nationalist China. On Thursday, June 29, the U.S. State Department received word that Chiang Kai-shek had volunteered to send 33,000 men to Korea. Truman's first impulse was to accept. For one thing, he favored the policy of Asians helping Asians. For another, the Chinese troops might ensure that it would be unnecessary to send in American ground troops. And he was eager for the burden of fighting to be distributed as fully as possible among UN members in order to demonstrate the effectiveness of collective security.

But Dean Acheson was strongly opposed to accepting Chiang's offer. First of all, the United States would have to reequip the Chinese troops completely and train them to use the new equipment. Even then there could be no certainty that Chiang's men would better the very poor showing they had made against the Communists on the mainland; during the Chinese civil war the Communists had captured intact nearly 75 percent of the weapons that the United States had supplied to the Nationalists. But, as Truman stated in his memoirs,

---

*The total number of American armed forces personnel stationed in Korea never exceeded 1 million at any given time.

a far more important factor in his decision to reject Chiang's offer was the secretary of state's fear "that if the Chinese troops from Formosa appeared in Korea, the Communists in Peiping*might decide to enter that conflict in order to inflict damage on the Generalissimo's troops there and thus try to reduce his ability to defend himself whenever they decided to try an invasion of Formosa."[5] The emphasis properly fell on the first part of that sentence rather than on the second. Acheson was afraid that the presence of Nationalist Chinese troops in Korea might prompt the Chinese Communists to become overtly involved, thereby expanding the conflict rather than helping to bring it to a conclusion both speedy and favorable to the West. Furthermore, the secretary of state suspected that Chiang might be making his offer simply to get the United States to transport a vanguard of his troops to a position on the Asian mainland from which he could strike at Manchuria, reopening the Chinese civil war in its most vital strategic area. Truman was categorically opposed to any such scenario, which not only risked dragging U.S. troops into the morass that he had been so determined all along to avoid, but which might also spark World War III.

*From 1928 until the Communist victory in 1949, Beijing ("northern capital"), Westernized to Peking, was officially called Beiping ("northern peace"), Westernized to Peiping. During most of that period the Nationalist Chinese capital was Nanjing ("southern capital"), Westernized to Nanking, though after the Japanese occupied that city in 1937, Chiang Kai-shek's government moved first to Hankow and then, in 1938, to Chungking, where the capital remained until 1945.

CHAPTER 15

The Commitment
of U.S. Ground Troops

WHILE THE UN SECURITY COUNCIL deliberated on Tuesday, June 27, Seoul was falling. When the council convened at 3:00 P.M., it was 4:00 A.M. on Wednesday in the South Korean capital, and Communist tanks were penetrating the northern defenses of the city, despite the efforts of ROK infantry and of American bombers and fighter planes. The minimum goal of this defensive rear guard was to delay the North Korean advance until the ROK army could evacuate as many men and as much matériel as possible across the Han River, which formed the southern boundary of the main part of the capital city. Once the South Koreans and their equipment were safely on the southern bank and the only bridge complex had been blown, the river would serve as a relatively defensible barrier. Most important, the North Korean juggernaut would be slowed by having to ferry its heavy tanks, under ROK fire, across the Han on primitive rafts.

The explosive charges on the bridges — a three-lane highway bridge and three separate railway spans — were already in place. (The bridges were only to be broken in the middle, not completely demolished.) But it was essential for the eventual rally of the ROK army that the charges not be detonated until the last possible moment: until, that is, the Communists were almost at the northern bank and no more South Koreans could be gotten across without danger of the North Koreans' seizing the bridges and preventing their destruction. Unfortunately, the entry of the Communist tanks into the outskirts of the city touched off a frenzied, terror-stricken exodus of both civilians and ROK soldiers, the latter being outnumbered nearly four to one by the attackers. Panic swept the city in the middle of the night; people grabbed whatever they could carry and threw themselves into a screaming, honking crush in the dark streets leading to the Han bridge. At 2:15 A.M. — while the enemy tanks were still far away on the other side of the city and the roadway bridge was choked with thousands of refugees on foot and with trucks carrying hundreds of soldiers — a hysterical official gave the order to blow the bridges. It was never established exactly who was responsible, but the results would have gratified a North Korean saboteur. Between 500 and 800 soldiers and civilians were killed, either directly by the explosions or by drowning when they plunged into the river. Most of the ROK defenders of the city were stranded, and those who were not killed or captured had to make their way across the river on boats commandeered at gunpoint or on whatever rafts they could improvise. But there was no way to transport heavy equipment to the southern bank before the enemy reached the Han. About one third of the ROK army's total supplies and equipment — including trucks, ammunition, and heavy weapons — was abandoned in Seoul, not only lost to South Korea but falling into the hands of the northerners. It was a disaster — tactically, logistically, and psychologically.[1]

On the evening of June 28, Major General John H. Church, who headed the group that MacArthur had sent to Korea the previous day to make an official assessment of the situation, reported back to Tokyo that Seoul was in the hands of the enemy. Moreover, only 1,000 ROK officers and 8,000 men were assembled at Suwon, twenty miles south of the capital, where he and the ROK chief of staff, General Chae Byong Duk, had established a joint headquarters. Church went on to inform MacArthur of his judgment that ROK troops stationed along the south bank of the Han could, at least for the time being, prevent any further enemy advance on that front. But the ROK army, he said, would be utterly incapable of mounting any sort of counteroffensive to push the North Koreans back to the 38th parallel. If that was the American goal, then nothing short of the commitment of U.S. ground troops could achieve it.[2]

This report was so discouraging, and its implications so serious, that MacArthur immediately decided to fly to Suwon the next day to take a look for himself. Despite bad weather, on Thursday, June 29, he and a small entourage that included four American news correspondents flew in his unarmed plane, the *Bataan*, to the Suwon airfield, which had been repeatedly subjected to enemy airborne fire. The general's plane was escorted by only four Mustang fighters, one of which narrowly succeeded in driving off a North Korean fighter — a Russian-made Yak — that was swooping down toward the *Bataan* just short of Suwon. Throughout the incident, as throughout the rest of the day's dangers, MacArthur comported himself like the very model of sangfroid.[3]

Although the airfield itself was protected by an American antiaircraft artillery battalion, four Russian planes attacked Suwon during the general's visit. According to the Associated Press reporter accompanying MacArthur, one bomb hit the airfield and another landed half a mile from where the general was conferring. Two American transport planes on the ground were damaged by strafing, and a private in the antiaircraft battalion was wounded — one of the very first American casualties.[4]

Waiting on the tarmac to welcome MacArthur was a remarkably calm and dapper Syngman Rhee, together with Ambassador John Muccio. Flying in from Taejon, where the Rhee government had established a temporary capital, they had had a close call. The two light observation planes in which they were flying were spotted by a North Korean fighter, but the evasive action of the South Korean pilots, maneuvering in a complex pattern at treetop level, had shaken it off.[5] Despite plenty of cause for distress, Rhee was calm, because MacArthur's visit gave him confidence that help was on the way. After all, MacArthur had promised him on a visit some months earlier, "I will defend South Korea as I would the shores of my own native land."[6]

The group went to a former schoolhouse on the periphery of the airfield to be briefed on the military situation by General Church, who said that only 8,000 ROK soldiers were fighting with their units — out of the total of 95,000 men the army had had at the beginning of the invasion. But as he spoke, he received a report that another 8,000 were on their way to Suwon and that ROK officers expected to send yet another 8,000 by evening.[7]

It wasn't for such a briefing, which he could have had in Tokyo, that General MacArthur was risking his life. Cutting Church short, MacArthur took charge of the situation and issued his order: "Let's go up to the front and have a look." Smoking his corncob pipe in the backseat of an old black Dodge sedan, and followed by a procession of jeeps, the general was driven north toward the Han. Because it was on the basis of his observations that day that MacArthur sent an urgent call to Washington for authorization to send American ground troops into combat, accounts of the scene that confronted him have been exaggerated, especially by his sycophantic officers. One of them who was in the entourage, Brigadier General Courtney Whitney, head of the section of MacArthur's headquarters that oversaw the Japanese government, later wrote that as they drove northward, they saw "the dreadful backwash of a defeated and dispersed army."[8] And General Charles Willoughby, MacArthur's intelligence chief, who was also along, wrote that the road was "clogged with retreating, panting columns of troops interspersed with ambulances filled with the groaning, broken men, the sky resonant with shrieking missiles of death and everywhere the stench and misery and utter desolation of a stricken battlefield."[9] This differs radically from the report made by the AP correspondent in the party, who wrote:

> Of his tour of the front, General MacArthur said the hundreds of South Korean soldiers seen along the road seemed to be in good shape and their morale appeared undiminished. Many saluted briskly. Most of them cheered or sang as the General's caravan passed their trucks. . . . None in a convoy of twelve trucks *returning to the front* seemed downhearted [emphasis added]. They all cheerfully waved flags. Even most of the hundreds of tired, discouraged refugees trudging southward along the highway stopped and applauded the general.[10]

Extreme as this discrepancy is, it would be a mistake to make too much of it, for even on the basis of the mildest reports of what MacArthur saw — distant and sporadic artillery fire, troops with good morale returning to the Han River front, scattered divisions re-forming themselves — the conclusions at which he arrived that day seem reasonable. Even when reports over the next several days revealed that the ROK army had some 54,000 effectives (a figure more than double the estimate given to MacArthur on the twenty-ninth, but one that still meant an appalling casualty rate of more than 40 percent for the first week), no one could have argued very convincingly that the South Koreans were capable of pushing the Communists back to the 38th parallel. Nor was the answer to supply South Korea with tanks and heavy artillery, for those would necessitate sophisticated training, and the rapidity of the North Korean advance made time a crucial factor. The enemy would have to be stopped at once, or so it seemed, before he could gain so much ground that he couldn't be dislodged. American air power was helping somewhat, but not nearly enough, for two major reasons: bad weather obscured the ground on many days and made operations impossible, and U.S. planes were so fully occupied with protecting South Korean ground forces that they had little time left over to attack enemy targets in the rear. In short, only U.S. ground troops trained in the use of tanks and heavy artillery could be expected to hold the North Koreans once they had built up enough strength to storm the Han River line. And for the ROK army to clear the south of enemy forces, even with the help of American air power, seemed out of the question. Under the circumstances, MacArthur was perfectly justified in recommending the commitment of American ground troops.

Back in Washington at 4:00 P.M. on Thursday, June 29, twelve hours after MacArthur had left Korea, Truman held his first press conference since the beginning of the crisis.[11] "Mr. President," said one reporter after the first few questions, "everybody is asking in this country: are we or are we not at war?"

"We are not at war," replied Truman. The curious protocol then in effect stipulated that unless the president gave his specific permission, newspapers were forbidden to print in quotation marks anything he said during a news conference. When pressed in this case, Truman consented to the direct quotation of his words.

After a few intervening questions, the president remarked that the members of the UN were acting to suppress a bandit raid on the Korean republic. (He later gave permission to put the word "bandit" in quotes.) The previous day Senator William Knowland had declared on the floor of the Senate: "The action this government is taking is a police action against a violator of the law of nations and the Charter of the United Nations."[12] Seizing on the key phrase that would come to haunt Truman, a reporter at the press conference asked the president, "Would it be correct to call this a police action under the United Nations?"

Yes, answered Truman, that was exactly what it amounted to. Thus it was not Truman but a man who had been, and would again come to be, one of his most virulent critics who first used — and in an approving sense — the term "police action" to characterize what would become the fifth most costly war in U.S. history.

Truman went directly from his press conference to a 5:00 P.M. meeting of the National Security Council, at which, upon the recommendation of his advisers, he decided to authorize U.S. planes and ships to attack military targets north of the 38th parallel, though they were to stay well away from the Soviet and Chinese frontiers.[13] Little did the conferees know that MacArthur had already given only slightly more limited authorization on his own initiative almost twenty-four hours earlier. On the flight to Suwon, General George E. Stratemeyer, commander of the Far Eastern Air Force, had explained to his superior the need to destroy North Korean airfields. MacArthur then reasoned, with egregiously slippery logic, that if he allowed North Korea to remain a "sanctuary" for the enemy's air force, he would not be giving South Korea a sufficient measure of the "assistance" for which the second UN resolution called. Capping his willful argument, he maintained that he was within his rights as a field commander to take action that the situation at hand demanded. Accordingly, he gave Stratemeyer permission to radio FEAF headquarters at once from the plane. The message was dispatched: "Take out North Korean airfields immediately. No publicity. MacArthur approves."[14] This was the first instance in the Korean War of MacArthur's unjustifiably creative interpretation of orders, if not outright insubordination. And it was made all the worse by being quickly followed by orders from Washington that, coincidentally, not only bore out MacArthur's decision but also enlarged upon it, to include *all* North Korean military targets, not just airfields. The general was inadvertently encouraged to think that wherever he led, Washington would follow. Furthermore, the decision to deprive the enemy of "sanctuary" on his home territory set the precedent for the potentially catastrophic strategy that MacArthur would advocate once the Chinese Communists sent troops into Korea.

Truman made a mistake in allowing American planes and ships to operate north of the 38th parallel. In fact, it was that decision, far more than the one to commit American infantry to combat, that set the United States irrevocably on a course to disaster. If the United

States had firmly limited its aims to pushing the North Koreans back above the 38th parallel, all might have ended well and soon, without three awful years of carnage and destruction. But the breaking of the legal and psychological barriers to the extension of warfare to North Korean territory made it almost inevitable that sooner or later U.S./UN/ROK forces would, if they could, invade North Korea with the goal of uniting the entire peninsula under the control of Rhee's government.

The National Security Council meeting on Thursday afternoon moved on to recommend, and Truman to approve, the use of American service troops (mainly signal corps and transport units) throughout South Korea. The ROK army's operations were seriously hampered by poor communications and transport; an American contribution to those services might, it was briefly hoped, raise the army's efficiency to the point at which it could manage without reinforcement by U.S. combat troops in the front lines. It was at least worth a try.

But Truman was inching steadily toward the ultimate commitment of American infantry to fight the North Koreans. Toward the end of the NSC meeting, he accepted the recommendation that a regiment of U.S. combat troops be transferred from Japan to Pusan in order to protect that vital port, through which South Korea would have to receive all seaborne shipments of supplies now that Inchon was in enemy hands — and through which the men of KMAG would have to be evacuated in the event of a complete ROK collapse. The American troops were to remain in Pusan, some two hundred miles from the front, but their presence would release the ROK soldiers stationed there to be moved up to the front.[15]

Truman was hesitant to commit any U.S. ground troops at all, for that was a psychological hurdle the jumping of which might bring in the Russians. Early in the week, the State Department had sent the Kremlin a note to ascertain whether it was willing to avow responsibility for the North Korean invasion. If so, then Stalin might send Soviet forces into Korea to help Kim Il-sung to conquer the south; but if the Kremlin replied with a disclaimer, then the Russians would probably remain aloof, at least as long as the existence of Kim's regime was not threatened. At the NSC meeting Dean Acheson informed Truman that a reply had at last been received: the Russians insisted that they had nothing whatsoever to do with events in Korea.[16] Just to be safe, however, the Joint Chiefs of Staff concluded their June 29 instructions to MacArthur with the proviso: "If Soviet forces actively oppose our operations in Korea, your forces should defend themselves, should take no action to aggravate the situation, and you should report the situation to Washington."[17]

Although the Soviet reply seemed to preclude the likelihood of Soviet entry, it still left the possibility that Stalin might send in the Chinese Communists. The previous day the government in Peking had released a statement charging that Truman's decision to use the Seventh Fleet to protect Formosa constituted "armed aggression against the territory of China," and asserting that "the fact that Formosa is part of China will remain unchanged forever." The statement, issued by Premier and Foreign Minister Chou En-lai, went on to accuse the United States of having ordered South Korea to attack the north as a "fabricated pretext" for American "aggression" against Formosa, North Korea, Indochina, and the Philippines.[18] The State Department viewed this extremely bellicose statement as just short of a declaration of war. But it was felt that the Chinese Communists had their hands full with the nearly overwhelming task of consolidating their rule over a nation devastated by two decades of fighting and still beset by hordes of anti-Communist "bandits."

It wasn't until 1:30 A.M. on Friday, June 30, that the Pentagon received MacArthur's firsthand report on the situation in Korea, along with his recommendations based on what he had observed. The tone of the message was businesslike and impersonal, but forceful; and its late-night timing was dramatic, perhaps intentionally so, since MacArthur had waited more than twelve hours after his return to Tokyo to send it off.

After a brief account of the ROK army's highly vulnerable condition, MacArthur went on to explain that if the Han River line didn't hold and if Suwon were to fall to the enemy, American planes would be left without a base in central Korea. The South Korean army, he concluded,

is entirely incapable of counter-action and there is grave danger of
a further breakthrough. If the enemy advance continues much

further it will seriously threaten [i.e., quite possibly bring about] the fall of the Republic.

The only assurance for the holding of the present line, and the ability to regain later the lost ground, is through the introduction of US ground combat forces into the Korean battle area. . . .

If authorized, it is my intention to immediately move a US regimental combat team to the reinforcement of the vital [Han-Suwon] area and to provide for a possible build-up to a two division strength from the troops in Japan for an early counter-offensive.[19]

Because MacArthur was an army officer, the JCS had given General J. Lawton Collins, the army chief of staff, primary responsibility to act as liaison between Tokyo and Washington. Accordingly, it was General Collins who was first notified when MacArthur's cable was received at the Pentagon. He was so disturbed by its contents that he felt he could not pass it along up the chain of command unless he had first consulted with MacArthur to determine whether the Far Eastern commander might not be overreacting in haste or emotion, to confirm that his soundest military judgment had convinced him that absolutely no other course of action would avail, and to make certain that he recognized the gravity of his recommendations. Collins immediately sent word to Tokyo that he wanted a Teletype conference — a "telecon," in military jargon — with MacArthur, to begin at 3:00 A.M. Washington time.

It was after 3:30 by the time the circuit was finally set up and all the participants assembled at both ends. The State Department was represented in the Pentagon's underground War Room by Dean Rusk, who, of all Truman's foreign-policy advisers, was the one most disposed to send U.S. ground troops into Korea.[20]

A telecon was a strange sort of meeting — the closest to a conference call that technology and the need for encryption would then allow. A message typed on the Teletype at either end was immediately projected onto screens in the darkened rooms at both ends. And so on that crucial early morning, the strongly worded messages flashed back and forth amid a voiceless clatter, often with a lengthy and tense wait while the unseen interlocutors, halfway around the world from each other, conferred with colleagues and composed responses.

After brief preliminaries, MacArthur got right to the point. What had earlier been phrased as a recommendation now became a demand.

The situation in Korea was critical, he contended, and there was no time to waste. He *must* receive authorization *immediately* to dispatch one regiment to the front and to begin moving two divisions to Korea for a prompt counteroffensive. Collins then reminded him that only the president could give such authorization and argued that Truman would certainly not make such a momentous decision until he had had an opportunity to discuss it with his advisers. That meant that MacArthur would have to wait at least another six hours for an answer.

At this point MacArthur's reason gave way to pride. The Far Eastern commander would surely have liked to be a military autocrat and probably felt that he deserved to be one; like Frederick the Great, he would have exercised supreme political authority and have been supreme commander in chief, leading his troops and making all decisions in the field. It was bad enough that he had to call upon Washington to rubber-stamp his demands at all; argument and delay were intolerable. If the great MacArthur, the most senior of all American generals, declared that immediate action was imperative in order to save the Korean republic, and with it American prestige and collective security against the worldwide Communist menace, how could the president possibly object to such a minor inconvenience as being awakened in the middle of the night? And how could Truman, a civilian, possibly question the general's judgment or fail to approve his demands?

By 4:30 MacArthur had succeeded in bullying Collins into agreeing to take steps to reach the president at once. The younger man, intimidated by his formidable elder, promised that he would try to have an answer within half an hour.

At the JCS meeting only a little more than twelve hours earlier, the majority had still been strongly opposed to the commitment of U.S. ground troops to combat, but Collins had maintained since Sunday that if the ROK army collapsed, American air and naval forces would not be able to turn the tide of battle without the help of U.S. infantry. He now, with Rusk's encouragement, took it upon himself to bypass the other members of the JCS and to ask army secretary Frank Pace, who had the authority to call the president directly, to present the question to Truman without further consultation. As JCS chairman Omar Bradley knew very well, Collins was a man of action who could be impetuous.

Pace reached Truman at 4:57 A.M. The president, who had never shaken the habit formed during his farm boyhood of rising between 4:00 and 5:00 A.M., had already been up for some time; he had shaved and was sitting in his bedroom, reading the early editions of the morning papers. (In her biography of her father, Margaret Truman remarked that even after he left office, reading the *New York Times* was a daily ritual "he did not propose to give up."[21]) That morning's *Times* carried the AP report of MacArthur's trip to Korea, as well as a story claiming that the South Koreans had finally stabilized the battle line and were "standing fast." Another story, however, held that the North Koreans had managed to get some of their tanks across the Han and that they were headed for Suwon. The paper's military commentator, Hanson Baldwin, not yet aware of the decisions made at Thursday's NSC meeting, wrote about the dangers of extending air operations to above the 38th parallel and of sending in American combat troops but conceded that in Washington there was "a growing conviction . . . that more quick and decisive action in the form of one or both courses may be necessary in the next few days if a wearing campaign of attrition is to be avoided."

Pace began by reading MacArthur's cable to Truman and then informed him that General Collins endorsed the recommendations in it. After only a few moments of reflection, Truman concurred. MacArthur was to be given immediate authority to send one regiment into combat. Consideration of the request to send in two divisions for a counteroffensive would have to wait until the president met with his advisers later that morning. But the crucial decision — whether to order any American infantry at all to fight the North Koreans — was made by Truman, alone and on the spot. The later decision would be one of numbers, not one of principle. Even though the official terminology would not acknowledge the fact, the Korean conflict had now irrevocably become the Korean War.

CHAPTER 16

The U.S. Army Begins to Fight

AT 9:30 ON THE MORNING of Friday, June 30, President Truman met once again with his principal advisers: Secretary of State Dean Acheson, Secretary of Defense Louis Johnson, the armed service secretaries, and the Joint Chiefs of Staff. The group now also included for the first time the president's newly appointed national security adviser for foreign affairs, Averell Harriman, just arrived from Paris, where he had been administering the Marshall Plan. Acquiescing to the inevitable, the men took only a few minutes to reach a consensus that MacArthur should be given the immediate permission he had demanded to begin transferring two American infantry divisions from Japan to the front lines in Korea.[1]

The orders that the JCS cabled to MacArthur a few hours later were, however, not so specific. Throughout the early months of the war, official orders sent to Tokyo were, in effect, doubly encoded. On the one hand there was the routine encryption to evade enemy intelligence; but there was also a subtle code in operation, cold and calculating, that dictated the wording of the instructions given to MacArthur. Its purpose was, quite simply, to shift onto MacArthur as much responsibility as possible for actions taken. Washington was, as the saying goes, covering its ass. Thus the orders dispatched to MacArthur on June 30 read, "Restrictions on use of Army Forces imposed by JCS 84681 are hereby removed and authority granted to utilize Army Forces available to you as proposed your C56942 subject only to requirements for safety of Japan in the present situation which is a matter for your judgment."[2] Truman recorded in his memoirs that MacArthur had been given "full authority to use the ground forces under his command,"[3] and from that statement much has been made of the administration's supposed willingness to grant MacArthur more than he had asked for. But that was really not the case at all. It then seemed inconceivable that MacArthur would endanger the security of Japan by transferring more than two divisions to Korea. The point was that he had permission to send as many men as he felt were necessary; the responsibility for deciding how many to send was his — as would be the blame if their assignment to Korea led, one way or another, to disaster.

The evasive ambiguity of the orders relayed to MacArthur was not only cowardly and irresponsible but also very dangerous, for it encouraged the general's proclivity for autocracy. He was not the least bit reluctant to accept the responsibility implicit in his orders from Washington. On the contrary, he wanted more and became convinced that it was his for the taking. MacArthur never wavered in his conviction that the greater the responsibility, and thus the authority, vested in him, the more complete would be the defeat of Communism in Asia, and the greater the glory with which he would consequently be crowned.

Once Truman had made his solitary, early morning decision to send a regiment of American infantry into combat — a decision that the Joint Chiefs had had no choice but to accept, since General J. Lawton Collins did not inform them until he had already passed the president's authorization on to MacArthur — the central problem took on a new complexion. No one questioned the prowess of the American navy and air force, but that of the radically depleted, undertrained, out-of-shape, and skimpily equipped U.S. Army was quite another matter. And yet it was upon that army that the hopes of NATO were largely based. In the event of a Soviet invasion of Western Europe, which is to say, in the event of World War III, the U.S. Navy would play a relatively small role in the West. The U.S. Air Force would pour an apocalyptic cataract of atomic bombs upon the Soviet Union. But the NATO allies were counting on the U.S. Army for help in turning back the tidal wave of the Red Army without obliterating the civilization whose rescue was at stake. If American ground troops proved unable to wallop the forces of little North Korea, the NATO states would surely have to reconsider the advisability of taking any stand that would antagonize the Soviet Union; it would then be wiser for them to appease the Soviets than to risk an invasion that they could not possibly resist. In other words, once Truman had committed American infantry to Korea, the United States was defending not only South Korea but also its own military credibility as the leader of the international system of collective security.

That being the case, it seemed prudent to err on the side of sending too many, rather than too few, American troops to Korea — though, of course, the larger the number of troops defeated by the Communists, in the always-to-be-considered worst-case scenario, the greater would be America's embarrassment. Once committed, however, with its prestige and credibility on the line, the United States simply could not afford the humiliation of withdrawal any more than it could afford defeat. Thus, at the slightest suggestion of impending disaster, thousands upon thousands of reinforcements would be rushed to the peninsula to guarantee the only denouement that could possibly be accepted: an ultimate American victory. More than ever, Truman felt constrained to do whatever the military situation seemed to demand in order to save both the Republic of Korea and the reputation of the United States. Unfortunately, a "limited" war (in this case, a war whose military objective was neither the destruction of the enemy's regime nor the occupation of its territory) fought with unlimited means is unlikely to remain limited for long.

The immediate dilemma was that in order to dispatch ever more troops to Korea, the U.S. Army had to rob Peter to pay Paul, and Peter was quite poor to begin with. In June 1950 the U.S. Army had a grand total of about 591,000 men on active duty. Of these, some 360,000 were stationed in America, a top-heavy percentage of them engaged in typing up and pushing around the mountain of paperwork upon which the self-esteem of the military bureaucracy so largely depended in a world more or less at peace. Many of the rest were teenagers who had enlisted after 1945 in the hope that the army would provide them with vocational training, and in the certainty that the UN and the American atomic monopoly meant they would never have to fight.

The army's remaining 231,000 men were stationed overseas, almost half of them in the Far East. In Japan alone were four out of the army's worldwide total of ten combat divisions. These four — the 7th, 24th, and 25th Infantry divisions and the 1st Cavalry, which, despite its vestigial name, was also an infantry division — constituted the Eighth U.S. Army, charged with the occupation and defense of Japan. It was from these four understrength divisions (like most other divisions at the time, they had only about 70 percent of their full wartime allotment of men) that MacArthur now had permission to choose two to send to Korea. The nagging question was, however, whether he could safely do so. With the abrupt removal of half the occupation force, might the Japanese Communist party possibly stage a comeback? Might the recently "rehabilitated" Japanese militarists stage a coup? Or might the Russians take advantage of the depletion of the defensive garrison to seize Hokkaido? Had the Kremlin, preparing to launch World War III, perhaps even ordered the North Koreans to invade the south precisely to lure American troops out of Japan? And what would happen to poorly defended Japan if the commitment of U.S. troops to Korea should spark a world war? These were very worrisome questions, but the combination of urgency and proximity dictated the choice of troops from Japan.

The logic of MacArthur's strategy during the first two and a half months of the American army's involvement in Korea, from July 1 to September 15, was very simple. Its underlying premise was that the enemy must, at all costs, be prevented from capturing Pusan, the greatest port in Korea, with a shipping capacity ten times that of Inchon. Through Pusan's harbor and airfield tens of thousands of men and millions of crates of equipment and supplies would arrive from Japan, from the United States, from Hong Kong and Australia, and from all over the world. Pusan and Japan were to be the two great staging areas and bases of operations from which, when enough strength had been built up, an irresistible, double-pronged counterattack would be launched.

The North Koreans understood the value of Pusan very well, and the primary goal of their strategy became the swiftest possible capture of the city — both to stop the flow of troops and matériel into the port and to cut off U.S. forces already in Korea from their supply base and only possible exit. In pursuit of their goal, the North Koreans planned to push down the corridor through which ran the main Seoul-to-Pusan road and railway line — passing through the key towns of Suwon, Osan, Chonan, Taejon, and Taegu — with supplementary drives along the secondary road and rail lines to the east and west, enabling them to swoop down on Pusan from all sides and to encircle their enemy.

The cumbersome logistics of military transport meant that MacArthur would be able to rush at once to Korea a contingent far too small to *stop* the North Korean onslaught; these first troops were to do their utmost to *delay* the enemy's main advance along the Seoul-Pusan road. The more they could slow down the North Koreans, the more time would be available in which to move troops and supplies into Pusan. The immediate tactic was to force the Communists to sacrifice as much time, as many men, and as much ammunition and fuel as possible. American planes would attack the lines of communication from the north to prevent reinforcements and supplies from reaching the front; since the U.S. Air Force had complete control of the air, the North Koreans would not be able to reciprocate. The enemy would thus inevitably be weakened by attrition while the Americans grew stronger. The farther south the front moved, the longer and more tenuous and vulnerable the enemy's supply lines would become — and the shorter and more secure the Americans'.

The two principal and generally interdependent methods of subduing an enemy army are by direct assault and by strangulation from behind (that is, by cutting the army off from its sources of supply). Like a car forced to keep on running without having its tank refilled, the army will eventually run out of gas and stop. The gas-guzzling American armed forces, with their emphasis on technology over manpower, had had great success with the strangulation method against equally mechanized opponents in North Africa and in the Pacific theater during World War II. But in both cases success was due largely to the enemy's dependence on maritime shipping, which is both concentrated and highly vulnerable. The sinking of a single ship means a considerable loss for the enemy — both because a ship carries so many troops and/or supplies and because ships are costly and time-consuming to replace — and a ship has nowhere to hide on the open sea. Furthermore, attacks on military shipping do not kill women and children, as even "surgical strike" bombing raids on urban military targets inevitably do. The destruction of shipping proved to be extremely effective in World War II, but American studies carried out after the end of the war argued very persuasively that strategic bombing of enemy cities, factories, and overland communications networks was not only ineffective but actually counterproductive, for — as in England during the blitz or in Germany late in the war — it galvanized the nation, encouraged defiant and resourceful improvisation, and strengthened the will to resist.

Nevertheless, because of the atomic bomb and parsimony, strategic bombing remained dominant in postwar American military planning, and it was expected to perform miracles in Korea, as it would again, even more in vain, be expected to do in Vietnam. Despite all the evidence, the American generals obstinately refused to acknowledge that bombing could do relatively little to impede overland transport and that the less industrial and mechanized an enemy was, the smaller the impact that strategic bombing would have on his war effort. In a country like Korea, where men on foot, equipped with A-frames, could carry extremely heavy loads on their backs with remarkable speed and endurance over long distances, bombing could do little. Such carriers could be widely dispersed, so that even saturation bombing would hit few of them. And they could hide during the day, traveling only at night and in bad weather, when planes couldn't spot them. In addition, the North Korean troops could manage very well, when they had to, on a flow of supplies so meager that a similar dearth would have stopped the Americans in their tracks.

Korea provided a demonstration of the futility of strategic bombing so dramatic that the subsequent fiasco in Vietnam can be attributed only to blind willfulness.[4] Operating from Pusan, from Japan, and from aircraft carriers offshore, the Far Eastern Air Force's hundreds of bombers and fighters had complete mastery of the air over North and South Korea early in the war. The bombers concentrated on hitting roads, bridges, railways, supply movements, trucks, tanks, artillery, airfields, munitions and steel factories, and oil refineries. But the vast and indefatigable labor battalions that the North Koreans recruited or forced into service repaired transportation arteries so quickly that American pilots began to complain that the roads and bridges must be made of rubber, since they seemed to bounce right back into shape after a hit. The Soviet Union and China sent munitions and fuel to make up for what was lost. And the tough North Korean soldiers foraged and robbed along the route of their advance, tightened their belts when they had to, and compensated for their dwindling technology with sheer manpower and ferocity.

Meanwhile, American and British naval forces gained control of the coastline of the entire Korean peninsula. Their blockade effectively prevented all foreign ships from entering ports in North Korean hands and stopped all coastwise movement of supplies to the Communist army in the south.

The combination of U.S./UN air and naval power certainly hurt the North Korean army, but not nearly to the extent that MacArthur and his subordinates had hoped and expected it would. If the enemy advance was going to be stopped well short of Pusan, American ground troops were going to have to do the job.

Some historians have judged the early performance of American troops in Korea very harshly. And yet the fact is that they were successful in carrying out their assignment. The North Koreans failed in their determined attempt to take Pusan. If there is blame, it must be ascribed to the complacency and thrift of the American people, who demanded minimal expenditures on military preparedness. That demand hobbled Truman, his advisers, Congress, and the Pentagon. And it meant that when the army was finally called upon to fight, its casualty rate was far higher than it would have been for an adequately trained and equipped force. American troops accomplished their mission during those first grueling months in Korea, but at terrible, and inexcusable, cost.

General MacArthur himself conceded that a delaying action is "the most difficult of military operations."[5] The men who were charged with this formidable task had been wrenched overnight — without warning, without physical or psychological preparation, and without anything like adequate combat training — from their very comfortable life in Japan, where, wrote Major General William F. Dean of the 24th Division, they had become flabby and accustomed to "Japanese girlfriends, plenty of beer, and servants to shine their boots."[6] Many of them had never heard the sound of artillery fire, and many didn't even know how to clean their rifles.

These inexperienced and out-of-shape men were suddenly thrown into savage fighting and hellish conditions that would have taxed to the utmost the fittest and most seasoned soldiers. Exhaustion was the first enemy of these poorly conditioned men; because of the urgency to move troops into position and the preciousness of every hour of delay that could be imposed on the North Koreans, there was very little time for sleep. Men often had to go for four or five days without more than two or three consecutive hours of sleep, grabbing a few minutes here and there whenever they could. But a much worse enemy was the heat, which incapacitated more soldiers than did North Korean fire. The temperature regularly went over 100 degrees Fahrenheit on sunny days, and there was very little shade in the harsh terrain covered mostly with low scrub, which also provided little cover from enemy sights. The heat compounded exhaustion and brought on excruciating ordeals of thirst. Water in canteens was quickly used up; men would then throw themselves into the first flooded rice paddy they came to and guzzle all they could hold. Since human excrement was used to fertilize the paddies, the result was dehydrating dysentery that felt like fire in the guts.

The weather tended to extremes. When the sun wasn't broiling the men alive, they were drenched by downpours that transformed the dusty countryside into oceans of mud. Slogging through the morasses, troops had to keep their ammunition dry and their weapons clean. The rain rusted guns and rotted supplies. It also reduced visibility both on the ground and from the air; the North Koreans took good advantage of rain and fog for mounting surprise attacks, and in bad weather U.S. planes couldn't provide close tactical support for ground troops.

In the beginning, American morale was generally bad. Many men could hardly believe that they were being required to fight. They were full of resentment and anger, of shock and fear. *New York Herald Tribune* correspondent Marguerite Higgins wrote of the first weeks of July, "I saw war turn many of our young soldiers into savagely bitter men. I saw young Americans turn and bolt in battle, or throw down their arms cursing their government for what they thought was embroilment in a hopeless cause."[7]

Many factors served to worsen morale even further. The first arrivals were confronted with two equally demoralizing spectacles: truckloads of ROK soldiers fleeing southward and trainloads of wounded ROKs coming from the front. Conditioned to believe that the North Koreans would turn tail as soon as they saw their first American uniform, the young U.S. recruits went to the opposite extreme when they discovered that they would really have to do battle, and fight to the limit, against a tough enemy who outnumbered them. Realizing that their contempt for the fighting abilities of the "gooks" was ill founded, many Americans concluded that they didn't stand a

Two of the principal players in the drama of the Korean War:
General Douglas A. MacArthur greets President Harry S. Truman on Wake Island,
October 15, 1950. (*National Archives*)

North Korean leader Kim Il-sung (*facing honor guard*) arriving at Moscow's Yaroslav railway station, March 1949. On his left are Anastas I. Mikoyan, the Soviet minister of foreign trade, and Andrei A. Gromyko, deputy foreign minister. (*AP/Wide World Photos*)

At a Seoul garden party celebrating the establishment of the Republic of Korea, 1948 (*from left*): John J. Muccio, U.S. diplomatic representative (later ambassador) to the ROK; President Syngman Rhee; and Lieutenant General John Reed Hodge, who had been head of the American Military Government of southern Korea. (*National Archives*)

The U.S. secretary of defense and the Joint Chiefs of Staff of the American armed forces in 1950. *Seated, from left:* Secretary of Defense Louis A. Johnson and General Omar N. Bradley, chairman of the JCS; *standing, from left:* General Hoyt S. Vandenberg, air force chief of staff; General J. Lawton Collins, army chief of staff; and Admiral Forrest P. Sherman, chief of naval operations. (*AP/Wide World Photos*)

Secretary of State Dean Acheson (*seated, right*) testifying on June 1, 1951, during the Senate hearings that followed Truman's dismissal of General MacArthur from all of his commands. The men facing Acheson across the table are (*left*) Senator William F. Knowland (Republican, California) and Senator Harry P. Cain (Republican, Washington). (*AP/Wide World Photos*)

John Foster Dulles (*right*), the Republican lawyer and diplomat who was then helping the State Department to lay the groundwork for a peace treaty between Japan and the Allied nations, with Dean Rusk, assistant secretary of state for Far Eastern Affairs, at the Washington airport, June 29, 1950. Dulles was returning from a trip to Japan and South Korea. (*AP/Wide World Photos*)

Warren R. Austin, U.S. delegate to the UN Security Council, displaying on September 18, 1950, a machine gun captured from North Korean troops. The gun bore markings that identified it as having been manufactured in the Soviet Union earlier that year. (*AP/Wide World Photos*)

South Korean soldiers on the march, July 5, 1950. They are wearing flimsy, canvas-topped shoes and carrying World War II–vintage Japanese rifles. (*National Archives*)

Lieutenant General Walton H. Walker (*left*), commander of the Eighth U.S. Army in Korea, confers with Major General William F. Dean, commander of the 24th U.S. Infantry Division, July 7, 1950. (*National Archives*)

U.S. Marines, a South Korean soldier, and a captured North Korean jeep, August 18, 1950. (*National Archives*)

U.S. Marines move out over mountainous terrain
along the Pusan Perimeter, summer 1950. (*National Archives*)

Bloody Ridge on September 6, 1951, after it was captured by the men
of the 9th Regiment, 2nd U.S. Infantry Division. (*National Archives*)

Spring rains slow the advance of the 1st U.S. Marine Division, March 1951.
(*National Archives*)

American tanks and infantry pass devastated buildings
in Hongchon, South Korea, March 1951. (*National Archives*)

Korean refugees, January 4, 1951. (*National Archives*)

Refugees fleeing Seoul, loading a ferry to cross the icy Han River, December 28, 1950. (*National Archives*)

Relatives identifying the bodies of some three hundred political prisoners
whom the North Koreans had executed before evacuating Hamhung, October 19, 1950.
(*National Archives*)

Korean refugees moving south as American tanks move north, April 28, 1951.
(*National Archives*)

General MacArthur watches the Inchon landings from the bridge of the USS *Mount McKinley*. Behind him are (*from left*): Vice-Admiral Arthur D. Struble, commander of the Seventh U.S. Fleet; Brigadier General Edwin K. Wright, MacArthur's assistant chief of staff; and Major General Edward M. Almond, commander of X Corps. (*National Archives*)

U.S. Marines scaling the seawall at Inchon, September 15, 1950. (*National Archives*)

Landing craft grounded on the Inchon mudflats. (*National Archives*)

U.S. Marines push through the streets of Seoul, September 1950. (*National Archives*)

chance against the North Koreans. Not only were they outnumbered — often ten to one and even fifty to one in some engagements — but they didn't even have available to them the technology that would have compensated somewhat for their shortage of manpower. During the first two weeks of combat, the Americans had no bazookas capable of penetrating the armor of the North Korean tanks, and they had no tanks of their own. They did have some artillery that could knock out the T-34s, but the special armor-piercing shells that fit them were in extremely short supply. The Americans were, of course, terribly dependent upon their supply lines, and it took a few weeks to get them well established. The men carried with them as much ammunition as they could, but when they ran out they had no choice but to retreat. Too, the haste with which men and matériel were sent to Korea inevitably led to a certain amount of disorder. Some ammunition turned out not to match the available weapons, and some was too old to be effective. Shortages were all that the army had in abundance. Early on, hunger and ill-fitting boots were chronic at the front. Old weapons malfunctioned, and there were never enough spare parts for guns or jeeps. Inadequate maps made for much confusion, and dead radio batteries meant the inability to direct artillery fire, to coordinate with supporting aircraft, to receive orders from headquarters, and to call for help. Good coordination of infantry, artillery, and air support can be developed only by extensive training and practice maneuvers; poor communications greatly exacerbated the lack. Misdirected U.S. artillery fire and aerial strafing cost an unconscionable number of American lives in the early days of the war. No wonder one exasperated lieutenant screamed at Marguerite Higgins, "Are you correspondents telling the people back home the truth? Are you telling them that out of one platoon of twenty men, we have three left? Are you telling them that we have nothing to fight with, and that it is an utterly useless war?"[8]

Discipline among the green American troops was poor, and insubordination was rampant. With so many factors depriving them of any hope of emerging from combat with victory, or even of emerging at all, many men balked at fighting or simply ran away. It wasn't enough for officers to issue orders from behind the lines; in many cases, unless they led the attack themselves, setting an example and giving direction, their men refused to attack. This led to the loss of a disproportionate number of officers early in the war, and, of course, the resulting shortage of experienced leaders only made units less able to stand up to the enemy effectively.

Higgins quoted one regimental commander who said that he had to be right up front with his men, taking personal charge of individual companies, because "before when I said, 'Withdraw,' these boys would just take off like a big bird. And panic — taking off every which way, dropping your weapons and such — gets too many people killed."[9] The syndrome he was describing was dubbed bug-out fever. The term has overtones of madness, and the men who succumbed did indeed seem to be temporarily insane. Their panic was wild, blind, and absolute. In their frenzy to escape, they flung aside any and all equipment that might slow them down. Those who crashed through the sometimes waist-deep water of flooded rice paddies even tore off the boots and shirts whose sodden weight impeded their flight. When units disintegrated, the wounded — in flagrant and shameful violation of a basic tenet of American army policy — sometimes had to be left where they had fallen, to be captured or murdered by the enemy.

The fears that engendered bug-out fever were far from irrational. The North Koreans were formidable, ruthless, and frightening. They maneuvered quickly and cleverly, responding flexibly to situations, in contrast to the road-bound, equipment-heavy, and tactically limited Americans. Using their greatly superior numbers, the North Koreans would engage a unit head-on and then send forces to outflank and surround it. And, not feeling themselves bound by the etiquette of Western warfare, they did not hesitate to shoot their prisoners.

Furthermore, despite the charges of international aggression leveled against them, the North Koreans had the advantage of being Koreans fighting in Korea. They spoke the language, were familiar with traditional customs, and, when not in uniform, were indistinguishable from the southerners, who happened, rather arbitrarily, to be their political adversaries. Consequently, North Korean soldiers had only to put the universally worn white robe over their uniforms and mingle with a column of refugees in order to infiltrate behind American lines. The enemy also had thousands of allies among South Korean civilians, many of whom posed as refugees and carried supplies for the Communists; the bundles that ostensibly contained the few personal possessions they had managed to salvage were actually full of food and munitions.

The dangers — both tactical and moral — implicit in such confusion and its attendant jumpiness were trenchantly summed up by the senior Time Inc. correspondent in the Far East, John Osborne. Henry Luce deemed his article so important that it appeared in the August 21 issues of both *Time* and *Life*. By the time Osborne visited Korea, the problem of bug-out fever was receding. "The American effort and the American soldier in Korea are magnificent," he exulted. "In a land and among a people that most of them dislike, in a war that all too few of them understand and none of them want, they became strong men and good soldiers — fast. . . . I have seen boys who by rights should have been freshmen in college transformed by a week of battle into men wise in the ways of this especially terrible war." Calling the conflict in Korea "an ugly war, perhaps the ugliest that Americans have ever had to fight," Osborne went on to say:

> No American, after seeing the actualities of war in Korea, could ever call it a "police action" or could dismiss it as merely the first of many "dirty little wars" that we must learn to take in our stride. Much of this war is alien to the American tradition and shocking to the American mind. For our men in Korea are waging this war as they are forced to wage it *and as they will be forced to wage any war against the Communists anywhere in Asia.*

Having made what seems an almost clairvoyant prediction of the dilemma that has dogged American policy ever since — in Korea, in Vietnam, in the Asian-style wars in Central America, and elsewhere — Osborne elaborated:

> Above all, our leaders must grasp one simple fact: war against the Communists of Asia cannot be won — not really won — by military means alone. To attempt to win it so, as we are now doing in Korea, is not only to court final failure but also to force upon our men in the field acts and attitudes of the utmost savagery. This means not the usual inevitable savagery of combat in the field but savagery in detail — the blotting out of villages where the enemy *may* be hiding; the shooting and shelling of refugees who *may* include North Koreans in the anonymous white clothing of the Korean countryside, or who *may* be screening an enemy march upon our positions.

In many terrible ways, Korea was a dress rehearsal for Vietnam. It should, on the contrary, have provided a warning clear and potent enough to avert the later exercise in savagery and futility.

At the very beginning of the great race for Pusan and for time, the North Koreans made a mistake that was to prove fatal in the long run. Having achieved their first major goal, of capturing Seoul, they eased off somewhat for a week while they got themselves and their equipment across the Han River. Threatened by an end run and badly shaken by their defeat so far, the South Koreans abandoned the Han line and retreated in disarray, though some units comported themselves honorably and inflicted surprisingly heavy casualties upon their overconfident foe. The NKPA took Suwon with little trouble on July 2 and then wasted a few precious days regrouping and waiting for supply lines to get organized. By slowing down for the week of June 28–July 4, instead of pressing relentlessly onward, the North Koreans gave the Americans just enough time to establish a toehold. From then on the Communist margin of advantage would steadily decrease, though the daunted Americans were slow to recognize the change and continued to think of themselves as outnumbered and outgunned for weeks after the balance had swung in their favor.

Almost as soon as the North Koreans resumed their advance south of Suwon, in the early hours of July 5, they ran into their first fire from U.S. ground troops — a unit known as Task Force Smith, which was part of a battalion from one of the 24th Infantry Division's regiments. Although the five-hundred-man force with a small battery of artillery managed to destroy a few T-34 tanks and to delay two enemy infantry regiments for a couple of hours, that accomplishment — sadly negligible in the strategist's cold eye — hardly warranted the 30 percent casualties (dead, wounded, missing, or captured) that were sustained. In fact, the damage done to American morale by news of the mauling was far worse than any damage done to the enemy. That the unit had actually performed remarkably well under the appalling circumstances gave small comfort to anyone. Eager to avoid opportunities to perform equally well under such conditions, the men of the 24th Division's other units, as they moved into position around the Kum River, did more retreating than delaying for the next few days, though they made up for it in the following weeks, during which they too suffered nearly 30 percent casualties.

On July 3, UN Secretary-General Trygve Lie proposed that an international committee be formed to direct the operations of the UN military forces in Korea. This was, however, unacceptable to the United States, which, since it was obviously going to contribute most of the troops and to bear most of the expense for supplies and equipment, felt entitled to unilateral control over their disposition. Unwilling to suffer the embarrassment of having to insist publicly in its own behalf, the United States prevailed upon Britain and France to sponsor a Security Council resolution calling for a "unified command under the United States." Far from establishing any sort of UN control or safeguards over American conduct of the war, the resolution, which was adopted by a vote of 7–0 with three abstentions on July 7, did no more than timidly "request" the United States "to provide the Security Council with reports as appropriate on the course of action taken under the unified command." The resolution called upon America to designate a commander for the UN forces in Korea and authorized those forces to fly the blue and white UN flag. The next day President Truman appointed MacArthur Commander in Chief, UN Command (CINCUNC). His appointment was in no way subject to UN approval.

Once MacArthur had begun to get reports of the disappointing results of the first engagements between American and North Korean troops, his estimates of the manpower that would be required for victory escalated rapidly. On July 7 he asked the Pentagon to send him without delay thirty thousand troops that he could use to bring the four divisions of the Eighth Army up to full combat strength. He went on to say that he would need an additional four to four and a half full-strength infantry divisions, an airborne regiment, and an armored group as soon as possible. Two days later he doubled his demands, saying he would need at least four divisions just to hold the area around Pusan and another four, plus a Marine division, for a counteroffensive strike behind enemy lines. To justify his demands — and to excuse the poor showing of U.S. troops so far — he argued that the impressive performance of the North Korean army clearly indicated that it was receiving help directly from the Soviets and the Chinese Communists.[10]

On July 10, the day after MacArthur's staggering demands were received in Washington, Generals Collins and Hoyt Vandenberg rushed off to Tokyo. In order to come anywhere near to satisfying the Far Eastern commander while maintaining national security and meeting commitments elsewhere in the world, Washington would have to draw heavily upon reserve units and the National Guard, and Congress would have to authorize the expenditure of a huge sum to equip and maintain these additional troops. The ceilings on military spending and manpower that Truman and his secretary of defense had imposed so firmly and defended so stalwartly would have to be lifted. All this meant, in effect, a leap toward the implementation of NSC-68, with its exorbitant price tag, which would necessitate a tax increase — and that only a few months before midterm elections. Recommendations with such momentous ramifications called for a face-to-face confrontation with MacArthur.

The impressive five-star general's arguments won over the two four-star emissaries. Upon their return to Washington, Collins and Vandenberg advised Truman to accept the inevitable. A few days later, on July 19, in what the *New York Times* afterward described as a mood of "anger and indignation" against Communist aggression,[11] the president made a national radio and television broadcast to announce that mobilization of National Guard and reserve units would begin immediately and that the size of all the armed forces was to be radically increased, the army alone by nearly 250,000 men.[12] To pay for this expansion, he called upon Congress to appropriate an additional $11 billion for the current military budget.[13] Congress gave its assent not only to that request but also eventually to two subsequent increases that would bring defense spending for fiscal year 1950–51 to $48.2 billion, only $1.8 billion short of NSC-68's revolutionary estimate. In fiscal year 1951–52 military expenditures exceeded $60 billion. It was no time for thrift. Communism had to be defeated and American prestige and security saved. The arms race was on.

Within a year the army tripled in size, while the navy and air force nearly doubled. By December 1951 the air force was up to ninety groups, twenty more than had been recommended in the controversial Finletter report. Production of planes, tanks, jeeps, ordnance, and the paraphernalia of a modern army — including sophisticated communications and electronic devices — boomed. The economy boomed along with it. By the end of August 1950 employment hit 62 million, 2 million more than the limit predicted by the most sanguine economists at the end of World War II. The value of the dollar, however, was falling fast; at the end of July 1950 a dollar bought only 59.3 percent of what it had bought in 1939. But inflation didn't prevent a nationwide buying spree. Remembering World War II shortages of all sorts of items ordinarily taken for granted, people began to hoard anything and everything made of metal and rubber. Matters went so far that in September Congress passed a bill that prohibited hoarding and gave the president authority to impose wage and price controls, to institute rationing, and to allocate vital materials to war-related industries.

By the end of July, three of the Eighth Army's four divisions had been transferred from Japan to Korea, and the fourth had been seriously depleted to reinforce the others. The soft army of occupation found itself tempered by fire. This development suited its commander, Lieutenant General Walton H. Walker, whom MacArthur appointed commander of all UN ground forces in Korea. (All non-U.S. troops except those of South Korea were incorporated into EUSAK, the Eighth U.S. Army in Korea.) Walker, a tough Texan built like a fire hydrant, was a fighter by nature, as feisty and tenacious as a bulldog. Patton, under whom he served in Europe, gave his supreme accolade to Walker when he referred to him as "my toughest son of a bitch." Nicknamed Johnnie Walker, he had none of the smoothness of his favorite scotch. On the contrary, he was a gruff man who barked orders and was perfectly capable of telling a lax subordinate that if he returned to headquarters before the successful completion of his mission, it had better be in a coffin. He meant it, too, and his officers and men knew that he did.

By mid-July, as the North Koreans steadily continued their advance despite frightful American sacrifices, General Walker had decided to turn an area of approximately four thousand square miles in the extreme southeastern corner of Korea into a fortress — the so-called Pusan Perimeter — to be held at all costs. On the south and the east this preserve abutted the sea and was safe from attack, since UN naval forces completely controlled Korean waters. Along most of the eighty-mile-long western front the snaking Naktong River served as a moat, and along the fifty-mile-long northern front the heights of rugged mountains were occupied and fortified. A quadrilateral network of roads, railroads, and communications connected Pusan with every corner of the defended area and ensured the flexible and expeditious movement of men and supplies to trouble spots anywhere along the front.

At the end of July, General Walker announced in his best style, compounded of intimidation and exhortation, that once the last American and ROK troops had withdrawn into the Pusan Perimeter, there would be "no more retreating, withdrawal, readjustment of the lines, or any other term you choose. There is no line behind us to which we can retreat. . . . There will be no Dunkirk, there will be no Bataan; a retreat to Pusan would be one of the greatest butcheries in history. . . . I want everybody to understand that we are going to hold this line. We are going to win."[14] On August 4 Walker ordered the destruction of the last of the bridges over the Naktong. EUSAK and the South Korean army settled in for a siege.

The main problem was that Walker had far too few troops to enable him to establish an adequately dense continuous defense all along the 130-mile length of the line of contact with the enemy. His strategy, therefore, was to distribute men and artillery as best he could among the many likeliest danger spots and then to hope that he could shift reinforcements quickly enough to meet any North Korean attack. It was a complex and hazardous juggling act — the peril being that if Walker moved too many men to counter what proved to be only a feint, the enemy might exploit the resulting weaknesses elsewhere for his main attack. For six weeks, from August 1 to September 15, emergencies were the norm. Men were constantly being rushed to "put out a fire" at first one place and then another. Although these maneuvers may sound quite simple, the defense of the Pusan Perimeter involved some of the most hellish, exhausting, heroic, and costly fighting of the entire war.

Those six weeks were also a period of maximum risk of world war. Washington feared that with most of the U.S. Army bottled up at the tip of the Korean peninsula, Moscow might consider the mo-

ment opportune for intervention to annihilate the American forces or
at least to drive them completely out of Korea. If it became clear that
the Russians were about to carry out such a plan, the United States
would have no choice but to launch a preventive nuclear strike on
the Soviet Union — in response to which the Kremlin, if it could,
would certainly retaliate in kind. The dangers were great enough for
Time to run in its August 21 issue a two-page spread addressing the
possibility of a Soviet nuclear attack on America. Among the questions
to which the magazine provided coldly objective answers: What are
the likeliest U.S. targets? What will happen if a bomb hits a city?
How will U.S. buildings stand up? ("Not much better than the Japanese ones.") How many casualties? (Within three thousand feet of
the blast, 80 percent would die. In the center of a major city during
business hours, casualties could far exceed those at Hiroshima.) Even
taking into consideration that this was still the era of relatively small
fission bombs, many of the precautions that *Time* advised its readers
to take in the event of an attack now sound fatally inadequate.

The North Koreans attacked the Pusan Perimeter persistently and
ferociously, but by early August they had lost their advantage. Now
they were the ones who were outnumbered, outgunned, outtanked,
and outsupplied. At first, the perimeter was defended by some 92,000
men — 47,000 Americans (three infantry divisions and a Marine brigade) and five divisions of the ROK army totaling 45,000. Having
sustained much heavier casualties than the Americans then realized,
the North Korean army was down to 70,000 men, and, of those,
thousands were untrained South Korean replacements drafted at gunpoint. By the end of August, combined U.S./UN/ROK strength had
risen to nearly 180,000 men — including 92,000 South Koreans, many
of whom, lacking combat training, had been recruited into labor units
for supply, construction, and other essential services. (MacArthur was
making efforts to supplement the training and equipment of the South
Korean army, which Syngman Rhee placed under his command on
July 14. Despite initial reverses, that army had played a considerable
and honorable part in the delaying action and had inflicted many
casualties on the North Koreans.) The 2nd U.S. Infantry Division
had arrived from Tacoma, and regimental combat teams had been
sent from Okinawa, Hawaii, and Puerto Rico. A brigade of 2,000

Englishmen and Scots that arrived from Hong Kong on August 28 was the first contingent from a UN member other than the United States.

By the end of August, U.S. forces had more than five hundred medium and heavy tanks, five times the number that the North Koreans could field. And the United States had an equally overwhelming advantage in artillery firepower. Nevertheless, the U.S./UN/ROK forces were strained to their utmost to prevent a North Korean breakthrough that would open the way to Pusan. Walker felt he needed every man he had and protested vociferously when, at the beginning of September, MacArthur withdrew the Marines in preparation for a great amphibious operation that would completely change the course of the war.

CHAPTER 17

Inchon

MACARTHUR WAS PLANNING an amphibious landing at the port of Inchon, from which his men would dash the few miles inland to Seoul, the hub of the transportation network serving all of southern Korea. With the main valve at Seoul shut off, as it were, supplies reaching the North Korean army, which was almost entirely concentrated against the Pusan Perimeter, would be reduced to a trickle. In an effort to reopen that valve, the Communists would be forced to rush troops northward to Seoul, which they garrisoned very sparsely both because they needed every possible unit for the southeastern front and because they simply didn't believe that the Americans could or would attempt anything so difficult as an invasion at Inchon. As soon as MacArthur had captured Seoul, his forces would begin to sweep toward Pusan; the Eighth Army would simultaneously break out of the Pusan Perimeter and push toward Seoul. The divided and strangled North Korean army would be unable to resist either advance; it would be crushed between the hammer of MacArthur's forces and the anvil of Walker's.

MacArthur argued that if the blow at Inchon was sufficiently massive, it couldn't possibly fail to bring the war to a favorable end within a few weeks at most. Without such a bold move, the war could drag on indefinitely, for the battle of the Pusan Perimeter had reached a stalemate. It was absolutely essential to break that stalemate before the onset of winter, when the arctic winds from Siberia would claim even more casualties than had the heat of summer.

MacArthur's Inchon plan was elementary in concept but audacious in its specifics. Every West Point plebe knew that an attack behind an enemy's back to cut his supply lines, followed by a pincer movement to encircle him, was one of the most dependable of strategies. And an unprecedented series of amphibious landings in both theaters of World War II had given the Americans great expertise in that most difficult of all types of invasion. The trouble was that the conditions prevailing at Inchon broke all the rules for a successful amphibious operation.

Inchon's most striking peculiarity is that its tides are among the most extreme in the world, with a difference of up to thirty-two feet between high and low watermarks within a single span of six hours. At high tide the ships carrying the invasion force would be able to negotiate the port's labyrinthine channels, past islands and break-waters, and maneuver into the inner harbor. At low tide, however, the approaches to the inner harbor would be reduced to vast, oozy mudflats upon which any unsuspecting vessel of even the shallowest draft would find itself mired and stranded like a beached whale until the tide returned.

MacArthur's plan was to have a battalion of Marines storm Wolmi Island (called Wolmi-do in Korean), whose guns protected not only the entrance to the inner harbor but also the sea approaches to the whole city. These Marines would land at the early morning high tide and establish themselves ashore very quickly, for their landing craft would have a maximum of three hours in which to get away before being grounded. Once the tide went out, there would be no possibility of either evacuation or reinforcement until the evening high tide, when a regiment of Marines would land north of Wolmi Island. Their landing craft would go right up to the seawalls that protected the most densely built-up part of the city of Inchon. A division of Marines would, at the same time, land just south of the city and swing around to approach its rear, where they could capture the main highway and railroad leading to Seoul, eighteen miles away. An armada of fighter-bombers would completely fill the airspace east of Inchon and prevent the North Koreans from moving any troops into the port once the invasion had begun. Two or three days later, once the Marines had secured Inchon, an infantry division would be landed, and the com-bined forces would advance upon Seoul.

The Joint Chiefs of Staff did their utmost to dissuade MacArthur from putting his plan into operation. They argued that the tides rendered a landing at Inchon excessively difficult, and they pointed out that a landing would be impracticable unless all the artillery on Wolmi Island was first destroyed. It was, moreover, probable that all the outer channels had been heavily mined. A ship knocked out by a mine or by artillery could block any of the narrow channels and

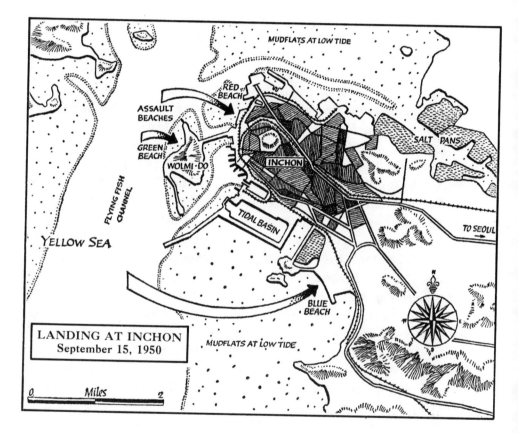

MUDFLATS AT LOW TIDE

RED BEACH

ASSAULT BEACHES

GREEN BEACH

WOLMI-DO

INCHON

SALT PANS

FLYING FISH CHANNEL

YELLOW SEA

TIDAL BASIN

TO SEOUL

BLUE BEACH

LANDING AT INCHON
September 15, 1950

MUDFLATS AT LOW TIDE

0   Miles   2

prevent the escape of other vessels. The Marines had never before made an amphibious entry directly into a city; they would have to clamber up scaling ladders in order to get over the twelve-foot-high seawalls. Furthermore, there were only two days a month on which the schedule and the level of high tides would permit amphibious operations; the North Koreans also had the tide forecasts and would certainly be vigilant on those days. Of the possible days in September and October, the earliest — and the one upon which MacArthur insisted all along — was September 15, right in the middle of the typhoon season, meaning that a storm could scatter the invasion fleet or otherwise disrupt the operation. And there were still more doubts and questions. MacArthur maintained that if the invasion was to be undertaken at all, it would have to be so massive that it couldn't possibly fail. But where could the Pentagon find the requisite number of men in time? MacArthur's demands would leave only one combat-ready infantry division (the 82nd Airborne) in reserve in the United States for any emergency that might arise elsewhere in the world. And what if the invasion failed after all? If such a large American force was defeated in Korea, the United States would be crippled and its allies demoralized, leaving the way clear for Communist expansion on any number of fronts all over the globe.

MacArthur's battle to win the JCS over to his plan was almost as arduous, from his point of view, as the invasion itself was to be. When General Omar Bradley first learned of the idea in mid-July, he thought it was "the riskiest military proposal" he had ever heard of,[1] and he later wrote that "Inchon was probably the worst place ever selected for an amphibious landing."[2] For two months MacArthur and the Pentagon engaged in increasingly testy telecons. Twice Washington sent high-level delegations to Tokyo in the hope of persuading MacArthur to shift the landing to a less treacherous site farther south. (Averell Harriman and General Matthew Ridgway made the trip early in August, and later that month, for the second time in six weeks, General J. Lawton Collins undertook the journey, which took two days each way. He was accompanied by Admiral Forrest Sherman.) Both times the charismatic commander mesmerized his visitors and sent them home full of enthusiasm for his plan. Nevertheless, it wasn't until September 8, only a week before the landing was to take place, that the Joint Chiefs finally gave MacArthur their formal and unqualified approval.

One of MacArthur's strongest arguments for Inchon was that all the objections leading the Joint Chiefs to consider the plan inadvisable would also lead the North Korean commanders to conclude that a landing there was most unlikely. Such an operation would thus give the U.S./UN/ROK forces the tremendous advantage of complete surprise. MacArthur claimed that his plan had been inspired and reinforced by his memories of Francis Parkman's classic account of the British general James Wolfe's attack on Quebec in 1759, during the French and Indian War.[3] By having his men scale what the French thought were the impregnable cliffs below the Plains of Abraham, Wolfe took General Louis Montcalm by surprise and scored a brilliant and decisive victory.

Indeed, MacArthur found it auspicious that the naval bombardment of Inchon began on September 13, the 191st anniversary of Wolfe's victory. On that day ten UN ships approached Wolmi Island in broad daylight and at fairly low tide (thus unexpectedly but crucially able to spot and to destroy all the mines that had been laid); once the island's hidden guns had revealed their positions by firing, the naval artillery zeroed in and annihilated them. There was, of course, the danger that this operation would alert the North Koreans that a landing at Inchon was imminent, but ships blasted several other locations along the Korean coast, planes carried out bombing raids, and UN troops even staged a small diversionary amphibious landing to the south. The ruses worked; no reinforcements were moved to Inchon. The maintenance of the crucial element of surprise was all the more remarkable given that a week before D day, press correspondents in Tokyo had begun to call Inchon "Operation Common Knowledge."

In the ports of southern Japan, MacArthur assembled an invasion force of nearly 70,000 men. This force, designated X Corps, consisted mainly of the 1st U.S. Marine Division and the 7th U.S. Infantry Division, which was brought up to combat strength by the rather desperate measure of incorporating into it some 8,600 raw Korean recruits — known as KATUSAs, from the official term "Korean Augmentation to the United States Army" — each of whom was paired with an American soldier in a buddy system. Just as the first of the flotilla of 260 transport ships and escorts from six UN nations (the United States, Britain, France, the Netherlands, Australia, and New Zealand) were setting sail, the fierce typhoon Kezia arrived on the scene; but, after giving everyone a good fright, it cooperatively veered away from the invasion route. From then on, all went very much according to plan.

Before the Marine battalion landed on Wolmi at 6:33 on the morning of Friday, September 15, the island had been so thoroughly pulverized and carbonized by air and naval bombardment that the 250 defenders remaining in bunkers were dazed and relatively innocuous. Less than an hour and a half later the island was securely in American hands; not a single Marine had been killed, and only 17 were wounded. Despite the absolute confidence that he had had to display in order to sell his plan to the Joint Chiefs, MacArthur had been very nervous about the invasion; news of the light casualties sustained on Wolmi greatly buoyed his spirits. "More people than that get killed in traffic every day," he exulted.[4]

The second wave of Marines landed at 5:30 P.M. They controlled the port by midnight, and by dawn they had all of Inchon in their possession. But then North Korean resistance became more stubborn and effective. The Marines didn't take Kimpo Airport until September 17, and they weren't able to cross the Han River into Seoul until the twentieth. MacArthur was adamant that the North Koreans were to be expelled from the city by the twenty-fifth, for he wanted the psychological advantage of being able to announce the recapture of the capital exactly three months after the beginning of the war. Even with the help of the 7th Infantry Division, the Marines were unable to make that deadline, for the enemy defended the city with furious and suicidal tenacity. But MacArthur was not to be deterred; he went right ahead and announced the fall of Seoul on the twenty-fifth anyway, even though the last barricades were not swept away and the final pockets of resistance eradicated until three days later.

The Inchon landings had no immediate effect on the Pusan Perimeter, for the North Korean command managed to keep the news from its troops. The UN Command airdropped a blizzard of broadsides over enemy lines to demoralize the men, but these were apparently dismissed as propaganda. General Walker began his attempts to push the Communists northward on September 16, but they wouldn't budge. Not until the nineteenth did the Eighth Army make any appreciable progress, and not until the twenty-third did the psychological and logistical impact of Inchon — as well as the physical impact of American firepower — upon the North Korean army become evident. Panic then began to spread within the North Korean ranks, many units began to disintegrate, and the army's ability to resist plummeted. Resistance had, in any case, even from the standpoint of the North Korean high command, become less important than escape. Certainly as many as 25,000 — and perhaps as many as 40,000 — North Korean troops managed to evade the U.S./UN/ROK net and to make their way, many of them disguised as civilians, northward to the 38th parallel. Early on the morning of September 27, however, troops from the Eighth Army finally made their first contact with troops from X Corps, and then the trap was closed.

On September 29 General MacArthur staged an emotional ceremony to restore Syngman Rhee's government to the blasted and burned-out city of Seoul. Washington afterward registered objections to the ostentatious prominence of American flags — and the shortage of UN flags — at the ceremony, since the Truman administration was eager to avoid being closely linked to Rhee, whose forces had been strongly criticized in the Western press for their brutality. But many Americans felt that the conspicuousness of their flag was entirely appropriate, for the United States had suffered 20,756 casualties so far in the Korean War;[5] without that sacrifice Rhee would not be back in Seoul. In any case, Rhee's stock rose soon after the recapture of Taejon, on the night of September 28–29. There the liberating forces discovered the bodies of several thousand South Korean civilians, 40 American GIs, and 17 ROK soldiers who had been executed (which is to say, murdered) by the North Korean "Security Police" during the final days the Communists held the city. In contrast — and faced with such a barbarous enemy — the conduct of Rhee's forces seemed excusable, if still not palatable.

For his part, MacArthur was immune to criticism after Inchon. His audacious plan had succeeded despite the doubts and warnings of nearly all of his military colleagues. Although the analogy must not be pushed too far, after Inchon MacArthur had a momentum akin to that which Hitler had gained when his remilitarization of the Rhineland had succeeded in the face of the doubts and warnings of most of his generals. After their stunning triumphs, no one dared to challenge or to restrain either leader. Inchon made its conceiver and commander a national hero in the United States. As Dean Acheson said to Harriman after the victory, there would be "no stopping MacArthur now."[6] U.S./UN forces were now virtually certain to cross the 38th parallel in an effort to unify Korea under an anti-Communist government.

Perhaps a truly great, wise, courageous, and powerful president could have convinced the American public that such a course of action would prove to be self-destructive. Or perhaps such a president would have acted decisively to end the war regardless of the political consequences. But Truman — fine, decent, sensible, and generous man that he was — lacked the power to sway the electorate and was too pragmatic a politician to override its mandate. How ironic it is that we must think less of a president of this democratic nation for his having yielded to the will of the people.

CHAPTER 18

Toward a "Unified, Independent, and Democratic" Korea

IF REASON rather than emotionalism had determined the policy of the U.S. government, the Korean War could, and would, have ended very shortly after the liberation of Seoul. The North Koreans had been expelled from South Korea, and Syngman Rhee's government had been restored to full power over the area below the 38th parallel. The United States and the UN had achieved the aims that they had declared in June. And that should have been the end of it. But America was determined to unify North and South Korea under Rhee. The story of the American failure to do so is the climactic chapter in the history of the Korean War.

Soon after Inchon the North Korean army ceased to be an effective fighting force. By the end of September, in the words of General MacArthur's report to the UN, "the backbone of the North Korean Army had been broken and their scattered forces were being liquidated or driven north with material losses in equipment and men captured."[1] His next report described the situation at the beginning of October thus: "More than half of the enemy's combat forces were entrapped in the south, and were no longer available to him. Thousands more were lost in their desperate flight north to the 38th Parallel. . . . An average of approximately 3,000 North Koreans had been captured daily since the end of September."[2] In mid-October MacArthur told President Truman, "There is little resistance left in South Korea — only about 15,000 men — and those we do not destroy, the winter will."[3] The U.S./UN/ROK forces had liberated South Korea. The North Korean army was in no shape to launch a counteroffensive, and even if it were to make a desperate attempt, there was no chance that the attempt could succeed. South Korea's survival was no longer in danger.

The Joint Chiefs of Staff, however, had been informed that the North Korean regime had recently drafted and partly trained a reserve of some 125,000 men; they feared that Kim Il-sung might employ such a sizable force for a new offensive, and they went on to argue that an invasion of North Korea should be undertaken to eliminate that danger. But in mid-October, by which time U.S./UN/ROK troops were fighting north of the parallel, MacArthur himself dismissed the danger posed by these troops. At his Wake Island meeting with President Truman he said that North Korea had "about 100,000 men who were trained as replacements. They are poorly trained, led and equipped." By continuing to fight, the enemy was "pursuing a forlorn hope" and was "only fighting to save face."[4] This was hardly a force that could have posed any real threat to South Korea in the near future. MacArthur was not, however, suggesting that the invasion of North Korea was unnecessary. On the contrary, his intention was simply to convince Truman that there was no danger in continuing the invasion and occupying the entire north. The Pentagon and MacArthur were equally guilty of interpreting intelligence so as to support the decisions each had already made.

If the war had ended in late September with the restoration of the status quo ante bellum, North Korea would certainly have proceeded to rebuild its army, and the Soviet Union would certainly have provided it with armaments and training. But that army would clearly, by dint of circumstance, have been consigned to a purely defensive role. The United States had forcefully demonstrated its commitment to South Korea, and the Communists had to assume that the commitment was to be permanent, especially since America had suffered more than twenty thousand casualties by the end of September in defense of Rhee's regime. The ROK army had been greatly enlarged and immeasurably strengthened by U.S. aid, and there could be no doubt that it would continue to receive millions of dollars a year for the defense of South Korea. Never again would the north have the military superiority over the south that had made possible the June invasion's early successes. If anything, the north would have to fear that the newly muscled south would feel able to make, and would feel justified in making, a retaliatory strike northward.

The United States had gone into Korea to reestablish its credibility in the eyes of the world, to end appeasement of Communism, and to demonstrate the effectiveness of the UN and of collective security. All of those goals had been achieved by the end of September. Moreover, although the Soviets had meticulously maintained their pose of noninvolvement, virtually all of the non-Communist world assumed the North Korean invasion of the south to have been abetted — and almost certainly ordered as well — by the Kremlin. The failure of the invasion entailed a loss of prestige for the Soviet Union and for the international Communist movement. Furthermore, the studied Soviet aloofness, and the USSR's failure to go to the aid of its satellite when the tide of battle turned after Inchon, suggested that Stalin was afraid of direct military confrontation with the West. All of this represented a great propaganda victory for the West.

The United States had emphatically made its point that it would not tolerate, and could effectively oppose, any further attempts to expand Communist hegemony. A dangerously unprepared America had gone all out to defend a region in which it had seemed to have relatively little interest. The Kremlin could draw only one conclusion from that fact: now that the United States was engaged in a crash program of rearmament and expansion of its armed forces, the nation would be prepared to respond massively and unhesitatingly to Communist aggression anywhere in the world. Stalin would have to understand that the enlargement of his empire was at an end. Containment had passed from theory into practice, and it had proven successful.

In this changed situation, a return to the status quo ante bellum would have left South Korea very secure. Kim would have recognized that North Korea alone didn't stand a chance of conquering the south, and Stalin would have realized that he would not again be able to use the North Korean army as a proxy. If he was really determined to subjugate South Korea, he would have to send in Soviet troops to help do the job. Since he could now be certain that any such Soviet move would be opposed by American troops, it was obvious that the conflict would almost inevitably escalate into World War III. Hence South Korea would be safe unless and until Stalin was ready to engage in global warfare, from which the American intervention in Korea had presumably dissuaded him (that was, after all, the whole point) and from which the massive buildup of American and Western European forces would discourage him even further.

The unification of North and South Korea under an anti-Communist regime would thus have added nothing to the security of Rhee's government. The U.S./UN forces attempted to conquer North Korea not because the security of the south demanded it — as Washington argued that it did — but rather because American domestic politics demanded it.

The central problem was that it would have been political suicide for Truman or Dean Acheson to have suggested that the United States settle for anything less than it was *possible* to achieve in Korea short of precipitating Soviet or Chinese Communist intervention that would lead to world war. Paradoxically, until America had already taken the one step too many and the Chinese Communists had actually intervened, no one could be absolutely certain what would trigger such intervention. In other words, the United States simply could not stop until it had gone too far. Recommendations of caution from within the U.S./UN camp were denounced, by right-wing Democrats as well as by extremist Republicans, as timidity and appeasement; and warnings from the Communist camp — even very specific ones stating exactly what would lead to Chinese intervention — were dismissed in Washington as bluff. Thus nothing but overwhelming Communist force could possibly have halted the American attempt to unify Korea.

On the surface it appears that the commitment of enormous numbers of American troops to Korea for the Inchon landing and Pusan Perimeter breakout, followed by the spectacular success of that dual operation, led the Truman administration to shift its ultimate goal from the rescue of South Korea to the destruction of the North Korean regime and the unification of Korea under an anti-Communist government. The administration did not, however, actually alter its goal at all; it simply changed its thinking about how best to achieve it.

At the outset Truman did indeed declare that the aim of American intervention was to repulse the North Korean invasion. But that was never regarded by the highest military and political leaders in Washington — including Truman himself — as more than an immediate *military* goal, the achievement of which would be followed by talks to achieve the *political* goal of the unification of Korea under the auspices of the UN. That this was not made more explicit early on had to do mainly with the desire of the U.S. government to keep the issues under discussion in the Security Council as simple as possible so as to ensure unanimity among America's friends and allies — and to win a high level of support from such nations as India and Egypt, which were trying to maintain a stance of neutrality in the Cold War. Since the majority of nations agreed that it was essential to take military action to repulse the North Korean invasion, the United States limited its initial proposals accordingly. Only later, once its allies were deeply committed to the UN action and once UN solidarity had been fully demonstrated, would America risk the introduction of more specific resolutions regarding North Korea's ultimate fate, a question that was certain to complicate matters and to cause dissension among the UN allies. By that time, however, sheer momentum would be a great help in getting more drastic resolutions adopted.

Such a manipulative strategy was shrewd, if not particularly admirable. It was, unfortunately, not the least admirable aspect of the way in which the United States shaped UN policy. Throughout the early stages of the Korean War, the United States consistently exhibited a rather unsavory legalistic deviousness, getting the UN to pass a vague and ambiguously worded resolution and then presenting the organization with a fait accompli that it claimed was based on that resolution, even though the action went far beyond a conservative interpretation of what had been authorized. The trick was to avoid explicitly stating the limits of any action, to eschew any statement that would close off any option. For example, a Department of Defense position paper dated July 31 noted that "no action of the Security Council has yet specifically limited military ground operations of the unified command to the area south of the 38th parallel."[5] That was true, strictly speaking, even though the UN resolution of June 27, by calling only for action "to repel the armed attack and to restore international peace and security in the area," seemed to imply that military operations would cease once the North Koreans had been driven back above the 38th parallel.

In all fairness, it must be said that America's allies understood quite well what it was up to. The crux of the matter was that they wanted, almost as much as the United States did, to see Korea united under an anti-Communist government. They simply didn't want any responsibility for the decisions, since they feared reprisals from Moscow and/or Peking. So an elaborate game developed in which the United States would introduce, or persuade a group of its allies to introduce, an ambiguous resolution. Next, the United States would proceed to interpret it in a radically permissive sense and undertake the action that all the allies wanted to see taken. The allies could then, for the benefit of their more conservative citizens and for that of the Communist capitals, ostentatiously disclaim all responsibility for the impulsive U.S. action, while America could self-righteously maintain that it was only the obedient servant of the UN. All of this disingenuous shirking of responsibility — all of this militancy in pacifists' clothing — set a very bad example for MacArthur, who was thereby encouraged to assume that Washington wanted him to do more than it was politic for Truman to state openly.

It would, however, be thoroughly mistaken to deduce that American policy was shaped by a carefully coordinated and relentless conspiracy. Reading through the comprehensive volume of official papers and correspondence for 1950 dealing with Korea, one gets a sense of overwhelming confusion. These papers (many of them written by the lawyers who held high office in the State Department) are full of heated arguments over the key questions: How much should the United States try to do in Korea? How much would it be *possible* for the United States to do? Would the Soviets and/or the Chinese Communists intervene? If so, at what point? And if so, in what strength? Would they intervene in limited numbers that America could defeat? Was the attempt to unify Korea worth the risk of world war? Debate over these questions led to endless drafts and revisions. Hypotheses, once stated, became too easily transmuted into axioms. On August 15 one member of the State Department's Policy Planning Staff complained in a memo to Acheson that "the papers on Korea are now so numerous that it is difficult to fit all the pieces together."[6] This was policy-making by drift and by compromise, by erosion and by stultification.

Running through all of this controversy are two principal lines of thought that most decisively influenced policy. The first of these hinged upon a sophistical interpretation of the UN resolution calling upon members to help "to restore international peace and security in the area." Those who focused on the word "restore" assumed that the phrase meant the restoration of the status quo ante bellum, for it is possible to restore only what has previously existed. But those who focused on the phrase "international peace and security" argued that since real security was impossible as long as Korea remained divided, a mere return to the status quo would not satisfy that demand. They suggested that the UN was calling for the "restoration" of the peace and security that would have, or should have, prevailed if Korea had been unified during the late 1940s, in accordance with the General Assembly resolutions of 1947 and 1948.

The most vehement proponents of this latter view within the U.S. State Department were John Foster Dulles, Dean Rusk, and John Allison, who was then serving under Rusk as director of the department's Office of Northeast Asian Affairs and as Dulles's chief assistant in drafting a peace treaty for Japan. Allison's temperament suited him well to work closely with Dulles, who would later become the leading advocate of "roll-back," or "liberation," as opposed to the "containment" of Communism. The principal liaison between the Democratic administration and the Republican right, Dulles was a very powerful man, and those who were in sympathy with him could be certain that their views would receive a wide and careful hearing.

Allison began his campaign for the liberation of North Korea on July 1, the day after Truman committed U.S. ground forces to the conflict. Having heard that some government officials were advising Truman to announce publicly that U.S. and ROK troops would not advance north of the 38th parallel, Allison wrote a memo to Rusk in which he strongly opposed any such announcement:

> I believe there is ample justification in the last part of the second Resolution of the Security Council for any action which may be deemed appropriate at the time which will contribute to the *permanent* restoration of peace and stability in the area [emphasis added]. I am convinced that there will be no permanent peace and stability in Korea as long as the artificial division at the 38th parallel continues. I believe the time has come when we must be bold and willing to take even more risks than we have already. . . . I personally feel that if we can, and I am by no means certain that we can, we should continue right on up to the Manchurian and Siberian border, and, having done so, call for a U.N.-supervised election for all of Korea.

Having read the memo, Rusk wrote in the margin, "Agree. D.R."[7] His agreement was crucial, for he had great influence upon Acheson's thinking. Before long, the secretary of state was arguing that MacArthur's troops could not "be expected to march up to a surveyor's line and stop."[8] American troops were destined to cross the 38th parallel.

Like the State Department extremists, the Joint Chiefs of Staff could be satisfied with nothing less than the unification of Korea under an anti-Communist government, but they hoped that such a result could be attained without a U.S./UN invasion of North Korea. General Omar Bradley wrote in his autobiography:

> The military was unanimous in its view about what to do in Korea, and that view never wavered. . . . The JCS agreed that in order to preclude another North Korean invasion of South Korea, the North Korean Army should be utterly destroyed. It was our hope that the North Korean Army could be destroyed in South Korea, but we believed that MacArthur should not be restrained at the 38th parallel. We urged that the whole country be occupied and guaranteed free elections. However, in order to minimize the possibility of Soviet or Chinese communist intervention, we felt that ground operations north of the 38th parallel should be conducted mostly by ROK forces, with continued American air and naval support.[9]

Unfortunately, the JCS did not hold that last belief quite strongly enough to prevent a full-scale U.S./UN invasion of North Korea in October.

The second line of thought that governed the formation of American policy in Korea held that it was vital to demonstrate that aggression does not pay. It wasn't enough to prove that aggression could not succeed. As Dulles wrote to Paul Nitze on July 14, "Neither equity nor good sense dictates that an unprovoked act of aggression should occur without risk of loss to the aggressor. If there can be armed aggression under conditions such that failure involves no permanent loss, then that puts a premium on aggression."[10]

The stated goals of the United States were defensive, but its real goals were punitive. North Korea had committed the international equivalent of attempted murder. It would have to be punished and rendered unable to commit such a crime ever again. More to the point, the Soviet Union was to be punished with the loss of North Korea.

What this meant in practice was that the war could not at that point be ended by negotiation, since it was generally assumed that nothing short of a military victory followed by the unconditional surrender of the North Korean government could force the Soviet Union to give up its satellite. Although the United States, in order to present itself as a peace-loving nation, had to declare itself open to negotiations, the fact was that Washington was not willing to settle for anything less than the unification of Korea under Rhee, and it knew perfectly well that the Russians would never agree to any such thing unless they were forced by military necessity to accept it. Hence the influential Defense Department position paper of July 31, "U.S. Courses of Action in Korea," recommended (as did its subsequent revisions) that until the United States was well on its way to achieving its objectives militarily, "the U.S. should use all its diplomatic means to forestall any Soviet effort to mediate the conflict on any terms short of the unification of all Korea on a free and representative basis under UN auspices."[11] In any case, most American leaders would have agreed with Pentagon official General Charles L. Bolté, who remarked in November that "history has proved that negotiating with Communists is as fruitless as it is repulsive."[12] Only the use of force could lead to an acceptable settlement with the Communists.

America, of course, cloaked its reasoning in impressive legal logic. Key to its plan was that no settlement could be acceptable if any of its conditions represented a gain for the Communists, for such a gain would be construed as a reward for aggression. The twist was that if the United States and the UN gave their formal consent to a return to the status quo ante bellum, that would imply their acceptance of the permanent division of Korea and thus also of North Korea's right to exist. Such concessions would represent a gain for the Communists and were therefore unacceptable. Similarly, no settlement involving the admission of Communist China to the UN could be considered, for those who believed that Communism was monolithic argued that any such move would reward Moscow as well as Peking.

To have ended the Korean War after the liberation of Seoul would have been the policy of wise moderation. But by invading the south,

North Korea had committed an extremist act. As we have seen, Americans are extremist only in their hatred of, and in their reaction to, extremism. It was inevitable, especially given the climate of extremism aggravated by Senator McCarthy, that the American response to North Korean aggression would be extremist. Truman's principle of doing whatever the military situation called for contained the seed of extremism. That principle was soon transformed into one of doing whatever the military situation *seemed to make possible*. Once those new goals had been affirmed, the United States felt bound to do whatever seemed necessary in order to achieve them. Like the sorcerer's apprentice, the United States didn't know how to stop the forces it had unleashed.

CHAPTER 19

Pushing China Toward War

GENERAL MACARTHUR had planned all along to invade North Korea. In mid-July 1950 he had told General J. Lawton Collins that his goal was the complete destruction of the North Korean army, not merely its expulsion from South Korea. He said that he intended to pursue the retreating North Koreans above the 38th parallel and, if necessary, to occupy all of the north with the ultimate aim of unifying Korea.[1]

According to the July 21 issue of the *New York Times*, General Dwight Eisenhower agreed that the North Koreans must be defeated "soundly" and must not be permitted to retire behind the 38th parallel to build up for another attack. "This meant, he indicated, that it might be necessary for U.S. forces to cross the 38th parallel. This would not violate the intent of the UN police action or draw the Soviet Union into the war."

George Kennan of the State Department was the most forceful and consistent proponent of restraint. Although he believed very strongly from the beginning that the United States should "react with all necessary force . . . to expel the North Korean forces from the southern half of the peninsula," he assumed that the U.S. government intended to do no more than to restore the status quo ante bellum.[2] As it began to become apparent that influential voices were advocating a final and permanent solution to the Korean problem, he warned of the grave dangers inherent in any attempt to put such a policy into practice.[3] Unfortunately, Kennan had been scheduled to leave the government at the end of June, and although Dean Acheson asked him to stay on as an adviser until the Korean crisis had passed, the secretary of state tended to regard him as an impractical idealist, an eccentric and a dreamer, a man whose proposals could not be implemented in the real world of American politics.

Kennan did, however, have the ear of Paul Nitze, who had succeeded him as director of the State Department's Policy Planning Staff. Thus Kennan's influence made itself felt in the draft memorandum written by George H. Butler of the PPS on July 22, the purpose of which was "to decide upon U.S. policy regarding the advance beyond the 38th parallel of U.S. forces now engaged in Korea as a part of the U.N. forces."[4] This paper clearly stated that "it is extremely unlikely that the Kremlin would accept the establishment in North Korea of a regime which it could not dominate and control." And, echoing the wisdom of UNCOK's report in the fall of 1949, it argued that "it seems likely that a satisfactory permanent solution of the Korean problem can be hoped for only when and if a substantial accommodation is reached between the U.S.S.R. and the noncommunist world."

The PPS paper warned that the South Korean government as well as American public and congressional opinion would probably press for the unification of Korea, but it advised that those pressures should be resisted, since "the disadvantages of a failure to attain the complete independence and unity of Korea after the North Korean forces have been driven back to the 38th parallel must be weighed against the risk of a major conflict with the U.S.S.R. or Communist China that such a settlement might well involve."

Perhaps it would not have made any difference if the PPS had stood firmly behind its conviction that the unification of Korea was simply not possible at any cost acceptable to the United States. But it hedged. The policy memo conceded that

> in the unlikely event that there is complete disintegration of North Korean forces together with a failure of the Kremlin and Communist China to take any action whatever to exert influence in North Korea, U.N. forces, acting in pursuance of an additional Security Council resolution, might move into North Korea in order to assist in the establishment of a unified and independent Korea.

By admitting that such a course of events was possible, however improbable, the PPS negated all of its other arguments, for the United States could not voluntarily stop short of what might be possible.

It is, however, unlikely that even the most unequivocal warnings could have prevailed against the self-righteous rantings of the extremists, Republicans and Democrats alike. John Allison of the State Department was certainly as extremist as any right-wing Republican fanatic in Congress, and his response to the PPS position paper so remarkably concentrates the attitudes that assailed Truman's better judgment that it deserves to be quoted at some length:

> The paper assumes we can buy more time by a policy of appeasement — for that is what this paper recommends — a timid, half-hearted policy designed not to provoke the Soviets to war. We should recognize that there is grave danger of conflict with the USSR and the Chinese Communists whatever we do from now on — but I fail to see what advantage we gain by a compromise with clear moral principles and a shirking of our duty to make clear once and for all that aggression does not pay — that he who violates the decent opinions of mankind must take the consequences and that he who takes the sword will perish by the sword.
>
> That this may mean war on a global scale is true — the American people should be told and told why and what it will mean to them. When all legal and moral right is on our side why should we hesitate? . . . Any member of the United Nations which did not support us would do so in the knowledge that its action was dictated by fear and not by doubt of the rightness of what we were doing. The free world cannot any longer live under constant fear. The issue is clear — we should now decide to stand up to what our President had called "raw aggression," or we should admit that Soviet Communism has won and be prepared to take the consequences.[5]

Not even Dulles went so far. In a memo to Paul Nitze dated August 1, he wrote:

> In my opinion, there is every reason to go beyond the 38th parallel except possibly one, and that is our incapacity to do so and the fact that the attempt might involve us much more deeply in a struggle on the Asiatic mainland with Soviet and Chinese Communist manpower because of the strategic bearing that the northern part of Korea has toward Port Arthur and Vladivostok.[6]

Allison's was a minority voice within the State Department, for none of the top officials was willing to provoke a major war with the Soviets or the Chinese. But rhetoric like his — in Congress and in the rightist press — was an important factor in making it politically impossible for the Truman administration to do anything less in Korea than it might be possible to do.

*   *   *

Throughout the month of July neither the Peking government nor its press expressed anything to suggest that China was even considering intervention in Korea.[7] The buildup of U.S. troops in Korea signaled the probability that the North Koreans would be expelled from the south, but the Chinese Communists seemed to regard with equanimity the prospect of a U.S./UN/ROK victory and the restoration of the status quo ante bellum.

In late July, however, while U.S. and ROK troops were retreating into the Pusan Perimeter, the U.S. government feared that a Chinese Communist move might be imminent. If the People's Republic of China was going to aid the North Koreans, that seemed to be the optimum moment for it to do so, though not necessarily by sending troops into Korea. The Pentagon surmised that the Communists might soon invade Formosa, since such an invasion would at the very least prompt the United States to divert some of its air and naval forces from Korea to help Chiang Kai-shek. The splitting of American forces in the Far East might enable the North Koreans to drive their enemies into the sea, and if it turned out that they couldn't manage that task alone, the PRC might send in some troops to assist them. The Communist Chinese army of five million men could easily cope with simultaneous operations on Formosa and in Korea. In any case, Washington thought that Peking probably figured it should seize Formosa while the Americans could ill afford to divert any of their forces from Korea.

Despite Truman's announcement on June 27 that the Seventh U.S. Fleet would neutralize the Formosa Strait, the Joint Chiefs of Staff feared in late July not only that the Communists were about to launch an invasion of Formosa but also that it might very well succeed. Most of the Seventh Fleet's aircraft carriers and battleships were in Korean waters; only a token force of a few destroyers was actually stationed in the Formosa Strait. The "neutralization" was largely a bluff, and the Pentagon assumed that Peking knew it.[8]

Military intelligence reported that the Communists were assembling on the coast opposite Formosa a fleet of several thousand vessels — ranging from concrete-reinforced junks to American landing craft that had been abandoned by the Nationalists when they fled the mainland. The Communists were also building airfields there and massing troops; estimates of their strength varied from about 200,000 to over 700,000. On July 20 Radio Peking quoted a speech made four days earlier in which General Ch'en Yi, commander of the PRC's Third Field Army, had said: "While we intensify preparations to liberate Taiwan [Formosa], we must not neglect our task of national economic recovery."[9] What this was presumably meant to signify may be rendered thus: "We are postponing the invasion of Formosa not because we are afraid of the Americans but rather because we have urgent matters to attend to at home. This delay can only work to our benefit, for when we finally invade Formosa, we shall be better prepared." The general was only trying to save face, but his statement increased Washington's fears.

They were increased all the more when, on July 22, the Communists attacked the two small Nationalist-held islands of Quemoy and Little Quemoy, located a few miles off the China coast and about one hundred miles due west of Formosa. Each side regarded Quemoy as an indispensable stepping-stone for the invasion it hoped to undertake — the Communists of Formosa, the Nationalists of the mainland. Thus when Quemoy was attacked, first by shelling from the nearby island of Amoy and then by an invasion force, the Pentagon automatically assumed that this move was preliminary to an amphibious assault on Formosa. The timing seemed right. On July 23 the *New York Times* observed, "One week hence — July 28 and 29 — there will be high tide at dawn along the Formosan coast. China's Red armies will have better conditions for an invasion of Formosa then than they are likely to see again for more than a month, because typhoons will whip the shallow Formosa Strait through most of August." It seems most likely, however, that the Communists, unwilling to risk an invasion of Formosa at that time, were trying to seize Quemoy as a consolation prize. Their possession of the island would not only be important for their eventual campaign against Chiang, but it would also remove the threat that Quemoy's major air and naval bases posed to the mainland.

In American eyes all Communist moves were aggressive, never defensive, and so the JCS were very worried about an invasion of Formosa in the last week of July. Since, as General Omar Bradley later wrote, the JCS "did not believe the Nationalist troops on Formosa had the will or the equipment to stop the invasion,"[10] they recommended at the National Security Council meeting on July 27 that the United States give matériel and supplies to Chiang, the corollary apparently being that American support would raise the morale of the Nationalist troops and give them the will they lacked. Although Truman had declared at the Blair House meeting on June 26, just one month earlier, that he wouldn't give the Nationalists "a nickel" for any purpose whatever, since "all the money we have given them is now invested in United States real estate,"[11] he immediately approved the JCS recommendation. To determine exactly what equipment and supplies were needed, and in what quantities, Truman authorized a military fact-finding mission to Formosa.

Truman's publicly stated position was that the Communists had to be deterred from invading Formosa while the fighting continued in Korea, for such an invasion would be a dangerous distraction from the principal business of settling the Korean problem. His predicament was to warn the Communists away from Korea without angering them to retaliatory or face-saving action, such as intervening in Korea, seizing Hong Kong, or perhaps even mounting the very invasion that he was hoping to prevent. Thus he was at pains to reassure Peking that the United States was not interested in controlling Formosa and that it had no intention of establishing military bases on the island. He even went so far as to make statements that could be interpreted as implying that America might condone a Communist Chinese invasion of Formosa once the Korean War had ended. But such statements were purposely misleading.

At the outbreak of the war Truman had accepted the arguments advanced by men as different as Acheson, Louis Johnson, General Bradley, and General MacArthur that the United States could never afford to let Formosa fall into the hands of a hostile power. That did not mean that he had changed his attitude toward Chiang. As Averell Harriman told MacArthur early in August, Truman was hoping that Formosa could be established as an independent nation under the auspices of the UN. It would be important to remove Chiang from power, continued Harriman, for he "had only the burning ambition to use Formosa as a stepping-stone for his re-entry to the mainland." American support of Chiang, he said, would not only heighten Chinese Communist antagonism toward the United States but would also run the risk of alienating "the British, Nehru and such countries as Norway, who, although stalwart in their determination to resist

Russian aggression, did not want to stir up trouble elsewhere."[12] Given all of these considerations, Truman wanted to deny Formosa to the Communists permanently, but he dared not say so. On the other hand, he wanted to make it clear that he had not decided to endorse Chiang and that he was still not willing to give him long-range aid, let alone to send American troops to help the Nationalists repulse any future Communist attempt to invade Formosa.

It was into this china shop that MacArthur charged like a bull. On July 29, having been informed of the decisions made at the NSC meeting two days earlier, MacArthur notified the JCS that he himself would make a brief visit to Formosa on the thirty-first "in order to determine its military capabilities for defense." Washington, concerned that such a visit might appear to have political ramifications, made a feeble attempt to dissuade the general from going and suggested that he send a senior officer instead. But, giving with one hand what it was trying to take away with the other, the Pentagon's July 30 message to MacArthur concluded, "Please feel free to go, since the responsibility is yours."[13] The Pentagon's punctilious and self-consciously deferential observance of military etiquette in its communications with MacArthur was a considerable factor in bringing about Chinese Communist intervention in Korea.

MacArthur, who had never met Chiang, was determined to go himself. He was welcomed as though he were a head of state; and for two days, between inspection tours and conferences, he and his entourage were entertained royally.[14] Peking quite naturally read sinister meanings into this visit. Just the week before, in its issue of July 24, *Time* magazine had stated that Chiang would like to see MacArthur put in charge of U.S. relations with Nationalist China. "The Generalissimo has unlimited confidence in MacArthur," continued the article, "and would be happy to place the fate of Formosa and of Nationalist China in his hands. . . . [I]t is of the first importance that General MacArthur be given full responsibility for all relationships, military and otherwise, between the U.S. and Nationalist China." Peking surely feared that MacArthur's visit meant the recommendation was being taken up.

Matters were made far worse by the statement that MacArthur issued to the press at the end of his visit, in which he said that "arrangements have been completed for effective coordination between the American forces under my command and those of the Chinese Government the better to meet any attack which a hostile force might be foolish enough to attempt."[15] That strongly implied that the United States would intervene on Formosa as fully as it had done in Korea, even though Washington had temporarily decided that no American forces except the Seventh Fleet would help to defend the island. The statement that Chiang issued after his meetings with MacArthur boasted that the talks had not only made arrangements for the joint defense of Formosa but had also laid the foundations for "Sino-American military cooperation" and for "final victory" against the Communists.[16] The paranoid regime in Peking, accustomed to expressing itself in phrases intended to mean either less or more than what they actually said, could easily interpret that to mean that the United States was prepared to help Chiang invade the mainland — especially since MacArthur's visit followed so closely on the heels of Truman's speech of July 19, calling for the radical expansion of American armed forces.

Truman became angry and worried when he read MacArthur's and Chiang's statements in the press, so much so that he dispatched Harriman to Tokyo at once to set the general straight on Washington's policy regarding Formosa and Chiang. Harriman's formal report to Truman gave fair warning of the dangers that lay ahead. "In my first talk with MacArthur," wrote the ambassador,

> I told him the President wanted me to tell him that he must not permit Chiang to be the cause of starting a war with the Chinese communists on the mainland, the effect of which might drag us into a world war. He answered that he would, as a soldier, obey any orders that he received from the President. . . . For reasons which are rather difficult to explain, I did not feel that we came to a full agreement on the way we believed things should be handled on Formosa and with the Generalissimo. He accepted the President's position and will act accordingly, but without full conviction.[17]

It seems that all this fuss had come about for no good reason, since MacArthur reassured Harriman that he was "satisfied the Chinese Communists will not attempt an invasion of Formosa at this time."[18] He thought that U.S. air and naval forces could destroy any invasion force and that the Chinese Nationalist troops could defeat any Communists who managed to get through. Just to be sure, Truman had the JCS send MacArthur a directive on August 14 stating in the usual roundabout way that if the Communists were to invade Formosa, he was not to send any American ground troops to the island, and that although he could employ American air and naval forces, they were not to be based there.[19]

Early in August there was much informal discussion at the UN of the possibility of pursuing the North Korean army above the 38th parallel and proceeding to unify Korea under an anti-Communist government. Peking would have been aware of these discussions through the intermediation of India. It appears that at this time the Chinese began to fear that such a development would expose them to the grave danger of an American invasion of Manchuria coordinated with an American-sponsored Nationalist invasion of southern China. The Russians — who were determined not to lose North Korea but were equally determined not to run the risks that overt Soviet military intervention would involve — apparently did all they could to exacerbate those fears so that Peking would come to believe that it was in its own interest to intervene if U.S./UN forces attempted to unify Korea. Just as Truman and MacArthur felt that it would be a strategic disaster for Formosa to fall into the hands of a hostile Communist China, so did Mao Tse-tung and Chou En-lai decide that it would be a strategic disaster for North Korea to fall into the hands of a hostile United States.

On August 17 the *New York Times* reported that "a Hong Kong paper with Nationalist leanings" had asserted that Soviet vice premier Vyacheslav Molotov had left Peking on August 10 after reaching an agreement with Mao specifying that "if U.N. forces should launch a full-scale offensive carrying them beyond the 38th parallel, the Chinese Communists would send 150,000 troops into Korea from Manchuria, with the Soviet Union supplying the military equipment." The *Times* dismissed the report with the comment that "rumors like this are frequent in Hong Kong," but the report may, in fact, have been true. On August 11 the American ambassador in London informed Acheson that the British military attaché in China had reported a number of observations that suggested preparation for war in northeastern China.[20] Two days later, Peking sent its first ambassador to Pyongyang. Since the PRC had as yet sent ambassadors to very few nations, that move certainly had more than casual significance.

The turning point came on August 17, when the chief American delegate to the UN, Warren R. Austin, made a speech before the Security Council in which he strongly implied that the United States would be satisfied with nothing less than the unification of Korea under an anti-Communist government.[21] This was the first public statement of that goal. The obvious meaning was that the United States was prepared to invade North Korea if necessary; the shift in the military balance within Korea at that time suggested that America would soon be in a position to pursue its goal. Austin's speech effectively put an end to the possibility that the war could end soon with a return to the status quo ante bellum, for once the United States had stated its real goal, failure to achieve it would involve a serious loss of face. The American public and Congress would denounce as appeasement the voluntary achievement of anything less than the unification of Korea, and they would decry as defeat the military achievement of anything less.

Three days later — apparently in direct response to Austin's speech — the Peking government, which had for some time said very little publicly about Korea, made an important pronouncement. On August 20 Chou sent a cable to the UN stating: "Korea is China's neighbor. The Chinese people cannot but be concerned about solution of the Korean question. . . . It must and can be settled peacefully."[22] What this meant was that the PRC was demanding a negotiated settlement — and such a settlement would, of course, mean the preservation of North Korea.

The Soviet delegate to the UN, Iakov Malik, warned the Security Council two days later: "Any continuation of the Korean War will lead inevitably to a widening of the conflict with consequences, the responsibility for which will lie with the United States and its Security Council delegation."[23] This was a very clear threat. If the United States pursued its goal of unifying Korea, the Communists would intervene militarily. But Washington chose not to take the threat seriously.

At that point attention again turned to Formosa. On the twenty-fourth Chou sent a cable to the UN demanding that the Security Council "condemn . . . and take immediate measures to bring about the complete withdrawal of United States armed invading forces from Taiwan [Formosa] and from other territories belonging to China."[24] Malik elaborated on this theme, charging that American aid to Formosa constituted "aggression" against the PRC and that the American goal was permanent control of Formosa. On August 25, in a letter to Secretary-General Trygve Lie that had been painstakingly drafted by the State Department, Ambassador Austin replied to the charges. The fate of Formosa, he suggested, should be decided by negotiations under UN auspices once the Korean War was over.[25] The intended implication was that PRC control of Formosa was by no means out of the question. This was, of course, not actually stated, for Washington was not willing to make explicit promises that it had no intention of keeping.

Truman hoped that Austin's letter would satisfy Peking for the time being. But the next day, August 26, the president received a copy of the statement that General MacArthur had written to be read at the annual National Encampment of the Veterans of Foreign Wars. This statement is rather strange, for it describes in considerable detail the value of Formosa to any enemy of the United States. MacArthur began by defining the U.S. defense perimeter in the terms already quoted* and then went on to argue that Communist possession of Formosa would render the defense perimeter very vulnerable. "Formosa in the hands of such a hostile power could be compared to an unsinkable aircraft carrier and submarine tender ideally located to accomplish offensive strategy and at the same time checkmate defensive or counter-offensive operations by friendly forces based on Okinawa and the Philippines."[26] Formosa would give the enemy bases 100 to 150 miles closer to Okinawa and the Philippines than any point in continental Asia. From it Communist fighter planes, which had a very limited range, would be able to reach the Philippines and to double their effectiveness against Okinawa.

In essence, MacArthur was saying that if we lost Formosa, we would lose the Pacific. So dramatic were his arguments that they could almost be taken as encouragement for the Communists to invade

*See pages 81–82.

Formosa at once. But the PRC's principal reasons for wanting Formosa were nationalistic and defensive, not aggressive. It wanted all of traditional Chinese territory, and it wanted to do away with the threat from Chiang's forces once and for all.

The import of MacArthur's statement was obvious. If Formosa was really that vital to American security, then the United States could *never* let the island fall into Chinese Communist hands, or at any rate not as long as the PRC remained hostile to the United States. (In December Truman would say to British prime minister Clement Attlee, "When we thought that Formosa was not strategically important to us, we never considered that the Chinese Government would be one which would be very hostile to the United States."[27]) What MacArthur had said was not really at variance with Truman's own position, but Truman's policy was to not make that position public. It was that latter policy that MacArthur had violated.

Truman was so furious that he considered relieving MacArthur of his command in Korea, though he would have left him in charge of the Japanese occupation. The Inchon landings were, however, scheduled to take place in less than three weeks, and MacArthur was indispensable to the completion of his plan. (For one thing, no one else wanted the responsibility of commanding at Inchon in case the operation failed.) So, instead of firing MacArthur, Truman simply ordered Secretary of Defense Louis Johnson to send the general a cable demanding that he withdraw his statement immediately.[28] It was too late. MacArthur issued a formal retraction, but the September 1 issue of *U.S. News & World Report*, in which the full text of the VFW message was printed, was already in the mails.

Perhaps MacArthur's removal would have reassured the PRC. As it was, Peking taunted America by saying (quite correctly) that MacArthur had embarrassed his government by revealing Washington's true policy. The fact that Truman didn't relieve MacArthur of his command surely suggested to Peking that even if Truman and MacArthur disagreed, the latter was more powerful and would prevail.

The Chinese Communist regime was terribly vulnerable, since it was still engaged in the suppression of hundreds of thousands of anti-Communist "bandits" and was wrestling desperately with the staggering economic problems caused by twelve years of war (1937–49).

If the United States was going to reopen the Chinese civil war, as many congressmen had been publicly demanding, then this was certainly the most favorable time to do so — before the Communist government could fully consolidate its position and develop a strong economic base. Peking's fears on this score were aggravated when, on August 27, an American plane accidentally strafed a Manchurian airfield just north of the Yalu River. It must then have seemed to Peking that perhaps the United States really was going to take up the call that navy secretary Frank Matthews had made in an August 25 speech in Boston. He had declared that America should launch a "preventive war" against Communism, arguing that this would "cast us in a character new to a true democracy — an initiator of a war of aggression — the first true aggressors for peace."[29]

Truman should have fired Matthews immediately, but he wanted to avoid the tremendous outcry from the Catholic anti-Communist extremists that such a move would trigger. Instead, on September 12, Truman finally fired Secretary of Defense Johnson. Hanson Baldwin had said in the *New York Times* that Matthews had made his speech at the instigation of Johnson, "who has been selling the same doctrine of preventive war in private conversations around Washington."[30] Truman pointedly replaced Johnson (who was widely known to agree with MacArthur in regard to China and Formosa) with General George Marshall, who, because of his efforts in 1945–46 to mediate between the Chinese Nationalists and the Communists, had the reputation of being less hostile to Mao's regime.

In late August Truman adopted a half-conciliatory and half-cautionary posture toward Peking. On the one hand, he said in a press conference on August 31 that the Seventh Fleet would be withdrawn from the Formosa Strait as soon as the Korean War had ended — the implication being that there would then be nothing but Chiang's weak forces to oppose a Communist invasion of the island.[31] That same day Ambassador Austin admitted to the UN Security Council that it was possible that an American plane had indeed mistakenly strafed a Manchurian airfield; if a UN commission confirmed the Communist charge, the United States would pay damages and discipline the fliers responsible for the accident.[32] On the other hand, in a speech that was broadcast over national radio on the evening of September 1, Truman warned Peking that if it intervened in Korea, it would soon come to regret that move. He assured the Chinese Communists that the United States and its UN allies had no intention whatever of attacking China, and he advanced the argument that if the Russians "misled or forced" China into entering the Korean War, the Soviet Union would take advantage of the resulting fray to seize more Chinese territory for itself.[33]

Truman stated unequivocally that "we do not believe in aggressive or preventive war." But he also stated: "We have had about one and a half million men and women on active duty in our Army, Navy, and Air Force. Our present plans call for increasing this number to close to three million, and further increases may be required."[34] He then went on to point out how well prepared the United States was for war. The *New York Times* summed up the meaning of Truman's speech by saying that the president "asserted that a world war would not develop unless the Communist masters drove new puppets against the United Nations in Korea. He made it plain, however, that we would not flinch if they made such a decision and that we would stay in the world conflict until we had achieved the kind of peace that free nations desired."[35]

To Peking, such a speech would surely have sounded far more bellicose and provocative than reassuring.

CHAPTER 20

Truman's Mistakes

IN MID-SEPTEMBER Truman made, almost simultaneously, two of his gravest blunders of the entire war. The first was his announcement on September 14, 1950, only a few hours before the Inchon landings began in Korea (where it was already the fifteenth), that, as the *New York Times* reported, "he had directed the State Department to begin a new effort to obtain a Japanese peace treaty. Behind this move was this country's resolve to produce a peace agreement, with or without Soviet participation."[1] At his press conference on August 31 Truman had said that the question of Formosa would be settled by the Japanese peace treaty. Now it was official that the Communists — the Soviets as well as the Chinese — would have no meaningful say in the shaping of that treaty. That was tantamount to saying that Peking would have no opportunity to establish its legal claim to Formosa.

On the morning of September 15 the banner headline of the *New York Times* read:

U.N. FORCES LAND BEHIND COMMUNISTS IN KOREA;
SEIZE INCHON, PORT OF SEOUL; MOVE INLAND;
U.S. WILL PRESS FOR A JAPANESE PEACE TREATY.

The conjunction of Inchon and the treaty was unfortunate, for it suddenly appeared that the United States might soon be in a position to invade North Korea. The Chinese Communists feared, or claimed to fear, that the Americans might enlist Japanese participation in such an invasion. This impression could only have been reinforced by a story in the next day's *Times* stating that "the United States will propose a Japanese peace treaty placing no restrictions on rearmament, allowing the maximum economic and commercial freedom and encouraging the admission of the former enemy into the United Nations and the community of anti-Communist allies." Under the circumstances, the Chinese Communists could hardly have failed to recall how, in February 1904, at the outbreak of the Russo-Japanese War,

Japanese troops had landed at Inchon and had then rushed northward to Manchuria, beginning the long process that led to the establishment of Manchukuo, in 1932.

Although there was not really even the slightest chance of an American-Japanese invasion of Manchuria in 1950, the fact remains that Japan and the Japanese were playing important roles in the Korean War. Japan was America's privileged sanctuary, a staging area safe from Communist attack. American planes took off from bases in Japan to attack North Korea. The United States employed many Japanese laborers to build airfields in South Korea and to unload ships in Korean ports. A number of Japanese ships were even recruited for the armada carrying UN troops to Inchon. And American military procurement orders to Japanese industry and trade during the Korean War were the decisive factor in the resurgence of Japan's economy. The Soviet representative on the Allied council that advised MacArthur in Japan was outraged by all this, but the great majority of Japanese were wholeheartedly in favor of U.S./UN intervention in Korea and were happy to support that effort.

The Japanese role in the Korean War provided much grist for the Communist propaganda mills, but the question of how genuinely the Chinese feared an American-Japanese invasion remains unanswered and, until Peking opens its archives, unanswerable. It seems most likely that Peking saw such an invasion as a very real danger in the long run if the United States/UN succeeded in unifying Korea. In the short run, talk of such an invasion was useful to mobilize the Chinese population and to embarrass the United States with charges that it was revealing its true fascist-imperialist nature by allying itself with Japan and sponsoring a revival of Japanese militarism.

Truman's second serious mistake of mid-September was to approve, on the eleventh, the National Security Council position paper known as NSC-81/1.[2] It was this paper, which had evolved directly from the State Department Policy Planning Staff paper of July 22, that provided the rationale for the United States to invade North Korea. The irony is that NSC-81/1 was really very cautious; it recommended that U.S. forces should probably *not* invade North Korea, and it predicted that America would probably have to accept a negotiated settlement that would preserve the North Korean regime. Because of this irony, General Omar Bradley in his autobiography called NSC-81/1 "a masterpiece of obfuscation."[3] It was no such thing. It was perfectly clear, consistent, and straightforward. (Perhaps the chairman of the Joint Chiefs of Staff didn't quite penetrate the paper's complex logic.) The real trouble with NSC-81/1 was that it was based entirely upon an erroneous analysis of probable Communist strategy.

The fundamental assumption of NSC-81/1 was that *before U.S./ UN troops crossed the 38th parallel*, the Soviet Union (and/or the People's Republic of China, acting on the Kremlin's orders) would either occupy North Korea and station troops immediately north of the border or else publicly deliver a formal and explicit ultimatum stating that if U.S./UN troops entered North Korea, the Soviets (and/or the Chinese) would oppose them militarily.

That incorrect conclusion was based on the correct assumption that the Soviets were not willing to give up North Korea but did not want world war. Given the tremendous importance of NSC-81/1, it is worth looking at the intervening logical steps, stripped of their legalisms and complexities. The drafters of the paper assumed that:

1. Both sides would assume that an overt *attack* by major Soviet forces upon U.S./UN troops — either north or south of the 38th parallel — would almost inevitably mean the outbreak of World War III.

2. The Soviets were not prepared to launch a world war to save North Korea. Thus the Soviets would take action that did not involve their attacking U.S./UN forces.

3. The PRC was not strong enough militarily to risk all-out war on its own with the United States/UN. The Chinese Communists would therefore launch a major attack on U.S./UN forces *only* if they had full Soviet support. But the Soviets would not give them such support, for a major Chinese attack with Soviet backing would inevitably escalate into the world war that the Soviets were determined to avoid. Hence Communist China would not attack U.S./UN forces on a scale that would lead to such a war. It was, however, possible that the PRC might soon send a relatively small

number of troops into South Korea to help the North Koreans fight a delaying action south of the 38th parallel while the Soviets occupied North Korea or mobilized their forces to back up an ultimatum warning U.S./UN forces not to cross the border. Since a small Chinese Communist force would not pose any serious threat to South Korea or to the U.S./UN troops, MacArthur was to deal with the Chinese as though they were North Koreans — to fight them as best he could within Korea but not to retaliate with any attacks upon the PRC.

4. If U.S./UN troops attacked Soviet and/or major Chinese Communist forces that had moved in to occupy North Korea, that would mean world war. Similarly, if U.S./UN forces crossed the 38th parallel in defiance of an explicit and public Soviet or Chinese Communist ultimatum, that would also mean world war.

5. It was most likely that the Soviets would occupy North Korea themselves, since, as NSC-81/1 stated, "the Soviet Union probably regards Korea as being in its own direct sphere of interest," and thus would not want the Chinese Communists to undertake an occupation that might entrench them in the area.

6. Washington assumed that Moscow understood the United States and its UN allies did not want world war, that all the UN allies might desert the United States if it tried to insist upon action that would probably lead to world war, and that the United States was not prepared to fight alone against the Communist bloc.

7. Given all of the above, Moscow would recognize that the only possible way in which it could save North Korea and yet avoid world war was to occupy North Korea or to issue an ultimatum before U.S./UN troops crossed the 38th parallel. Since that course of action would not involve a Soviet *attack* on U.S./UN forces, it would not provide a casus belli for World War III. Once the U.S./UN/ROK forces had crossed the parallel, however, the only way the Soviets could attempt to save North Korea would be by attacking those troops and trying to push them south of the parallel. Since that would mean world war, the Soviets would not choose that course. They would have to act *before* the United States and its allies had crossed the parallel.

This conclusion seemed so obvious to the drafters of NSC-81/1 that they felt that Moscow could hardly fail to reach it also. Indeed, they felt certain that this scenario would actually take place. They recommended that if all went as fully expected, the United States should accept that its goal of a unified, independent, and democratic Korea could not be achieved at the present time. When the Soviets occupied North Korea or issued their ultimatum, the United States would get the UN General Assembly to condemn the Communist move. The United States was then to engage in negotiations that would, unfortunately but inevitably, lead to the preservation of North Korea. The United States should, however, negotiate a settlement that would, in the words of NSC-81/1, "not leave the aggressor in an advantageous position that would invite a repetition of the aggression and that would undermine the authority and strength of the United Nations."

It would have been an easy and satisfactory ending to the war. The U.S./UN/ROK forces would have repulsed the North Korean invasion and saved South Korea. Truman could say that the UN had accomplished its original mission and that it would stop at the 38th parallel because it wished to spare the world an unimaginably devastating war. Since America's UN allies would certainly veto any action that was likely to lead to world war, Truman would not even have to bear the responsibility himself for deciding not to pursue the Communists into North Korea.

The serious problems all began with the paragraph of NSC-81/1 that stated,

> It is possible, but politically improbable, that no action will be taken by the Soviet Union or by the Chinese Communists to re-occupy Northern Korea or to indicate in any other way an intention to prevent the occupation of Northern Korea by United Nations forces before the latter have reached the 38th parallel. *In this unlikely contingency there would be some reason to believe that the Soviet Union had decided to follow a hands-off policy, even at the expense of the loss of control of Northern Korea* [emphasis added]. Only in this contingency could the U.N. ground forces undertake to operate in or to occupy Northern Korea without greatly increasing the risk of general war.[4]

The paper asserted that existing UN resolutions authorized UN troops to cross the 38th parallel in pursuit of North Korean forces in order to bring about their military defeat. A new UN resolution would be needed only to authorize the political goal of unifying Korea.

The main trouble with NSC-81/1 was that its predictions were wrong. Its error sprang from the fact that Moscow and Peking did not know that if they occupied North Korea or issued an explicit and public ultimatum, the U.S./UN/ROK forces would halt at the 38th parallel and negotiate an armistice. As far as the Soviets knew, if they occupied North Korea or issued an ultimatum, they would be running a grave risk of precipitating a world war. (Where were Kim Philby, Guy Burgess, and Donald Maclean when we needed them?) Of course, the United States couldn't very well announce its policy, for then the Communists could simply go ahead and issue an ultimatum with impunity, whether they were prepared to back it up with force or not. Alas, the United States could stop at the 38th parallel only if it could argue that the Soviets were definitely ready and willing to engage in world war in the event that U.S./UN forces entered North Korea. But NSC-81/1 held that the Soviets would occupy North Korea or issue an ultimatum precisely because they were *not* willing to risk world war in order to save North Korea.

Thus, although the logic of NSC-81/1 was superficially consistent with its stated terms, the deeper logic underlying the paper was hopelessly fallacious. There was never any real chance that things would come to pass as it predicted. And yet it stated its predictions with such conviction that when the Soviet Union failed to act as it was expected to, the United States proceeded confidently, despite many signs of danger, on a course of action that would ultimately cost the lives of perhaps a million people and that would wound, injure, or leave homeless several million more.

CHAPTER 21

Crossing the 38th Parallel

ONCE THE INCHON OPERATION had succeeded and Truman had accepted the faulty logic of NSC-81/1, events began to move swiftly and inexorably toward disaster. The success of Inchon indicated that the U.S./UN/ROK forces would probably be able to crush the remainder of the North Korean army and to unite Korea under Syngman Rhee if the Soviets didn't intervene. In that light, Senator William Knowland predictably declared that to halt the UN advance at the 38th parallel would be to appease the Communists. A Gallup poll early in October showed that 64 percent of the American public agreed.[1] Midterm elections were coming up on November 7, and Truman couldn't afford to ignore such sentiments. In order for the Democrats to retain their majority in both houses of Congress, he would have to appear, at least until the elections were over, militant enough to satisfy American voters but not so militant as to frighten the Chinese Communists.

Early in September the Truman administration continued its efforts to convince Peking that the United States had no intention of invading Manchuria and to dissuade the Chinese Communists from intervening in Korea. This, it seems, would have been the moment for America to demonstrate its good faith by making the magnanimous gesture of allowing the People's Republic of China to gain admission to the UN. But, of course, the problem of Formosa made such a move impossible. Therefore, as the September 19 opening of the General Assembly session approached, the United States took steps to counter anticipated resolutions to admit the PRC.

When Averell Harriman had visited MacArthur in Tokyo early in August, he had (as he wrote in his report to Truman) "emphasized" to the general

> the importance of getting evidence on the participation of the Chinese Communists in supporting the North Korean attack and present operations. There will be considerable support in seating

the Chinese Communists at the next meeting of the Assembly. I explained that if we could obtain real evidence of direct support for the North Koreans, this might be the reason by which we could prevent the seating of the Communists on the moral issue involved.[2]

MacArthur was more than happy to oblige. In his mid-September report to the UN, read at the Security Council meeting on the eighteenth, he stated that the Chinese Communists

> had furnished substantial, if not decisive, military assistance to North Korea by releasing a vast pool of combat-seasoned troops of Korean ethnic origin which provided the means for expansion of the North Korean army. A substantial percentage of all prisoners-of-war so far interrogated had received training in Manchuria, or had performed active service with the Chinese Communist Army.[3]

MacArthur conceded that most of the Koreans who returned from China had done so "during the year prior to the invasion," and he did not accuse the PRC of having aided North Korea since the invasion began. But his charges were effective enough. When the General Assembly convened the next day, the very first order of business was the vote on an Indian proposal to admit the PRC to membership. The proposal was defeated 33–16, with ten abstentions. The vote revealed an embarrassing rift between the United States and its principal ally, for Britain was among the nations that voted in favor of admitting the Chinese Communists.

A few ominous rumblings from Peking followed, but nothing strong enough to deter the United States/UN from crossing the 38th parallel. Nor, despite the obviousness of U.S./UN intentions and capabilities by the last week of September, was the expected bellicose ultimatum forthcoming from Moscow. Quite the contrary, in fact. Soviet foreign minister Andrei Vishinsky, who was representing his nation at the UN General Assembly session, was behaving in an uncharacteristically mild and friendly manner. His deportment was widely interpreted to signify that Moscow was in a mood to negotiate an end to the Korean War; he was apparently trying to create confidence in Soviet cooperativeness and pacifism so that the UN would negotiate a settlement leaving North Korea intact. But his behavior was taken as a sign of weakness. The United States and its UN allies perversely reasoned that if the Soviets were so eager for a negotiated peace, then it was probably safe to invade North Korea.

There was some hesitation in Washington about crossing the 38th parallel, but not much. The consensus was that the United States/ UN really had no other choice. For one thing, Rhee had announced on September 19 that ROK troops would pursue the North Korean army across the parallel whether U.S./UN forces did or not. That presented Washington with an awkward predicament. Although the Soviets and the Chinese Communists probably would not dare to attack U.S. troops, they might very well feel that they could safely render enough covert assistance to the North Koreans to enable them to defeat the ROKs. What if Rhee wouldn't listen to reason and, when South Korea was cleared of the enemy, persisted in ordering his men to cross the parallel? It would be most unseemly for American troops to have to restrain them forcibly in order to avert a calamity in the north. Besides, so went another argument, even a successful ROK invasion of North Korea could be a terrible embarrassment to the United States and the UN, for unless U.S./UN troops went along to police them, the South Koreans would probably indulge in a rampage of retributive atrocities and looting. Of course none of these arguments was decisive; they only provided additional rationales for the United States to do what it was determined to do anyway.

On September 27, two days before MacArthur restored Rhee's government to Seoul, the Joint Chiefs of Staff cabled orders based on NSC-81/1 to Tokyo. The orders stated MacArthur's goal unequivocally: "Your military objective is the destruction of the North Korean armed forces."[4] As long as neither the Soviet Union nor the PRC had occupied North Korea, had announced its intention to do so, or had issued "a threat to counter our operations militarily in North Korea," he could then cross the 38th parallel at once if it was necessary to do so in order to complete the destruction of the North Korean army. He was not, however, to make any statements about unifying Korea until the UN had passed a new resolution calling for unification. Furthermore, under no circumstances were MacArthur's ground forces to cross the Chinese or Soviet borders; neither was he to use his air or naval forces to attack Manchuria or Soviet territory in support of his ground operations within Korea. As an added precaution to allay Chinese and Soviet fears, no non-Korean ground forces were to operate "in the northeastern provinces bordering on the Soviet Union or in the area along the Manchurian border," though it was all right for U.S./UN planes to attack those areas of North Korea.[5] Truman, Dean Acheson, George Marshall, and the JCS all approved of these orders.

The next day MacArthur supplied the JCS with the details of his plan to invade North Korea.[6] General Walton Walker, who had not yet been informed of MacArthur's plans, was quoted in the American press the same day as having said that the troops under his command, including the ROK army, would halt at the 38th parallel for regrouping. Commentators speculated that Walker was awaiting explicit authorization from the UN to cross the border. But what the United States and its UN allies wanted most to avoid at that moment was any debate over whether to cross the parallel. The issue was simply too explosive, and no nation was willing to go on record as having proposed the move. The United States evaded responsibility for the decision by maintaining that the UN resolution of June 27 provided the legal basis for MacArthur to cross the parallel for the purpose of destroying the remainder of the North Korean army; by invading the north, he would simply be carrying out the UN's orders. As for America's allies, they were happy to be presented with a fait accompli.[7]

Accordingly, Secretary of Defense Marshall sent MacArthur a cable on September 29 "for his eyes only." The message, composed by Marshall and General Omar Bradley, said: "We want you to feel unhampered tactically and strategically to proceed north of the 38th parallel." Any further announcements like Walker's might "precipitate embarrassment in UN where evident desire is not to be confronted with necessity of a vote on passage of 38th parallel, rather to find you have found it militarily necessary to do so."[8]

Although America's allies maintained that the decision to cross the 38th parallel was a military one, to be made by the theater commander, they recognized the need for a new resolution to deal with the political situation that would, they felt certain, soon be created by MacArthur's conquest of North Korea and the unconditional surrender of Kim Il-sung's regime. Hence on September 29, at U.S. instigation, eight of America's friends and allies — Australia, Brazil, Britain, Cuba, the Netherlands, Norway, Pakistan, and the Philippines — introduced a resolution to the UN General Assembly recommending:

> (a) That all appropriate steps be taken to ensure conditions of stability throughout Korea,
>
> (b) That all constituent acts be taken, including the holding of elections, under the auspices of the United Nations for the establishment of a unified, independent and democratic government in the sovereign state of Korea.[9]

The connotation was clear enough. If the General Assembly adopted the resolution, MacArthur's plan to invade and conquer North Korea would have the tacit sanction of the UN. Peking responded swiftly and outspokenly. In a September 30 speech Chou En-lai declared: "The Chinese people enthusiastically love peace, but in order to defend peace, they have never been and never will be afraid to oppose aggressive war. The Chinese people absolutely will not tolerate foreign aggression, nor will they supinely tolerate seeing their neighbors being savagely invaded by the imperialists."[10] Washington dismissed the warning, which seemed to suggest that the Chinese Communists might give some token assistance to North Korea — certainly nothing to worry about.

The next day the first ROK troops crossed the 38th parallel, and MacArthur broadcast an ultimatum calling upon Pyongyang to surrender unconditionally, since "the early and total defeat and complete destruction of your armed forces and war-making potential is now inevitable."[11] No response came either from Pyongyang or from Moscow. But at midnight on the night of October 2–3, Chou dramatically summoned the Indian ambassador, K. M. Panikkar, to the Ministry of Foreign Affairs and informed him that if American troops crossed the 38th parallel, China would send troops across the Yalu River to participate in the defense of North Korea. He said, however, that if only ROK troops crossed the parallel, China would not intervene.

Panikkar immediately sent a report of the meeting to New Delhi, whence it was relayed to London and then on to Washington, where a State Department official awakened Acheson shortly after 5:30 A.M. on October 3 to give him the news.[12] The secretary of state dismissed the warning as "the mere vaporings of a panicky Panikkar."[13] The Indian ambassador did, in fact, have a reputation for overreacting to

Chinese Communist propaganda statements. In August, for example, he had claimed to have it on good authority that Peking was ready to attack Formosa unless the United States withdrew the Seventh Fleet. The fleet stayed, but no attack was forthcoming.

Although Chou's warning could easily have been taken as the ultimatum that NSC-81/1 had predicted, the manner of its communication suggested that Peking might not really be prepared to act on it. For Washington to forbid a U.S/UN invasion of North Korea on the basis of a threat that it judged to be a bluff would be to stop short of what might possibly be achieved in Korea. Only a public and unequivocal ultimatum from which Peking could not possibly back down without a severe loss of face could suffice to prevent the United States/UN from crossing the 38th parallel.

Acheson maintained that Chou had made his statement to Panikkar in an attempt to frighten America's allies away from supporting the eight-power resolution that would soon be submitted to a vote in the General Assembly. The UN, he said, could not give in to such "blackmail." Besides, Washington believed that the PRC neither would nor could intervene in Korea on a scale that would make any real difference to the outcome. Consequently, Peking probably wouldn't intervene at all, for fear that its action might lead to U.S./UN retaliation and involve China in a major war for which it was thoroughly unprepared. One U.S. official summed up the consensus when he said at this time, "I don't think that China wants to be chopped up."[14]

Why didn't Peking publicly issue a formal ultimatum? The answer is probably that the Chinese Communists, obsessed as they were with saving face and ignorant of the logic of NSC-81/1, assumed that a privately communicated warning would enable the United States and its allies to halt at the 38th parallel without losing face. The warning could remain a secret, and the United States and the UN could then claim that they had decided on the basis of their own sense of justice and superior morality that now that the original goal of repulsing the North Korean invasion had been achieved, the killing should be stopped and peace restored at once. Surely Peking would have reasoned that America and the UN would find it excessively embarrassing to halt in reaction to a publicly delivered threat from China.

The first U.S. ground troops — reconnaissance patrols from the 1st Cavalry Division — crossed the 38th parallel near Kaesong shortly past 5:00 on the afternoon of October 7. It was then very early in the morning of the seventh in New York. That afternoon the UN General Assembly passed the eight-power resolution calling for the unification of Korea, 47–5, with seven abstentions. The Soviets and their satellites had voted against the resolution, but the Russians had not sent troops into North Korea or issued an ultimatum. The logical time for such moves was now past. It appeared most likely that no insurmountable obstacle would block the way to a unified, independent, and democratic Korea.

However, Washington did at least acknowledge the possibility that substantial — though certainly not overwhelming — Chinese Communist forces might go to the aid of the North Koreans. On October 9 Truman approved a JCS directive to MacArthur instructing him:

> Hereafter in the event of the open or covert employment anywhere in Korea of major Chinese Communist units, without prior announcement, you should continue the action as long as, in your judgment, action by forces now under your control offers a reasonable chance of success. In any case you will obtain authorization from Washington prior to taking any military action against objectives in Chinese territory.[15]

Translated into straightforward English, that meant: "If the PRC sends forces into North Korea without first announcing publicly that the continuation of UN military operations in North Korea will mean all-out war with China, you should not hesitate to engage those troops, as long as you feel reasonably certain that you can defeat them without calling for reinforcements. Do not, under any circumstances, attack Chinese territory unless you have first received explicit instructions from Washington to do so."

On the morning of October 9 the Eighth U.S. Army began to advance in force across the 38th parallel near Kaesong. MacArthur's plan was to execute an encirclement across the narrow neck of the Korean peninsula, not far north of Pyongyang. The Eighth Army was to move up the western coastal corridor, capturing the North Korean capital along the way. After making an amphibious landing at the port of Wonsan, on the east coast, X Corps was to proceed northward to Hungnam and then inland. ROK troops would operate between the two U.S./UN forces, in the central mountains, where they could maneuver more easily than could the road-bound and equipment-heavy American troops. MacArthur hoped to entrap most of the North Korean army south of a line stretching from Chongju, on the west coast, to Hungnam, on the east, a line whose distance from the Manchurian border ranged from fifty to a hundred miles. Only ROK ground forces (assisted, however, by U.S./UN air power) would pursue any North Koreans who managed to evade the trap and make their way farther north.

The JCS felt that MacArthur's plan was flawed. They especially disliked the idea that the two main U.S./UN forces would be separated and unable to reinforce each other. Such a large gap between the Eighth Army and X Corps would make for poor communications and difficult coordination. They argued further that transporting X Corps by sea, rather than overland from Seoul, would create a logistical nightmare. They were right. Outloading the 1st Marine Division and its equipment so strained Inchon's limited facilities that for almost a week few incoming supplies for the Eighth Army could be unloaded there. Moreover, the 7th Division had to be moved by truck from Seoul to Pusan for its embarkation, choking the rather primitive highway, so that the northward flow of supplies from that major port to Seoul and on to the Eighth Army was greatly impeded.[16] But after Inchon the JCS were unable to prevail over MacArthur, who apparently liked the prospect of following the phenomenally successful Inchon landing with another amphibious operation.

MacArthur got his comeuppance. The X Corps landing at Wonsan was humiliatingly anticlimactic, since ROK troops advancing overland up the east coast captured the city on October 10–11 and the ships carrying the 1st Marine Division didn't arrive in the port until October 20; then it took another five days to clear the harbor of mines. On October 26 the Marines made what MacArthur called, in his report to the UN, an "administrative landing" at Wonsan.

On October 9, the day on which the Eighth Army began to cross the 38th parallel in force, President Truman decided that the need to avoid provoking the Chinese Communists and the Soviets into intervention during this final stage of the war was so great that he should have a face-to-face meeting with MacArthur to impress upon him the necessity for tact and caution. At this point one of the general's unauthorized broadsides or pronouncements could be disastrous. If he didn't fully concur with the administration's China policy, it was vital that he at least keep his dissenting views to himself.

Truman was already scheduled to speak in San Francisco on October 17. Since he would have to fly to the West Coast anyway, it seemed a relatively simple matter to leave Washington early and fly on to an island in the middle of the Pacific — Wake Island was selected, nearly five thousand miles from San Francisco and slightly less than half that distance from Tokyo — to meet the general on October 15. Secretary of Defense Marshall and the JCS felt that Truman shouldn't ask MacArthur to travel all the way to San Francisco to meet him, for that would take the general away from his Tokyo headquarters for too long during a crucial period of operations in Korea.

When Ambassador-at-Large Philip Jessup learned of Truman's plan, on the morning of October 9, he had some misgivings. That afternoon he wrote a memo to Acheson in which he said:

> In thinking over since lunchtime the plan for a meeting between the President and General MacArthur, I incline more and more to the view that such a meeting would be interpreted to foreshadow some major new American move in the Far East.
>
> If it is true, as I believe it is, that both the Chinese Communists and the Russians really believe that we are intent upon maintaining a foothold in Korea, they will interpret this meeting as bearing upon our plans to that effect. I think it reasonable to assume that the Chinese Communists fear that we are mobilizing forces in North Korea to invade Manchuria or to engage the Chinese armies there while Chiang Kai-shek makes a landing on the mainland to the south.[17]

Jessup didn't suggest that Truman discard his plan to meet with MacArthur, but he felt that in order to allay Peking's fears the president should issue statements, both before and after the meeting, stating its purpose and emphasizing his desires to localize the conflict, to end it as soon as possible, and to withdraw American troops from Korea.

Truman took Jessup's advice.[18] Nevertheless, it may very well have been the October 10 announcement of Truman's upcoming meeting with MacArthur that finally convinced the Chinese Communists that they had no choice but to intervene in Korea. It would have been difficult for Peking to believe that Truman would make such a long trip except to discuss with MacArthur policy of the very gravest and most momentous nature, such as a decision to reopen the Chinese civil war. That Truman would travel so far to meet MacArthur seemed to imply that the president might be capitulating to the general's aggressive views.

Another negative result of the meeting, less speculative and less dire than its possible influence on Peking's decision to intervene, was that it aggravated MacArthur's dislike of Truman into outright contempt. The conceited general couldn't imagine why Truman would want a meeting except to garner some reflected glory from the hero of Inchon in order to help the Democrats in the upcoming elections. The publicity-obsessed MacArthur claimed to despise the president for such motives and vowed that he would do or say nothing upon which Truman could capitalize for political advantage. Thus, as Truman noted in his memoirs, MacArthur did not bother to wear a tie on Wake Island; he left his shirt collar unbuttoned; and "he was wearing a cap that had evidently seen a good deal of use."[19] Furthermore, lest one of the photographers present snap a compromising shot of the gesture, he even refused to salute his commander in chief. That was all just posturing; what really mattered was that because MacArthur discounted the meeting as a political stunt, he refused to take seriously the very serious admonitions that Truman gave him regarding the delicacy of the situation in the Far East.

During the course of the principal meeting on Wake, Truman asked MacArthur directly, "What are the chances for Chinese or Soviet interference [in Korea]?" The general replied, "Very little. Had they interfered in the first or second months it would have been decisive. We are no longer fearful of their intervention. We no longer stand hat in hand. The Chinese have 300,000 men in Manchuria. Of these probably not more than 100–125,000 are distributed along the Yalu River. Only 50–60,000 could be gotten across the Yalu River.

They have no air force. Now that we have bases for our air force in Korea, if the Chinese tried to get down to Pyongyang, there would be the greatest slaughter."[20]

MacArthur's observations simply reconfirmed what the delegation from Washington already believed, namely, that neither the Soviets nor the Chinese Communists were likely to intervene in Korea. Truman and his advisers still accepted the logic of NSC-81/1, and the conclusions of that paper were supported by briefing memos that the CIA had given to Truman on October 12 to prepare him for Wake Island. The CIA analysis of Peking's intentions stated:

> While full-scale Chinese Communist intervention in Korea must be regarded as a continuing possibility, a consideration of all known factors leads to the conclusion that barring a Soviet decision for global war, such action is not probable in 1950. During this period, intervention will probably be confined to continued covert assistance to the North Koreans.[21]

As for Soviet intentions, the CIA averred:

> It is believed that the Soviet leaders will not consider that their prospective losses in Korea warrant direct military intervention and a consequent grave risk of war. They will intervene in the Korean hostilities only if they have decided, not on the basis of the Korean situation alone, but on the basis of over-all conditions, that it is to their interest to precipitate a global war at this time.[22]

Truman and his Wake Island delegation (which included General Bradley, Dean Rusk, and Jessup) returned to Washington full of optimism that the Korean War would very soon be brought to a gratifying conclusion. They believed that with each passing day, Chinese Communist intervention in Korea became less and less likely. That belief was strengthened by the reports beginning to filter out of Tibet in mid-October regarding the movement of Chinese troops into that nation. If China really were on the verge of intervening in Korea, they reasoned, then surely it wouldn't choose that moment to launch an invasion of Tibet.

MacArthur returned to Tokyo from Wake Island feeling as certain that the Chinese Communists would not intervene massively in Korea as he had been in 1941 that the Japanese wouldn't attack the Philippines. (He had then asserted that Japan realized possession of the Philippines would do very little for its economy, that the need to defend the islands after capture would be a strategic liability, and that an attack on the Philippines would expose the Japanese to retaliation from the United States. Therefore, an attack was out of the question.[23])

On October 17, two days after the Wake meeting, MacArthur's confidence prompted him to move the projected restraining line for U.S./UN operations northward, some sections of it by as much as sixty miles. The shift in the line meant that American troops would operate all around the crucial Chosin (Changjin) and Pujon reservoirs, vital parts of the hydroelectric system that supplied Manchuria with much of its power. This change was still in accord with the orders MacArthur had received from the JCS on September 27, for those orders specified only that he was not to use non-Korean troops in the areas immediately bordering on Manchuria and Siberia.

Two days later, meeting relatively little resistance, the Eighth Army occupied Pyongyang, which had been abandoned at the last minute by Kim Il-sung and his government. A great disappointment was that the parachute drop of the 187th Airborne Regiment at dawn the next day some thirty miles north of Pyongyang, along the main highway from the capital to Manchuria, failed to intercept the leaders of the North Korean regime as they fled northward.

What MacArthur did not know was that on October 14, Chinese Communist forces had begun to cross the Yalu in great secrecy. By October 24, when they were ready to strike, they would number nearly two hundred thousand in North Korea — more than three times the size of the largest force that MacArthur had estimated they could possibly get across the river. There would indeed be "the greatest slaughter," as MacArthur had predicted, but it would by no means be only of Chinese Communists.

CHAPTER 22

Peking's Decision to Intervene

WHY DID THE PEOPLE'S REPUBLIC OF CHINA
intervene in the Korean War, and what was its minimum goal?
The latter was certainly the preservation of a Communist North
Korean state, though it is possible that Peking could have accepted
the maintenance of such a state with greatly diminished territory — perhaps limited to the area above the Chongju-Hungnam line
(just below the 40th parallel), somewhat more than half the size of
North Korea on June 25.

Peking's position regarding North Korea was virtually identical to
the American position regarding Formosa. The Chinese Communists
were not out to impose their suzerainty on North Korea or even to
establish military outposts there. They were simply determined that
it not fall into enemy hands. Especially now that Japan was to be
rearmed in alliance with the United States, it was absolutely vital,
from Peking's point of view, that North Korea be Communist and
friendly and that it continue to exist as a buffer between Manchuria
and South Korea, the latter of which could be expected to fall increasingly under American and Japanese influence. Stalin undoubtedly held, even more strongly, similar views about North Korea's role
as Siberia's first line of defense. Neither the Soviet Union nor China
could possibly tolerate, directly on highly sensitive stretches of its
borders, an anti-Communist Korea allied with the United States and
Japan.

Consider how the United States would feel if the situation were
reversed. Let us imagine, for instance, that Florida was not a state
but rather two independent nations, a pro-American one north of the
29th parallel and, south of that line, a Communist one with close ties
to the Soviet Union and to Cuba. Let us then imagine that events
had taken place in Florida exactly mirroring the course of the Korean
War between June 25 and mid-October 1950. Communist troops from
the south — including South Floridians, Soviets, units from Eastern-
bloc nations, and possibly Cubans as well — would by then have

advanced well into North Florida. The United States would obviously be gravely concerned, if not downright hysterical, especially if an agricultural and industrial concentration like Manchuria's happened to be located in Georgia and Alabama and to receive much of its electric power from North Florida. Despite announcements by the Communists that they simply intended to unify Florida under an anti-American government and had no intention of invading the United States, it is unthinkable that Washington would stand by passively, even if it believed that the Communists really did have no immediate intentions of invading Georgia or Alabama. The American government and people simply would not tolerate such a next-door neighbor. (Think how disturbed we have been by a Communist Cuba, which is one hundred miles offshore.) Although the Communists might not have any present intentions of invading the southeastern states, they would be in a superb position from which to do so at their future convenience. Communist control of the southeastern electrical supply would be of immense value for diplomatic blackmail. And in the event of a world war, a Florida unified under an anti-American government would be a grievous liability to the United States. In such circumstances it would be bad enough to have only an anti-American South Florida, which would provide the Communists with a staging area on the continent of North America.

In that light, it was inevitable that any U.S./UN attempt to unify all of Korea would lead to Chinese Communist intervention. Neither the Soviet Union nor the PRC could afford to permit the creation of a unified, anti-Communist Korea. Since it seemed excessively dangerous for the Soviets to intervene directly, the Chinese would have to do the fighting, while the Russians would supply them with guns, tanks, planes, and other matériel. That Stalin required the Chinese to pay for all this equipment suggests a masterful twist of psychology. He evidently managed to convince the Chinese that a unified Korea posed much more danger to them than to the Soviet Union, which would refuse to intervene not because it was afraid of a war with the United States but rather because Korea was not really all that important. By forcing China to pay for its equipment, the dissemblingly nonchalant Kremlin would imply that Korea really was China's problem and that the Chinese were not doing the Russians any great favor by intervening. Mao Tse-tung would thus have no grounds for demanding any favors or concessions from Stalin in return.

The Chinese Communist intervention in North Korea was quite exactly the mirror image of the American intervention in South Korea in June. The Chinese wanted to do no more than was absolutely necessary for the achievement of their minimum goal, the permanent preservation of a Communist North Korean state. But they were willing to do *whatever* proved to be necessary in order to achieve that goal. (The U.S./UN invasion of North Korea was also quite exactly the mirror image of the North Korean invasion of the south. Kim Il-sung had believed that he could unify Korea under a Communist government because the United States would not intervene. The United States came to believe that it could unify Korea under an anti-Communist government because neither the Soviet Union nor Communist China would intervene.)

Only when the warning that Chou En-lai delivered through K. M. Panikkar failed to deter the United States and the UN from authorizing MacArthur to conquer all of North Korea did Peking decide that it had no recourse but to send troops into Korea. The memoirs of General Peng Teh-huai, who commanded the Chinese Communist troops in Korea, were published in Peking in 1984, as were those of General Nieh Jung-chen, who was chief of staff of the PRC army in 1950. Both suggest that Peking wrestled with the question of intervention for a full month after Inchon. Hu Yao-bang, a former secretary-general of the Chinese Communist party, stated in 1986 that Mao was so preoccupied and distraught by the issue that he didn't shave for a full week while reaching a final decision.[1] It appears that until about October 14 the Chinese were still hoping that U.S./UN restraint might spare them the necessity of intervening militarily in Korea on a massive scale. By that date, however, it was clear that unless China intervened the United States/UN could and would unify all of Korea under Syngman Rhee.

Chou told Panikkar at their midnight meeting that if only ROK troops crossed the 38th parallel, China would not intervene. We may assume he said that only because Peking believed that the North Koreans, with covert Chinese help if necessary, could defeat the ROKs. We may be certain that if only ROKs had crossed the 38th parallel and if they had shown signs of being able to inflict a total defeat on the North Koreans, so that only massive and overt Chinese Communist intervention could have prevented the unification of Korea, the PRC would not have hesitated to intervene. It makes no sense whatsoever to argue that Peking could have accepted the unification of Korea as long as it was carried out exclusively by ROK troops.

The question of Chinese Communist fears about a U.S./UN invasion of Manchuria is fascinatingly complex. On November 1, General Walter Bedell Smith, head of the CIA, stated in a memo to President Truman that "the Chinese Communists probably genuinely fear an invasion of Manchuria despite the clear-cut definition of UN objectives."[2] It seems unlikely, however, that Chinese Communist intervention in Korea was motivated primarily by any real fears in Peking that if its forces didn't halt the advance of U.S./UN troops in North Korea, those troops would keep right on going — across the Yalu River and into Manchuria. Peking would certainly have regarded that as a possibility, but not as a probability. The United States and the UN had, after all, strongly implied during the early stages of their intervention that they would not cross the 38th parallel and then, when they had reached it, had gone ahead and crossed without hesitation. On the other hand, an unprovoked invasion of China would be a very different matter — morally as well as militarily — from a punitive invasion of North Korea.

Peking's fears were probably of a more long-range nature, and those fears were not entirely groundless. A U.S. Department of Defense paper dated August 7, 1950, had emphasized the importance of Manchuria to the Soviet Union and had asserted that a unified Korea would weaken the Soviet and Chinese Communist hold on the region. "The bonds of Manchuria, pivot of this complex outside the U.S.S.R., would be weakened," stated the paper, "for a free and strong Korea could provide an outlet for Manchuria's resources and could also provide non-communist contact with the people there and in North China."[3] The United States may have had no intention of invading Manchuria, but that didn't mean that it had no designs upon the region.

The prospect of the unification of Korea also posed a more immediate threat to Manchuria short of an invasion. In his November 1 memo to Truman, General Smith mentioned that a South Korean general had recently said that, as soon as possible, ROK forces would cut off all electrical power supplied to Manchuria from northern Korea.[4] This was a plausible threat, since North Korea had abruptly stopped supplying the south with electrical power very shortly after the South Korean elections in May 1948. Such a danger alone would probably not have precipitated Chinese intervention in Korea, but it certainly added some incentive. The fact that most of the reservoirs, dams, and power stations of North Korea's hydroelectric system were located north of the Chongju-Hungnam line would probably also have helped to induce China to accept, if necessary, a reduced but very securely armed Communist North Korea with a southern border along that line.

The paradox is that although the Chinese Communists probably did not intervene in Korea because they feared an imminent U.S./UN invasion of Manchuria, they certainly did fear U.S./UN air attacks on Manchuria as a result of their decision to intervene. These fears were perfectly reasonable and genuine, and it was as a result of them that Peking evacuated the civilian population of some Manchurian cities and moved a number of vital Manchurian factories to Inner Mongolia. By doing so, Peking was able to give substance to its claims that it was intervening in Korea because it feared a U.S./UN invasion of Manchuria. This was terribly important, for if Peking could convince the world that its intervention was motivated by genuine fears of an invasion — that it was acting defensively against what it perceived as a real and immediate danger — the likelihood that the UN would authorize retaliatory strikes against Chinese territory would be greatly reduced.

Peking's strategy worked quite well. Witness, for example, General Smith's November 1 memo to Truman. On November 6, UN Ambassador Warren Austin told Dean Acheson that the Yugoslavian delegate to the Security Council was convinced the PRC "feels hydroelectric works are threatened and that UN forces constitute a genuine threat to Manchuria."[5] And on November 17 the U.S. consul general in Hong Kong informed the secretary of state that "strong feeling exists among Western Europeans in Hong Kong that Chinese Communists acted independently as result genuine fear that U.S. threatening Manchuria."[6]

If China was going to have to attack U.S./UN troops, it wanted to do so under conditions that would maximize the effectiveness of the strike and minimize the risks of retaliation against Chinese territory. Accordingly, Peking decided that it would make no declaration of war and that it would disavow responsibility for the presence of Chinese troops in Korea. The official line would be that the troops were volunteers who had been granted permission to go to the aid of their North Korean comrades.

The Chinese troops were not to attack until the U.S./UN forces had begun to penetrate the northernmost regions of Korea. For one thing, that tactic would reinforce the argument that China was really intervening only to protect the Manchurian border. For another, the fact that the Chinese supply lines would be very short and secure at that point, while the U.S./UN supply lines would be tenuous and vulnerable, would give the Chinese their greatest possible advantage over the supply-obsessed Americans. Moreover, the extremely harsh and mountainous terrain of the far north favored the agile Chinese over the road-bound U.S./UN forces. And finally, if anything went terribly wrong, Peking would be able to withdraw its troops quickly across the Yalu.

Washington's overly zealous determination to unify all of Korea under an anti-Communist government and Peking's unyielding resolve to prevent such a development were now set to collide.

CHAPTER 23

China Enters the War

IN HIS REPORT of December 28, 1950, to the UN, General MacArthur stated,

> By the middle of October 1950, the UN forces held in prisoner-of-war enclosures more than 130,000 North Korean military personnel, and had killed or wounded an additional 200,000. Thus, the personnel of the North Korean forces were eliminated, their equipment was captured or destroyed, and all but the northern borders of Korea was held by United Nations forces. For all practical purposes, the conflict with the armed forces of the former North Korean regime had been terminated.[1]

All of these claims were somewhat exaggerated, but MacArthur apparently believed them because he wanted to believe them. During the second half of October he felt certain that the successful completion of his mission was in sight, and he was eager to occupy the remainder of North Korea before anything could go wrong.

On October 24, which happened to be United Nations Day, MacArthur ordered his generals (in the words of the official Joint Chiefs of Staff record) "to drive forward toward the north with all speed and with full utilization of their forces."[2] In other words, he seemed to be overriding, on his own authority, the JCS proviso that only ROK troops were to be employed "in the northeastern provinces bordering on the Soviet Union" and "in the area along the Manchurian border." When the Joint Chiefs registered what was for them a strong protest, MacArthur replied that the ROK forces were insufficiently numerous to occupy the far north along the Yalu River and that most ROK units were effective only when they were integrated with U.S./UN forces led by experienced and dependable officers. He went on to invoke General George Marshall's cable of September 29, which instructed him "to feel unhampered tactically and strategically," and he claimed further that he was acting in accordance with what Truman had authorized on Wake Island — though the specifics of tactics had not been discussed there at all.

The profusion and the vague generalities of Washington's communications with MacArthur since June now began to hurt. The general could cite chapter and verse to justify whatever he wanted to do. In all fairness to him, it must be said that he did not exactly violate his orders at this point. He directed no U.S./UN troops toward "the northeastern provinces bordering on the Soviet Union" but instead sent the ROK army's best division. As for "the area along the Manchurian border," that could easily have meant a strip only a few miles wide south of the Yalu; here, too, only ROK troops reached the river in late October. Moreover, the restraining line that MacArthur had abolished was one of his own devising, not one that the JCS had drawn. Disturbed though the Joint Chiefs were by the orders that MacArthur issued on October 24, they did not countermand them.

Some Marxist-oriented historians have suggested that MacArthur decided to dispatch American troops toward the Yalu in the hope of provoking the Chinese Communists to intervene, thus giving him an excuse to attack China and to reopen the civil war. It seems most likely, however, that MacArthur based his decision on a precisely opposite line of reasoning. His only immediate goal was to complete the conquest of North Korea, and he wanted nothing to interfere with the achievement of that goal. He probably ordered American forces into the far north because he believed that although the Chinese Communists might feel they could safely attack ROK troops — perhaps making a lightning strike against them that would diminish their ability to defend a united Korea — the Chinese would not dare to attack Americans. Thus, if U.S./UN troops were in the vanguard of the drive toward the Yalu, so MacArthur must have reckoned, the Chinese Communists would stay out of Korea. He was wrong, but it was not his error of judgment that brought about the Chinese intervention.

As the Eighth Army continued its advance northward from Pyongyang against decreasing resistance, many American soldiers came to believe that the war was essentially over and that they would thenceforth be engaged in occupation duty. Many discarded the heavy ammunition and even the steel helmets that weighed them down, for they felt certain they would have no further need for such encumbrances.

While the 24th U.S. Infantry Division progressed up the western coastal road, ROK troops on its right flank swept in a northeasterly direction toward the Yalu. It was against these vulnerable ROK forces that the Chinese Communists launched their attack. On October 25 the Chinese annihilated a ROK battalion at Pukchin, about forty miles south of the Yalu. The next day a reinforced ROK reconnaissance platoon reached the town of Chosan, on the river, but it was promptly ambushed and decimated by Chinese troops wearing North Korean uniforms. Between October 26 and the twenty-ninth, the greatly out-numbered ROK 6th Division took a terrible beating in the area around the towns of Onjong and Huichon, and in the following days another ROK division just to the south was also hit hard. Many of the ROK units that were not wiped out broke and ran. By the afternoon of November 1 the ROKs were incapable of offering effective resistance; their dissolution exposed the right flank of the Eighth Army and created the threat of a Chinese attack on its rear.

As late as October 29 Washington was informed that the Eighth Army was "not inclined to accept reports of substantial Chinese par-ticipation in North Korean fighting,"[3] and for several days thereafter the State and Defense departments were still seriously considering a plan to send home many non-American UN troops in order to ease the burden they placed on U.S. supply services.[4] By November 1, however, extensive Chinese Communist intervention was becoming an accepted fact in Washington. On that date O. Edmund Clubb, director of the State Department's Office of Chinese Affairs, sent a memo to Dean Rusk explaining why the Chinese, if they were really intervening, would probably do so in great numbers: "It seems un-likely that the Chinese Communists would be prepared to venture into the Korean theater in such a limited manner as would confront them with the danger of being promptly bloodied and thrown out by a force which they themselves have consistently characterized as 'a paper tiger.' "[5]

Nevertheless, MacArthur's estimates of Chinese Communist strength in Korea remained deludedly low. On November 2 he told the JCS that although the Chinese had vast forces in Manchuria that could conceivably be used to reinforce those in North Korea, Peking had so far sent in a total of only about 16,500 men. There were, in fact, already more than ten times that many Chinese Communist soldiers in Korea.[6]

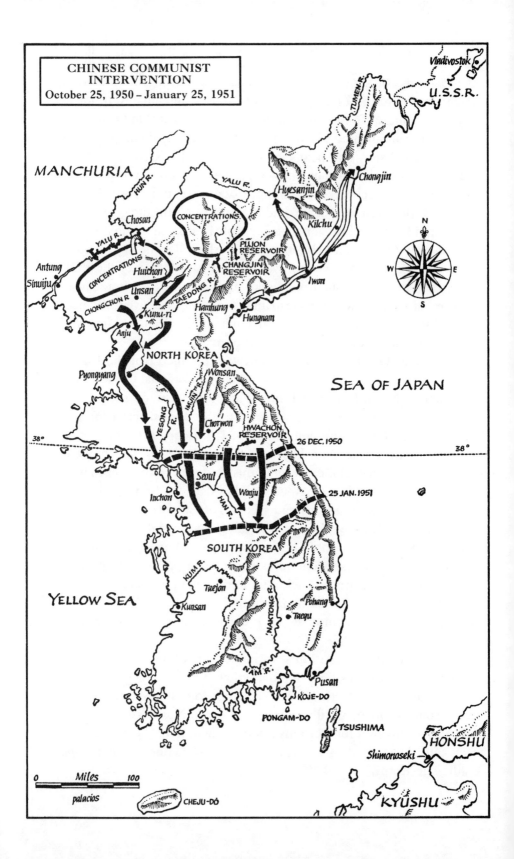

CHINESE COMMUNIST
INTERVENTION
October 25, 1950 – January 25, 1951

Vladivostok

U.S.S.R.

MANCHURIA

HUN R.

YALU R.

Hyesanjin

Chongjin

Kilchu

Chosan

CONCENTRATIONS.

YALU R.

CONCENTRATIONS

Huichon

Unsan

PUJON
RESERVOIR

CHANGJIN
RESERVOIR

Iwon

Antung

Sinuiju

CHONGCHON R.

TAEDONG R.

Kunu-ri

Hamhung

Hungnam

Anju

NORTH KOREA

N

W   E

S

Pyongyang

Wonsan

SEA OF JAPAN

YESONG R.

IMJIN R.

Chorwon

HWACHON
RESERVOIR

26 DEC. 1950

38°   38°

Seoul

Inchon

Wonju

25 JAN. 1951

HAN R.

SOUTH KOREA

YELLOW SEA

KUM R.

Taejon

NAKTONG R.

Kunsan

Pohang

Taegu

NAM R.

Pusan

KOJE-DO

PONGAM-DO

TSUSHIMA

HONSHU

Shimonoseki

0   Miles   100

palacios

CHEJU-DO

KYUSHU

The most serious problem at this stage was the failure of MacArthur's reconnaissance forces to detect the movement of 180,000 Chinese troops across the Yalu. The lightly equipped Chinese moved mostly on foot and at night; during the day they hid in the mountainous terrain that could easily swallow up even such huge numbers of men; and they were under strict orders not to light any fires, either in the daytime or at night. They thus managed to evade completely detection by the air reconnaissance upon which the United States/ UN depended.

The initial Chinese successes against the ROKs did not necessarily suggest that Peking had committed a large number of troops to Korea, for the Chinese had the tremendous advantage of surprise. Furthermore, because the ROK units were scattered, and difficult to reinforce on account of the terrain, the UN commanders concluded that the damage could have been done by a relatively small number of Chinese.

The first battle between American and Chinese Communist troops began late on the afternoon of November 1, as darkness was falling. The Chinese, having broken through the panicked ROKs around Onjong and Huichon, were swooping southwestward to hit the Eighth Army on its right flank and from behind. At about 5:00 P.M. the men of the 8th U.S. Cavalry Regiment, overconfidently occupying the town of Unsan, were startled by the frantic cacophony of blaring bugles and screeching whistles with which the Chinese, in the hope of inducing panic, regularly accompanied their attacks. Thousands of Chinese swarmed against American positions in the town and its vicinity. Attacking with mortars, grenades, rifle and machine-gun fire, and bayonets, they managed to surround some American units and to force others to retreat. At the end of two days of vicious fighting, nearly half of the 8th Cavalry's men had become casualties, and the regiment had lost much of its equipment, including tanks and artillery.

In the eastern sector of North Korea, ROK troops approaching the Chosin Reservoir were fired upon by Chinese forces on October 27. The ROKs then withdrew and waited a week for the arrival of a U.S. Marine regiment that had just disbarked at Wonsan. The Marines promptly engaged the Chinese, and in five days of heavy fighting south of Chinhung-ni (November 3–7) they inflicted casualties severe enough to force the battered Chinese division to flee northward.

It wasn't until November 2 that General Walton Walker, finally acknowledging that his forces had encountered a powerful new enemy, ordered the Eighth Army to retreat to the safety of the Chongchon River. MacArthur, reluctant to accept any fact that threatened to interfere with the swift completion of his conquest of North Korea, thought that Walker was overreacting. On November 4 the supreme commander conceded in a cable to the JCS that it was possible "that the Chinese Communist Government proposes to intervene with its full potential military forces," perhaps even that it would announce its decision. While "many foreign experts predict such action," he continued, "there are fundamental logical reasons against it and sufficient evidence has not yet come to hand to warrant its immediate acceptance." The general speculated that the Chinese would intervene cautiously and with very limited forces in the hope of achieving limited goals — of, as he put it, "salvaging something from the wreckage."[7]

Within two days MacArthur felt that more than sufficient evidence had come to hand. The Chinese, he believed, were now beginning to introduce enormous forces into Korea. To stop the movement of these forces he ordered the destruction of the North Korean end of the twin bridges across the Yalu connecting the Manchurian city of Antung with the North Korean city of Sinuiju, to which Kim Il-sung had moved his government. MacArthur did not bother to clear this radical order with the JCS, but General George Stratemeyer, commander of the Far Eastern Air Force, felt that it behooved him to check with Washington before carrying it out. It was early in the morning of November 6, Washington time, when Stratemeyer telephoned air force chief of staff Hoyt Vandenberg, who promptly called air force secretary Thomas Finletter, who in turn continued up the chain of command to Assistant Secretary of Defense Robert Lovett. Shortly after 10:00 A.M. Lovett arrived at the State Department for an emergency meeting, at which he informed Dean Acheson and Rusk that ninety B-29s were scheduled to take off from Japan less than three hours later.

The danger was that some of the bombs might accidentally land on the Manchurian side of the river, therby inciting China to even more drastic action than it was already taking. The British had made it clear to Washington that if the United States pushed China to all-out war, London would withdraw its forces from the UN Command. The prospect of losing Britain's moral support, far more than that of losing its military support, terrified the Truman administration and served as a salutary reinforcement of its resolve to avoid war with China.

As soon as Lovett had apprised him of the danger, Acheson called Truman, who had gone to Kansas City to vote in the next day's election. The president said that he would approve the action if it was "immediately necessary to protect our forces."[8] Otherwise, the mission should be canceled. At 11:40 A.M. Eastern Standard Time, only one hour and twenty minutes before the scheduled takeoff, the JCS sent MacArthur an order postponing the bombing, pending further assessment of the situation. General Omar Bradley wrote in his autobiography that "this was the first time Washington had ever directly (or even indirectly) countermanded a MacArthur order. It may even have been the first time the JCS had ever overridden a theater commander on a tactical operation."[9]

MacArthur was outraged and shot back a reply that ranted:

> Men and material in large force are pouring across all bridges over the Yalu from Manchuria. This movement not only jeopardizes but threatens the ultimate destruction of the forces under my command. . . . I cannot overemphasize the disastrous effect, both physical and psychological, that will result from the restrictions which you are imposing. I trust that the matter will immediately be brought to the attention of the President as I believe your instructions will result in a calamity of major proportion for which I cannot accept responsibility without his personal and direct understanding of the situation.[10]

Truman would not have been unjustified in relieving MacArthur of his command for such insolence. Instead, he authorized the bombing. MacArthur was, after all, the field commander, and if in his expert estimation a large portion of the U.S. Army was in danger of "ultimate destruction," then there really was no choice — unless Washington were to replace him with a commander who might assess the situation differently.

The JCS conveyed Truman's approval to MacArthur in a tone that bordered on sarcasm:

We agree that the destruction of the Yalu bridges would contribute materially to the security of the forces under your command unless this action resulted in increased Chinese Communist effort and even Soviet contribution in response to what they might well construe as an attack on Manchuria. Such a result would not only endanger your forces but would enlarge the area and U.S. involvement to a most dangerous degree.[11]

The reciprocal antagonism between Washington and MacArthur was now such that the Joint Chiefs' failure to recommend that the general be replaced must be condemned as irresponsible, since mutual antipathy and distrust were interfering with the prudent conduct of the war.

MacArthur certainly deserved to be relieved at that point, for his judgment had been rendered unreliable by his unyielding, and indeed obsessive, determination that he would let *nothing* stop him from achieving his goal of unifying all of Korea under Syngman Rhee. He felt that it was imperative to do whatever needed to be done to that end. Although he surely believed in all sincerity that total victory in Korea was vital to America's interests, there was clearly also a large element of personal ambition in his idée fixe. His tenure as the "Arkansas Mikado" was being brought to an end by the Japanese peace treaty preliminaries. And, although MacArthur told Truman on Wake Island that he had no political ambitions, it seems probable that he envisioned himself returning to the United States in the near future — as the victor over Japan, as the great statesman of the Japanese occupation, and as the heroic general who had defeated Communism in Korea — and being elected by overwhelming acclaim to the presidency. In any case, the Korean War would undoubtedly be his last military campaign, and he abhorred the thought that it could end with anything less than a resounding victory, an exclamation point to his career.

MacArthur was dangerous because he was blinded by his sense of destiny, by his evident certainty that God meant for him to liberate North Korea from Communism. The general certainly never doubted for a moment that if Washington would give him carte blanche, he would accomplish his mission in short order. As he had done in World War II, he viewed Washington as the adversary who foolishly prevented him from inflicting a swift and decisive defeat on their common enemy.

Reading through MacArthur's Korean War correspondence with Washington, one can hardly avoid suspecting that some of the general's messages were expressly manipulative rather than honestly informative, that some of his evaluations were tendentiously exaggerated or understated, that he often told Washington not what he really believed but rather what he calculated was most likely at that moment to lead the administration to authorize him to do what he passionately believed the situation called for. Those are some of the most serious charges that can be leveled against a military commander. They would be grounds not only for removal but also for court-martial. But the criterion that distinguishes a lie from an error is sincerity, and as unreliable, erratic, and unstable as MacArthur was, he seems to have been sincere. The problem was that he was such an egregious egotist that, in his view, a claim qualified to be considered a fact only when it happened to support what he believed — and he felt fully justified in believing only what he wanted to believe.

What about his abrupt shifts from one line of argument to another almost diametrically opposed, and then back again? MacArthur appears to have been afflicted with a manic-depressive syndrome. His mood swings were genuine, though pathological, and they clearly affected his judgments. His was an all-or-nothing personality, and overstatement was his natural mode of expression. Unfortunately, he had a history of living up to his overstatements, and so Washington had to take them seriously — especially after Inchon. No matter how questionable his evaluations may have seemed, or how inadvisable his plans, Truman could not afford to remove him, for too many powerful Republicans believed that MacArthur was certain to be right again.

The key exchange between MacArthur and Washington took place on November 8–9. On the eighth the Joint Chiefs sent the general a cable the effect of which, if not the intention, was to call his bluff. It said, in essence, that if the Chinese Communists were really committing forces to Korea on the scale that MacArthur had claimed two days earlier, then the United States/UN might have to accept that it would not be possible to complete the mission of destroying the North Korean armed forces. The obvious corollary was that the United States/UN would have to settle for an anti-Communist Korea that would incorporate something less than all of North Korea.[12]

Behind that cable, as revealed in a JCS memo read at the National Security Council meeting the next day, lay the thinking that it simply was not in America's best interest to undertake "a determined military operation" to drive major Chinese Communist forces out of Korea. "From the military standpoint," stated the memo, "the continued commitment of U.S. forces in Korea is at the expense of the more useful strategic deployment of those forces elsewhere." The Joint Chiefs recommended that "every effort should be expended as a matter of urgency to settle the problem of Chinese Communist intervention in Korea by political means, preferably through the United Nations, to include reassurances to the Chinese Communists with respect to our intent." In other words, the JCS were hoping that if the Chinese could be convinced that the United States/UN had no intention of attacking Manchuria, then perhaps they would agree to a compromise peace in Korea, possibly on the basis of a North Korea with reduced territory. Alas, all those sensible recommendations were undercut by the last paragraph, which stated that "pending further clarification as to the military objectives of the Chinese Communists and the extent of their intended commitments," MacArthur's orders to conquer all of North Korea "should be kept under review, but should not be changed."[13]

Horrified by the JCS cable of November 8, MacArthur replied with all the very considerable vehemence at his command. His message set forth his views so candidly that it is worth quoting extensively:

> In my opinion it would be fatal to weaken the fundamental and basic policy of the United Nations to destroy all resisting armed forces in Korea and bring that country into a unified and free nation. I believe that with my air power, now unrestricted so far as Korea is concerned except as to hydroelectric installations, I can deny reinforcements from coming across the Yalu in sufficient strength to prevent the destruction of those forces now arrayed against me in North Korea. I plan to launch my attack for this purpose on or about November 15 with the mission of driving to the border and securing all of North Korea. Any program short of this would com-

pletely destroy the morale of my forces. . . . It would condemn
us to an indefinite retention of our military forces along difficult
defense lines in North Korea and would unquestionably arouse
such resentment among the South Koreans that their forces would
collapse or might even turn against us. . . .

That the Chinese Communists after having achieved the complete success of establishing themselves within North Korea would
abide by any delimitations upon further expansion southward
would represent wishful thinking at its very worst. . . . To give
up any portion of North Korea to the aggression of the Chinese
Communists would be the greatest defeat of the free world in
recent times. Indeed, to yield to so immoral a proposition would
bankrupt our leadership and influence in Asia and render untenable
our position both politically and militarily.

I recommend with all the earnestness that I possess that there
be no weakening at this crucial moment and that we press on to
complete victory which I believe can be achieved if our determination and indomitable will do not desert us.[14]

Would that Truman or Acheson or the JCS could have said at this
point: "The Chinese Communists are perfectly capable of preventing
us from conquering all of Korea at a cost that we are willing to bear,
and it is now clear that they are prepared to do whatever they must
to that end." Unfortunately, Peking's intentions were far from clear
to Washington's highest echelon. The uncertainty was heightened by
the fact that on November 7 the Chinese Communists withdrew from
all the battlefronts in Korea and vanished into the hills. That they
did so was at least partly due to their inability to sustain combat for
more than about ten days at a stretch, after which time (in accordance
with a pattern that would govern their tactics throughout the remainder of the war) they would have to draw back for resupply and regrouping. But the Chinese must have believed that the spectacular
success of their attacks in the west, where they had concentrated their
main efforts, had demonstrated that they were capable of preventing
the complete conquest of North Korea and that it would be fruitless
for the United States/UN to persist. The Chinese surely hoped that
they had made their point and could therefore avoid further conflict.

Contrarily, optimists in the anti-Communist camp concluded that
the Marine victory in the eastern sector had convinced the Chinese

that they would do well to cut their losses and get out of Korea before it was too late.

On only one point was the Truman administration adamant: it was determined to avoid a full-scale war with China. In a November 7 memo to Dean Rusk, O. Edmund Clubb trenchantly articulated the philosophy to which the president and all of his principal advisers subscribed:

> Even if strikes against Manchuria meant nothing more than hostilities with China, it would be practically impossible to disengage from such a war, and while we were sinking slowly in the quagmire of that vast nation over which no victory could be anything but pyrrhic, we might see Japan, Germany, and all of Europe be lost before our eyes — and the United States placed in a danger such as it had never known before.[15]

But, calamitously, Truman did not dare to call a halt to MacArthur's advance, for it was not *certain* that one more step would lead irrevocably to full-scale war with China. Arguments for continuing the advance were in fact rife, foremost among them the NSC-81/1 chestnut that Peking could not possibly afford to risk all-out war with the United States/UN unless China could count on massive aid from the Soviets, who would not give such aid, since they feared that they would then be dragged into the war, which would inevitably become global. Furthermore, argued some diplomatic strategists, if Washington were to call for immediate negotiations, the Communists would claim that the United States was suing for peace after having suffered a stunning reversal. Such a scenario not only would place the United States at a bargaining disadvantage but might also encourage further Communist aggression. On the other hand, even if the complete conquest of Korea would not be possible, a new U.S./UN victory would strengthen the anti-Communist hand.

The results of the November 7 congressional elections were also a factor in limiting the administration's options. Many Americans saw the elections — the first since the Soviet development of an atomic bomb and the Communist victory in China — as a referendum on Truman's foreign policy, and many hearkened to the words of Harold E. Stassen (an unsuccessful candidate for the Republican presidential nomination in 1948), who declared on November 5 that the Truman administration had been "five years of coddling Chinese Communists, five years of undermining General MacArthur, five years of snubbing friendly freedom-loving Asiatics, and five years of appeasing the arch-Communist, Mao Tse-tung."[16] Rhetoric of this sort got Richard M. Nixon promoted from the House to the Senate and won Senator Robert A. Taft the most emphatic victory of his career. Although the Democrats retained small majorities in both houses of Congress, the alliance between the Republicans and many southern Democrats (the Dixiecrats) meant that Truman could not count on getting any measure passed automatically. In order to accomplish anything with the new Congress, the president would have to appease the Mac-Arthurites.

On November 6 MacArthur bombastically charged Peking with having

> committed one of the most offensive acts of international lawlessness of historic record by moving, without any notice of belligerency, elements of alien Communist forces across the Yalu River into North Korea and massing a great concentration of possible reinforcing divisions with adequate supply behind the privileged sanctuary of the adjacent Manchurian border.[17]

Five days later Peking replied indirectly through a spokesman for its Ministry of Foreign Affairs, who acknowledged that "the Chinese people" were fighting in Korea and claimed that they were following the example set by "the progressive people of France, inspired and led by Lafayette" in the American Revolution and by the Americans of the Abraham Lincoln Brigade in the Spanish civil war. The spokesman concluded by saying that "since the expression of the Chinese people's will . . . is so reasonable, so just, so righteous, magnanimous, and so flawless, the People's Government of China sees no reason to prevent their voluntary departure for Korea."[18] These were hardly the words of a regime that had any intention of backing down in Korea.

CHAPTER 24

"An Entirely New War"

BY MID-NOVEMBER the Eighth U.S. Army had retreated to secure positions along the Chongchon River, in western Korea. That would have been a good place to dig in and to establish a permanent boundary. But MacArthur was unshakably determined to launch a new offensive that would, he felt certain, speedily complete the unification of Korea and bring the war to an end.

In preparation for his new attack, MacArthur initiated a two-week-long aerial bombardment of the area between U.S./UN lines and the Yalu River. He hoped that by destroying the Korean end of all the Yalu bridges he would make it impossible for China to send any more troops into Korea or to supply the men who were already there. Having sealed off North Korea from Manchuria, his planes would so severely pound the enemy forces hidden in the northern wastes that the U.S./UN/ROK advance to the Yalu, encountering little resistance, would take only about ten days. To this operation MacArthur allocated every available bomber in his command and ordered that their crews fly missions without respite until they were utterly exhausted. On November 17 the general told Ambassador John Muccio that "the Air Force was . . . destroying all resources in the narrow stretch between our present positions and the border. Unfortunately, this area will be left a desert."[1]

Because of the need to take extreme measures to avoid hitting the Chinese end of the Yalu bridges, MacArthur's planes succeeded in rendering useless only four of the twelve major bridges along a 150-mile stretch of the border. Over those that remained, as well as over hastily emplaced pontoon bridges, the Chinese continued to pour men and matériel across the Yalu in numbers that jeopardized, and even threatened ultimately to destroy, MacArthur's forces. By the beginning of the fourth week in November, when the United States/UN was ready to launch its end-the-war offensive, the Chinese Communists had 300,000 to 340,000 troops in Korea, most of them well concealed in the central mountains; in addition, approximately 65,000

North Koreans had been regrouped and reequipped. Neither Mac-
Arthur's reconnaissance forces nor his bombers found these legions.
All the thousands of tons of bombs dumped on North Korea during
November seem to have missed the Communist forces completely.

American military intelligence reported rumors from various
sources claiming that Peking had 200,000 men in Korea, but it was
not at all convenient for MacArthur to credit any such figure — and
so he didn't. On November 17 he told Muccio (as the ambassador
informed the State Department) that he was "sure the Chinese Communists had sent 25,000, and certainly no more than 30,000, soldiers
across the border" and insisted that "they could not possibly have
got more over with the surreptitiously covert means used."[2] A week
later, at the beginning of the UN Command offensive, his headquarters' estimate was larger but still irresponsibly far from accurate:
40,000 to 80,000 Chinese Communists and 83,000 North Koreans.

Even if MacArthur had had accurate figures at his disposal, and
had chosen to believe them, he might very well have been confident
anyway. Against the Communists was ranged a U.S./UN/ROK army
of approximately 440,000 men, of whom about half were service-and-
supply troops. Since in the Communist forces the logistical "tail" was
much smaller than the combat "head," the Communist combat troops
in North Korea outnumbered those of their enemies. Nevertheless,
the Americans were contemptuous of Chinese fighting abilities and
would have maintained that any Communist numerical advantage
would be canceled out by vastly superior American armor, artillery,
and air power.

The Chinese were, in fact, a formidable enemy. Chinese soldiers
were inured to hardship; they were accustomed to living in the open
in all extremes of weather and to subsisting on small amounts of food.
They were trained and experienced in guerrilla warfare and were
adept at hiding, at improvising, and at maneuvering on foot in the
most inhospitable terrain. And they had been indoctrinated to believe
that they were defending their homeland against the monstrously
vicious American imperialists, who were as bad as the Japanese, if
not worse.

MacArthur's battle plan was an extension of that which he had pursued
in October. Some units of the Eighth Army were to advance northward

along the west coast, while others were to move inland in a northeast-erly direction. The ROKs were to be responsible for the area around the central mountains and for the northeastern provinces nearest the Soviet border. X Corps was to move northwestward from the east coast to meet up with the Eighth Army near the Yalu and close a giant trap upon the enemy, which would be surrounded and de-stroyed. Meanwhile, U.S./UN planes would continue to prevent the movement of Chinese reinforcements across the river, which would then (as MacArthur saw it) provide the most secure possible northern boundary for a unified Korea.

MacArthur felt that it was imperative to complete this operation before the worst of the winter weather set in, for although U.S./UN/ROK ground troops could finally blow up the Korean end of all the bridges once they had reached the Yalu, the freezing over of the shallow river would render the bridges irrelevant. U.S./UN/ROK troops would by then have to have established an unbroken defensive line along the river to keep the Chinese from sending reinforcements across the ice. An added incentive for haste was the fact that the UN Command troops were not adequately clothed, equipped, or trained for fighting in the Siberian cold of a North Korean winter.

The JCS were worried about the separation of the Eighth Army and X Corps, for if the Communists threw all of their weight against one of these forces, and if that weight was sufficient to pose a real danger, the other major force would not be able to cross the seventy-five miles of impassable mountains to provide relief. Except through a few narrow passes, the forbidding central mountains — a labyrinth of treacherous, knifelike ridges and precipitous, uncrossable gorges — were penetrable only over a few single-file paths. Assuming that rem-nants of the North Korean army had taken to the mountains and would adopt guerrilla tactics to harass his forces, MacArthur assigned the central area to the ROKs, at least some of whom had experience in fighting Communist guerrillas in the mountains of South Korea. But he simply couldn't believe that enemy troops could assemble or maneuver in such terrain in numbers sufficient to endanger, let alone to defeat, his forces. It is ironic that his strategy should have hinged on such blind confidence, for the success of his masterstroke at Inchon had been based on the enemy's belief that he couldn't possibly land enough troops there to make a difference. MacArthur scorned the idea that the Chinese Communists could be as daring and as determined as he had been at Inchon.

He was not, however, totally oblivious to the dangers that would be raised by his campaign. On November 14 he had a discussion with his principal political adviser, Ambassador William J. Sebald of the State Department, who prepared a memo of the conversation and sent it to Dean Acheson and Dean Rusk. Sebald reported that MacArthur had said,

> Should the planned operation fail and the Communist Forces continue to stream into North Korea from Manchuria, he saw no alternative, from a military point of view, to bombing key points in Manchuria. He said that if this should become necessary "the fat would be in the fire," because such operations would, in his opinion, bring about a counter-move by Soviet Russia. Such counter-move, he felt, could only lead to a spreading of the war and he therefore hoped that it would not be necessary to resort to such drastic action.[3]

But all of that remained quite comfortably hypothetical in MacArthur's mind, since he was sanguine about the likelihood that his operation would succeed.

By mid-November Washington was convinced that Peking had intervened in Korea because it feared an invasion of Manchuria. The Truman administration naively hoped that if Peking's fears could be assuaged, then the Chinese forces would withdraw and allow MacArthur to get on with his conquest of North Korea. Both Truman and Acheson made major speeches to reassure the Chinese Communists.[4] But the primary American effort was the submission (together with Britain, Cuba, Ecuador, France, and Norway) to the UN Security Council of a draft resolution calling upon Peking to withdraw its forces from Korea and affirming "that it is the policy of the United Nations to hold the Chinese frontier with Korea inviolate and fully to protect legitimate Chinese and Korean interests in the frontier zone." In the hope that a threat might succeed if reassurance failed, the resolution went on to call "attention to the grave danger which continued intervention by Chinese forces in Korea would entail for the maintenance of such a policy."[5] Peking responded by charging that the United States had intended all along to invade Manchuria and that Washington was engaged in a propaganda campaign to convince the world that Chinese action in Korea was providing both provocation and justification for such an invasion.

The British government was especially worried about the possible escalation of the war and strongly advocated reassuring the Chinese and the Russians by a UN promise to create a demilitarized zone on the Korean side of the Manchurian and Soviet borders. The British also voiced strong objections to letting U.S./UN troops advance all the way to the Yalu, even if they had promised to withdraw once the enemy had been defeated.[6] But such proposals did not appeal to the Truman administration, which had to contend with such influential characters as Senator William Knowland, who said that the UN should insist on a demilitarized zone *north* of the Yalu.

Some historians have charged that MacArthur went ahead with his November 24 offensive despite pleas from Washington. This is simply not true. On the afternoon of November 21 there took place in the Pentagon what amounted to a meeting of the National Security Council without Truman; present were the JCS, the secretaries of state and defense, and key officials of those departments. The minutes of that meeting record that "General Marshall expressed satisfaction that Mr. Acheson had stated his belief that General MacArthur should push forward with the planned offensive."[7] The nearly unanimous assumption at the meeting was that the offensive would succeed. Afterward, General J. Lawton Collins informed MacArthur that "the consensus of political and military opinion was that there should be no change in your mission" to complete the destruction of the enemy forces.[8]

Collins did, however, warn the general that it was possible America's UN allies might insist that the offensive be halted short of the Manchurian and Soviet borders and that a demilitarized zone be created. MacArthur replied with his usual cries that anything short of the occupation and unification of all of Korea would be disastrous,[9] to which Collins responded with nothing more than a few tentative suggestions for the commander's consideration.

November 23, the day before MacArthur's big offensive was to begin, was Thanksgiving. Despite the priority that might reasonably have been given in such circumstances to supplying units at the front with ample reserves of ammunition, the energies of the American logistical services were strained to provide every man, even in the most remote advance outposts (reaching them by airdrop if necessary), with a turkey dinner including all the traditional trimmings: mashed potatoes, gravy, cranberry sauce, buttered squash, mince pie, and even after-dinner mints.

The next day MacArthur flew into Sinanju to fire the starting gun for the race to the Yalu. His message, proclaiming that China would not intervene further and that the war would be over in two weeks, was meant to raise morale, but its effect was to send his men into battle totally unprepared for the immense struggle that lay ahead. Believing that they would be home by Christmas, the U.S./UN forces set off for the north. [10]

Three days earlier a small detachment of the 17th Regiment of the 7th U.S. Division had reached the Yalu at Hyesanjin, in the eastern sector. They were the only Americans ever to reach the river.

The Eighth Army began its advance in the west without any ominous portents. By the afternoon of the twenty-fifth, some units had progressed as much as eight miles against token resistance. But as soon as darkness had fallen, the Chinese Communists struck the ROK II Corps near Tokchon, on the Eighth Army's right flank. Overwhelmed, most of the poorly trained and poorly led ROK divisions quickly collapsed into chaotic fragments. By November 27 it was becoming clear to General Walton Walker that there was hardly any effective barrier between two hundred thousand Chinese Communists and his Eighth Army and that — despite the vaunted superiority of American armor, artillery, and air power — the U.S./UN forces were in serious trouble. That same day huge Chinese forces descended upon U.S. Marines and infantry around the Chosin Reservoir, in the eastern sector.

During the night of November 27–28 (Washington time), MacArthur sent the Pentagon one of his most accurate messages of the war:

> The developments resulting from our assault movements have now assumed a clear definition. All hope of localization of the Korean

conflict to enemy forces composed of North Korean troops with alien token elements can now be completely abandoned. The Chinese military forces are committed to North Korea in great and ever increasing strength. No pretext of minor support under the guise of volunteerism or other subterfuge now has the slightest validity. We face an entirely new war.[11]

CHAPTER 25

World War III?

THE "POLICE ACTION" was becoming "a major war confined to a small area." The question on everyone's mind was whether the Korean War was going to escalate uncontrollably into World War III.

At least until the middle of January 1951 the United States and its allies feared that it might. On December 9, Truman wrote in his diary that despite his having "worked for peace for five years and six months," and despite "conference after conference on the jittery situation facing the country," it looked to him "like World War III is here."[1] One of the greatest triumphs of his administration — one would have to say the greatest if the measure of a triumph is proportionate to the horror of its alternative — was its success after all in preventing the crisis precipitated by massive Chinese Communist intervention in Korea from developing into a world war.

The administration was held on a steady course by a new analysis of Communist global strategy. According to its logic, since the People's Republic of China had entered the Korean War on a scale that might enable it to drive U.S./UN forces completely out of Korea, that could mean only that Stalin was now willing to risk world war. Perhaps he was even planning to launch a world war in the near future and had ordered the PRC to intervene in Korea specifically in order to get the United States so bogged down and overcommitted in Asia that it would be forced to neglect the buildup of NATO. The Soviets could then safely invade vulnerable Western Europe.[2]

Given such a possibility, felt the Truman administration, the United States should disengage from Korea as soon as possible and should under no circumstances allow itself to become embroiled in a major war with the PRC. The United States should instead focus its attention and resources on countering the Soviet threat to Western Europe. Korea was a sideshow, a distraction that had to be kept in proper perspective. As for a major war with China, that, said Truman, would be "a gigantic booby trap."[3] At the MacArthur hearings in the spring of 1951 General Omar Bradley explained, "So long as we regarded the Soviet Union as the main antagonist and Western Europe as the main prize," a full-scale war with China would have been "the wrong war at the wrong place at the wrong time and with the wrong enemy."[4]*

Although the United States was beginning a rapid and massive buildup of its armed forces at home and abroad, MacArthur's forces in Korea still comprised most of the U.S. Army's trained and active divisions. The destruction of those forces would obviously be a catastrophe with the gravest international repercussions. If the U.S. Army were decimated in Korea, then the Soviets might very well seize the opportunity to invade Western Europe and/or Japan before America could train and equip replacements.

During the first week of December, Washington feared that the destruction of the U.S./UN forces in Korea was a real possibility. The safety of those forces therefore became the paramount consideration in determining U.S. military policy. The adopted strategy was to withdraw the Eighth Army into a defensive perimeter around Seoul-Inchon and hope that the Chinese wouldn't pursue it below the 38th parallel. X Corps was to be withdrawn into a defensive perimeter around Hungnam, from which it could be transported by sea to reinforce the Eighth Army, at Seoul. If the Chinese surrounded the Seoul-Inchon beachhead, the Eighth Army could be shipped to Pusan to establish a new defensive perimeter there. Or, if it was deemed futile to try to maintain a position in Korea, the U.S./UN forces would already be in beachheads from which they could immediately be evacuated to Japan.

Since the Communists seemed to be in an aggressive mood, Washington feared that an invasion of Japan might be next on Stalin's agenda. If it became clear that this was Stalin's plan, then U.S. forces would have to abandon Korea and rush to the defense of far more important Japan, where not even a single American regiment remained. The Joint Chiefs of Staff made it very clear to MacArthur

---

* Bradley's "wrong war" wording has often been misapplied to refer to the Korean War itself.

that, aside from ensuring the safety of his forces, his foremost responsibility was to guarantee the safety of Japan.[5]

From early December 1950 until mid-January 1951 it was U.S. policy to withdraw the U.S./UN/ROK forces into the safe refuge of beachheads as quickly as possible and with a minimum of casualties, since it seemed hopeless to try to stand and hold. The worst of the fighting occurred at the very beginning of December, when the Chinese were able to mount heavy attacks against U.S./UN escape routes. Once the United States/UN had managed to break out of the Communist traps, the fighting tapered off, since the mechanized U.S./UN forces moved faster than could the Communists and thus had relatively little need to engage in delaying actions.

Along the western sector of the front, the Eighth Army began its general retreat on November 28. On its right flank the 2nd U.S. Division, which the ROK collapse had exposed to ferocious Chinese attacks from the north and the east, had the job of blocking the Communist advance, while the Eighth Army divisions closer to the west coast moved southward. On November 29 the 2nd Division was ordered to begin its own retreat. The next afternoon it ran into an ambush in which it suffered more than 3,000 casualties and lost most of its equipment. Only scattered remnants of the division managed to reach safety. But most of the Eighth Army — thanks largely to the speed of its retreat, covering 120 miles in ten days — was able to make its way south fairly intact. That force evacuated Pyongyang on December 5 and kept on withdrawing, racing for the 38th parallel.

The going was much tougher in the X Corps sector, in the east, where the 1st Marine Division's retreat from the Chosin Reservoir — not only battling through a gauntlet of Chinese hordes but also struggling with "General Winter's" relentless subzero winds — took on the epic proportions of Napoleon's retreat from Moscow.

On November 27 a force of 10,000 Marines had begun its advance along the only road — a primitive dirt track — that led northwestward from the western side of the Chosin Reservoir, through the central mountains, to the junction of Mupyong-ni, from which they could proceed to join up with Eighth Army forces near the Yalu. That first night they were attacked by 30,000 Chinese Communists. Additional

Marines were strung out all along the one road that led from the reservoir back to the beachhead of Hungnam. Some 50,000 Chinese troops had taken up positions dominating key points along that road, and another 40,000 were in reserve nearby.

The Marines west of the reservoir began fighting their way southward on December 1 along the tortuous, barely negotiable, deep-frozen trail, through near-lunar wastes, to Hagaru, at the Chosin's southern tip. There, on December 3, they met up with the survivors of three battalions of the 7th U.S. Division, which had been savaged a short distance to the northeast. Out of the battalions' 2,500 men, only 1,000 had reached Hagaru, and of them only 385 were able-bodied.

As the Marines had moved northward in mid-November, their commander, Major General Oliver P. Smith, had been very apprehensive about massive Chinese intervention and had been careful not only to advance as slowly as possible but also to leave detachments of men and to stockpile supplies at every village along the road that was the Marines' umbilical cord to Hungnam. Now his caution paid off, for his men were going to have to fight their way out. If he had been less circumspect, the Chinese might well have succeeded in surrounding the Marine division and annihilating it.

Smith meant what he said when, on December 4, he exhorted his men, "Retreat, hell! We're only attacking in another direction." Against all odds, he shepherded his division to safety by the end of another week of valor. During the exodus more than 700 Marines were killed, another 3,500 wounded, and hundreds stricken with severe frostbite. It was estimated that some 15,000 Chinese Communists had been killed by the Marine ground forces and another 10,000 by their air cover.

While the Eighth Army and X Corps withdrew into their beachheads, Washington contemplated the possibility of disaster. The administration decided that if the Communists penetrated the defensive perimeter around Seoul or Hungnam and seemed likely to massacre the U.S./UN forces before they could be evacuated, then the United States/UN should resort to such drastic measures as bombing Manchuria in order to force Peking to call off its troops.[6] The military was admirably reluctant to use atomic bombs.

Truman and his advisers considered the possibility of evacuating all U.S./UN forces from Korea as soon as they reached their beach-heads, without waiting to see whether the defensive perimeters would hold. But that policy was rejected. The United States could not just pull out of Korea and leave the South Koreans to their dismal fate. Such a cowardly and dishonorable course of action would imperil all of America's alliances and, the administration feared, would probably consign all of Asia, in the long run, to Communist domination. There was some talk of establishing Syngman Rhee's government and army on the island of Cheju (Cheju-do), off the southern coast of Korea, just as the Chinese Nationalists had sought refuge on Formosa.[7] But that idea was also rejected except as a last resort. Washington concluded that a Dunkirk-style forced evacuation in the face of dire military necessity, terrible emergency though it would be — posing the danger of atomic warfare if it looked as though the U.S./UN troops would not be able to escape in time otherwise — was the only honorable way in which those forces could leave Korea. Short of that, they would have to hang on as best they could.

One thing seemed very clear. The United States would now have to renounce, once and for all, its goal of unifying Korea militarily. Under the present circumstances, the United States/UN would have to redefine its maximum military aim as the restoration of the status quo ante bellum. The United States/UN would fight with limited forces and limited strategy for a limited purpose, while continuing to advocate the unification of Korea by political means. Although the Truman administration firmly embraced these revised war aims during the first week of December, it did not, then or later, send MacArthur any official and unequivocal statement of the new policy. This lapse in communications was due partly to the fact that the South Korean ambassador in Washington repeatedly informed the U.S. State Department that his government was "unalterably opposed" to a return to the status quo. Rather than risk trouble with Rhee during this critical period, Truman decided to present him with a fait accompli when the time came.

Truman's limited-war policy was anathema to MacArthur. On November 30 he had informed the JCS that "everything leads to the conclusion the Chinese forces have as their objective the complete destruction of the United Nations forces and the securing of all of

Korea."[8] The PRC, in other words, was not going to fight a limited war for the limited objective of pushing the United States/UN out of North Korea. The PRC had bottomless reserves of men and, MacArthur argued, was prepared and able to send unlimited reinforcements into Korea from Manchuria and even from more remote areas of China. MacArthur, extremist as always, seemed to imagine that if Washington didn't heed his warnings and entreaties, he would soon be fighting in Korea the entire Chinese Communist army of five million men. Indeed, on December 3 he cabled the JCS, "This small command actually under present conditions is facing the entire Chinese nation in an undeclared war and unless some positive and immediate action is taken, hope for success cannot be justified and steady attrition leading to final destruction can reasonably be contemplated."[9]

Nothing less than "ground reinforcements of the greatest magnitude" and permission to bomb Manchuria could satisfy MacArthur. As he told General J. Lawton Collins on December 7, he wanted his forces augmented by 75,000 U.S./UN troops, in addition to which he wanted Washington to allow Chiang Kai-shek to send between 50,000 and 60,000 Chinese Nationalist troops to Korea. He also wanted authorization to blockade the Chinese coast. He felt that if Washington was not prepared to grant those demands, and if the Chinese Communists were not willing to halt their advance at the 38th parallel, then the United States should abandon Korea at once.[10] The JCS notified MacArthur that he would have to manage with the men he already had. As for the Chinese Nationalists, the JCS countered that if Chiang sent men to Korea, the far more efficient and valuable British troops would leave.

When MacArthur continued to press his demands throughout December, the JCS finally told him, in mid-January, that they would consider the possibility of U.S./UN naval and air attacks on mainland China only "at such time as the Chinese Communists attack any of our forces outside Korea." In the same message, however, they informed the general that they would recommend to the National Security Council that the United States "remove now restrictions on operations of the Chinese Nationalist forces and give such logistic support to those forces as will contribute to effective operations against the Communists."[11] The NSC shelved the recommendation.

MacArthur was outraged that the JCS refused to grant his demands but nevertheless ordered him to hold the Korean beachheads. He blustered to a *U.S. News & World Report* interviewer that the refusal put him under "an enormous handicap, without precedent in military history."[12] (Ironically, on Wake Island he had given the presidential press secretary a double-talk statement, saying, "No commander in the history of war has had more complete and admirable support from the agencies in Washington than I have during the Korean operation."[13]) In another interview he blamed America's allies for insisting upon the restrictions against drastic action and accused them of selfishness and shortsightedness.[14] He wanted the historical record to be clear: it would not be his fault if the United States/UN lost the Korean War.

Truman became so fed up with MacArthur's defeatist and buckpassing blather that on December 5 he ordered American military officers and diplomatic officials from then on to clear with the State Department all public statements regarding foreign policy — including those made during interviews — before releasing them for publication.[15] The Republican right was incensed by what it correctly interpreted as a move to gag MacArthur.

Many powerful Republican senators and congressmen, accurately reflecting the sentiments of a large and vocal percentage of their constituents, thundered that since the Chinese Communists had attacked U.S./UN forces in Korea, America should strike back with everything it had. Because Communist China was waging war upon the United States, they contended, it was outrageous for the Truman administration to insist that MacArthur fight the red hordes with one hand tied behind his back. If the president was not prepared to acknowledge that the United States was already engaged in a major war with China and to respond accordingly — authorizing MacArthur to bomb Manchurian airfields and troop concentrations, to attack supply lines within China, and even to bomb Chinese cities — then the United States should withdraw from Korea at once. To make U.S. troops fight against an enemy whose bases were safe from attack was, they said, un-American. One draft board in Montana went so far as to announce that it would call up no more men until MacArthur had been given permission to use the atomic bomb against China.

Influential voices in the press echoed the Republican congressional demands and even added fuel to the flames. In an editorial in the December 11 issue of *Life*, John Osborne (who had written so perceptively of the Korean situation that summer but who had since become a rabid anti-Communist) stated, "World War III moves ever closer. . . . The Chinese Communist armies assaulting our forces . . . are as truly the armies of the Soviet Union as they would be if they wore the Soviet uniform." And in the issue of January 8 he wrote, "*Life* sees no choice but to acknowledge the existence of war with Red China and to set about its defeat, in full awareness that this course will probably involve war with the Soviet Union as well."

CHAPTER 26

Mr. Attlee Goes to Washington

AT HIS PRESS CONFERENCE on November 30, three days after MacArthur had declared that the U.S./UN/ROK forces were now engaged in "an entirely new war," President Truman said, "We will take whatever steps are necessary to meet the military situation, just as we always have."

"Will that include the atomic bomb?" inquired a reporter.

"That includes every weapon that we have," replied Truman.

"Mr. President, you said 'every weapon that we have.' Does that mean that there is active consideration of the use of the atomic bomb?"

"There has always been active consideration of its use. I don't want to see it used. It is a terrible weapon, and it should not be used on innocent men, women, and children, who have nothing whatever to do with this military aggression. That happens when it is used."[1]

Truman's reply to a subsequent question was misconstrued to mean that the decision of whether to use the atomic bomb would be left up to MacArthur. In a desperate attempt to undo the damage, the White House issued a clarification later that day: "Naturally, there has been consideration of this subject since the outbreak of the hostilities in Korea, just as there is consideration of the use of all military weapons whenever our forces are in combat. Consideration of the use of any weapon is implicit in the very possession of that weapon." The statement went on to give reassurance that only the president could authorize use of the atomic bomb. MacArthur would only "have charge of the tactical delivery of the weapon."[2]

The administration had, of course, for some time been considering the advisability of using atomic weapons against China. On November 8 the planning adviser of the State Department's Bureau of Far Eastern Affairs had prepared a paper for Dean Rusk entitled "Use of the Atomic Bomb in China." The paper emphasized that the bomb should be used only as a last resort and pointed out that China offered "few suitable A-bomb targets, in view of the scattered cities, low degree of industrialization, and immense area." It then went on to argue that use of the bomb might do more damage to America's reputation than to China's ability to wage war. "The A-bomb has the status of a peculiar monster conceived by American cunning and its use by us, in whatever situation, would be exploited to our serious detriment." The Soviets would claim its use was proof that the United States was bent on initiating a world war, and its use against China would lead people throughout the world to accuse the United States of a racist inclination to employ such an inhuman weapon only against Asians. Such accusations might turn all of Asia against the United States. Furthermore, stated the paper, America's UN allies would never agree to the use of the bomb, and for the United States to go ahead and use it anyway might put an end to America's international system of collective security.[3]

Nevertheless, in the dark days when the very survival of the U.S./ UN forces in Korea seemed to be in question, the Truman administration feared that there might be no alternative to using the bomb. Even the profoundly humanitarian Eleanor Roosevelt stated at the UN (as Ambassador Warren Austin reported to Dean Acheson on December 1) that "although she hoped that it would not be necessary to use the A-bomb in Korea, the choice of weapons would have to be decided in terms of the military situation at the particular time."[4]

Reports of Truman's November 30 press conference threw the British Parliament into a furor. One hundred members of Parliament, many of them from Prime Minister Clement Attlee's own Labour party, signed a letter to Attlee stating that they were aghast at the thought that MacArthur, under whom British troops were serving, might have the power to decide whether to use the atomic bomb. Surely, they protested, even if control of the bomb remained in Washington's hands, Britain should have a veto over a decision that might involve it in a world war.

Attlee immediately contacted Truman and said that he wanted to fly to Washington almost at once for talks. Truman accepted the proposal and agreed to hold a series of meetings between Monday, December 4, and Friday the eighth, dealing not only with the Korean War but also with other aspects of Anglo-American relations. This was very short notice for such complex and delicate talks, in which dozens of American and British officials would participate. Indeed, they were so inclusive that even the U.S. postmaster general was present at the last meeting.

Attlee, whom Churchill once unfairly described as "a sheep in sheep's clothing," was regarded by the McCarthyites and the MacArthurites as the arch-appeaser of Communist China. They were intensely disappointed that he failed to carry an umbrella when he arrived in Washington, for the umbrella that Neville Chamberlain had carried at Munich in 1938 had become a symbol of appeasement. They claimed to believe that Acheson took orders from Attlee and that the latter was responsible for inhibiting the United States from meting out harsh justice to the Chinese Communist aggressors. In point of fact, the only serious disagreements between the British and the Americans during the Truman-Attlee talks concerned U.S. policy toward China.

The overall tenor of the talks was friendly, albeit somewhat strained, and Attlee assured Truman that America would continue to have Britain's full support in Korea. "We're in this with you and we stand together," he told the president.[5] Like the Americans, the British were eager to end the war, were willing now to accept a cease-fire on the basis of the restoration of the status quo ante bellum, and were extremely anxious to avoid a full-scale war with China.

The obstacle to such a resolution of the hostilities was Peking's announcement that it would discuss a cease-fire only if the United States first agreed to yield on Formosa and China's UN seat. The United States just as stubbornly insisted that it would discuss those matters only after a cease-fire had been arranged. What Washington wouldn't say, but what everyone correctly assumed, was that America had no intention of making any concessions, either before or after a cease-fire in Korea. Indeed, Washington regarded the prospect of being driven completely out of Korea as preferable to buying a cease-fire on Peking's terms. Acheson told Attlee that if the United States appeased Peking by relenting, then the Communists would probably demand a veto in the Japanese peace treaty negotiations and would end up in control of both Japan and Indochina.[6]

The British, however, were trying to establish a friendship with Peking, for they were concerned about the safety of Hong Kong and they wanted to protect and develop their trade with China, long a mainstay of their economy. Consequently, Britain had voted for the seating of the People's Republic of China in the UN and had refused to participate in the neutralization of the Formosa Strait. Attlee argued that American opposition to Peking's demands was unreasonable. If it meant bringing the Korean War to a prompt and satisfactory end, he maintained, then the United States should be willing to make concessions. Besides, he added, China would probably behave better if it was "in the club." Since the Chinese Communists were excluded from the UN, they didn't feel bound by its principles or resolutions.[7]

Attlee pointed out that the Cairo Declaration had promised the return of Formosa to China. But Acheson retorted that in America's view the legitimate Chinese government was already in possession of Formosa.[8] By this time he had completely given up his old line of reasoning, that the PRC might be led to view the Soviet Union as its real enemy and the United States as its real friend. During the meetings with Attlee, both Truman and Acheson made it clear they now believed that Peking was totally subservient to Moscow, that no gesture of friendship could possibly nudge Peking's sympathies away from the Soviet Union and toward America, and that the only argument to which the Chinese Communists would respond was that of force. Acheson rather pathetically whined to Attlee,

> For fifty years we have tried to be friends with the Chinese. They have now attacked us with their armies and have denounced us violently. They have done great harm to the work of fifty years. . . . If the Chinese Communists take an attitude of hostility to the United States, they will suffer more than we do. Instead of our making an effort to prove that we are their friends, we ask them to prove that they are ours. Formosa is too dangerous a thing for them to have to play with.[9]

Attlee disagreed with Truman and Acheson. For one thing, he firmly believed that the Chinese Communists were Chinese nationalists first and Soviet puppets second. Hence he thought there was a good chance of Titoism in the PRC.[10] Attlee — who, after all, was himself a moderate Socialist — maintained that the Chinese Communists could be sincere Marxists and yet not be Stalinists. In light of that, he felt that U.S. policy regarding Formosa was unsound and unwisely provocative. He said he could understand that the United

States wanted to deny Formosa to an actively hostile PRC for military reasons, but he suggested at least getting rid of Chiang Kai-shek and putting Formosa under a UN trusteeship "until the Chinese Communists behave." Although they genuinely wanted Formosa on the grounds of nationalistic principle, they were, he said, far more immediately concerned about the threat that Chiang posed to them. Eliminate him and the problem of Formosa might be defused for the time being.[11]

But Truman and Acheson now believed that the Soviets were eager for the Chinese Communists to get Formosa because of its strategic value in a war with America. Acheson told Attlee that no UN commission could keep the Communists off Formosa. Only U.S. air and naval power could do that. Knowing that, if the United States agreed to a UN commission, "we would be merely going through a form and then letting them take it."[12] That would be appeasement. In any case, Truman confessed, American domestic politics would not permit him to repudiate Chiang or to allow the PRC to occupy China's UN seat.

The British and the Americans were, however, in full agreement over the need to avoid a full-scale war with China. To that end, the British adamantly opposed taking any action whatsoever against Chinese territory and, together with all of America's other UN allies, refused to approve the "hot pursuit" of Chinese planes into Manchurian airspace. MacArthur argued that this restriction permitted the Chinese to engage in hit-and-run air strikes, for his aircraft often didn't have time to shoot down the attacking Chinese planes before they crossed the Yalu River to safety. His argument convinced Acheson, but the Joint Chiefs of Staff countered that since Chinese planes weren't doing much harm to U.S./UN forces, and since hot pursuit might cause the war to escalate, the restriction should remain.[13]

As for the atomic bomb, Truman made it very clear to Attlee that he had no intention of using it unless there was no other way to prevent the destruction of the U.S./UN forces. The prime minister hesitantly accepted that policy, on the condition that Truman promise not to authorize an atomic attack without first consulting the British government. Truman gave his word.[14] The Republicans howled that Truman had given Attlee a veto over the use of the bomb, but the "veto" was de facto, not de jure, and it would pertain only if Washington began to view the bomb as a weapon of choice rather than as one of desperation. Since the British would have the option of dissociating themselves from the UN Command before the atomic bomb could be used, and since the United States would not use the bomb unless it had British backing, the United States would not use the bomb — except, that is, to prevent the total destruction of the U.S./ UN forces in Korea. Truman had in any case resolved to use the bomb only in those circumstances and would use it then with or without British concurrence, therefore rendering the British veto meaningless.

From all indications, it appeared by the time of the final meeting, on December 8, that there would be no immediate need for the atomic bomb. At that meeting General J. Lawton Collins, just off the plane from an emergency trip to Tokyo and Korea, was able to assure the assembled officials that the worst of the current crisis seemed to have passed and that although the situation remained serious, "from a military point of view, our troops are not in a critical condition today."[15]

CHAPTER 27

The Great Debate

FROM MID-DECEMBER 1950 ONWARD, the course of the Korean War was governed entirely by the need to find a compromise that would allow the United States and the People's Republic of China to disengage honorably. Each side naturally wanted to end the war on terms that would enhance its prestige and that would guarantee the security of its Korean client. Hence each side now pressed military and diplomatic offensives mainly in the hope of strengthening its bargaining position. There was no longer any question of an extremist solution. The United States/UN recognized that it would not be able to unify Korea by force of arms and accepted, albeit most reluctantly, that the North Korean regime would continue to exist. For their part, the Chinese Communists recognized that they would not be able to drive the United States/UN out of Korea. Given the forces that each side was able and willing to commit to Korea, it was clear that the most either side could hope for was a balance close to the status quo ante bellum, with only minor gains. In the end, the anti-Communists proved to be marginally stronger than the Communists and were thus able to secure slightly advantageous terms in the final armistice.

The threat of imminent destruction of the U.S./UN troops in Korea by the Chinese Communists had been mitigated by December 8, but the even more ominous threat of a Soviet-instigated world war seemed greater than ever — and it was upon counteracting that threat that the Truman administration focused its most urgent attention in mid-December.

Although the doubling of the size of America's armed forces that Truman had announced in September represented a giant step toward the full implementation of NSC-68, it wasn't until December 11 that the National Security Council resumed its formal consideration of the paper's recommendations. The Joint Chiefs of Staff now wanted an army of 18 divisions, a navy with 400 major warships, and an air force of 95 groups, 25 more than the 70 that had seemed such a radical proposal in 1948. That would translate into defense expenditures of $55 billion for fiscal year 1952, more than four times the pre–Korean War military budget ceiling of $13 billion. The NSC decided that it was no time for thrift.[1]

Much of America's increased military strength was to be devoted to the defense of Western Europe. During their talks, Truman and Attlee agreed that the United States must very soon assign a sizable number of its troops to the NATO command and station those troops in Europe. The need to do so, they also agreed, was the overriding reason to avoid a full-scale war with China. In order to facilitate congressional approval for this departure from America's hallowed tradition of never stationing its troops abroad except to perform occupation duties, the supreme commander of NATO (it was decided) should be an American. The British were especially eager that NATO should proceed as rapidly as possible to organize a European army incorporating West German units. In December, in accordance with these recommendations, the JCS drafted a revised defensive strategy for a world war. The new war plan, REAPER, called for using NATO forces to halt a Soviet invasion of Europe much farther east than had been thought possible when the previous plan, OFFTACKLE, had been formulated.[2]

To sell this expensive program to the American public, Truman decided to declare a state of national emergency. His public relations task was going to be a very difficult one, for the obvious emergency seemed to be that created by massive Chinese intervention in Korea, and yet his thesis (a perilously abstract one for a mass democracy) was that the *real* emergency had been created by Stalin's apparent readiness for world war. "Our homes, our nation, all the things we believe in, are in great danger," Truman told a national radio and television audience at 10:30 P.M. on December 15. "This danger has been created by the rulers of the Soviet Union." He then recounted how, when the UN "had all but succeeded" in putting down the act of aggression in Korea, "the Communists [i.e., the Russians] threw their Chinese armies into the battle against the free nations. By this act, they have shown that they are willing to push the world to the brink of a general war to get what they want."[3]

To meet this worldwide emergency, Truman continued, the

United States would increase its armed forces as rapidly as possible to 3.5 million men, and U.S. industrial production for military requirements ranging from electronics components to aircraft would more than quadruple. A new entity called the Office of Defense Mobilization would have the authority to impose price and wage controls so that the inflation these increases might stimulate would be minimized. As for measures directed specifically against Communist China, Truman announced nothing more drastic than the freezing of its assets in the United States and a total embargo on America's already greatly diminished trade with that nation. That was a far cry from the atomic holocaust with which militant Americans wanted to see treacherous China punished.

Truman's declaration of a national emergency was carefully coordinated with Secretary of State Dean Acheson's trip to Brussels for a meeting of the NATO Council on December 19. It had been largely prearranged that the council would ask the United States to appoint an American general to the post of supreme commander of NATO forces and that it would recommend General Dwight Eisenhower as the most desirable candidate.[4] In order to get around any possible constitutional objections that Republican congressmen might pose to stationing American troops in Europe, Eisenhower would be both Supreme Commander Allied Forces Europe and Supreme Commander U.S. Forces Europe; there would thus be no danger that American troops might be ordered into battle by a foreign power. The NATO Council did exactly what was expected of it on the nineteenth, and Truman announced that same day both Eisenhower's appointment and the impending dispatch of American troops to Europe. Thus began what became known as the Great Debate, which would rage in Congress and in the press until early April.

The central issue in question was whether an anti-Communist Europe or an anti-Communist Asia was more important to America's security and well-being. Those Republicans who gave their allegiance to General MacArthur and to Senators Joseph McCarthy and Robert Taft felt that the great developments of the future would be in Asia and that American influence in Asia would thus be far more valuable in the long run than would the retention of American connections with Europe. In their eyes Europe was the sinful Old World, hardened in its ways and not very amenable to American suggestions or grateful for American help. It was riddled with trade barriers and provided relatively few opportunities for lucrative investment. It was, in other words, essentially a lost cause. Asia, on the other hand, was docile and eager to be led into the modern world under American guidance — witness the alacrity with which the Japanese under the occupation had adopted American laws, values, and styles. The dream of the American Century, which Henry Luce had articulated so forcefully in *Life* magazine in February 1941, could be realized only if all of Asia, with its huge markets and burgeoning industries, was pro-American. Hence, insisted the fanatic Republicans, the United States had an obligation to save Asia from Communism before it became too late to do so.

This anti-Europeanism found one of its most extreme expressions the day after Truman's announcements. On December 20 former president Herbert Hoover declaimed, in a speech that became known as "Fortress America," that if Europe didn't have the will and the moral strength to defend itself, no amount of American aid could provide the undeserving continent with those qualities. (This was, of course, precisely the line of argument that the Truman administration had used against Chiang Kai-shek and the Chinese Nationalists.) If the nations of Europe proved that they could work together in unity, and if they raised a great NATO army, then and only then should the United States send troops or give aid to Europe. "The foundation of our national policies," pontificated Hoover, "must be to preserve for the world this Western Hemisphere Gibraltar of western civilization. . . . We can, without any measure of doubt, with our own air and naval forces, hold the Atlantic and Pacific Oceans with one frontier on Britain (if she wishes to cooperate), the other on Japan, Formosa, and the Philippines."[5] This was the creed of the neo-isolationists, of whom it was said that they were willing to fight only in Asia.

The Republican extremists were outraged that the administration was, on the one hand, imposing (as they saw it) possibly fatal restrictions on MacArthur and refusing to send him the reinforcements for which he continued to call while, on the other hand, proposing to send a large detachment of American troops to Europe. Surely, they shrieked, Acheson must be behind this most insidious of all acts of appeasement and subversion. Having schemed to allow the Communists to gain control of China, was he now trying to give them an opportunity to inflict a mortal defeat on American military forces in Korea? The clamor for Acheson's dismissal reached new heights.[6]

It was Acheson's ordeal, inextricably related to the Great Debate, that prevented Truman from relieving MacArthur of his command in December. At his press conference on November 30 Truman had said that the general had done a good job and had not exceeded his authority,[7] but, in fact, both the president and the Joint Chiefs of Staff felt that they could no longer trust him. The problem was that the uproar against Acheson would sound euphonious in comparison to that which would inevitably follow MacArthur's removal, and it was possible that the indispensable NATO legislation might get voted down in the midst of the commotion. Truman believed that the future of the world might well depend upon a favorable outcome to the Great Debate, and he was unwilling to do anything that might lose him the necessary senatorial consent. Once the Senate had given its approval to sending American troops to Europe, then MacArthur could be dealt with.

CHAPTER 28

Enter General Ridgway

THE SITUATION in Korea was gradually becoming stabilized. On December 15, 1950, the day on which Truman declared a national emergency, the Eighth Army withdrew below the 38th parallel, hoping that the Communists would stop when they reached that line. In the three weeks since November 25, General Walton Walker's forces had suffered some 13,000 casualties — a deplorable loss, but not one that endangered American security. Morale was the most serious problem as the Eighth Army continued its retreat into the Seoul-Inchon beachhead, for the American troops had been unnerved by the Chinese Communist intervention that they had been so confident would not occur.

In the eastern sector of North Korea, the evacuation of Hungnam was completed on Christmas Eve. Over the course of two weeks a fleet of aircraft and a flotilla of ships had transported to safety a staggering number of people and an astounding amount of matériel: 105,000 American and South Korean troops and other military personnel, more than 90,000 Korean refugees, more than 17,000 vehicles, and several hundred thousand tons of supplies. To deprive the enemy of the considerable stores that had to be left behind, demolition experts from the U.S. Army Corps of Engineers set charges throughout the port of Hungnam, which was blown to smithereens in a spectacular explosion as soon as the last American ship had departed.

All the while, MacArthur kept up his predictions of disaster and his litany of demands, to which he added a new one at the end of December: "Release existing restrictions upon the Formosan garrison for diversionary action (possibly leading to counter-invasion) against vulnerable areas of the Chinese Mainland."[1] As we have seen, the Joint Chiefs of Staff entertained this suggestion in January but were forced to abandon it.

The import of MacArthur's messages to the JCS was: Do it my way, or else it isn't worth even trying. Hoping that he could either shame or frighten Washington into letting him fight the war his way —

with massive reinforcements of American and Chinese Nationalist troops in Korea and with attacks upon China — he insisted that the loss of Korea would render Japan more vulnerable and that consequently America would have to reinforce Japan and the Pacific defense perimeter in order to hold them against "determined assault." As for whether the Soviets would respond if the United States attacked the People's Republic of China, that was "a matter of speculation." He now predicted that the Soviets would intervene only if they believed that a world war at that time would be to their overall advantage. The clincher, MacArthur contended in reference to the Great Debate, was that an American acceptance of defeat in Asia "could not fail to insure later defeat in Europe itself."[2]

Late in December the fates provided Washington with a way of lessening MacArthur's tactical control over the U.S./UN forces in Korea without actually relieving him of his command. On December 23 General Walker — who, like his hero and former superior George Patton, was a notorious speed demon, constantly goading his driver to perform daredevil maneuvers — was killed when his jeep collided with a ROK army truck. Lieutenant General Matthew Ridgway, a distinguished World War II paratroop commander then stationed in Washington as the army's deputy chief of staff for operations and administration, was immediately notified that he was to replace Walker as the commander of the Eighth Army, into which X Corps was now to be incorporated. Ridgway would thus be in command of all U.S./UN/ROK ground forces in Korea.

The highly intelligent and cultivated Ridgway, a man with all the virtues of an ancient Stoic, was the ideal choice for the job, since he was liked and trusted both by Washington and by MacArthur. The supreme commander had in fact designated Ridgway months earlier as his preferred standby for Walker, whom he had never liked.[3] MacArthur's confidence in Ridgway was such that at their meeting in Tokyo on December 26, he told his newly arrived subordinate, "The Eighth Army is yours, Matt. Do what you think best."[4] Because of both MacArthur's delegation of authority and Ridgway's close ties to the JCS (he had been slated to replace General J. Lawton Collins as army chief of staff in 1952), Washington was able to deal less with MacArthur and more directly with Ridgway, who was fully in sympathy with Truman's policies. The new commander felt confident not only that the United States/UN would not have to withdraw from Korea but also that, with proper tactics, his forces could inflict defeats on the Communists that would strengthen the U.S./UN bargaining position.

When Ridgway arrived in Korea, his forces were holding a line just below the 38th parallel. There had been relatively little Communist activity for several weeks, but a major offensive was now expected daily, especially since Chou En-lai had boasted on December 22 that the Chinese would push the U.S./UN forces out of Korea. The offensive finally came on New Year's Eve, when the Chinese hit several ROK divisions with massive force. When the ROKs disintegrated in panic, the Eighth Army was forced to fall back to the strong defensive positions that Ridgway had prepared north of the Han River, around Seoul, which was linked to the south bank only by two pontoon bridges.

On January 4, feeling (as he later wrote) that he "had not yet found sufficient basis for confidence in the ability of the troops to hold their positions, even if they were ordered to," Ridgway decided to evacuate Seoul and, with it, the vital supply base of Inchon.

> Jammed into a tight bridgehead on the north bank of the Han, we had more than a hundred thousand UN and ROK troops with all their heavy equipment. . . . And pressing upon us was the imminent possibility that panic-stricken refugees by the thousands might overwhelm our bridge guards and hopelessly clog our bridges — while enemy artillery, if resolutely pushed forward at night, might soon have the crossings within range.[5]

While military guards restrained the refugees at gunpoint, the Eighth Army got all of its men and equipment safely across, including even the huge tanks under the weight of which the bridges sagged dangerously deeply into the river's strong currents. By the next day the enemy offensive appeared to be losing its momentum, for the Communist supply lines were now overextended. About forty miles south of Seoul, sixty miles south of its position at the beginning of the offensive, and a few miles below Osan (near where Task Force Smith had, on July 5, fought the war's first engagement between Americans and Communists), the Eighth Army established a secure defensive line. There, at last, ended that force's 275-mile retreat from the advance positions it had held on November 25 — the longest retreat in American military history. At no point during the remainder of the war would U.S./UN/ROK forces be pushed farther south.

Ridgway's first priority was to restore the confidence and fighting spirit of his men. He began with the basics. In response to complaints he heard all along the front, he ordered his supply services to provide better food, to make sure that there was plenty of it, and to see that it was served hot. He ensured that his men received warmer clothing for the bitter Korean winter, and he even requisitioned a huge supply of stationery for GI letters home. Ridgway also took steps to improve the Mobile Army Surgical Hospitals (MASH), later boasting that no army had ever had better medical and surgical services in the field.[6] He emphasized such services not only on humane grounds but also because he knew that his men would take greater risks and fight harder if they knew that they would have a decent chance of survival once wounded.

Giving his men a sense of security was central to Ridgway's philosophy of command. He felt that if his men believed in the army's overall effectiveness, reasonableness, and concern for their well-being, they would fight better. To that end, he undertook a radical overhaul of his forces. He replaced officers whom he suspected of defeatism or incompetence. He placed great emphasis on improving reconnaissance and intelligence gathering so that his men could be confident they would not be sent into any more traps like the one in the far north. He also assured his men that only when his personal assessment demanded it would they be ordered to hold a position at all costs and that U.S./UN forces would pursue the enemy "only to the point where we were still able to provide powerful support or at least manage a timely disengagement and local withdrawal."[7]

Any military unit will fight its best when it knows that it can count on all the other units around and supporting it to perform well — if the units on its flanks will hold and prevent encirclement by the enemy, and if artillery and air cover can be depended upon to respond promptly and accurately to calls for assistance. Hence Ridgway emphasized the three *C*'s: coordination, cooperation, and communications. He trained his men intensively to develop maximum flexibility and efficiency in responding to enemy moves, encouraging them to become less road-bound in order to hold a solid line that would resist penetration by the enemy and drilling them in the coordination of infantry, artillery, and air power.[8] He felt certain that with such coordination, with carefully planned tactics, and with their great superiority of firepower on the ground and in the air, the UN Command forces were more than a match for the Communists, whose frontline combat troops outnumbered those of the anti-Communist coalition more than two to one. As in World War II, the United States would use its technological advantage to overcome the enemy's greater manpower.

Ridgway's program instilled great confidence and esprit de corps, yielding dramatic results almost at once. Indeed, the discrepancy between his glowing reports and MacArthur's pessimistic grumblings became so great that the JCS sent General Collins on yet another trip to the Far East to investigate. On January 17 he cabled his colleagues: "Eighth Army in good shape and improving daily under Ridgway's leadership. . . . On the whole Eighth Army now in position and prepared to punish severely any mass attack."[9]

Ridgway was ready to fight. His restored forces were well deployed along a curving line that stretched across the peninsula, with the Eighth Army responsible for the westernmost sector, X Corps in the middle, and ROK troops in the mountainous terrain along the east coast. On January 15 he initiated Operation Wolfhound, a "reconnaissance in force" in which an Eighth Army regiment established contact with the enemy near Osan. The bulk of the enemy forces, however, were farther east, ranged against X Corps, which lost the town of Wonju in bloody fighting the next day. A gap then developed between the opposing forces along much of the line, as the Communists withdrew to better tactical positions.

On January 25 the U.S./UN/ROK forces went on the offensive for the first time in two months, as Operation Thunderbolt began with a northward advance toward the Han River in the western sector. At first the Eighth Army moved forward against little opposition, but after six days Chinese resistance stiffened considerably. Heavy mortar and artillery fire greatly slowed the UN Command until, on February 9, the Chinese along the west coast abruptly eased off and withdrew. The Eighth Army swiftly advanced to the Han and on the tenth was able to occupy Inchon and Kimpo Airport without firing a shot. The Communists, however, were determined to hold Seoul, which they reinforced.

The advance was much slower on the Eighth Army's right flank, where X Corps encountered heavy resistance as it pushed northward to reach a position from which it could envelop Seoul from the east. The Communists threw the men they had withdrawn from Inchon against the vulnerable ROK forces on the X Corps front near Hoeng-song on the night of February 11–12. Those men succeeded in opening a gap through which they could pour to cut supply lines and to set up ambushes on U.S./UN/ROK troops retreating southward. Pandemonium resulted. On the thirteenth the U.S./UN forces abandoned Hoengsong and withdrew into Wonju. In general, however, Ridgway's training paid off; U.S./UN forces — including the 2nd U.S. Division, which had been reconstructed since its terrible beating in late November — fought bravely and capably.

The Communist offensive had spent most of its energy by February 18. Ridgway then immediately seized the initiative and ordered X Corps to attack while the Chinese were most vulnerable. They had expended their supplies of food and ammunition, were able to forage little in the frozen countryside, had inadequate protection against frostbite, were suffering from an epidemic of typhus, and had been badly hurt by U.S./UN ground and air action. They withdrew so hastily from the line of contact that they were forced to abandon a considerable amount of equipment at the front.

The pursuit that Ridgway ordered was designated Operation Killer. Its ostensible aim was for X Corps to reach a line stretching more or less due east from Seoul. But, as far as Ridgway was concerned, its primary purpose was simply — as the operation's code name avowed — to kill as many Communist soldiers as possible. "We are not interested in real estate," Ridgway had told his men not long after he arrived in Korea. "We are interested only in inflicting maximum casualties on the enemy with minimum losses to ourselves. To do this we must wage a war of maneuver, slashing at the enemy when he withdraws and fighting delaying actions when he attacks."[10] He didn't even care about recapturing Seoul, but MacArthur convinced him that possession of the capital would have great psychological value.

The main aim was, as Truman told MacArthur in a letter dated January 13, to "deflate the dangerously exaggerated political and military prestige of Communist China, which now threatens to undermine the resistance of non-Communist Asia and to consolidate the hold of Communism on China itself."[11] From Ridgway's standpoint, his declaration that his forces need concern themselves with nothing except the day-to-day slaughter of Communists obviated any need for him to try to explain to his men the war's long-range political goals or to specify under what circumstances the war might end. Unlike MacArthur, he wasn't going to make any promises that he might not be able to keep.

The weather was a more serious hindrance to the progress of Operation Killer than was Communist firepower. As an early spring thaw set in with heavy rains, mud and swollen streams in the mountainous terrain slowed the advance on the ground, while poor visibility hampered air support. The Chinese engaged in delaying actions, but by February 28 all enemy resistance south of the Han had collapsed.

Only the flooding of the river delayed further U.S./UN advances, until March 7, when Ridgway launched Operation Ripper. After pounding the Communists with the heaviest artillery barrage so far in the war, Eighth Army forces in the west pushed across the Han near Seoul and occupied the nearly deserted city on the night of March 14–15. In the central sector of the front, X Corps steamrollered northward to the key junction and supply depot of Chunchon, inflicting tens of thousands of casualties along the way.

From late January onward, Ridgway's successes angered MacArthur, since they undermined all the reasons that he continued to adduce in favor of attacking Chinese territory. MacArthur still felt that if Washington was not willing to go all out to unify Korea under Syngman Rhee, then the United States should withdraw altogether. The new U.S./UN offensives, he felt certain, could lead to nothing more than a stalemate and a compromise, which would be tantamount to defeat.

Ridgway, in an effort to maintain the morale that he had so assiduously rebuilt, studiously avoided discussion of such matters in his briefings and statements. But MacArthur shamefully tried to subvert his efforts. On March 7 the supreme commander flew into Korea for the jump-off of Operation Ripper. That afternoon, in Suwon, he held a press conference at which he read a statement that detailed his prognosis of an eventual stalemate. Among the U.S./UN troops the gist of his analysis was summed up by the demoralizing slogan "Die for Tie."[12]

CHAPTER 29

MacArthur Goes Too Far

DURING JANUARY 1951, while General Ridgway was preparing to turn the tide of battle, Washington was taking steps to ensure that a negotiated peace in Korea would not give China's UN seat or Formosa to Peking. In the middle of the month the Chinese Communist government had informed the UN that it would agree to a temporary cease-fire as soon as a seven-nation (People's Republic of China, Soviet Union, United States, Britain, France, India, and Egypt) conference convened to discuss the withdrawal of all foreign troops from Korea, the seating of the PRC in the UN, and the fate of Formosa. Once these questions had been satisfactorily resolved, the cease-fire in Korea would become permanent and the specifics of a settlement could be negotiated. The United States naturally rejected this proposal out of hand.

On January 19 the U.S. House of Representatives adopted, by an almost unanimous voice vote, a resolution demanding that the UN condemn the Chinese intervention in Korea as an act of aggression rather than excuse it as a defensive move. Four days later the Senate passed a similar resolution, by a vote of 91–0. The thinking behind these moves was that if the PRC was officially branded an aggressor, it would be unable to gain admittance to the UN community of peace-loving nations. Although no country was willing to assume the risks of cosponsorship, the United States went ahead and presented to the UN General Assembly's First Committee a draft resolution censuring the PRC as an aggressor and demanding the immediate withdrawal of its forces from Korea.

The Chinese Communists warned the UN on the twenty-ninth that if it accused them of aggression, they would reject all future calls for a negotiated peace in Korea. Nevertheless, on February 1 the General Assembly voted 47–7, with nine abstentions, to adopt the American resolution. Two days later Peking denounced the verdict of aggression as "an insult to the Chinese people" and affirmed that it "blocked the path to a peaceful settlement."[1]

There matters stood on the diplomatic front while Ridgway's forces advanced in Korea. With the recapture of Seoul on March 15, however, Truman felt that the time was auspicious for a new attempt to reach a settlement with Peking. The United States/UN would very soon be in a position to pursue the Communists northward across the 38th parallel, and there was strong feeling in the UN that although minor tactical thrusts across the line were permissible, U.S./UN troops should not enter North Korea in force unless Peking rejected a new call for negotiations.

Truman was now, in any case, very eager to end the war, which had become extremely unpopular with the American electorate. The Gallup poll showed that two thirds favored withdrawal from Korea if Washington was not prepared to authorize attacks on Chinese territory. A great many Americans, in other words, agreed with MacArthur's win-or-get-out position and felt that it was wrong for the United States to continue to suffer an average of thirteen hundred casualties a week in a frustratingly limited war for confusingly limited objectives.

The Truman administration decided that the best way to approach the Communists would be for the president to issue a moderate and unemotional statement devoid of condemnations or threats. The statement, painstakingly drafted in consultation with America's UN allies, was to point out that since "the aggressors have been driven back with heavy losses to the general vicinity from which the unlawful attack was first launched last June," and since the United States and the UN wanted "to prevent the spread of hostilities and to avoid the prolongation of the misery and the loss of life," they were ready to negotiate an armistice. The planned statement went on to imply that the United States/UN would now settle for the restoration of the status quo ante bellum and would agree to the removal of all foreign military forces as long as the future security of South Korea could be guaranteed. It was to conclude with a clause suggesting that "a prompt settlement of the Korean problem would greatly reduce international tension in the Far East and would open the way for the consideration of other problems in that area by the processes of peaceful settlement envisaged in the Charter of the United Nations."[2] The intentionally misleading insinuation was that once the Korean War was over, the United States might submit the questions of China's UN membership and of Formosa to arbitration by the UN.

On March 20 the Joint Chiefs of Staff alerted MacArthur that such an overture was forthcoming.[3] He, of course, was dead set against it. Only a few days earlier he had told Hugh Baillie, the president of the United Press, that he opposed any end to the war short of the "accomplishment of our mission in the unification of Korea." Secretary of State Dean Acheson later claimed that MacArthur "had been told over and over again that this was not his mission."[4] But, of course, the JCS had never bothered to send the general a message stating unequivocally that the United States had permanently abandoned that goal.

MacArthur decided to take matters into his own hands and on March 24 published what was in effect an ultimatum to Peking, threatening that if the Chinese Communists did not withdraw their troops at once and permit the unification of Korea, the United States/UN would force China to its knees.[5] The first two paragraphs of his statement represented a dumbfounding turnabout for a man who a short time earlier had predicted that the sheer number of troops the Chinese could field would bring about the ultimate destruction of his command. Because of the United States/UN's "round-the-clock massive air and naval bombardment" of enemy supply lines, began MacArthur, the Chinese troops at the front were so short of all essential supplies that they no longer had the stamina or the ammunition they needed in order to fight effectively. The U.S./UN forces were taking full advantage of that situation.

> Of even greater significance than our tactical successes [he continued] has been the clear revelation that this new enemy, Red China, of such exaggerated and vaunted military power, lacks the industrial capacity to provide adequately many critical items necessary to the conduct of modern war. He lacks the manufacturing base and those raw materials needed to produce, maintain and operate even moderate air and naval power, and he cannot provide the essentials for successful ground operations, such as tanks, heavy artillery and other refinements science has introduced into the conduct of military campaigns. Formerly his great numerical po-

tential might well have filled this gap . . . [but now] the resulting disparity is such that it cannot be overcome by bravery, however fanatical, or the most gross indifference to human loss.

In other words, Communist China was backward and primitive. It was a paper tiger that didn't stand a chance against the highly advanced United States and its Western European allies.

MacArthur went on to point out that, given the United States/UN's success despite its self-imposed restrictions,

the enemy . . . must by now be painfully aware that a decision of the United Nations to depart from its tolerant effort to contain the war to the area of Korea, through an expansion of our military operations to its coastal areas and interior bases, would doom Red China to the risk of imminent military collapse. These basic facts being established, there should be no insuperable difficulty in arriving at decisions on the Korean problem if the issues are resolved on their own merits, without being burdened by extraneous matters not directly related to Korea, such as Formosa or China's seat in the United Nations.

MacArthur was, his message concluded, "ready at any time to confer in the field with the commander-in-chief of the enemy forces."

What exactly did MacArthur want? Was he a madman hankering for an apocalyptic war that would purge China of Communism even if it meant colossal suffering and destruction worldwide? The answer appears to be a qualified no. He would have settled, in the short run, for the unification of Korea under Syngman Rhee, since he believed that the achievement of that goal would so badly damage both the strategic position and the prestige of international Communism that it would mark the beginning of an irreversible decline of the Kremlin's power.

And yet there was certainly a frightening element of madness in the lengths to which MacArthur was prepared to go in order to unify Korea. It was his conviction that if he could prevent Peking from sending supplies and reinforcements to its troops in Korea, then the U.S./UN/ROK armies (substantially reinforced by Chinese Nationalists from Formosa) could defeat the Communist forces that were currently there. Bombing attacks on Chinese industry and on troop concentrations in Manchuria would be one way to accomplish that. Another would be to "seal off" the Korean peninsula so that there would be no possibility of intercourse between it and China. To that end MacArthur submitted a preposterous plan to the JCS on February 11. He would, he said, first "clear the enemy rear all across the top of North Korea by massive air attacks." Then, "if I were still not permitted to attack the massed enemy reinforcements across the Yalu, or to destroy its bridges, I would sever Korea from Manchuria by laying a field of radioactive wastes — the by-products of atomic manufacture — across all the major lines of enemy supply" immediately to the south of the Yalu River. Thereupon he would administer the coup de grace: "I would make simultaneous amphibious and airborne landings at the upper end of both coasts of North Korea, and close a gigantic trap. The Chinese would soon starve or surrender. Without food or ammunition, they would become helpless. It would," he concluded, invoking the almost magical aura of his greatest victory, "be something like Inchon, but on a much larger scale."[6]

Truman wrote in his memoirs, "General MacArthur was ready to risk general war. I was not."[7] It would have been more accurate to say that MacArthur — his judgment distorted by his obstinacy — felt it would be safe to take action against Chinese territory, while Truman believed such a move would probably bring about a world war. Reversing his appraisal of late November and December, the general had convinced himself that, because of its internal problems and its commitments in Tibet and Indochina and along the coast opposite Formosa, Peking would not be able to respond to U.S./UN attacks on China by sending massive reinforcements into Korea. Because the principal goal of the first U.S./UN bombing attacks would be to destroy China's air force and bases, there would be little danger of retaliation from the air. Moreover, since Chinese industry could easily be wiped out (so he believed), and since the Soviet Union wasn't producing enough surplus to supply the Chinese forces without endangering its own security, Peking's forces would soon collapse from deprivation.

As for the threat of Soviet intervention, it was no longer convenient for MacArthur to believe, as he had told Ambassador William Sebald on November 14, that if the United States/UN bombed Manchuria, "the fat would be in the fire." He now had made up his mind that

Stalin was not yet ready to launch a world war and hence would refuse to help China overtly. For one thing, the crippling of the Soviet Union's ally China by the initial U.S./UN strikes would make Stalin less willing than ever to engage in global warfare. Conversely, there was much speculation in Washington — and MacArthur may have agreed with it — that the Soviets would not be unhappy to see the PRC weakened or preoccupied by a major war with the United States, for then they could hope to strengthen their hold on northeastern China. Much of MacArthur's analysis was undoubtedly grievously mistaken, but where he joined the lunatic fringe was in his blithe assertion that if the Soviet Union intervened after all, it too could be destroyed.

It is virtually inconceivable that the Soviets would have stood passively by while they lost North Korea, while the Chinese Communists were in danger of being deposed, and while America was supposedly preparing to rearm Japan. They would surely have felt compelled to make a desperate move, regardless of its cost, before the entire Far Eastern balance of power shifted overwhelmingly against them. Otherwise, they could expect a repetition of the scenario that had led from the Russo-Japanese War to Manchukuo, this time with Japan in alliance with the United States. But MacArthur did not choose to accept such reasoning.

Even after the Chinese Communists intervened in Korea, MacArthur did not want to undertake an invasion of China by U.S./UN troops. He was being perfectly honest when he said to Congress on April 19, "[N]o man in his right mind would advocate sending our ground troops into continental China, and such was never given a thought."[8] He seems, rather, to have believed very sincerely that if Washington allowed him to bomb China and to blockade its coast, those operations would force Peking to withdraw its troops from Korea and would render the mainland extremely vulnerable to an invasion by Chiang Kai-shek's forces from Formosa, especially if (as he anticipated) that invasion received extensive air, naval, and logistical support from the United States. (The Pentagon feared that if the bungling Nationalists suffered a few initial reverses, they might defect en masse to the Communists, as so many of Chiang's troops had done during the civil war, and that Formosa would then be left without a garrison.) In sum, MacArthur believed that Communism could be eradicated from Asia at relatively little cost if the United States acted soon, before the Chinese Communists developed China's industrial potential and consolidated their hold on the nation and its neighbors. Otherwise, the opportunity would be lost forever, and Communist power would mount irresistibly throughout the world. Thus his boundless frustration in the face of what he viewed as Washington's misguided timidity.

The testimony of MacArthur's aides and of officials who visited him during March supports the thesis that the general knew perfectly well when he made his March 24 statement that he was risking dismissal. He had nothing much to lose. He was at the end of a distinguished career, close to retirement from active duty (though, by law, a five-star general remains on call for life), and his work in Japan had been effectively completed. Optimally, the publication of his statement might arouse American public opinion sufficiently to force Truman to back him, or it might frighten Peking into withdrawing from Korea. At worst, he would be relieved of his command and would thus serve his cause by becoming a martyr. Perhaps political martyrdom would even catapult him into the White House.

In any case, MacArthur had the outlook of a martyr. Whereas Sir Thomas More defied his king to serve God, MacArthur was prepared to defy his president and commander in chief to serve his country. After his dismissal he candidly averred, "I find in existence a new and heretofore unknown and dangerous concept that the members of our armed forces owe primary allegiance and loyalty to those who temporarily exercise the authority of the executive branch of government rather than to the country and its Constitution which they are sworn to defend."[9] MacArthur, with the overweening conceit of a man who believes that he is in possession of the absolute truth, was prepared to violate the Constitution in order to defend it.

CHAPTER 30

The Dismissal of MacArthur

TRUMAN RELATED in his memoirs that after he had read MacArthur's March 24 statement, he decided he would relieve the general as soon as possible.[1] Why not at once? Because the Great Debate had still not ended. The Senate would soon be voting on the troops-to-Europe resolution, and the president wasn't about to sabotage his assiduous politicking by making MacArthur a martyr before the vote.

A number of Republicans, including such party heavyweights as John Foster Dulles and Governor Thomas Dewey, had supported the resolution all along. A few Republican senators, including Henry Cabot Lodge of Massachusetts and (most surprisingly) William Knowland of California, had even made speeches in favor of it as early as January. But it was the then carefully nonpartisan Dwight Eisenhower who swung a decisive number of moderate skeptics behind Truman. Early in February, having just returned from an inspection tour of NATO countries, he told an informal joint meeting of Congress that European morale was good, that an anti-Communist Europe was vital to American security, and that the United States had a moral obligation to provide NATO with leadership and troops.[2]

Two months later, on April 4, 1951, by a vote of 69–21, the Senate finally passed a resolution hailing the formation of NATO as a turning point in history, endorsing the concept of a unified NATO command to be headed by Eisenhower, authorizing Truman to send four American divisions to be stationed in Europe (in addition to the two that were already there performing occupation duties), and urging the use of German, Italian, and Spanish resources for the military defense of Europe. Truman had won the Great Debate. The passage of the resolution amounted to a vote of confidence for the president and his Europe-first policy. MacArthur, whose gravest offense was to attempt to subvert that policy, could now safely be fired.

Since Truman had waited, he needed a new excuse. One came along very quickly — the next day, in fact. On March 8 Republican congressman Joseph W. Martin, Jr., of Massachusetts, the House minority leader, had written to MacArthur to seek his views on America's Far Eastern policy. He enclosed a copy of a speech he had delivered in Brooklyn on February 12 suggesting that Chinese Nationalist troops invade the southern part of mainland China, thereby opening "a second Asiatic front to relieve the pressure on our forces in Korea."[3] As the man who had read MacArthur's August message to the Veterans of Foreign Wars into the *Congressional Record*, in defiance of Truman's attempt to suppress MacArthur's statement entirely, Martin had reason to assume that he enjoyed the general's confidence.

On March 20 MacArthur cordially replied that his own

> views and recommendations with respect to the situation created by Red China's entry into the war against us in Korea, . . . follow the conventional pattern of meeting force with maximum counterforce as we have never failed to do in the past. Your view with respect to the utilization of the Chinese forces on Formosa is in conflict with neither logic nor this tradition.[4]

Martin had asked MacArthur for his views "on a confidential basis or otherwise," but in his reply the general said nothing about confidentiality. After receiving the letter, Martin waited ten days for some indication that MacArthur did not wish to have it made public. Finally, on April 5, having decided that he "owed it to the American people to tell them the information" that he had received "from a great and reliable source," Martin read the letter to the House of Representatives.[5] Although neither Martin's own letter nor MacArthur's reply suggested the use of Chiang Kai-shek's forces in Korea, the lead of the Associated Press report read: "House Republican Leader Martin of Massachusetts told the House today General MacArthur favors use of Chinese Nationalist troops in Korean fighting."[6]

MacArthur had made his remarks in a private letter, but since he had not requested that it be kept private, he must have assumed, and probably hoped, that a firebrand like Martin would make it public. In effect, therefore, the general had violated Truman's December 5 injunction against foreign-policy statements that had not been cleared by the State Department. Truman now had his pretext.

The following morning, Friday, April 6, Truman met with Dean

Acheson, Averell Harriman, Secretary of Defense George Marshall, and General Omar Bradley to discuss what to do about MacArthur. So as not to influence their advice, he didn't tell them that he had already made his decision, for he wasn't prepared to act on it unless he had the nearly unanimous support of his political and military advisers, including the Joint Chiefs of Staff. Acheson told Truman at that meeting, "If you relieve MacArthur, you will have the biggest fight of your administration,"[7] and the president knew that it would be so. Unshakable unanimity would be vital if the administration was to withstand the tirades that were certain to follow MacArthur's removal.

General Marshall, worried that the relief of MacArthur might interfere with the passage of a huge military appropriations bill then before Congress, hesitated to recommend such an extreme step. But Truman asked him to read all the correspondence between MacArthur and the JCS for the past two years and then to think about it overnight. No decision could be made for a couple of days anyway, since General J. Lawton Collins was on a speaking and inspection tour in the southern states from which he wasn't scheduled to return until Saturday night. General Bradley feared that if Collins were suddenly summoned back to Washington and forced to cancel his remaining engagements, the press might indulge in alarming or embarrassing speculation.

That afternoon Acheson, Harriman, Marshall, and Bradley met again, this time without Truman. Marshall suggested bringing MacArthur home for consultation before making a decision, but the others were all strongly opposed. Acheson wrote in his memoirs that he had replied to Marshall, "The effect of MacArthur's histrionic abilities on civilians and of his prestige upon the military had been often enough demonstrated. To get him back in Washington in the full panoply of his commands and with his future the issue of the day would . . . gravely impair the President's freedom of decision."[8] It would be better to present the nation with a fait accompli.

Truman met once again with his key advisers on Saturday morning, at which time they urged that he defer making any final decision until Monday. The president's feelings were, however, evident enough so that when Bradley and Marshall met later in the day, they decided to set the machinery in motion to prepare for the probability that MacArthur would have to be notified. They wanted the relief orders to be conveyed with tact and courtesy. And that meant they didn't want them to go over the Pentagon's line to Tokyo, since by the time the message had been decoded and relayed to MacArthur, half of his headquarters staff would already have heard the news. It happened that army secretary Frank Pace was then in Tokyo; Marshall ordered him to go to Korea at once and to await further instructions there. The State Department could then send the relief orders through its own channels to Ambassador John Muccio in Pusan, and he could give them to Pace, who would immediately fly back to Tokyo and deliver them to MacArthur in person.

Truman wanted to relieve MacArthur primarily for political reasons, but the Joint Chiefs of Staff had their own urgent military reasons for replacing him with a more levelheaded commander. They knew that the Communists were building up their forces in North Korea for a powerful new offensive, and they felt that they couldn't trust MacArthur to respond prudently to what might well prove to be the war's greatest crisis so far.

MacArthur himself was well aware of the coming offensive. As early as March 7 he had announced that the Communists were preparing for a major spring campaign and implied that he hoped the impending blow would finally induce America's UN allies to remove the restrictions under which he was chafing.[9]

By early March it was clear to all, Communists and UN allies alike, that General Ridgway's forces stood a good chance of being very soon in a position to cross the 38th parallel once again. And as far as the Communists could divine, the United States/UN might intend to make a second attempt, even more determined than the first, to unify Korea by force. It was to put a permanent end to any such plans that the Communists undertook a massive buildup for what they viewed as a counteroffensive.

Ridgway recorded in his history of the war that late in March he received from MacArthur's headquarters a report, originating from a source deemed reliable, claiming

that a Soviet Far Eastern Committee, with the redoubtable Vyacheslav M. Molotov at its head, was planning a large-scale offensive

in Korea toward the end of April. Extensive use would be made, according to this report, of Soviet aircraft and of regular Soviet troops of Mongolian extraction, under the guise of volunteers, while the Soviet Far Eastern Command was under instructions to render all necessary assistance to insure victory, regardless of the risk of full-scale war.[10]

It seems quite possible that the Kremlin deliberately started this rumor in the hope of bluffing the United States/UN into halting its northward advance at the 38th parallel.

If so, the strategy failed. The JCS decided that since the Communists were obviously readying for a huge offensive, it was imperative for Ridgway to maintain heavy pressure on them so as to drain resources and distract attention that they could otherwise concentrate on their preparations. Accordingly, the first anti-Communist troops — the ROK I Corps — entered North Korea near the east coast on March 27, and the first American troops crossed the parallel north of Seoul four days later. On April 5 Ridgway launched Operation Rugged, the goal of which was a topographically desirable line roughly twenty miles above the border, where U.S./UN/ROK troops could entrench and brace themselves for the expected Communist attacks.[11]

The Joint Chiefs of Staff viewed the impending Communist offensive with considerable dread. So far the Chinese had used their Manchurian-based air force mainly to attack U.S./UN planes operating over North Korea and had refrained from carrying out concerted operations against U.S./UN ground forces, presumably because they correctly surmised that such operations would lead the United States/UN to make retaliatory strikes against the Manchurian bases. But intelligence had recently reported, as Truman was to mention in his April 11 broadcast explaining why he had relieved MacArthur, that there had been "large increases in the enemy's available air forces."[12] The JCS feared that this, and the report of possible Soviet intervention, might mean the enemy was now planning to bomb and strafe U.S./UN infantry. If such a major air attack were to come, the survival of the U.S./UN forces could depend entirely upon the JCS's ability to order the immediate destruction of the Manchurian bases, without having to wait for authorization to work its way through the Washington hierarchy. And so it came to pass on April 5, the day on which Martin read MacArthur's letter to the House, that the Joint Chiefs resolved to seek prior presidential approval to cover such an eventuality.[13] Within the next two days, with the concurrence of Acheson and Marshall, Truman gave the JCS permission to authorize attacks upon "enemy air bases and aircraft in Manchuria and the Shantung peninsula in the immediate vicinity of Weihaiwei . . . if and when the enemy launches from outside Korea a major air attack against our forces in the Korean area."[14] The whole point of expediency, however, was undermined by Britain's demand that it be consulted before Washington actually ordered any attacks.

The telling fact is that General Bradley, as he later admitted, "deliberately withheld . . . all knowledge" of this development from MacArthur.[15] Knowing that MacArthur desperately wanted to bomb China, Bradley feared that he might trump up some minor incident and possibly even proceed to attack the Chinese bases without bothering to request the necessary permission from the JCS, afterward justifying his move by insisting that he couldn't have afforded to delay the implementation of what the president had already approved in principle. Such fears were the basis of the Joint Chiefs' unanimous decision, reached on Sunday, April 8, to recommend that MacArthur be relieved of his command.

The matter was settled on Monday morning. The four men with whom Truman had first discussed the problem now told him that neither they nor the Joint Chiefs had any doubts or reservations about relieving MacArthur of all of his commands. It was decided that the orders would be sent to Secretary Pace in Korea the next day with instructions for him to give them to MacArthur at 10:00 A.M. (Tokyo time) on Thursday, April 12 (8:00 P.M. on Wednesday the eleventh, Washington time). The meeting then turned to the question of MacArthur's successor. Marshall, Bradley, and Collins had already decided to recommend Ridgway to replace MacArthur as Supreme Commander for the Allied Powers; Commander in Chief, Far East; and Commander in Chief, UN Command. Truman was pleased. Lieutenant General James A. Van Fleet would take Ridgway's place as commander of the Eighth Army.

The meticulously choreographed relay of MacArthur's relief orders failed to go as planned. Early Tuesday evening the managing editor of the *Chicago Tribune* received a tip from Tokyo that "an important resignation" would take place the next day. Assuming that MacArthur might be resigning under pressure from Truman, the editor called the paper's Washington correspondent, Walter Trohan, who immediately went to the White House to query Joseph H. Short, the president's press secretary. Although Short denied everything, his obvious discomfort led Trohan to disbelieve him. For his own part, Short felt certain that Trohan was going to go ahead and write his story.

This led to a crisis. It seemed quite possible that MacArthur really was planning to resign the next day and that the anti-Truman *Tribune* might have received a valid tip. On the other hand, perhaps the *Tribune* had picked up nothing more than a groundless and merely coincidental bit of information. Nonetheless, the story that the paper was probably going to run the next morning might become a self-fulfilling prophecy. Immediately after Trohan's visit, Short relayed the correspondent's suspicions. Some of the president's advisers (Acheson among them) felt that there was no problem. They should go ahead exactly as planned. If MacArthur beat them to the punch and resigned, that would spare the administration the attacks that would result if Truman relieved him. But when, about 10:30 that evening, a delegation consisting of General Bradley, Dean Rusk, Harriman, and Short went to the Blair House to alert Truman, the president exclaimed, "The son of a bitch isn't going to resign on me. I want him *fired*."[16]

Although the State Department had cabled the relief orders to Pace that afternoon, as Acheson later recalled, "something went wrong with the commercial cable line through which the Department had to transmit," and by the time of the Blair House meeting the requested confirmation of receipt had still not come from Ambassador Muccio.[17] There was, in any case, no time for the nicety of having Pace inform MacArthur in person nearly twenty-four hours later. Truman ordered Bradley to send the relief orders directly to MacArthur over the Pentagon-Tokyo wire at once. Meanwhile, Short was to get word out that a special announcement would be made at the White House in two hours, at 1:00 in the morning. Because of delays in amending and encoding the relief orders, Bradley's cable wasn't sent until 12:30 A.M.

When reporters gathered for the extraordinary middle-of-the-night announcement, many speculated that Truman must have died or that some event was leading the president to ask Congress for a declaration of war. The actual announcement came as a surprise to all but Trohan, who like everyone else raced to find a phone from which to call in the sensational news. As it turned out, the *Tribune* had killed his earlier story, since a follow-up in Tokyo had disparaged the source of the original tip. All the frantic abandonment of Washington's carefully laid plans had been needless.

Within minutes word of the White House announcement reached Tokyo (where it was the afternoon of April 11) and was broadcast at once as a flash following the 3:00 P.M. news. MacArthur was at home entertaining guests from the United States over lunch, but one of his aides heard the broadcast at headquarters and immediately telephoned the general's residence. Mrs. Jean MacArthur took the call and was thunderstruck. When she told her husband, he took the news very calmly, quite possibly because he had been forewarned through an official leak. Such a leak would not have led him to resign, for he was determined that if he had to go, it would be as a martyr. He had no intention of letting Truman off the hook.

MacArthur didn't receive Bradley's cable until about fifteen minutes after the radio broadcast. That fact outraged many Americans as much as did the actual dismissal. They complained that it was inexcusable to treat so shabbily a man who had served his nation with such distinction, and they conjectured that the botched delivery had been an intentional affront arranged by Truman. Perhaps if MacArthur's dismissal had been carried out with appropriate protocol and dignity, there would have been somewhat less of an uproar. It is ironic, given the Joint Chiefs' usual bending over backward to be courteous to MacArthur, that when the situation really demanded tact, discourtesy prevailed.

On the evening of April 11 Truman addressed the nation on radio and television to explain why he had relieved MacArthur. The overly complicated speech was ineffective. Its main point was that the whole purpose of American involvement in Korea was to prevent a third world war. "A number of events have made it evident that General MacArthur did not agree with that policy," said the president blandly. "I have therefore considered it essential to relieve General MacArthur so that there would be no doubt or confusion as to the real purpose

A soldier of the 2nd U.S. Infantry Division, in the Yongsan area, looks for Communist snipers during the breakout from the Pusan Perimeter, September 16, 1950. (*National Archives*)

A grief-stricken American infantryman whose buddy has been killed in action is comforted by another soldier, near Haktong-ni (along the Pusan Perimeter), August 28, 1950. At left a medical corpsman impassively shuffles through casualty tags. (*National Archives*)

General MacArthur presents a Distinguished Service Cross to Master Sergeant Curtis D. Pugh of Columbus, Georgia, on February 13, 1951. Pugh, of the 25th U.S. Infantry Division's 24th Regiment, had heroically held a position against determined enemy assaults. (*National Archives*)

As U.S. Marines fight their way from the Chosin Reservoir to the sea, a Chinese Communist concentration is hit with napalm, December 1950. (*National Archives*)

During their December 1950 exodus, Marines rest at Hagaru. (*National Archives*)

South of Koto-ri, on the road from the Chosin Reservoir, soldiers and tanks pass over a temporary bridge installed by the U.S. Army Corps of Engineers to replace a span that the Chinese had dynamited. (*National Archives*)

Generals Douglas MacArthur (*left*) and Matthew B. Ridgway (who had recently assumed command of the Eighth U.S. Army) during the former's visit to Korea, January 25, 1951. Their expressions reflect MacArthur's pessimism and Ridgway's optimistic view of the war at that point. (*AP/Wide World Photos*)

General Ridgway (*second from left*) pays a farewell visit on May 8, 1952, to the Munsan headquarters of the UN's delegation to the armistice negotiations, accompanied by his successor as commander in chief of the UN forces, General Mark W. Clark (*second from right*). At the far left is Vice-Admiral C. Turner Joy, the chief UN delegate to the talks, and at the far right is General James A. Van Fleet, commander of the Eighth U.S. Army. Ridgway was leaving Korea to succeed General Dwight D. Eisenhower as commander in chief of the NATO forces in Europe. (*AP/Wide World Photos*)

During his visit to South Korea in December 1952, General (and President-Elect) Eisenhower is briefed on the disposition of ROK units, as represented on a sand-table model of the terrain along the front. (*AP/Wide World Photos*)

Communist delegates to the armistice negotiations at Panmunjom, June 17, 1952
(*from left*): Rear Admiral Kim Won Mu (North Korean navy); Major General Lee Sang Cho,
North Korean People's Army; Lieutenant General Nam Il, NKPA, the chief delegate;
and Major General Hsieh Fang, of the Chinese People's Volunteers. (*National Archives*)

UN delegates to the armistice negotiations, June 16, 1952 (*from left*):
Brigadier General Han Lim Lee, ROK army; Major General Howard H. Turner,
U.S. Air Force; Major General William K. Harrison, Jr. (who had replaced Admiral
C. Turner Joy as chief delegate), U.S. Army; Rear Admiral Ruthven E. Libby,
U.S. Navy; Brigadier General Frank C. McConnell, U.S. Army; Lieutenant Colonel
Earl H. Robinson, U.S. Air Force, staff officer. (*National Archives*)

and aim of our policy.''[18] That was perfectly true, but it wasn't nearly punchy enough to justify to the American public the cashiering of one of the greatest generals in American history. Incredibly, Truman mentioned neither MacArthur's March 24 ultimatum nor his letter to Martin — nor any other specifics. He said nothing about the constitutional need to maintain civilian control over the military; neither did he draw the analogy, to which he had referred frequently from the beginning of the crisis, between his own position and Abraham Lincoln's dismissal of General George McClellan, in 1862. All in all, Truman's speech left many Americans more confused than ever. The concept of fighting to prevent a third world war was too cerebral. Are we at war or aren't we? they wanted to know. If so, let's give 'em all we've got and get it over with.

Early that morning pro-MacArthur Republican congressmen, led by Senator Robert Taft and Congressman Martin, had held a war conference. They resolved to invite MacArthur to address a joint session of Congress, and they demanded a full congressional inquiry into the circumstances of the general's relief and into the administration's Far Eastern policy. Speaking to the press after the meeting, Martin ominously mentioned that "the question of possible impeachments" had been discussed.[19] Although congressmen were deluged with telegrams calling Truman everything from stupid to treasonous and demanding his impeachment, the Republicans never did attempt to institute impeachment proceedings.

Public outrage against Truman was wildly vociferous. The president was burned in effigy in many towns across the country, and many flags were lowered to half-mast. Of the 27,363 letters and telegrams that the White House received in the first twelve days after the announcement, more than 95 percent excoriated Truman. The ratio of nearly twenty to one in favor of MacArthur held for the next 60,000 messages, after which the White House mail room stopped counting. In a more representative survey, the Gallup poll found 69 percent championing MacArthur and only 29 percent defending the president. The California, Florida, and Michigan state legislatures censured Truman, and the Illinois Senate passed a resolution stating, "We express our unqualified confidence in General MacArthur and vigorously condemn the irresponsible and capricious action of the President in summarily discharging him from command."[20]

Much of the press, however, threw its weight behind Truman, and even many newspapers that habitually criticized the administration supported the president, primarily on the grounds that MacArthur's high-handedness had jeopardized the sacred principle of civilian control over the military. A poll of the correspondents covering the story revealed that more than 80 percent of them thought that Truman was justified in removing MacArthur but that he had handled it badly.

The reaction abroad was generally enthusiastic, especially since America's UN allies had been very worried that Truman was losing control over MacArthur and that the United States might consequently drift into a major war with China. There were loud cheers in the House of Commons when British foreign secretary Herbert Morrison announced that MacArthur had been relieved, and reactions in other European capitals were comparable. Unfortunately, this foreign endorsement of Truman's action gave fuel to the Republican extremists who were claiming that MacArthur had been relieved at the insistence of the British. Senator McCarthy observed in his self-parodying style that "Truman is the President in name only. . . . The real President who discharged MacArthur is a rather sinister monster conceived in the Kremlin and given birth to by Acheson, with Attlee and Morrison as midwives, and then nurtured into Frankenstein proportions by the Hiss crowd, who still run the State Department."[21] McCarthy also gloated that the dismissal was "perhaps the greatest victory the Communists have ever won" and sneeringly accused Truman of having made his decision "after a night of bourbon and benedictine."[22]

The Japanese were at first very disturbed by the news of MacArthur's relief, but the Truman administration dispatched John Foster Dulles to reassure Prime Minister Shigeru Yoshida that the move meant no change in U.S. policy toward Japan. In the end, the Japanese — whose civilian politicians had been terrorized by the military for several decades before 1945 — were greatly impressed to see how easily a single order from the civilian authorities in Washington could remove from power a military figure who seemed almost to have assumed the divinity that the emperor had renounced.

Upon MacArthur's return to the United States for the first time since 1937, the nation indulged in a cathartic orgy of hysterical adulation. After receiving a tumultuous welcome in San Francisco on

April 17, the general proceeded to Washington to address a joint meeting of Congress. (A joint meeting is somewhat less formal and prestigious than a joint session; the Democrats had insisted upon the former.) When MacArthur entered the House chamber at 12:31 P.M. on April 19, most of the congressmen and visitors in attendance gave him a standing ovation, though some Democrats remained pointedly seated. Neither Truman nor his cabinet attended, but the president was among the thirty million Americans who watched the speech on television, the largest audience that any broadcast had reached up to that time.

MacArthur devoted about half of his speech to an assessment of the general situation in the Far East, including observations regarding America's Pacific defense perimeter that were taken almost verbatim (and no doubt with a malicious sense of satisfaction) from his suppressed message of August 1950 to the Veterans of Foreign Wars. He then went on to reiterate his perennial arguments in favor of going all out to unify Korea, concluding, "In war there is no substitute for victory. There are some who, for varying reasons, would appease Red China. They are blind to history's clear lesson, for history teaches, with unmistakable emphasis, that appeasement but begets new and bloodier war." Waxing maudlin, he closed by saying that after fifty-two years of service, "I now close my military career and just fade away, an old soldier who tried to do his duty as God gave him the light to see that duty. Good-bye."[23]

The thirty-four-minute speech was interrupted thirty times by applause, and when it was over the television cameras focused on congressmen who were weeping. Truman dismissed the speech as "a bunch of damn bullshit,"[24] but a fellow Missourian, Congressman Dewey Short (a Republican who had been educated at Harvard, Oxford, and Heidelberg), gushed when it was over, "We heard God speak here today, God in the flesh, the voice of God!"[25]

The next day MacArthur was given the most extravagantly enthusiastic welcome in New York City history. His cavalcade took more than seven hours to cover the nineteen-mile route from the Battery to St. Patrick's Cathedral and back again, MacArthur standing all the way in an open Chrysler. An estimated 7.5 million people turned out to pay homage to the martyred hero, twice as many as had come out in 1945 for Eisenhower, who was just a victorious hero. Many people crossed themselves as MacArthur rode by; others fainted. At times, those who were watching the procession on television had trouble seeing anything through the blizzard of ticker-tape streamers, shredded newspaper, and phone-book pages torn into coarse confetti, all cascading out of windows overlooking the route, from along which the New York City Department of Sanitation reported that it afterward removed a record 3,249 tons of litter.

Between May 3 and June 25, 1951, the Senate Foreign Relations and Armed Services committees held joint hearings to investigate MacArthur's relief. The seven million words of testimony delivered over the course of seven weeks laid bare every aspect of post–World War II American political and military strategy regarding the Far East. Although a complicated system of censorship had been set up to provide the press with daily reports from which the most highly classified information had been deleted, diligent reporters were able to fill in most of the gaps with the help of loose-lipped senators, leading Truman to grouse in his memoirs that the Soviet leaders must have gotten "a great deal of satisfaction out of the hearings."[26]

And yet the hearings performed an extremely valuable service for the Truman administration. They effectively discredited MacArthur's cause and revealed the man himself to be pompous, arrogant, and tedious, bearing out Ralph Waldo Emerson's dictum "Every hero becomes a bore at last." After the backfire of the hearings that the Republicans had demanded to vindicate MacArthur, the American public lost most of its interest in him, and, except for a brief revival when he made his abortive bid for the 1952 Republican presidential nomination, he faded away.

CHAPTER 31

Stalemate

ON MARCH 7 General MacArthur had predicted,

> Assuming no diminution of the enemy's flow of ground forces and
> matériel to the Korean battle area, a continuation of the existing
> limitations upon our freedom of counter-offensive action, and no
> major additions to our organizational strength, the battle lines
> cannot fail in time to reach a point of theoretical military stale-
> mate.[1]

His prediction was reasonably correct, and the Truman administration
did not vehemently disagree with his analysis. The difference in
outlook between the two was that MacArthur abominated such a
development, while Washington saw the stabilization of the line of
battle just north of the 38th parallel as the only acceptable way to
end the war, given the hard realities of international diplomacy that
constrained its freedom of action at every turn. With the ending of
what was commonly called the accordion-war phase of the fighting,
in the spring of 1951, Truman felt that the United States/UN would
be in a position strong enough to dictate peace terms sufficiently
disadvantageous to the Communists to guarantee the future security
of South Korea.

In mid-April 1951, however, the front was still very much in flux. At
that time the fighting was mainly concentrated in the center of the
peninsula, where U.S./UN forces were inching northward to the base
of what was known as the Iron Triangle, a level area of about fifty
square miles protected on all sides by steep hills running between
the towns of Pyonggang (not to be confused with the North Korean
capital) at its apex in the north, Chorwon at the southwestern angle
of the base, and Kumhwa in the southeast. As long as the Communists
held the heavily fortified Iron Triangle, they could use it as a secure
staging area from which to dispatch large numbers of troops to either
the eastern or the western sectors of the front. Furthermore, road and

rail links between the Iron Triangle and Manchuria could keep those troops well supplied.

The progress of the U.S./UN advance was not slowed by the changeover of command. General James Van Fleet assumed tactical command of the Eighth Army on April 14, though General Ridgway would still play a very active role in directing the war from Tokyo. A thoroughly military man who was no more enthusiastic about the prospect of a stalemate than MacArthur had been, Van Fleet urged his troops forward and favored a policy of pushing the Communists once again deep into North Korea. Ridgway had the thankless job of restraining him. There was, in any case, little amity between the two generals. Ridgway regarded Van Fleet as not very smart and tried to prevent his assignment to Korea. But Van Fleet was esteemed in Washington as the victor in the Greek civil war. He had worked miracles in Greece, whipping the ragtag Greek army into shape and getting along remarkably well with the mercurial Greek government. Truman hoped that Van Fleet could now work his magic on another mountainous peninsula threatened with Communist domination.

As the Eighth Army moved northward in mid-April, it encountered relatively little resistance, for the Chinese were simply fighting delaying actions while they amassed a huge force farther north for their long-anticipated offensive — their most powerful of the entire war, an all-out attempt to inflict a stunning defeat that would force the UN Command to accept terms decidedly favorable to the Communists.

The Chinese forces in Korea also had a change of command at this time. To ensure the success of their venture, Peking installed the experienced general Peng Teh-huai as head of the Chinese People's Volunteers. Like the North Korean high command, he received directions and guidance from the Russian military staff under Colonel General Terenty Shtykov, the Soviet ambassador to Pyongyang. By the time they were ready to launch their spring offensive, the Communists had a total of about 700,000 men in North Korea. Ranged against them was a U.S./UN/ROK ground force of approximately 420,000, some 230,000 of them in the front line.

The Communists struck just as the Eighth Army was about to reach Chorwon, at the southwestern corner of the Iron Triangle. By the light of the full moon on the night of April 22, all hell broke loose.

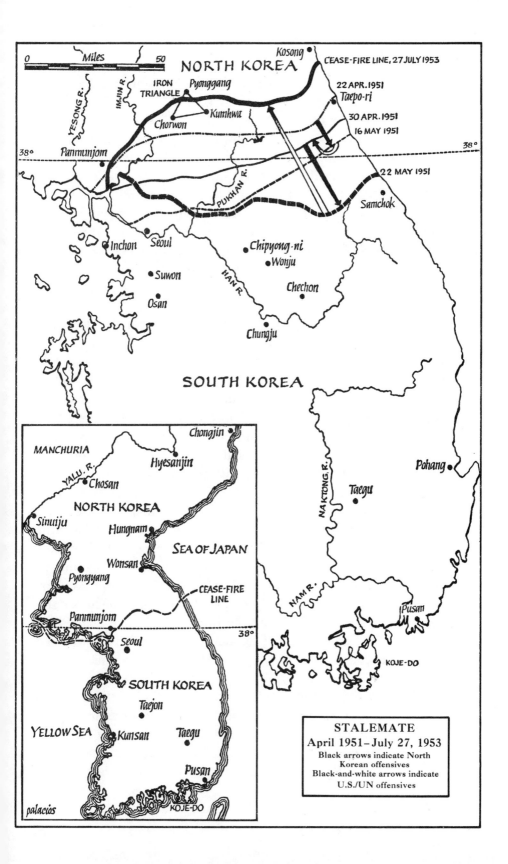

STALEMATE
April 1951–July 27, 1953
Black arrows indicate North
Korean offensives
Black-and-white arrows indicate
U.S./UN offensives

After the Communists had pounded the UN Command troops with an exceptionally intense artillery barrage, the Chinese threw most of their weight against the approaches to Seoul all along the western two thirds of the front — especially down the roads that passed through Chunchon, Uijongbu, and Kaesong, the roads on which the North Koreans had advanced at the beginning of their invasion ten months earlier. At first the UN Command troops successfully resisted the onslaught, but poorly officered ROK troops in the center of the attack soon gave way. As usual, the Communists hoped to pour through the ROK gap in order to get behind the U.S./UN forces. Creating confusion within the U.S./UN lines, the Chinese could isolate units and surround them, cutting them off from supplies, reinforcements, and retreat.

The Communists were being exhorted to capture Seoul as a May Day present for Stalin, and for a while it looked as though they might succeed. This was clearly meant to be their own version of Mac-Arthur's end-the-war offensive. They threw everything they had into it. Immense waves of manpower surged relentlessly forward despite horrific casualties inflicted by U.S./UN firepower. In the face of such sheer weight, Van Fleet decided to move his forces back to a better defensive line and to do so as quickly as possible. That tactic would accomplish several ends. Moving faster than the Communists were capable of doing would prevent them from getting around behind the U.S./UN/ROK lines. If the Communists kept up their pressure against the withdrawing UN Command forces, the former would soon outrun their supply lines and their offensive would collapse. Furthermore, Van Fleet wanted to spare his troops direct man-to-man fighting. He preferred instead to use artillery and air power to slaughter the enemy. The strategy worked. The UN Command fell back as much as thirty-five miles at some points along the front and endured about 7,000 casualties. But some 70,000 Communists were killed or wounded. And despite such appalling sacrifices, Stalin didn't get his May Day present.

One of the westernmost of the key approaches to Seoul passed through the positions along the Imjin River (about thirty miles north of the capital) that were held by the British 29 Brigade, consisting of four infantry battalions, three of them British and the fourth Belgian, a total of about 4,000 men. On April 22, the first night of the offensive, a Chinese force numbering well over 10,000 slammed into the bulwark of the 29 Brigade. For three days the British allowed the Communists only minimal gains for a maximal price; the original attacking force was shattered, and its reinforcements fared little better. An estimated 11,000 Communist soldiers became casualties. By stemming the Communist tide, the 29 Brigade protected the entire left flank of the U.S. I Corps and enabled it to withdraw safely to more defensible positions.

The Britons' stand was heroic, and it cost them dearly. One Gloucestershire battalion of about 700 men was surrounded on a hilltop, "Gloucester Hill," above the hamlet of Solma-ri, a few miles south of the 38th parallel. They attempted a breakout on the morning of April 25, but just over 40 men reached the American lines. Well over 100 men had died on the hill, and the rest, including the more than 200 wounded, were taken prisoner. General Van Fleet later MacArthuresquely called the Gloucesters' stand at Solma-ri "the most outstanding example of unit bravery in modern warfare."[2] The praise should really have gone to the British 29 Brigade as a whole, which had suffered more than 1,000 casualties in three days of fighting.

By April 30 the Communists had exhausted themselves, and their offensive had faded away. Across most of the peninsula they had managed to push UN Command forces south of the 38th parallel, although in the eastern mountains the ROKs had held firm against North Korean attacks and remained above the line. The UN Command had halted the Communists just above Seoul and held good positions north of the Han River. What's more, the offensive had actually been of considerable benefit to U.S./UN/ROK morale. The terrifying Chinese Communists had done their utmost, and the UN forces had weathered the furious storm quite well. The Chinese had lost not only the offensive but their psychological edge as well.

The front was relatively quiet for two weeks, as the bulk of the Communist force withdrew about ten miles to lick its wounds, leaving inadequate units in place to ward off any UN Command attempts to recover the real estate it had lost during the offensive. The U.S. Marines were able to fight their way into Chunchon by May 7, and the other key junction, Uijongbu, fell simultaneously to the 1st U.S. Cavalry Division.

The Eighth Army did not, however, expend its energy driving northward. Intelligence had reported that the Communists had committed only half of their available strength to the April offensive; a renewal was bound to follow shortly. Van Fleet accordingly ordered most of his forces to devote their attention to making their positions impregnable. They strung more than five hundred miles of barbed wire in front of their lines, laid minefields and set out drums of gasoline and napalm that could be detonated electronically, emplaced artillery and calculated its range, and carefully plotted interlocking fields of machine-gun fire.[3]

Although the men of the UN Command were well prepared to defy the Communists yet again, Washington feared that the Chinese, determined that the second phase of the spring offensive must not fail, might at last resort to the desperate measure of attacking U.S./UN infantry from the air. It was in light of this quite reasonable fear — and in the aftermath of the British 29 Brigade's ordeal on the Imjin River — that London now reversed one of its most stubbornly held policies. Through his foreign secretary, Herbert Morrison, Prime Minister Clement Attlee assured Washington that if planes from Manchuria attacked U.S./UN forces heavily, the British government would assent to retaliatory strikes against the Manchurian airfields.[4]

The anticipated ground offensive finally began on the night of May 15–16, with another heavy artillery barrage. This time the weightiest Communist blow fell in the mountainous terrain near the east coast, just above the 38th parallel. This sector of the front, where the rigors of topography should have given the defenders a tremendous advantage, was manned entirely by ROKs. The Communists obviously planned to knock them out and, long before U.S./UN reinforcements could arrive on the scene, to outflank the whole Eighth Army.

The offensive was an utter failure. Although the Communists launched their attack with some 300,000 men, including twenty fresh divisions to spearhead the assault, they gained very little ground and inflicted relatively light casualties on the U.S./UN forces. The ROKs in the east did yield, but the Chinese who swept through the gap soon ran into an immovable barrier of U.S. Marines and ROKs north and east of Chunchon. The ROKs also redeemed their honor by thwarting a Communist feint toward Seoul. The strong Eighth Army defensive positions held, and UN Command air power took its usual frightful toll.

On May 18, even before the Communist offensive had fully lost its momentum, Van Fleet ordered his forces onto the counteroffensive. It was a case of "hit 'em while they're down." Badly hurt, disorganized, and running short of ammunition, the Communists could offer little resistance. Their offensive was stopped cold by May 20, and in the course of the next few days the UN Command moved northward all along the front. In the western sector the Eighth Army moved up the main road through Uijongbu to Kumhwa (at the southeastern corner of the Iron Triangle), along the way securing the Hwachon Reservoir, which, before the division of Korea, had supplied much of Seoul's water and electricity. On the east coast ROKs reached Kansong, the terminus of a good road from Seoul. In the end it was not enemy force but heavy rains, rendering roads and valleys impassable, that slowed the advance. By that time enemy casualties for the month of May amounted to 17,000 killed, as many taken prisoner, and several times that number wounded.

By May 30 U.S./UN forces along most of the front were back on the line north of the 38th parallel that they had occupied in mid-April. Making it clear to Ridgway that continued pursuit of the Communists was out of the question, the Joint Chiefs of Staff rather reluctantly accepted his proposal for Operation Piledriver, to begin on June 1 with the primary objective of seizing as much as possible of the Iron Triangle. Chorwon and Kumhwa fell on June 11, and two days later U.S./UN forces entered the abandoned town of Pyonggang, at the triangle's apex. (Truman's memoirs and several histories of the war state that UN forces occupied the North Korean capital on June 13. They were confused by the similarity of names. U.S./UN/ROK forces did not enter Pyongyang at any time after December 5, 1950.) Pyonggang was soon relinquished, but Chorwon and Kumhwa were retained and are in South Korea today. With the hills at the base of the Iron Triangle in U.S./UN/ROK possession, the Communists were deprived of an important staging area not only for a new offensive but also for any postwar attempt to invade South Korea.

During May the Truman administration came to feel that it was an auspicious time to end the war. By the close of the month their spring offensives had cost the Communists a total of nearly 200,000 casualties. Even populous China could ill afford to continue paying such a price for long. Moreover, it was imperative for the United States/UN to conclude a truce before the Chinese Communist air force could become strong enough to hold its own against UN Command air power. If Chinese planes could radically curtail U.S./UN air operations over North Korea, and if the Communists could build and defend jet airfields that would base their planes sufficiently far south to facilitate attacks upon U.S./UN/ROK forces or the bombing of South Korea, then the United States/UN would once again be confronted with "an entirely new war." Equally important, the American public was rapidly losing its patience with a confusing and frustrating war that had already cost America nearly 75,000 casualties.

The United States wanted to open negotiations that would deal with no issue except that of ending hostilities; all discussion of political issues was to be postponed. At its meetings on May 2 and 16 the National Security Council confirmed that the United States would seek what would essentially be a restoration of the status quo ante bellum. Washington would continue to pay lip service to the long-range goal of creating a unified, independent, and democratic Korea through political negotiations. But on June 1, during his testimony in the MacArthur hearings, Secretary of State Acheson said of the unification of Korea, "I do not understand it to be a war aim." This was the first publicly reported and unequivocal official statement of the change of heart that had taken place in December. (That same day Secretary-General Trygve Lie made a similar statement on behalf of the UN.) When he returned for more questioning the following day, Acheson was asked whether he was suggesting "the possibility of a cease-fire at or near the 38th parallel." He replied: "If you could have a real settlement, that would accomplish the military purposes in Korea. That is if the aggression would end and you had reliable assurances that it would not be resumed, then you could return to a peacetime status, and we would hope gradually to remove the troops from Korea, both Chinese troops and United Nations troops."[5]

The Truman administration rather naively hoped that the Chinese Communists would behave sensibly and, under pressure of military necessity, accept these reasonable terms — and indeed be grateful that America was allowing them to extricate themselves from Korea at so little cost. By halting its advance just above the 38th parallel, the United States/UN was — so Washington claimed — demonstrating that it had adopted a policy of restraint and moderation. It was hoped that the Communists would follow this good example.

At the same time, however, to intensify the pressure on the Chinese Communists and to make it clear to them that their cooperation would not be bought with any concessions regarding China's UN seat or Formosa, the United States launched a diplomatic offensive. On May 18, despite a Soviet-bloc boycott of the proceedings, the UN General Assembly passed an American-sponsored resolution (48–0, with eight neutral nations abstaining) calling upon all members not to supply Communist China or North Korea with military equipment or materials (including petroleum) vital for their war effort. Even the British voted in favor. The Communist spring offensives had rallied America's cautious allies squarely behind its policies, and Washington felt that this increased level of unity within the UN alliance would be a powerful factor in convincing Peking that it was time to cut its losses.

Also on May 18, addressing the China Institute in America at New York City's Waldorf-Astoria Hotel, Dean Rusk delivered a major foreign-policy speech in which he removed any doubts that might have lingered about U.S. endorsement of Chiang Kai-shek's regime on Formosa as the legitimate government of China. "We do not recognize the authorities in Peiping for what they pretend to be," he declared. "The Peiping regime may be a colonial Russian government — a Slavic Manchukuo on a larger scale. It is not the Government of China. It does not pass the first test. It is not Chinese." He then went on to say, without intentional humor, "We recognize the National Government of the Republic of China, even though the territory under its control is severely restricted." That government, he affirmed, would "continue to receive important aid and assistance from the United States."[6] Indeed, Washington had very recently sent a hundred-man Military Assistance Advisory Group to Formosa and had promised Chiang that a $300 million first installment of resumed military aid would soon be forthcoming.

The Truman administration was now fully and publicly committed to the support of Chiang, both on Formosa and in the UN. However, although Rusk had properly cleared his speech with Acheson, the president had not been forewarned and was quite upset about it. As Acheson recorded in a memo, he had to reassure Truman that Rusk "had not suggested or in any way made any change in policy, but had merely repeated what had been said by both the President and me many times in the past."[7] But never so forthrightly or so publicly.

Developments now began to come quickly on the diplomatic front. The main barrier to the beginning of negotiations was that neither side was willing to announce its eagerness for peace talks, for then it would appear that weakness was forcing it to sue for peace, thereby giving the enemy a propaganda advantage and encouraging him to demand concessions in return for agreeing to end the fighting. But Washington hit upon a solution. It would announce that it understood that the Communists wanted to open negotiations and that it would not reject any reasonable and serious proposal regarding peace talks. The Communists could then save face by claiming that the United States had made the first move, but Washington could also save face by saying that its move had been made in answer to Communist feelers. First, however, it was necessary to ascertain that the Communists wouldn't embarrass the United States by responding to its announcement with silence or with excessive demands.

George Kennan, who was then on an extended leave of absence from the State Department, was the perfect man to make the preliminary contact. His status had the right balance of official and unofficial. The Communists would correctly understand him to be speaking for the U.S. government, but if there was a foul-up, the State Department could disavow Kennan and claim that he had been speaking as a private citizen without authorization.

On May 18 Acheson asked Kennan to contact the chief Soviet UN delegate, Iakov Malik, and to inform him in a private conversation that the United States was ready to negotiate if the Communists were prepared to be reasonable. By June 5 he had accomplished his mission and had received an encouraging response from Malik. The talks soon bore fruit. Speaking on a UN radio program on the twenty-third, Malik said that "the Soviet people" believed that an armistice on the basis of the 38th parallel was now possible if both sides really wished to stop the fighting. Two days later, on June 25, the first anniversary of the North Korean invasion, the Peking *People's Daily* stated that the Chinese people agreed with the Soviet people.[8]

Shortly thereafter, the Soviet deputy foreign minister, Andrei

Gromyko, assured the American ambassador in Moscow that Malik had accurately represented the Kremlin's point of view and that the Soviets favored negotiations in which the military commanders of the forces engaged in Korea would confine their discussions to purely military matters.[9] Indeed, all would understand that the explosive political issues were simply beyond the province of such negotiators. This arrangement also suited the Americans and the Chinese Communists, for Peking still disclaimed responsibility for the Chinese "volunteers" in Korea, and Washington feared that any dealings with Chinese Communist diplomats might imply recognition of their regime.

By this time it was clear to everyone that the Korean War had gravely harmed the Soviet Union's strategic position in the Cold War, and that continuation of the fighting in Korea was only making things worse. As a direct result of the Korean War the United States and Great Britain had both embarked on extremely ambitious programs of enlarging their armed forces and arming them with a profusion of sophisticated weapons; Anglo-American accord and cooperation had been greatly increased; the United States had gained complete control of the UN and had actually managed the incredible feat of getting the organization to field an anti-Communist army; the NATO alliance had been solidified — to the point where a pan-European army led by an American general now appeared to be on the verge of becoming a reality; West Germany was well on its way to sovereign status and rearmament; and Japan seemed about to be rearmed and allied with the United States. Soviet diplomatic efforts to reverse these trends had failed miserably. On June 21, only two days before Malik's radio speech, a Paris conference of Big Four deputy foreign ministers had collapsed in anger when the Soviet delegate tried to force through an anti-NATO tactic. Evidently the Kremlin decided sometime during June that the only way to destroy the momentum of American diplomacy and military buildup was to turn down the heat in Korea.

Assured now that a public overture would not meet with an embarrassing rebuff, Washington drafted a message addressed to the "Commander in Chief Communist Forces in Korea" and instructed Ridgway to broadcast it openly, in his own name, from Tokyo on June 30. "I am informed," the message began, putting the burden of initiation upon the Communists, "that you may wish a meeting to discuss an armistice providing for the cessation of hostilities and all acts of armed force in Korea, with adequate guarantees for the maintenance of such armistice."[10] It all sounded so simple.

On July 2 the Communists broadcast a response signed by Kim Il-sung (as commander of the Korean People's Army, not as head of the North Korean government) and by General Peng Teh-huai, commander of the Chinese People's Volunteers. They agreed that it was desirable to begin talks and proposed that representatives of the two sides meet in Kaesong, just below the 38th parallel. Since Kaesong was then in no-man's-land between the lines, Ridgway found the proposal acceptable and sent his reply the next day. Communist and U.S./ROK liaison officers met at Kaesong on July 8, and two days later the chief delegates met for the first time.

Since the talks were to deal exclusively with military questions, America's monopoly of command of the UN forces was carried over to the negotiating table. The chief UN delegate was an American, Vice Admiral C. Turner Joy, Commander Naval Forces, Far East. The remainder of the UN delegation was composed of an American rear admiral, an American army general, an American air force general, and a South Korean army general. No other UN nation with forces in Korea was represented, and none objected very loudly to this arrangement.

The principal Communist delegates were General Nam Il, chief of staff of the North Korean army, and Major General Hsieh Fang, chief of staff of the Chinese People's Volunteers. Although the former would do most of the talking for the Communists, he clearly deferred to the latter for guidance. Hsieh was the éminence grise, and his hard features called to Admiral Joy's mind Shakespeare's lines: "Yond Cassius has a lean and hungry look;/ . . . such men are dangerous."

Washington's expectation that the negotiations would take from three to six weeks might have been tempered if note had been taken of a disturbing historical precedent. After the Japanese had invaded Korea in 1592 and Chinese troops from Manchuria had gone to the rescue of the Ming dynasty's tribute state, peace talks between the Chinese and the Japanese dragged on for three years, largely because neither side would agree to any terms that implied it had suffered even a minor defeat.[11]

*   *   *

The Communists began the first session, on July 10, by proposing an immediate cease-fire, but the United States/UN insisted on continuing the fighting until satisfactory terms had been negotiated. Washington felt that this would put pressure on the Communists to accept its terms quickly. This initial exchange also gave the United States/UN a psychological edge, for Communist eagerness to disengage suggested weakness. Such subtleties would count for much in the war of nerves that lay ahead.

After the defeat of the second phase of the Communist spring offensive, General Van Fleet had wanted to pursue the Communists far into North Korea, since he felt that by pressing them as hard as possible the United States/UN would get the most prompt and advantageous settlement. He later complained that such pursuit could have been undertaken with little risk, since, he said, "we had the Chinese whipped. . . . They were in awful shape." But the JCS insisted that the UN Command forces halt a short distance above the 38th parallel. They agreed with Ridgway that it was especially important that the Communists be deprived of the Iron Triangle and that North Korea be punished by the loss of a significant amount of territory. (At some points the U.S./UN/ROK line was as much as forty miles above the parallel, though the Communists partially offset that loss by holding some territory below the parallel in the west.) But Ridgway and the JCS also agreed that it would be a mistake to continue deep into North Korea, since the longer the American supply lines grew, the greater the disadvantage at which the U.S./UN/ROK forces would find themselves. Conversely, as the Communists were pushed northward, the increased flow of supplies and reinforcements over their shortened and thus more secure supply lines would strengthen their fighting capacity.[12] Even MacArthur had acknowledged in his Die-for-Tie statement that once a stalemate had been reached, "thereafter our further advance would militarily benefit the enemy more than it would ourselves" unless the United States/UN accompanied that advance by air attacks against Chinese territory.[13]

Although many hawks, both within the U.S. military and outside it, accused the Truman administration of letting the Communists off the hook by halting arbitrarily just north of the 38th parallel, Ridgway and the JCS felt that by stopping where they did, they would actually be able to put maximum pressure on the Communists. Their logic was that by keeping the Communists pinned down near the parallel, they would render the enemy's attenuated supply lines very vulnerable to air attack.

Ridgway and the JCS were now hoping that by bombing, mercilessly and continuously, all of the major roads over which the Communist forces at the front received supplies and reinforcements, they could pressure the Communists into accepting a reasonable armistice. Military intelligence had reported that the Communists were becoming far more dependent on truck transport than they had been earlier in the war; it stood to reason that if UN Command bombers could keep long stretches of all the major north-south roads knocked out, few trucks could get through to the front. At the same time, UN naval forces would not only continue their blockade of North Korea but also maintain heavy shelling of ports, including Hungnam and Wonsan, the latter a vital depot on a major railway line from Manchuria. By appearing to pose a threat of amphibious landings at those ports, the UN Command would also force the Communists to station substantial numbers of troops there.

The code name of the bombing program, Operation Strangle, announced its purpose. But even after the operation had been expanded in August to include railways and bridges as well as roads, it failed to strangle the Communists into submission. Indeed, it didn't seem to do much at all either to impair their performance in battle or to make them more acquiescent at the negotiating table. The problem was that no matter how hard the U.S./UN planes hit their targets, the Communists would repair, improvise, or reroute with astonishing speed and ingenuity. They maintained huge forced-labor battalions that would be rushed to the site of an attack and have a damaged road back in usable shape within hours, or a bombed railway serviceable within days. When necessary, they reverted to using armies of carriers who would travel on foot, hiding during the day and moving at night. The Communist soldiers at the front needed relatively few supplies, and enough got through to enable them to manage.

In a series of articles in the *New York Times* in late November 1951, Hanson Baldwin declared Operation Strangle a failure and observed that "the enemy's supply lines can be cut finally and irretrievably only when ground forces are firmly astride them."[14] All this should have demonstrated, once and for all, the futility of strategic bombing in a war against Asian Communists. But the U.S. Air Force found all sorts of excuses for the failure of Operation Strangle and tried the same hopeless — and unprofitably murderous — program all over again in Vietnam.

When the peace talks began, in July 1951, the enemies were ranged along a line at which their strength was more or less balanced — pitting Communist manpower, frugality, and resourcefulness against U.S./UN firepower and supplies. As both sides took great pains to fortify their positions with barbed wire, mines, deep tunnels, and artillery emplacements, the fighting along this increasingly static line became much like the trench warfare of World War I, punctuated by desperate and extremely costly sorties to capture an occasional hilltop.

From that time on, the fighting had two main functions: to gain control of certain topographical features that had tactical value, and to prod the enemy into making concessions at the negotiating table. The United States/UN also launched some attacks for a third, less publicized reason: to keep its men in fighting trim. On September 30 General Van Fleet admitted that he felt it was "imperative that the Eighth Army remain active to forestall the dreaded softening process of stagnation . . . I could not allow my forces to become soft and dormant."[15]

The next two years saw some of the most savage and bitter fighting of the war, but there were no more chases up and down the peninsula. Gains were measured in yards rather than in miles. And the battles that made headlines were for the relatively minor outposts to which the U.S./UN forces gave such names as the Punchbowl, Heartbreak and Bloody ridges, Capitol Hill, White Horse Hill, Sniper's Ridge, the Hook, Luke the Gook's Castle, and Pork Chop Hill. This fighting was terribly costly, especially in proportion to what was gained. The United States alone would suffer 63,200 casualties (12,300 of them killed in action) during the two years the peace talks lasted, and the Communist losses were many times heavier. An appalling number of men were indeed going to die for tie.

CHAPTER 32

The War of Nerves

THE NEGOTIATIONS were like an obsessive, horribly frustrating nightmare from which it is impossible to awake. The Americans soon came to feel that General Bolté had been right: negotiating with the Communists really was proving to be as fruitless as it was repulsive.

One problem was that both sides had mixed feelings about ending the war. Although President Truman was a decent man who genuinely deplored the carnage in Korea, his administration felt a certain need to continue the war for the same reasons that the Kremlin wanted to end it: the war was a powerful stimulus for American and NATO military buildup and for American diplomatic leadership. On the other hand, the American public had lost its enthusiasm for the war, and its disenchantment threatened to translate into a Republican victory in the 1952 presidential election. The Kremlin certainly viewed with pleasure the damage that the war was doing to American domestic morale, and it well suited Stalin's purposes to have the war drag on, at a simmer, as long as the continuation could be blamed on American aggressiveness and imperialism. The Communists could then win international sympathy by portraying themselves as the champions of peace — and could convert pacifists into Communists, just as they had done with antifascists in the mid-1930s, in both cases because no other major power was as effectively, albeit self-interestedly, espousing the cause in question.

The major obstacle to the swift negotiation of an armistice was the American position that the United States had the moral right and responsibility to demand terms that, although essentially restoring the status quo of a divided Korea, would tip the balance sufficiently in South Korea's favor so as to guarantee its future security. The United States was perfectly justified in making such demands; after all, North Korea had invaded the south. The United States had, at enormous cost, led a successful effort to repulse that invasion, and it wanted to be certain that the Communists would not soon be in a position to make another attempt.

The Chinese Communists would eventually yield to all the major American demands, but they went to extraordinary lengths to make it appear that they were not prompted to do so by American strength. For weeks and months on end they would refuse to yield one iota, no matter how much pressure was applied by UN Command forces in the field. At length, having demonstrated their indifference to the minor annoyance of U.S./UN/ROK attacks, the Communists might finally make a counterproposal that was close enough to American demands so that the U.S. delegation could accept it. The Communists could then say that the Americans had yielded to them, not vice versa.

The negotiations were thus characterized by endless and exasperating face-saving and sparring for psychological advantage. To apply pressure each side would from time to time threaten to break off the talks — or actually carry out such threats — always assigning the responsibility for the breakdown to the other side's perfidy, even fabricating incidents to support the charges. Both sides would then protest that although their peace-loving instincts led them to favor talks, if the enemy insisted on continuing his aggression, there was no point in talking until he was prepared to be reasonable. Until then, to insist on continuing the talks would be to show weakness.

Responsibility for the absurdly excessive duration of the peace talks must be shared by the Americans and the Communists. For all their stubbornness, the Communists did show themselves willing to concede to reasonable demands. But each such concession only lengthened the war, for the United States would take it as a sign of Communist weakness and increase its demands on other issues. In the negotiations, as in the military conduct of the war during its first months, the United States felt that it could not afford to stop until it had extracted *every possible* concession. Each gain only made it appear that further gains might be possible. Then the negotiating process would begin all over again with each side viciously accusing the other of bad faith. The delegates would exchange coarse insults, and the talks would degenerate into orgies of vituperation and recrimination. Meanwhile, the hillside massacres and the fierce bombing of North Korea continued relentlessly.

*   *   *

When the talks began, at Kaesong in July 1951, one of the first Communist demands was for the withdrawal of all foreign troops from Korea. The UN delegation insisted that this was a political issue beyond the jurisdiction of the negotiators. The talks remained deadlocked over this question for nearly two weeks. Finally, on July 24, General George Marshall told a press conference in Washington that "withdrawal of foreign troops from Korea will naturally follow a satisfactory peace settlement."[1] The Communists then proposed a clause stating that the military commanders would recommend to their governments that a postwar political conference be held to discuss troop withdrawal and other such matters. The United States agreed, and both sides were surprised by how easily that dispute had been settled. It gave everyone a sense of optimism that would soon prove to be thoroughly groundless.

On July 27 the negotiators turned to the question of the demarcation line between North and South Korea. The United States insisted that the new boundary be the line of contact between the military forces at the time an armistice agreement was signed. The Americans argued that the topography along the 38th parallel made that line difficult to defend. They could accept only a line farther north, where hills and ridges could be well fortified. The Communists professed to be outraged. They insisted upon the 38th parallel and maintained that they had agreed to negotiations only because the United States and the UN had said that they would accept a return to the status quo ante bellum. America countered that surely it was worthwhile to give up a bit of territory in return for an end to U.S./UN air attacks on North Korea. What really made this issue so emotional for both sides was that the loss of territory would be seen by the world as North Korea's punishment for its aggression.

To prod the Communists into submission, the United States/UN bombed Pyongyang heavily on July 30. But the Communists remained impassive and adamant. On August 4 a small group of heavily armed Chinese soldiers violated the neutrality of the conference zone and menaced the UN delegation. General Ridgway immediately broke off the talks but ordered their resumption a few days later, having received assurances from the Communists that there would be no more such incidents. The tough American response had done nothing to change the Communist bargaining position. On August 10, the day the talks resumed, General Nam Il reiterated, yet again, his arguments in favor of the 38th parallel and then declared, "At present we have nothing more to say."

"Neither do we," responded Admiral C. Turner Joy. The delegates then sat facing each other in unbroken silence for two hours and eleven minutes before at last curtly adjourning the session.[2]

Ridgway was so furious that he recommended to the Joint Chiefs of Staff that the talks be suspended unless the Communists accepted the proposed UN line within three days. He believed that a good dose of fire and steel would bring the Communists to their senses and wrap up the war in short order. But the JCS counseled restraint and patience. President Truman didn't want to let anything interrupt the talks. He believed that the Communists were eager to end the war but that they felt they could do so only after some face-saving delay. If the United States could be patient just a little longer, the Communists would surely yield.

And indeed they very soon showed signs of doing just that. During the course of the week after August 10, they gradually manifested an increasing willingness to compromise on the issue of the 38th parallel, which many observers felt was the key question of the negotiations. If that point could be resolved, a truce might be in the offing.

What followed is one of the cloudiest episodes in the history of the Korean War. On August 19, and again on the twenty-second, the Communists protested that UN Command forces had violated the neutrality of the Kaesong conference zone. Ridgway insisted that the charges were false and refused to apologize, whereupon the Communists suspended the negotiations. (They would not resume until late October.) It is entirely possible that South Korean guerrillas, or even regular troops, were responsible for the alleged attacks, if they did indeed take place. Syngman Rhee was dead set against an armistice that would leave Korea divided, and he may well have given orders to sabotage the talks. But it is also possible that the charges were a Communist ruse to embarrass the UN Command.[3]

Regardless of who was responsible, the fact is that, from the American point of view, a truce in Korea at that juncture would have been inopportune, for it would have made the Soviets appear cooperative and would have removed one of the principal reasons for rushing ahead with a lenient Japanese peace treaty. The ending of the immediate crisis in the Far East might even have induced some of the more moderate of the neutral nations in Asia to call for a treaty that the Soviets would be willing to sign.

On August 13 the United States and Great Britain circulated their final draft of the treaty to all the nations that had been at war with Japan — all, that is, except China. The Americans and the British had reached a compromise on the Chinese issue. Washington refused to deal with Peking, and London refused to deal with Chiang Kai-shek; therefore both Chinese regimes were to be excluded. The volatile issue of Formosa was handled similarly. The treaty simply stated that the Japanese renounced their sovereignty over the island, without specifying the government to which it was to be transferred. In what was an unnecessarily provocative move, the Kurils and southern Sakhalin Island were given the same treatment, even though the Yalta agreement had specifically awarded them to the Soviet Union.[4]

The draft treaty was presented as a virtual fait accompli. The Allied nations were to read it and to send delegates to a conference that was to open in San Francisco on September 4. Provision was made for minor changes and amendments, but debate was to be minimal, and the main business of the conference was simply to sign the treaty. The Soviet Union had been invited, in the hope and expectation that it would angrily decline. To the great consternation of Washington, the Soviets replied that they would attend to present their own proposals. Dean Acheson was especially worried that the sole Soviet intention was to "wreck" the conference. At his direction Dean Rusk prepared a memo for the National Security Council warning that

> the USSR, finding itself unable to prevent the signing of the treaty by parliamentary means, might resort to "shock tactics" to reduce the number of signatories, reduce the effect of the treaty in Asia, delay it, amend it, or arouse Japanese fears. The USSR might also produce a competing treaty, attack our security arrangement, start a major offensive in Korea, or submit an ultimatum of some sort.[5]

It was no time to be negotiating with the Communists in Korea.

In the end, Acheson's fears proved baseless. Denied by parliamentary tactics any chance to present their proposals, the Russians walked out of the conference. On September 8 the treaty was signed by forty-eight nations, none of them Communist. The treaty was to go into effect on April 28 of the following year. By September 1951, however, the transition from occupation to self-government in Japan had progressed so far that the treaty did little more than provide a legal basis for the already existing situation. MacArthur's relief had effectively meant the end of the occupation, for Ridgway had not tried to live up to his predecessor's image, instead encouraging the Japanese to take over ever more of their own government, with occupation authorities playing an increasingly minimal and inconspicuous role.

Late in August, Ridgway ordered his troops to begin a new series of attacks east of the Iron Triangle, presumably both to intensify Communist eagerness to end the war and also to gain the strongest possible defensive positions before agreement on an armistice would preclude further movement.

The most intense fighting from August to October, while the armistice negotiations were suspended, was for the hills dominating the deep valley that the Americans nicknamed the Punchbowl, about twenty miles from the east coast. The U.S. Marines concentrated on gaining control of the Punchbowl itself, while the 2nd U.S. Infantry Division (which was reinforced with ROKs) struggled to secure two ranges of hills a short distance to the west. The names tell the story: Heartbreak Ridge, for the acquisition of which the 2nd Division suffered 3,700 casualties, and Bloody Ridge, which cost 2,700. By October 15 all of these objectives were in American hands. Similar gains were made at a number of points along the front, giving the United States/UN a line of contact that it felt South Korea could hold securely in the future. These gains had been made at staggering cost; between August and October the anti-Communist forces incurred some 60,000 casualties, of whom 22,000 were Americans. General Van Fleet estimated that the Communists had sustained approximately 234,000 casualties, and although his figure was grossly inflated to make the U.S. losses sound less awful, the Communists had indeed lost huge numbers of men.

Ridgway had vowed that the U.S./UN negotiators would not return to Kaesong, for it was effectively in the Communist zone. He would resume the negotiations only at a site that was truly neutral, so that the Communists could not play any more tricks. After a long and bitter argument, the Communists proposed on October 7 that the talks be resumed, this time at the village of Panmunjom, five miles east of Kaesong. Ridgway agreed, and after two weeks of preliminary meetings the chief delegates finally met, on October 25, for the first time since August 22.[6]

On that same day, October 25, the Conservatives bested the Labour party in a British general election, largely because the Labourites had become so bitterly divided over issues relating to the Korean War. The crux of the disagreement was that Prime Minister Attlee had for the most part approved of the American conduct of the war. He had also sponsored an enormously costly program of expansion and equipping of the British armed forces. He had done so both because the United States insisted that the British do their part for NATO and because only increased military strength would permit Britain to hold on to its great-power status and to avoid becoming a virtual American colony. The huge sums spent on the military, however, meant less for the social welfare programs so central to the traditional Labour policy. A large faction of the party, led by Aneurin Bevan (who had been minister of health and then minister of labor before resigning in protest from Attlee's cabinet in April), strongly criticized Attlee's pro-Americanism and his defense budget. The deep split within the party ranks led to defeat at the polls. Churchill then became prime minister once again, and Britain became more supportive than ever of U.S. policy.

Within a week of the resumption of talks the Communists had made a major concession: they gave up their insistence on the 38th parallel and agreed that the new demarcation line between North and South Korea should be approximately along the present line of contact. But they gave with one hand and took with the other, demanding a line that would not only acknowledge their disputed control of Kaesong but that would also require the UN Command to give up all its holdings in the Iron Triangle and Punchbowl areas, including Heartbreak and Bloody ridges. This was obviously unacceptable.

Then, on November 6, the Communists made a startlingly dramatic offer. They would accept the actual current line of contact as the permanent demarcation line if the United States/UN would accept the proposal at once. That would mean that a de facto cease-fire would go into immediate effect on the ground (though U.S./UN air and naval action against North Korea would continue) and would last until an armistice had been signed, since there would be no point in fighting for gains that would have to be given up in the end. Ridgway rejected the offer out of hand, because he felt that a cease-fire would remove much of the incentive for the Communists to agree to reasonable terms for the remaining items on the agenda, and because the current line would give Kaesong to the Communists. Ridgway had something of an obsession about Kaesong, and it led him into heated arguments with the JCS, who thought he should yield on such a minor point. But Ridgway wanted Kaesong for a number of reasons: from the tenth century A.D. until 1392 it had been the capital of Korea and thus had a certain nostalgic prestige; it was astride one of the main invasion routes toward Seoul; it was south of the 38th parallel; and the Communists held it only because they had violated its neutrality.

Ridgway's obstinacy infuriated the JCS, who argued that the American public would never understand why what seemed like such a reasonable offer had been rejected. They felt that he should relent on Kaesong and accept the Communist proposal, with the stipulation that the deal would remain valid only if all other armistice-related issues were settled within a stated time. Ridgway gave in — and Kaesong is today part of North Korea.

Anticipating the abatement of the fighting, Ridgway issued on November 12 orders specifying that the U.S./UN forces were to adopt a policy of "active defense." Units larger than a battalion were not to initiate attacks without special permission from Tokyo. Meanwhile, Communist and UN Command officers argued over the line of contact and drew it on the map. On November 27 the chief delegates agreed that if complete accord on all remaining items had not been reached within thirty days, the demarcation line would no longer be binding.

The U.S./UN/ROK forces were not to be inactive during this period. On November 12 Ridgway had launched the inhumanly named Operation Ratkiller to eliminate the Communist guerrillas who, operating from the mountains of South Korea, harassed the UN Command's rear and supply lines. By January 1952 the operation had succeeded in killing or capturing more than 20,000 guerrillas and bandits. Both sides also used the December lull to fortify their defensive positions and to catch their breath.

The December 27 deadline passed without an agreement, largely because of the issue of prisoners of war, which came to the fore in the negotiations that month. Early in the war the United States/UN and both Korean regimes had announced that they would abide by the terms of the Geneva Prisoners of War Convention of 1949. To prevent any situation similar to Stalin's holding of huge numbers of POWs long after the end of World War II, the International Red Cross had adopted the principle that all prisoners must be repatriated without delay once hostilities had ended. However, by the time negotiations were about to begin at Kaesong in the summer of 1951, the United States had decided that it did not want to return all of its nearly 100,000 North Korean prisoners, for to do so would be to provide North Korea with practically a whole new army. On July 3, 1951, Dean Rusk informed America's allies that the United States wished to exchange POWs on a one-for-one basis. Since the Communists had killed many of their ROK prisoners (and some of their U.S./UN prisoners as well, though not as many as some estimates held), and since many U.S./UN soldiers had died of illness or starvation while in captivity, the Communists held only about 10,000 POWs. When they returned them, they would get just 10,000 of their own men in exchange.[7]

The American delegates said nothing about this even during the first weeks of December, when the negotiations turned to the prisoner-of-war issue, and in fact the Communists agreed to exchange lists of POWs only because the UN Command promised to release all prisoners as soon as an armistice was signed. The lists, presented on December 18, showed that the UN Command held a total of 132,474 prisoners, of whom approximately 95,500 were North Koreans, 20,700 were Chinese Communists, and 16,200 were pro-Communist South Koreans who had joined the North Korean army. The UN Command held an additional 38,000 anti-Communist South Koreans (mostly men, but some women) who had been recruited at gunpoint by the North Koreans; they were reclassified as civilian internees. Another 6,000 POWs had either died or escaped.

The Communists held less than one-tenth as many POWs. They reported a total of 11,559, of whom approximately 7,100 were South Koreans, 3,200 were Americans, and 1,200 were from Britain and other UN countries. When these figures were published in the American press, they caused a great wave of revulsion and moral outrage against the atrocities that they implied. The United States/UN had officially reported 11,224 Americans as missing in action; the Communist figures meant that something like 8,000 Americans had died — one way or another — after capture. Nearly 80,000 South Koreans were unaccounted for. The Communists disingenuously countered that 53,000 prisoners had been "sent home" or "released at the front." Many of the South Koreans had, in fact, either been murdered or else forced to serve in the North Korean army.

Once these figures had been released, it was unthinkable for the United States to agree to an all-for-all exchange — to give the Communists 132,000 men in return for 11,000. At Panmunjom on January 2, 1952, the U.S./UN delegates finally announced the American demand that would prolong the war for another year and a half — and that would cost the United States another 37,000 casualties. The UN Command said that it would repatriate only those POWs who expressly stated that they wished to return home. All those who said they did not want to return to life under a Communist regime would be released after the signing of an armistice and given political asylum. The Koreans could remain in South Korea; the Chinese would be given transportation to Formosa.

America stated its case in moral terms. It was common knowledge that Stalin had executed or sent to Siberia huge numbers of Russians who had been captured by the Axis during World War II. (Their crime had been to allow themselves to be captured.) The United States and Britain, in an effort to maintain their shaky friendship with Stalin, had forced many of these men to return home, against their will, from POW camps in areas liberated by Anglo-American troops. Now the United States vowed that it would never again appease the barbaric Communists by agreeing to forced repatriation.

The Communists were beside themselves with rage. Did America really mean to say that it would shamelessly violate the Geneva Convention? they shrieked. However, the Communists were not particularly worried about the well-being of their men. They feared, rather, that if a large percentage of North Koreans and Chinese refused to return home, the West would score a great propaganda victory. That would be a loss of face that they simply could not tolerate. Hence they were incredibly fanatic in their opposition to the American position, vowing that they would never yield. The equally determined United States/UN attempted to sway them with insincere assurances that the great majority of POWs would probably want to return home, but to no avail.

On January 24, 1952, Ridgway reported to Washington that the truce talks had reached "a complete state of paralysis."[8] Truman's sense of frustration was so great that three days later he confided to his diary:

> Dealing with Communist governments is like an honest man trying to deal with a numbers racket king or the head of a dope ring. It seems to me that the proper approach now would be an ultimatum with a ten-day expiration limit, informing Moscow that we intend to blockade the China coast from the Korean border to Indochina, and that we intend to destroy every military base in Manchuria, including submarine bases, by means now in our control, and if there is further interference, we shall eliminate any ports or cities necessary to accomplish our peaceful purposes.

He went on to write, "This means all out war," and he elaborated that it meant that every major city "and every manufacturing plant in China and the Soviet Union will be eliminated. This is the final chance for the Soviet government to decide whether it desires to survive or not."[9] Fortunately, once Truman had gotten this off his chest, he returned to deal sensibly and realistically with the situation.

The Communists responded to the challenge of the POW issue in several drastic and desperate ways. First of all, they greatly intensified their efforts to indoctrinate the POWs they held — to brainwash them — so that they would refuse repatriation at the end of the war. Second, they launched a campaign of violent disorders in the UN Command POW camps, within which the pro- and anti-Communist prisoners had organized themselves into extremely militant factions. A significant number of trained Communist cadres even allowed themselves to be captured by U.S./UN/ROK forces so that they could direct disruptive activities within the camps and also attempt, through brainwashing and intimidation, to convert the anti-Communists held by the UN Command. Here, as elsewhere in the war effort, the Communists displayed extraordinary determination and resourcefulness. They managed to smuggle into the camps radios over which they could receive instructions from Pyongyang and Peking; they established a network of contacts with locals outside the camps who would see that messages were relayed to the north; and, at the largest camp, that on Koje Island, or Koje-do, offshore from Pusan, they improvised an enormous arsenal of homemade, but nonetheless very effective, weapons. They then, ostensibly to protest inhuman conditions in the camp, proceeded to riot so violently and in such large numbers that the disorders could not fail to attract the attention of the Western press. The Communist press, meanwhile, raged that Koje was like a Nazi concentration camp and assured the world that the North Korean and Chinese camps were like resorts in contrast.

Beginning in February, and continuing through the rest of 1952, unrest smoldered on Koje and occasionally exploded into full-scale riots. When the first major riot broke out, on February 18, U.S. troops had to be sent into the compounds to suppress it. Seventy-seven POWs were killed and another 140 wounded. (One American soldier died; 38 were wounded.) The climax came in May. On the seventh of the month POWs managed to capture the American general in charge of Koje. Three days later, threatening to kill him, they extracted a statement that implied that the United States/UN had been treating POWs inhumanely and had forced some to state that they did not wish to be repatriated. (To the American demand of "no forced repatriation," the Communists replied with the counterdemand of "no forced retention.") The U.S./UN High Command repudiated the commandant's forced confession and, after several weeks of attempting to settle the issue peacefully, followed by warnings of force, sent a regiment of American paratroopers and a squad of tanks to Koje on June 10 to break up the Communist organization. At the end of a two-and-a-half-hour battle, 31 POWs and one American were dead, and many more were wounded. In the Communist arsenal the United States/UN found 3,000 spears, 1,000 Molotov cocktails, and

4,500 knives. Although the Chinese Communist prisoners and the South Korean civilian internees were removed from Koje soon thereafter, disturbances continued into December.

The third aspect of the Communist reaction to the U.S./UN demand for voluntary repatriation was a huge campaign to turn international public opinion against the United States by charging it with having waged bacteriological warfare in Korea. On February 18, 1952, Radio Moscow accused the United States of having poisoned wells in North Korea, of having spread typhus and smallpox viruses, and even of having sent lepers into the country to infect the population. The campaign crescendoed rapidly. Peking and Pyongyang were soon claiming that the United States was dropping disease-ridden rats and germ-carrying insects into North Korea. In May 1952, to back up these absurd charges, the Communists released the filmed "confessions" of two captured U.S. airmen who had been brainwashed into believing that they were serving the cause of peace by stating that they had dropped "explosive germ bombs" over North Korea in January.

The truth of the matter is that devastated North Korea was then in fact ravaged by epidemics. But they were due to the unimaginably horrible conditions in which people were living — suffering terribly from malnutrition, shivering amid ruins, and having pitifully few medical services available. The Communist propagandists were simply trying to salvage some benefit from a horrendous situation and were confident that the ignorant populace would believe them. Less excusable than the Communist propaganda effort was the fact that many leftists in the West, who should have known better, were also very willing to believe.

The negotiations made no appreciable progress on the POW issue until March 1952, when the Communists agreed to drop their demand for the delivery of the 38,000 South Korean anti-Communists if the UN Command would drop the question of what had happened to the 53,000 POWs whom the Communists claimed to have released. The United States/UN agreed and in subsequent discussions assured the Communists that a total of more than 100,000 North Koreans and Chinese would probably want to return home. Such a figure was acceptable to the Communists, but both sides agreed that no further negotiations could be meaningful until concrete figures had been obtained by screening the prisoners. On April 19 the UN Command presented a provisional list indicating that only about 70,000 of the 132,000 prisoners it held wished to be repatriated. The Communists found that figure totally unacceptable.

On April 28 the Japanese peace treaty went into effect, and the occupation of Japan officially ended. That same day President Truman announced that as of May 12 General Mark W. Clark, who had led the American forces in Italy during World War II, would replace Ridgway as Commander in Chief, Far East, and Commander in Chief, UN Command. Ridgway, in turn, was to be the new supreme commander of NATO, replacing Dwight Eisenhower, who by then was a candidate for the Republican presidential nomination.

It was also on April 28 that the U.S./UN delegation, on instructions from Washington, presented a new offer at Panmunjom. It consisted of two demands, one of them major, and a significant concession. The Communists had had the gall to require that the Soviet Union be one of the "neutral" nations represented on the commission that was to ensure that both sides would adhere to the terms of the armistice. The United States/UN insisted that the Communists drop that preposterous and impudent demand at once, as they had already indicated some willingness to do. The major U.S./UN demand was that the Communists accept, without further argument, the principle of voluntary repatriation. In return the United States/UN would allow the Communists, after the signing of an armistice, to reconstruct and rehabilitate airfields in North Korea that had been destroyed by bombing. Since that would shift Communist air power closer to South Korea, it represented a substantial concession.

In a public statement on May 7, the day that the POW camp commandant was captured on Koje, President Truman said that the United States was absolutely adamant on the POW issue: "There shall be no forced repatriation of prisoners of war — as the Communists have insisted. . . . It would be repugnant to the fundamental moral and humanitarian principles which underlie our action in Korea. . . . We will not buy an armistice by turning over human beings for slaughter or slavery."[10]

The Communists rejected the offer. The negotiations had now apparently reached an unbreakable deadlock over the POW issue.

That was all that was standing between war and peace, but it was enough. Both sides refused to yield, and each accused the other of purposely stalling the negotiations so as to gain time to build up forces in Korea for a new offensive.

Admiral Joy was so exasperated that he asked to be relieved of his job of chief U.S./UN negotiator. His request was granted, and he was rewarded with the comfortable post of superintendent of Annapolis. On May 22 his place was taken by Major General William K. Harrison, Jr., a direct descendant of William Henry Harrison (the ninth American president) and of Benjamin Harrison (the twenty-third president). Harrison, who had for some time been a member of the U.S./UN delegation, would soon become as frustrated as Joy had been.

As the second anniversary of the North Korean invasion approached, the United States was determined to break the deadlock and end the war. It was time to put unprecedented pressure on the Communists — time, even, to remove one of the restrictions that had so bothered MacArthur. The general's orders from the JCS on November 6, 1950, which gave him permission to bomb the North Korean end of the Yalu bridges, carefully stipulated that "the above does not authorize the bombing of any dams or power plants on the Yalu River." In June 1952 Washington decided to remove that limitation. The primary target would be the power plant at the Supung Dam across the Suiho Reservoir, on the Yalu. The dam itself, the northern end of which was on the Manchurian side of the river, would not be bombed. The target would be the power-generating station (the fourth largest in the world), which was on the North Korean side. In addition, four power stations within North Korea, some distance from the river, would be hit at the same time. The rationale that Washington gave to the public for this move was that the North Korean power system was supplying electricity both to the Manchurian airfields from which Communist planes were operating against UN Command forces and to the North Korean radar system.

On June 23 more than 250 U.S./UN planes attacked the Suiho power station, while another 250 hit the four other generating and distribution plants, depriving much of North Korea of electric power. Another raid on the same targets followed the next day. The British were furious that they hadn't been consulted before the attacks, which they feared might touch off a world war. It happened that Acheson was in London at the time and could thus personally assure a meeting of outraged members of Parliament that Washington had fully intended to consult with Prime Minister Churchill and had failed to do so only because of a "snafu."[11]

The attacks had no discernible influence on the negotiations at Panmunjom. Indeed, the Communists didn't betray any reaction at all. So the United States/UN decided to increase the pressure a bit more. On July 11 (the day after the first anniversary of the beginning of the truce talks) some 1,200 U.S./UN fighter-bombers and dive-bombers spent the entire day dropping 1,400 tons of bombs and 23,000 gallons of napalm on Pyongyang. They concentrated on factories, warehouses, railroad yards, military barracks, and airfields, but they inevitably also killed many civilians.

The Communists still refused to yield on the POW issue — and, if anything, became more emphatically firm than ever after July 13, when the United States/UN released the final results of its screening of POWs. Out of the total of 132,000 that it held, only 83,000 (76,600 North Korean soldiers and pro-Communist South Koreans, and 6,400 Chinese) wanted to go north at the end of the war.

After the bombing of Pyongyang, the United States/UN warned that heavier raids would follow if the Communists insisted on "prolonging the war," and from mid-July onward U.S./UN planes hammered at approximately eighty North Korean industrial and transportation centers. Radio broadcasts from the south and air-dropped leaflets warned people living in those centers that their towns and cities had been marked for destruction and should be evacuated, but the Communists nevertheless accused the United States of "blind and wanton bombing of civilians."[12] When these raids failed to produce results at Panmunjom, Washington decided to hit Pyongyang again, on August 29. This was the biggest air attack of the war, with 1,403 planes from Korea, Japan, and carriers offshore participating. But it, too, accomplished nothing.

One reason for Communist intransigence at this time was that the United States/UN began to release the 38,000 prisoners it had classified as anti-Communist South Korean civilians who had been pressed into service by the North Korean army. Some 27,000 of them were set free during August, and the remainder were freed during the following months. The Communists, furious that they would not have any further chance to win these people over to their cause, declared in a fit of rage that the U.S./UN action rendered the armistice talks "null and void," though they soon decided that that reaction was imprudently extreme.

The United States/UN was greatly embarrassed at this same time by the outrageously manipulated presidential election that Syngman Rhee held on August 5. As the end of his first four-year term approached, Rhee had made himself more unpopular than ever with a majority of the members of his legislative assembly. His problem was then that under the South Korean constitution, the president was to be elected by a vote in the assembly. Confident that the people of South Korea would elect him if they were given a chance to do so (since the war had inflamed anti-Communist passions and had brought a great influx of anti-Communists from the north), Rhee ordered the assembly to change the constitution to allow for a popular vote. When it refused, he arrested dozens of hostile legislators, charging them with pro-Communist sympathies. A new vote changed the constitution, and Rhee proceeded to win a popular election with his usual methods of intimidation. All this gave some pause to people who were under the impression that the United States/UN was fighting in Korea to preserve democracy.

By August the war had reached a military and political impasse. On August 14 Kim Il-sung, sounding uncharacteristically discouraged, made a speech in Pyongyang in which he conceded that the war was stalemated. He said that he would accept an armistice by the terms of which the Americans would not be the winners and the Korean people the losers.[13] For their part, the Americans wanted an armistice whose terms would at the very least embarrass the Communists and guarantee the future security of South Korea. After months of hopeless deadlock, the talks were suspended indefinitely on October 8.

CHAPTER 33

Referendum on Korea

THE REPUBLICANS expressed the issues of the 1952 presidential campaign in terms of a chemical formula: K_1C_2 — the Korean War, Communist influence within the federal government, and the corruption of government officials (a number of whom had recently been accused of graft, influence peddling, and taking kickbacks). Of these three issues, the Korean War was the decisive one. The Republicans could well have returned to their slogan of the 1946 congressional campaign, "Had Enough?" The question underlay the entire campaign, and the answer on Election Day was to be a resounding yes.

On March 29, 1952, President Truman announced that he would refuse to run for reelection. By the time of the next inauguration he would have served nearly the two full terms that had been made the legal limit by the twenty-second constitutional amendment, ratified in February 1951 to prevent any repetition of Franklin Roosevelt's lengthy tenure in office. Although the amendment stated that it would not be binding upon the president who was in office at the time of its ratification, as early as April 1950 Truman had written in a memorandum for himself, "In my opinion eight years as President is enough and sometimes too much for any man to serve in that capacity."[1] His decision on the basis of principle was reinforced by the simple fact that, long before the spring of 1952, Truman himself had had enough.

In December 1951 he wrote to General Eisenhower (who was still politically neutral) at NATO headquarters in Europe, implying that if the general would run for the presidency as a Democrat, he would have Truman's full support. Eisenhower replied sincerely, "The possibility that I will ever be drawn into political activity is so remote as to be negligible."[2] He had been little more encouraging to the Republicans, most notably Senator Henry Cabot Lodge, who had first approached him a few months earlier. Eisenhower had made it very clear to Lodge that he would not campaign for the party's nomination and that he might not accept it even if it was offered to him. Ike still wouldn't even say whether he was a Republican or a Democrat.

Undeterred by this uncooperativeness, Lodge proceeded in January 1952 to place Eisenhower's name as a Republican candidate upon the ballot for the New Hampshire primary. Somewhat reluctantly, Ike then publicly acknowledged that he was indeed a Republican, but he would say no more. In February, however, he decided, and let it be known, that although he would not actively seek the Republican nomination, he would run if nominated. After winning several state primaries in March, he wrote to Truman asking to be relieved of his NATO duties as of June 1. On that date the opening of the Republican National Convention would be only five weeks away. Truman promptly granted the request on April 11, exactly one year after he had relieved General MacArthur under very different circumstances.

Before their convention, the Republicans were divided sharply into two camps. Those who supported Senator Robert Taft for the nomination were in sympathy with McCarthy and MacArthur. They were obsessed by their fears (or, in some cases, were cynically aware of the political utility of inciting the public to fear) that American foreign policy had long been shaped by Communist agents and sympathizers and by men whose lack of courage led them to appease the Communists. Believing that Asia was far more important to American interests than was Europe, they advocated unifying Korea by military force, even if it meant all-out war with China and the Soviet Union. Senator Taft's affinity for the latter position was so great that before the convention he promised unofficially to ask General MacArthur to be his running mate if he received the nomination. (The general had by then pretty much surrendered his own presidential hopes; on the convention's first ballot he would receive only 10 votes out of a total of more than 1,200.) MacArthur, in turn, let it be known that he would accept if Taft would give him more than the usual powers of that office. The senator replied that he would appoint MacArthur deputy commander in chief of the armed forces. (Taft died of cancer in July 1953. One shudders at the realization that had he been elected, MacArthur would then have become president.)

Taft was the favorite of the Republican old guard. Younger Republican leaders, including Lodge, ridiculed him as a dinosaur and joked that he "had the best mind in Washington until he made it up." His views were dangerously out of date; he seemed like a throwback to the arrogant and aggressive American spirit of Teddy Roosevelt's time, a spirit inappropriate to the world that had been ushered in by Franklin Roosevelt. Furthermore, Taft had spent the previous fourteen years as a leader of the conservative Republican opposition to the policies of the Democratic administrations. Much of the public therefore perceived him as essentially negative in his outlook; it seemed that he was most passionate in his views against but had very little in the way of a positive program. Thus it was that Eisenhower prevailed over Taft at the convention, when, after the first ballot — in which the former received 595 of the necessary 604 votes, to the latter's 500 — the Minnesota delegation announced that it had decided to shift 19 of its votes for its favorite son, Harold Stassen, to the general.

Eisenhower was favored by the Republican "young guard." He was widely regarded as moderate and sensible, and his position was indeed basically a middle-of-the-road compromise between recent Republican and Democratic lines. He endorsed the Truman administration's pro-Europe policy and promised no major changes in foreign relations except to take a somewhat tougher stand against Communism and to end the Korean War. In domestic policy he pledged no radical changes other than to reduce military spending and thus to lower taxes, as well as to eliminate corruption from the federal government. Eisenhower was so uncritical of the New Deal–Fair Deal record that his Democratic opponent, Adlai Stevenson, quipped, "I've been tempted to say that I was pleased to stand on that record if only . . . the General would move over and make room for me."[3]

On June 5, at his first U.S. press conference since his return from Europe, Eisenhower admitted that he "did not have any prescription for bringing [the Korean War] to a decisive end." He stated that he did not think any major new UN offensive could succeed in unifying Korea and added, "I believe we have got to stand firm . . . and try to get a decent armistice out of it."[4] This, of course, was identical to Truman's own position. To his credit, Eisenhower courageously and honorably stood by his convictions throughout the campaign, even though his doing so enraged the Republican hawks.

Eisenhower proposed no radical or imaginative ways to bring the Korean War swiftly to a satisfactory conclusion. But he had to offer the public something that would suggest his election wouldn't simply mean more of the same. Thus he emphasized his intention to step up the expansion, the equipping, and the training of the ROK army so that it would soon be able to take over completely the manning of the front lines. (This policy was obviously the forerunner of "Vietnamization," which Richard Nixon would institute upon assuming the presidency, in 1969.) Troops from the United States and other UN nations would be held in reserve just behind the lines. As Eisenhower's foreign-affairs adviser John Foster Dulles argued, that plan would put an end to the Soviet propaganda claiming that the United States was waging "a race war, with white men killing yellow men by methods white people would not use against each other."[5] It would also permit America to withdraw some of its forces from Korea for deployment elsewhere. Eisenhower said that since the Soviets wanted the war to drag on mainly because it tied down a large number of American troops in remote Korea, the reduction of American forces there might lead the Kremlin to conclude that it was no longer worthwhile to continue the war. Finally, and most important to the American public, was the prospect that once the ROKs took over the front lines, the U.S. casualty rate would plummet. By July 1952 more than 110,000 American soldiers had been killed, wounded, or captured in the Korean War. At home, many Americans were fed up with heavy losses that all seemed to be for nothing. In the eyes of these voters, a decisive factor in the election campaign was that Eisenhower himself had a son fighting in Korea and could thus be counted on to stop the apparently senseless slaughter as quickly as possible.

Although Eisenhower played up his proposal to substitute ROKs in the front lines as if it were a departure from the Truman administration's policy, it was no such thing. Since early in the war, Syngman Rhee had been protesting that he had large reserves of manpower that could be employed if only the United States would provide equipment for them. In January 1951 MacArthur had recommended against doing so, for he felt it was more important to give available equipment to the Japanese paramilitary police force, which had assumed primary responsibility for the security of a Japan largely stripped of American occupation forces.[6] At the time of the Communist offensives in the spring of 1951, the Joint Chiefs of Staff returned to the idea of enlarging the ROK army, but General Ridgway told them it would be pointless until the South Koreans could develop a more professional officer corps. Poorly led ROK units were always the first to break under enemy pressure, and they had already abandoned in the field enough equipment to outfit several divisions. Only after the stabilization of the combat line north of the 38th parallel were the Americans able to turn to the task of providing the South Koreans with the additional training they needed. Ridgway focused particularly on enabling the ROKs to take over the manning of heavy artillery, which until then had been almost entirely the responsibility of Americans, and he even sent ROK officers to artillery schools in the United States. As a result of the massive training programs that he sponsored, nearly three quarters of the frontline troops at the end of 1952 — which is to say, before Eisenhower took office — were South Koreans.[7]

In the face of cries from Republican zealots that Truman should never have started what he wasn't prepared to finish properly, Eisenhower staunchly maintained that the president had done the right thing by intervening in June 1950. But he strongly criticized the administration's pre-invasion policy regarding Korea, insisting that if the United States had made it clear that it would respond militarily to any such Communist move, the North Koreans would never have invaded the south in the first place.

Moreover, Eisenhower and Dulles argued that the Korean War had proven that the doctrine of containment did not offer a satisfactory way of dealing with Communist aggression. The Soviet Union, the real culprit, would emerge from the conflict unblamed and unscathed. The war would also have shown the Soviets that they had the initiative: they could decide when and where to strike, and America and its allies would be obliged to send large numbers of troops in response. Even with the buildup of its armed forces, the United States would have to divert some troops from strategic areas to defend small backwaters. The Kremlin might find a series of simultaneous small-scale aggressions scattered around the globe a very advantageous way of dissipating American strength, thus clearing the way for a Soviet invasion of Western Europe. Or it might elect to erode American resolve through an endless sequence of nuisance attacks. Whatever the Soviet strategy, so Eisenhower and Dulles asserted, the containment doctrine of responding to aggression locally with U.S. ground troops would continue to cost many American lives. It would also, as the Korean War had demonstrated, lead to the devastation of the area to be rescued. Finally, there was something deeply repugnant about the concept that the aim of American intervention should be simply to kill as many Communist soldiers as possible, until at last the enemy relented, withdrew, and agreed to an armistice. It was for all of these reasons that Dulles denounced containment as "negative, futile, and immoral." This epithet failed to prevent the fiasco in Vietnam, which bore out many of his objections to containment and for the genesis of which he was among those most responsible.

Dulles articulated many of these ideas in an article entitled "A Policy of Boldness," published in the May 19, 1952, issue of *Life*. There he set forth what would eventually (after a January 1954 speech in which he first used the term) become known as his doctrine of "massive retaliation." The central idea was that the United States must make it absolutely clear to the Communists that in the future it would be prepared to respond to any act of aggression like the Korean invasion by launching a major attack upon the Soviet Union. He didn't then specify that the attack would be atomic, but that was obviously implicit — and in 1954 was made perfectly explicit. Such a policy, Dulles avowed, would deter the Russians from attempting to expand their hegemony and would thus remove the need for America to intervene militarily in remote and inconvenient regions. During the campaign Eisenhower did not declare himself in favor of the policy of deterrence, but Dulles's role as heir apparent to the post of secretary of state made it a tacit issue.

As an army general who favored the stationing of American troops in Europe, Eisenhower never advocated a return to the small defense budgets and minimal forces of the late 1940s. But neither did he approve of the huge military budgets recommended by NSC-68 and pushed through Congress by Truman. What Eisenhower wanted was a substantial U.S. Army, Navy, and Air Force maintained by a level of spending that the American economy could comfortably afford. In particular, he deplored the fact that in Truman's budget for fiscal year 1952–53, government expenditures would exceed revenues, largely because of the grossly inflated size of the defense budget. The projected deficit of well over $10 billion in that budget led many Americans to fear that the Democrats were putting the United States on the road to economic ruin. On September 25 Eisenhower said in a campaign speech: "We must achieve both security and solvency. In fact, the foundation of military strength is economic strength. A bankrupt America is more the Soviet goal than an America conquered on the field of battle. . . . Our defense program need not and must not push us steadily toward economic collapse."[8] Those words resonate today with as much common sense, and at least as much urgency, as they did in 1952.

Eisenhower's promised reduction of military spending would, he assured the public, accomplish several goals. It would ensure the economic stability of the nation. It would make possible lower taxes. And it would return the overheated economy to a more normal and healthy state. Many voters believed, with considerable justification, that the enormous military expenditures brought on by the Korean War were directly responsible both for the rapid increase of inflation and for the nation's recent economic boom. For that very reason, a large portion of the public was not enjoying its new prosperity; it felt that the extra dollars in American pockets were "blood money," cursed by the deaths of thousands upon thousands of U.S. soldiers in Korea. Consequently the Democratic campaign slogan — "You Never Had It So Good" — offended many people. The Republicans charged that the Korean War, not Democratic fiscal savvy, had created the new prosperity. Referring to the deficit and to Alger Hiss, respectively, Senator William Knowland chided that 1952 was the year to get rid of "red ink and red herrings,"[9] red being the color both of Communism and of blood.

While Eisenhower held out the attractive prospect of moderate change, Adlai Stevenson seemed to many voters to offer nothing more than a continuation of the status quo. He was widely viewed as Truman's handpicked successor, and his cultivated manner and sardonic wit reminded many of Dean Acheson's. To the rednecks who revered

Senator McCarthy and General MacArthur, Stevenson looked like a pinko — a graduate of "Dean Acheson's cowardly College of Communist Containment,"[10] as Eisenhower's running mate, Richard Nixon, so demagogically put it during the campaign. The Korean War, for the drawing out of which even many moderate Republicans found it expedient to blame Truman, had led the nation to desire "a policy of boldness." But Stevenson didn't seem very bold. To the simple man in the street he was an egghead, too intellectual, too introspective, too indecisive. Governor Thomas Dewey summed up the reservations of many voters when he asked rhetorically, "Who is Stalin more afraid of, Adlai Stevenson or Dwight Eisenhower?"[11]

Much of Eisenhower's appeal was personal rather than ideological. The catchy Republican campaign slogan, "I Like Ike," was right on the mark. A great number of people simply liked and trusted Eisenhower. They responded favorably to his apparent qualities of honesty, trustworthiness, competence, confidence, sincerity, and wholesomeness, even if his policy pronouncements sometimes seemed rather vague. This was the first presidential campaign in which television played a major role, and the advertising executives in charge of Eisenhower's publicity packaged him well to take maximum advantage of the unprecedented sense of intimacy between candidate and voter fostered by the new medium.

Not the least aspect of Eisenhower's appeal was his status as the general who had led the Allies to victory in Europe during World War II. Now, despite all the fuss over civilian command of the military that had been occasioned by Truman's relief of MacArthur, many people seemed to think it might be useful to have an experienced and victorious military man in the White House. Perhaps he could end the Korean War successfully and promptly, as Captain Harry Truman of a World War I artillery battery had proven unable to do, and as the World War II assistant secretary of the navy Stevenson might also fail to do. To allay any fears that a general might lead the nation more deeply into war with the great Communist powers, Governor Dewey pointed out during the campaign that eleven generals had become president of the United States and that during none of their administrations had a major war broken out.[12]

*   *   *

Many reporters covering the campaign chided Eisenhower for the dullness of his speeches and for his "five-star generalities." It was, they joked, a case of the bland leading the bland. After yet one more boring speech, one newsman quipped, "He just crossed the thirty-eighth platitude." Then, in an October 24 speech delivered in Detroit and broadcast on national television, Eisenhower startled everyone with a specific and dramatic promise. "The first task of a new administration," he said,

> will be to review and re-examine every course of action open to us with one goal in view: to bring the Korean War to an early and honorable end. . . . That job requires a personal trip to Korea. I shall make that trip. Only in that way could I learn how best to serve the American people in the cause of peace. I shall go to Korea.[13]

Upon reading an advance copy of the speech, one reporter on Eisenhower's campaign train ventured, "That does it. Ike is in."[14]

The promise was a political gimmick, but a very effective one. Stevenson denounced it as "a slick idea that gets votes by playing upon our hopes for a quick end to the war."[15] But by that rebuttal he did himself more harm than good, for he implied that he expected the war to drag on.

On Election Day, November 4, Eisenhower received nearly 34 million votes, more than had ever before in American history been garnered by a presidential candidate. Stevenson, who carried only nine states, received a very respectable 27.3 million votes (44.3 percent of the total, to Eisenhower's 55 percent), but that earned him only 89 electoral votes to his opponent's 442. Truman claimed that the election had been swung by millions of onetime voters who cast their ballots for Eisenhower but not for the Republican party. It was true that the Republican congressional slate had not scored a landslide, making only small gains to win a one-seat majority in the Senate and an eight-vote lead in the House. But the new voters were not one-timers. They were the Americans to whom television had given a new interest in politics.

As he claimed in the title of the first volume of his White House memoirs, Eisenhower had indeed received a mandate for change.

However, even in regard to the Korean War, it was a mandate for *moderate* change. The majority of Americans did not want him to expand the war to China nor, certainly, to make dangerous concessions to the Communists. They simply wanted him to extricate the United States promptly, honorably, and decisively from its terrible dilemma.

CHAPTER 34

Eisenhower Takes Over

EISENHOWER kept his promise. He set out for Korea on November 29, accompanied by his designated secretary of defense, Charles E. Wilson (who had left his job as president of General Motors to accept the cabinet post), by General Omar Bradley, and by a few other advisers, as well as by a group of hand-picked journalists and photographers. In order to prevent any attempts to assassinate the president-elect in Korea or en route, all facts concerning the journey were classified top secret until Eisenhower was safely on his way home. The newsmen who habitually congregated on the sidewalk outside Ike's New York City apartment were told that he would be staying in for a few days while he was under pressure to make his final cabinet selections.[1] The Secret Service even enlisted a few important personages to visit the empty apartment so that the reporters would never suspect that the president-elect was anywhere but at home.

The trip, which was nothing but a gesture, didn't change Eisenhower's thinking about the war in any fundamental way. He had said all along that he wanted a prompt and honorable truce. General Mark Clark wrote in his memoirs that he had prepared for Eisenhower "a detailed estimate of the forces and plans required to obtain a military victory in Korea should the new administration decide to take such a course."[2] But Ike, who knew from General Bradley that the plan involved the bombing of Communist China and the use of Nationalist Chinese troops in Korea, didn't even give Clark an opportunity to present it. After arriving in Korea on December 2, Eisenhower visited the front and met with all the principal commanders. But just before he left Korea, at the press conference in Seoul on December 5 that ended the news blackout regarding his trip, he admitted that he had "no panaceas, no tricks" for bringing the war to a swift and satisfactory end. He conceded that it would be "difficult . . . to work out a plan that would bring positive and definite victory without possibly running a grave risk of enlarging the war."³ He was still crossing the thirty-eighth platitude.

Eisenhower was not, however, willing to let the armistice negotiations drag on indefinitely. He knew long before he went to Korea that the patience of the American people was running out, and he knew that was one of the main reasons for his having been elected. He realized that if American firmness at the bargaining table didn't soon yield a solution, then he would be forced at least to threaten to take some drastic, stalemate-breaking action. He certainly didn't want a major war with Communist China, let alone a world war against the Soviet Union. He was even unwilling to make a public threat of expanding the war, for fear that if such a threat failed to produce results at the negotiations in Panmunjom, he would be obligated to carry it out. After the MacArthur hearings, in the spring of 1951, the Communists would not have taken seriously a threat from the Truman administration to attack Chinese territory. But Eisenhower hoped that were American officials and military commanders to drop hints that he was considering radical action, such threats would be credible enough so that he would not have to act on them. He was, after all, a Republican president who was a great general and whose secretary of state was a notorious hawk.

Eisenhower knew all along that something would have to be done — something, he hoped, that would not precipitate a world war. He later wrote that his conclusion as he left Korea was "that we could not stand forever on a static front and continue to accept casualties without any visible results. Small attacks on small hills would not end this war."⁴ He had surely realized that before he ever set foot in Korea.

One of the first actions Eisenhower took concerning Korea after he assumed office was to replace General James Van Fleet as commander of the Eighth Army. Van Fleet had come to find the endless hillside engagements of limited warfare unbearably frustrating and longed for permission to mount an all-out offensive, which he felt certain could at least push the Communists back to a line above Pyongyang and Wonsan, at the narrow neck of the peninsula. Eisenhower gave Van Fleet a fourth star and brought him home to retirement. On February 11, 1953, Lieutenant General Maxwell D. Taylor, until then the army's deputy chief of staff for operations and administration, took over command of the Eighth Army. Taylor — an urbane soldier-statesman who spoke several languages and who would go on to become chairman of the Joint Chiefs of Staff under John Kennedy and then Lyndon Johnson's ambassador to Saigon — was fully in sympathy with Eisenhower's ideas regarding the proper conduct of the war.

By the end of 1952 the negotiators at Panmunjom had made no further progress on the POW issue. The talks, adjourned on October 8, had still not resumed. On October 24 the United States had submitted to the UN General Assembly's Political Committee a resolution endorsed by twenty other nations, including Britain, calling upon the Communists to accept the principle of voluntary repatriation. But soon thereafter Soviet foreign minister Andrei Vishinsky told the committee that the Communists would "never budge" from their opposition. On that issue, he said, no compromise was possible.

The military stalemate continued. In January the Communists made a determined effort to evict the UN Command from its positions along the base of the Iron Triangle, but the attempt failed. The reinforced U.S./UN/ROK forces now numbered 768,000, including service and supply units and the South Korean paramilitary security forces. Twelve ROK and eight U.S./UN divisions, more than 300,000 combat troops, were stationed along or near the front line. By this time the Communists had a total of nearly a million soldiers in Korea, more than half of them at or just behind the front. The delicate balance was still maintained by the Communist advantage of manpower on the one hand and the U.S./UN superiority of firepower and control of the air on the other hand.

Beginning on January 9, 1953, the UN Command launched what was apparently a last-ditch attempt to force the Communists to yield before the Truman administration left office. That night several hundred B-29 bombers blasted the rail and road bridges near Sinanju (on the west coast, about forty miles north of Pyongyang), where three major railway lines from Manchuria converged, as did a number of important roads. If all eleven of the bridges in the area could be destroyed beyond the possibility of repair, a huge amount of traffic carrying supplies from China would very quickly become backed up there, and then U.S./UN bombers could swoop in and attack the concentrations. By inflicting such a devastating loss of supplies, the UN Command might at last force the Communists to capitulate on the POW issue and to conclude an armistice.

The attack on the Sinanju bridges continued without respite for five days. U.S./UN planes flew a total of 2,292 combat sorties during the operation and succeeded in knocking out all of the bridges. But, with their usual resilience, the Communists had pontoon bridges in place within a week and were carrying supplies across them under cover of darkness. A huge army of laborers at once set about building a rail detour, and enough supplies got through to sustain the troops at the front, who were inured to shortages.

On Inauguration Day, January 20, 1953, the problem of the Korean War was officially handed over to Eisenhower. Two weeks later, on February 2, in his State of the Union message to Congress, the new president announced that he had ordered that the Seventh Fleet "no longer be employed to shield Communist China" from attack by Chiang Kai-shek's forces on Formosa. He assured the Communists that "this order implies no aggressive intent on our part," but, he asserted, "we certainly have no obligation to protect a nation fighting us in Korea."[5] Headlines the next day proclaimed that Ike was "unleashing Chiang."

In his speech Eisenhower mentioned that Nationalists from islands just offshore China had already been making forays to the mainland to contact anti-Communist guerrillas, and that Chiang had even sent such expeditions from Formosa without interference from the U.S. Navy. Within days Chiang announced that although his forces were not adequately equipped for a full-scale invasion, they could not afford to wait until they were totally prepared. It looked as though MacArthur's long-called-for second front might finally be opened. But it turned out that the Nationalists had to content themselves with bombing attacks and minor raids against mainland China — some two hundred of the latter during the first five months of 1953 alone.

On February 4, just two days after Eisenhower's State of the Union message, Chou En-lai announced that China was "ready for an immediate cease-fire on the basis of the agreement already reached in Panmunjom."[6] In other words, if the United States would yield on the issue of voluntary repatriation, the hostilities could end at once. His statement was surely prompted by two factors. The first was the threat of new trouble from Chiang. If he was really going to attack the mainland, Peking did not want to have major forces tied down in Korea. The second factor was China's eagerness to end the war, contingent upon not losing face, so that it could get on with desperately needed economic improvement. It was certainly no random occurrence that on the very day of Chou's appeal for the reopening of the peace talks, Peking announced the 1953 production goals of its initial and incipient Soviet-style five-year plan to bring about a quantum leap in industrial and agricultural progress.[7] The Korean War was a drain on Chinese manpower and resources that the Communists could no longer afford. In 1952 China had a lower per capita production of pig iron, steel, and cotton textiles, and fewer miles of railway track per square mile, than Russia had had in 1900.[8] If China was going to take its rightful place in the modern world, it would have to stop squandering its strength on an enterprise in Korea that was outlasting its usefulness as a propaganda exercise.

Washington responded to Chou's unsatisfactory overture by saying that the United States would return to the negotiating table only if and when China would stop insisting upon the forced repatriation of POWs. Having observed, however, that the Communists were more likely to agree to a very specific plan proposed by the UN Command than they were to concur in any statement of principles, the State Department and the JCS decided to try to make some headway toward practical cooperation through a channel other than Panmunjom. At their instruction General Mark Clark sent a letter, dated February 22, to the Communist commanders in Korea suggesting an exchange of sick and wounded prisoners. The Communist reply was contemptuous silence.

But then fate intervened. On the morning of March 6 the Soviet news agency Tass reported that the seventy-three-year-old Stalin had died during the night, following a stroke suffered several days earlier. On the fifteenth Stalin's designated heir, the conciliatory Georgi Malenkov — who was soon to be punished for his self-confessed "ignorance of and disregard for" Lenin's emphasis on heavy industry over the production of consumer goods — made a speech in which he declared that there was no existing dispute between the Soviet Union and the United States that "cannot be decided by peaceful means, on the basis of mutual understanding."[9] John Foster Dulles dismissed this as mere propaganda, an attempt to represent the Soviet Union as a peacemaker rather than as the troublemaker that it always had been and always would be.

It soon began to appear as though Malenkov had meant what he said. On March 28, two weeks after his speech, and presumably in response to it, Kim Il-sung and Peng Teh-huai sent a letter to General Clark accepting his proposal for an exchange of sick and wounded prisoners and adding, in a most uncharacteristically friendly tone, that they hoped the exchange would "lead to the smooth settlement of the entire question of prisoners of war."[10] Two days later Chou En-lai, recently returned from Stalin's funeral in Moscow, issued a statement that retreated from the cardinal Communist demand that all prisoners be repatriated immediately after the signing of an armistice. Saving face with the claim that the UN Command had brainwashed or coerced many of the prisoners it held into renouncing their home-lands, Chou stated (as reported by Clark) that "the governments of Red China and North Korea had agreed that in order to attain an armistice they would accept a plan in which all prisoners opposed to repatriation would be turned over to a neutral agency so that their right to return home could be explained to them."[11] In short order the new Soviet foreign minister, Vyacheslav Molotov, endorsed Chou's statement. It now began to seem — almost incredibly, to a world that was coming to accept the talks at Panmunjom as an ap-parently permanent fixture in current events — that an armistice might soon be forthcoming.

U.S./UN/ROK and Communist liaison officers met at Panmunjom on April 6 to begin discussions of the exchange of sick and wounded prisoners. Five days later they reached agreement. It was to be an all-for-all swap, each side handing over all of the sickest and most seriously wounded prisoners it held, regardless of numbers. Little Switch, as the operation came to be called, began on April 20. Over the course of the next two weeks the UN Command returned 6,670 men and women (5,194 of them NKPA soldiers, 1,030 Chinese Com-munists, and 446 civilian internees) and received only about one-tenth as many in exchange — a total of 684 prisoners, of whom 471 were South Koreans, 149 were Americans, and 32 were Britons. In order to gain maximum propaganda advantage, the Communists had chosen for the exchange many prisoners who were relatively healthy and who had been treated well because they had seemed to respond favorably to Communist indoctrination. Moreover, Communist propagandists were soon retailing fabricated accounts of the "abuses" the Chinese and North Koreans had endured in the UN Command camps.

Before the exchange had gotten under way, the Communists took action to let the UN Command know that they hadn't suddenly grown softhearted. Their aim was to show that although they were willing to cooperate, it was not because they were afraid to fight. On the night of April 16 numerically superior Chinese forces attacked the soldiers of the American 7th Division who were manning the outpost on Pork Chop Hill, just west of the Iron Triangle. For two days the enemies struggled fanatically for control of the hill, while artillery fire from both sides reduced the tree cover on the hillsides to barren stubble. The attack finally subsided on the eighteenth, leaving the hill still occupied by American troops.

On April 26 the chief delegates to the negotiations at Panmunjom met for the first time since October 8, 1952. U.S./UN hopes were high, for Chou En-lai's March 30 statement and the fact that Little Switch was successfully under way encouraged speculation that the Communists were now eager to end the war and would make dramatic concessions in order to do so. Furthermore, the world was waiting breathlessly to see whether there would be any discernible Communist reaction to a speech entitled "The Chance for Peace," which Eisenhower had delivered on April 16 before the American Society of Newspaper Editors at the Statler Hotel in Washington. In the speech, which Eisenhower's biographer Stephen E. Ambrose has called the finest of his presidency, Eisenhower stated that with the death of Stalin, "the new Soviet leadership now has a precious opportunity to awaken, with the rest of the world, to the point of peril reached and to help turn the tide of history." He went on to promise that if the Russians demonstrated a real change of heart by permitting the settlement of "an honorable armistice" in Korea, by ending Communist aggression in Indochina and Malaya, by agreeing to a free and united Germany, by liberating the nations of Eastern Europe, and by other such deeds, then he in return was prepared to negotiate, under the auspices of the UN, an agreement to abolish atomic weapons and to limit other armaments.[12]

The hopes of the free world were disappointed at once. As soon as the first session of negotiations convened, General Nam Il made a proposal that fell far short of what the United States was expecting. The proposal did indeed drop the Communist demand that all POWs be repatriated immediately after the signing of an armistice. But it insisted that all POWs who requested political asylum be moved within three months of the truce to POW camps in a neutral state and held there for six months while agents from their governments tried to persuade them to accept repatriation. Any prisoners who could not be cajoled into relenting would, after the end of the six months, remain in the camps until a UN-Communist political conference could decide what to do with them. That might take years. Most prisoners would probably conclude that even being sent back to their Communist homelands was preferable to languishing indefinitely in a prison camp.

Endless haggling and vituperation ensued over where the POWs should be interned while they were being screened and induced to return home, who should guard the prisoners during that process, how long the "persuading" period should last, and what should be done with those who remained unwilling to accept repatriation. On May 7 the Communists finally abandoned their stubborn commitment to the cumbersome procedure of transporting the POWs to a neutral state and agreed that they could be screened and persuaded in Korea. That was an important step toward a settlement, but major obstacles remained. The United States was still hoping that only the Chinese prisoners would have to undergo the screening and persuading procedures and that all the North Korean anti-Communists could simply be given civilian status and released in South Korea as soon as an armistice was signed. The Communists naturally found this proposal totally unacceptable. Moreover, the Communists would not agree to a fixed time limit after which all the nonrepatriates would be set free.

Washington accordingly decided that it was time to put more pressure on the Communists, by employing a tactic that had theretofore been rejected on the grounds that it would jeopardize the lives of too many civilians. From May 13 through the sixteenth U.S./UN bombers attacked two of North Korea's twenty major irrigation dams; the two chosen for the first attack were about twenty miles north of

Pyongyang. The timing was calculated so that the resulting floods would not only wash out roads and railways but would also destroy much of the local rice crop just before it was due to be harvested. The raids were quite effective, wreaking more havoc with transport than had any of the previous interdiction attempts and confronting North Korea with the prospect of widespread famine if the Americans attacked more of the dams, as they in fact did, hitting three more during the next few weeks. The Communists had by then taken the precaution of lowering the water levels behind the dams to reduce flooding, but the damage was nevertheless extensive.

On May 22 Washington sent General Clark what it termed its *final* proposal on the POW question. It represented a substantial concession to the Communists, for it allowed all nonrepatriates, North Korean as well as Chinese, to be submitted to screening and persuasion. It also insisted that while those procedures were being carried out, the nonrepatriates were to be interned in camps in the demilitarized zone to be established between North and South Korea and were to be guarded only by Indian troops; within six months of the signing of the armistice, all the remaining nonrepatriates were to be released.[13]

The Eisenhower administration sincerely regarded this position as one beyond which it simply could not and would not make more than the most minor concessions. Washington's patience and its room for maneuver had run out. If the Communists would not respond reasonably, the United States/UN would have no alternative but to resort to massive force. As Secretary of State Dulles told Indian prime minister Jawaharlal Nehru on May 21, the United States would not abandon its concept of political asylum. "Perhaps in this matter we were idealistic," Dulles observed, "but the one thing for which Americans had been willing to fight and die was their ideals. We did not apologize for this."[14]

The new proposal was thus, in effect, an ultimatum. But Washington bent over backward to avoid presenting it publicly as such, lest the Communists feel that they could not agree to its terms without losing face. On May 19 Undersecretary of State General Walter Bedell Smith cabled the American embassy in Tokyo: "Thinking here is that presentation final position and any subsequent meetings should be in executive [i.e., closed] session doing all possible to avoid ul-

timatum connotations, couched to maximum in terms acceptance
Communist position, that is, do all possible facilitate Communist
acceptance while making clear firmness our position."[15]

That same day Smith told a group of British Commonwealth
diplomatic officials (as recorded afterward in a memo):

> When decisions have been reached on the position which we were
> discussing, the UN Command would have reached the end of its
> bargaining position and in the absence of clear indications from
> the Communists that agreement could be reached upon the basis
> of these positions within a reasonable period there would be no
> purpose in carrying on negotiations any further. General Smith
> pointed out that if it should come to a break-off in the negotiations
> it cannot be expected that military operations can just sit where
> they are. The people of the U.S. would not stand for such a
> situation and it must be expected that the military operations will
> have to be intensified.[16]

General Clark wrote in his memoirs that "if the Communists rejected
this final offer and made no constructive proposal of their own," he
was authorized to terminate the negotiations and, as he ominously
put it, "to carry on the war in new ways never yet tried in Korea."[17]
Foremost among the "new ways" under consideration was the use of
atomic bombs.

By the spring of 1953 the United States had regained a formidable
nuclear advantage over the Soviet Union. On October 31, 1952, the
Americans had successfully tested a hydrogen fusion bomb many
times more powerful than the Hiroshima-style fission bomb; the Russians did not yet have an H-bomb. (They were, however, not far
behind; they would detonate one in August 1953.) The United States
had an arsenal of sixteen hundred fission bombs, many of them at
bases overseas and ready to be dropped on the Soviet Union or Communist China within hours of an order; American military intelligence
held that the Soviets had no atomic bombs deployed operationally.
Furthermore, in January 1953 America had perfected an artillery-sized
fission bomb to be used tactically on the battlefield.

By May 1953 Eisenhower was perfectly willing to use atomic
bombs against targets in Korea. The minutes of the National Security
Council meeting on May 6 record that

General Bradley had pointed out that the Communists seemed to be attempting to put planes back on four airfields in North Korea, and the Air Force had been making these fields targets for recent attacks. With regard to this, the President inquired whether these airfields might not prove a target which would test the effectiveness of an atomic bomb. At any rate, said the President, he had reached the point of being convinced that we have got to consider the atomic bomb as simply another weapon in our arsenal.

General Bradley squelched Eisenhower's suggestion by expressing "some doubts as to the usefulness of any of these fields as a target for an atomic bomb."[18]

But Ike was back the following week, at the NSC meeting on the thirteenth, with yet another proposal for using nuclear force:

The President seemed not wholly satisfied with the argument that atomic weapons could not be used effectively in dislodging the Chinese from their present positions in Korea. . . . [He] thought it might be cheaper, dollar-wise, to use atomic weapons in Korea than to continue to use conventional weapons against the dugouts which honeycombed the hills along which the enemy forces were presently deployed. This, the President felt, was particularly true if one took into account the logistic costs of getting conventional ammunition from this country to the front lines.[19]

Eisenhower was indeed considering the atomic bomb as simply another weapon in the American arsenal. But that did not mean that he was now willing to launch a world war.

The president was determined to expand the war beyond Korea only as the very last resort — only, to be specific, if it became apparent that the Communists really had no sincere interest in ending the war and were content to let it and the truce negotiations drag on indefinitely. He wrote in his memoirs that he and his advisers gave much consideration to what to do "in the event that the Chinese Communists refused to accede to an armistice in a reasonable time."[20] The key to his position was his notion of what constituted "a reasonable time." He was a fairly patient and reasonable man, certainly far more so than was Dulles, who consistently took an aggressive stand on the issue of expanding the war to Communist Chinese territory.

If there really was no alternative, Eisenhower was prepared to seek a "military solution" to end the war on acceptable terms. "It was obvious that if we were to go over to a major offensive," he wrote, "the war would have to be expanded outside Korea — with strikes against the supporting Chinese airfields in Manchuria, a blockade of the Chinese coast, and similar measures. . . . Finally, to keep the attack from becoming overly costly, it was clear that we would have to use atomic weapons."[21] Indeed, at its meeting on May 20 the NSC officially adopted the policy statement that "if circumstances arose which would force the United States to an expanded effort in Korea," the United States should probably be prepared to make massive atomic strikes against Communist Chinese territory.[22] The strategy was to deal China such a swift and devastating blow that it would be knocked out of the war before the Soviets would have a chance to intervene, for Eisenhower "stressed his anxiety lest the United States become involved in global war commencing in Manchuria."[23]

These were, however, long-range plans; at the NSC meeting on the twentieth the president mentioned May 1954 as a possible target date, since it would take that long to coordinate all the elements of such an offensive so well that it would go off without a hitch. It might also take that long to win over America's allies. "It was the President's view," state the minutes, "that we ought at once to begin to infiltrate these ideas into the minds of our allies. If the ground were prepared and the seeds planted in a quiet and informal way, there was much better chance of acceptance than if we suddenly confronted the allied governments with a full-fledged plan to end the war in Korea by military decision." General Smith countered that "a quick victory would go far to sell our allies on even the most drastic course of action in Korea."[24]

But Eisenhower was still hoping that a threat indirectly conveyed to Peking would suffice. While in New Delhi to discuss the Indian role in the implementation of a Korean armistice, Dulles told Nehru on May 21 (in the words of the former's memorandum about the conversation) that "if the armistice negotiations collapsed, the United States would probably make a stronger rather than a lesser military exertion, and that this might well extend the area of conflict. (*Note:* I assumed this would be relayed.)"[25] Relayed to Peking, that is. He did not mention atomic weapons or any other specifics, but the implication was clear. Nehru was so disturbed by Dulles's statement that he brought it up again the next day, saying that if hostilities became more intense, "it would be difficult to know what the end might be."[26] At the end of their meeting that day Nehru returned to the subject yet again, but Dulles refused to elaborate. It is generally assumed that Nehru acted in his wonted manner as diligent go-between and that his report to Peking of what Dulles had said was an important factor in prompting the Communists to respond reasonably to the final POW proposal that the UN Command delegates placed on the table at Panmunjom on May 25, four days after the New Delhi conversation.

During the days immediately following the United States/UN's presentation of its final POW proposal, the Communists launched a series of attacks at several points along the front. The heaviest of these attacks fell on the ROK troops around Kumsong, just east of the Iron Triangle, where the line of contact bulged northward. The ROKs caved in, but General Maxwell Taylor rushed South Korean reserves to the scene, and they were able to halt the Communist advance. Although the attacks created a brief military crisis, they were actually regarded as an encouraging sign by the UN Command, which assumed that the Communists were moving because they believed that an armistice was imminent and that it therefore behooved them to modify the future border before it was too late to change it, and also to apply moderate pressure so as to get the most lenient possible terms.

Whatever influence Dulles's veiled threat through Nehru may have had on the negotiations, the decisive factor was probably that Washington's May 25 proposal was an eminently reasonable one. The Communists considered it for ten days, while their attacks were in progress, and then finally on June 4 replied by demanding changes minor enough to be acceptable to Washington. A mutually satisfactory compromise on the obstructive POW issue had at last been reached. All prisoners in UN Command and Communist hands were to be turned over to the Indian troops of the newly created Neutral Nation Repatriation Commission as soon as the armistice was signed. There would then be a period of two months during which all POWs who expressed their desire to return home would be repatriated. After that, the governments involved would have ninety days to try to change the minds of their unwilling citizens. If by the end of an additional thirty days a political conference hadn't resolved the question of what to do with those who still wanted political asylum, they would all revert to civilian status and be released. (In the end, approximately 70,000 of the North Koreans held by the UN Command at the end of the war chose to return home, while 7,600 remained in South Korea. Only 5,640 of the Chinese prisoners opted to return to the People's Republic of China; the remaining 14,200 were eventually sent to Formosa. Beginning early in August 1953 the Communists returned 12,773 POWs, of whom 3,597 were Americans and 946 were Britons. One Briton, 21 Americans, and 325 South Koreans refused repatriation.)

On June 8 Generals William Harrison and Nam Il signed the Terms of Reference, spelling out in full the intricacies of the POW deal. No other issues of principle remained to be settled. Now only the detailed mapping of the final front line and of the demilitarized zone to be created on both sides of it had to be undertaken before a truce could go into effect.

Along most of its length the border runs north of the 38th parallel. South Korea gained 2,350 square miles north of latitude 38 degrees north, while North Korea gained 850 square miles south of the parallel. Three horrific years of war thus yielded a net gain of 1,500 square miles of territory for South Korea.

CHAPTER 35

Final Crises

THE SIGNING of the Terms of Reference prompted the heaviest Communist attack since the 1951 spring offensives. Beginning on June 10, 1953, the Communists once again concentrated on the ROKs guarding the critical terrain around Kumsong, between the Iron Triangle and the Punchbowl. The fighting raged for about a week and then, as usual, sputtered out. Along an eight-mile stretch the UN Command line on June 20 was about three miles farther south than it had been ten days earlier. Atypically and forebodingly, these gains had cost the Communists fewer casualties than they inflicted on the ROKs, who reported a total of 7,300 killed, wounded, or missing. The UN Command estimated the Communist casualties at 6,600.

By the time that round of fighting ended, a major crisis developed that threatened to extend, and possibly to expand, the war just as it had seemed about to end. Ever since the beginning of the truce talks, in July 1951, Syngman Rhee had repeatedly told Washington, in the most forceful possible terms, that he was unalterably opposed to any settlement short of the unification of Korea under his government, and especially to a settlement that would leave Chinese Communist troops in North Korea. Pleased and encouraged by the lack of progress that so infuriated and exasperated Washington, he never gave up hope that America might lose its patience and renew its attempt to drive the Communists out of North Korea, regardless of the cost.

Those hopes — indeed, the hopes and dreams of his entire life — suddenly seemed in jeopardy when the negotiators began to approach a compromise in April 1953. On April 24, just before the talks at Panmunjom were to resume after a six-month hiatus, the South Korean ambassador in Washington told Eisenhower that if the United States agreed to an armistice that would permit the Chinese Communists to remain south of the Yalu River, Rhee was prepared to withdraw the ROK forces from the UN Command and to fight on — alone, if need be — to unify Korea. In such a case, he would demand that all UN members unwilling to support his venture remove their forces from Korea at once.[1]

The idea was quixotic, to say the least. But Rhee was desperate enough that he might actually attempt to carry out his preposterous plan, thereby quite possibly — indeed, almost certainly — bringing about the unification of Korea under the Communists. The United States, quite naturally, was determined not to permit Rhee's unrealistic intransigence to cancel out all the gains that it and the UN had made in three years of horrendous sacrifice. Washington accordingly began to formulate contingency plans, the most extreme of which — code-named EVERREADY — called for American troops to "seize custody" of Rhee and other "dissident military and civil leaders." If the ROK army then refused to take orders from American generals, its supplies were to be cut off; it was to be subdued by force if necessary; and the American commander was to "proclaim military government in the name of the UN."[2]

Late in May, when Washington was about to present its final POW proposal at Panmunjom, it instructed General Clark to make a very generous offer to Rhee that might finally induce him to cooperate. Clark was authorized to make several major promises, among them:

1. As soon as an armistice was signed, all sixteen UN members who had sent forces to Korea would issue a joint statement declaring that if the Communists violated the truce, all sixteen nations would again send forces to defend South Korea. The statement would warn the Communists that if they broke the truce, the sixteen nations "might not confine their retaliatory efforts to Korea." (The countries involved had agreed upon the terms of the so-called Declaration of Sixteen in January 1952.)

2. The United States would underwrite the expansion of the ROK army to "more or less twenty divisions (plus one Marine brigade)" and would also enable South Korea to build up "appropriate air and naval strength." (During the first months of 1953 America had already provided Rhee with equipment for two new divisions, bringing the total to fourteen ROK divisions.) With such forces at its disposal, South Korea should be able to deter any Communist attempt to violate the truce. Clark made it very clear to Rhee, however, that if at any time in the future he initiated aggressive

action against the north, the United States would abandon South Korea to its inevitable fate.

3. The United States would give South Korea $1 billion over the course of the next few years for the reconstruction and economic rehabilitation of the nation.

4. In the political conference to follow the signing of the armistice, the United States would make every effort to secure the withdrawal of the Chinese Communist forces from northern Korea and to bring about the unification of the entire Korean peninsula under Rhee's government.[3]

Rhee was noncommittal. From May 25 onward the ROK delegate boycotted the talks at Panmunjom. But Washington's offer stood, and Rhee promised not to take any action without first consulting Clark.

Early in June, in response to a letter dated May 30 in which Rhee protested to Eisenhower that the impending armistice would mean "a death sentence for Korea," the American president reassured the Korean that the United States would "not renounce its efforts by all peaceful means to effect unification of Korea." He also told Rhee that he was prepared to negotiate, as soon as a satisfactory armistice was signed, a mutual-defense treaty with South Korea.[4]

All this was still not enough for the seventy-eight-year-old Rhee, who feared that unless he took drastic action, he would not live to see the fulfillment of his lifelong dream of a unified, independent, and democratic Korea. Refusing to believe that he was destined to fail in what he had regarded as his God-given, messianic mission, he resorted to a desperate measure in mid-June, by which time all of the individual articles of the armistice had been drawn up and signed by both sides. He ordered the South Korean guards of the UN Command prison camps to begin releasing the approximately 35,000 anti-Communist North Koreans who had requested political asylum. In the hours before dawn on June 18, some 25,000 prisoners were set free, and another 2,000 were released over the course of the next few nights. General Clark recorded in his memoirs that the operation, of which he knew absolutely nothing in advance, was very well planned. "Everyone concerned in the mass release was well briefed," he wrote. "The prisoners knew when they would go, what to take, where to shed and burn their prison garb, where to get civilian clothing and where to hide." In response to an official radio broadcast announcing the release and asking the populace to aid the POWs, many citizens hid the fugitives in their homes while "South Korean police stood watch to warn of the approach of American soldiers on a manhunt."[5] Only 1,000 of those released were ever recaptured, making a total of only 9,000 North Korean antirepatriates to be handed over to the Communists for persuasion.

The UN Command and the governments of all the UN members with forces in Korea were aghast. Hardly anyone could imagine that after a year and a half of excruciating negotiations over the issue of voluntary repatriation, the Communists would simply acquiesce to the release of nearly one quarter of all the North Koreans held in the south. Hardly anyone, that is, except for Secretary of State Dulles, who insisted that if the Communists wanted a truce as badly as he thought they did, they would overlook Rhee's impetuous action and would go ahead and sign an armistice, provided they were given proper assurances.[6] Most officials feared that the Communists would now denounce the negotiations and mount an all-out offensive to drive the UN Command from Korea. Washington was resigned to ordering atomic attacks on PRC territory if the Communists made such an attempt.

General Clark wrote to the Communist commanders to apologize formally for Rhee's release of the POWs and to disavow any complicity in the action. He could not resist telling the Communists that it would be as impossible for the United States to recapture the men "as it would be for your side to recover the 50,000 South Korean prisoners 'released' by your side during the hostilities."[7] The Communists did suspend the armistice talks, on June 20, but they left the door open by saying that they would come back to the negotiating table once the United States could demonstrate that it had Rhee under control. The most powerful offensive that the Communists mounted at this time was a propaganda one, though they also resumed their battlefield attacks on June 24.

Eisenhower, for his part, issued a statement deploring Rhee's action and saying that every effort would be made to ensure that he would abide by the terms of the armistice. That, however, was more easily said than done. Washington decided to give Rhee one last chance to promise that he would cooperate. If he refused, he would be removed forcibly from office.

The seemingly near-impossible mission of persuading Rhee was given to Walter Robertson, who had Dean Rusk's old job as assistant secretary of state for Far Eastern Affairs. Robertson arrived in Seoul on June 25, the third anniversary of the North Korean invasion, and spent the next two weeks inveigling, wheedling, flattering, convincing, reassuring, and tactfully threatening the stubborn old man. Robertson's ace in the hole was that he had been authorized to tell Rhee (untruthfully) that the United States/UN was prepared, if Rhee continued to withhold his cooperation, to sign a simple cease-fire agreement with the Communists immediately and withdraw from Korea. General Clark was instructed to take measures that might lead Rhee to believe that the United States was preparing to carry out this threat.[8]

The Communists had tacitly accepted General Clark's apology and President Eisenhower's statement, but while Robertson was still doing his best to bring Rhee around, they managed to get some tangible revenge for the American failure to keep Rhee reined in. Two hours before midnight on July 6 the Chinese Communists attacked American positions on Pork Chop Hill, which the United States had defended at such great cost in the spring. Now, in four days of brutal fighting, the Communists finally managed to force the 7th U.S. Division off the hill for good.

On July 8 the Communists informed the UN Command that they were ready and willing to resume the truce talks, which had been recessed since Rhee's sabotage, though they would not sign an armistice until they felt assured that Washington could handle Rhee. General Clark accepted the offer, and the talks got under way again, on July 10.

The previous day Rhee had finally relented and had given Robertson a letter promising that he would not obstruct the conclusion of an armistice and that he would accept its terms as binding upon him "so long as no measures or actions taken under the armistice are detrimental to our national survival."[9] He agreed to hand over to the Neutral National Repatriation Commission all the remaining anti-Communist prisoners, but he said that he would not allow any South

Korean to sign the armistice. That didn't matter to the Communists, as long as the United States signed.

In return for Rhee's reluctant cooperation Eisenhower confirmed all the terms of the offers that he and General Clark had made previously. Moreover, Eisenhower agreed to hold a high-level U.S.– South Korean political conference soon after the signing of the armistice in order to enable the two nations to present a united front at the postwar UN-Communist political conference called for in the armistice. Dulles, who would go to Seoul in August for the conference, was so much in sympathy with Rhee that he had said at a National Security Council meeting in April that if the Communists wouldn't agree to the peaceful unification of Korea, then America would have to break the armistice. But, of course, the more moderate and reasonable Eisenhower prevailed.

The war's last round of fighting began on the night of July 13, when the Chinese Communists threw three divisions against the elite ROK Capitol Division near Kumhwa, at the southeast corner of the Iron Triangle, and nearly overwhelmed it. In grave danger of being completely surrounded, the South Korean division retreated in confusion. The resulting gap in the main line of resistance enabled substantial Chinese forces to attack the flanks of several other ROK divisions, pushing them relentlessly to a new line on the south bank of the Kumsong River by July 20, when the attack abated. As usual, the Communist advantage in manpower had been outbalanced by the U.S./UN superiority in firepower. But firepower alone could never defeat an offensive. This last battle of the war cost the UN Command more than fourteen thousand casualties, most of them South Koreans. Casualties were considerably higher on the Communist side. But the Communists had made their point. If Rhee had still entertained any plans of invading the north after the armistice, the severe mauling given to the ROKs demonstrated that without American support South Korean troops wouldn't stand a chance against the Communists.

On July 19 the negotiators at Panmunjom reached final agreement on all points. The fighting was to end twelve hours after Generals Harrison and Nam Il had signed the armistice; each side would then withdraw two kilometers from its positions to create a demilitarized zone. (Thus many topographical features that had been won and held at such terrible cost were relinquished, though they were still denied to the enemy.) Once the armistice went into effect, neither side could increase the number of non-Korean troops stationed in Korea. (At the last minute Eisenhower shifted two additional infantry divisions from Japan to Korea and dispatched the 3rd Marine Division from the United States.) Finally, a military armistice commission composed of representatives from five UN Command nations and five Communist nations was to supervise execution of the agreement.

Truman later remarked that if he had concluded an armistice on the terms that Eisenhower accepted, the Republicans "would have tried to draw and quarter" him.[10] In the summer of 1953, however, most Republicans refrained from making a great outcry against the armistice for the simple reason that it had been concluded under a Republican president.

The battlefront was relatively quiet after July 20, making it possible for staff officers of the two delegations to chart the position of the cease-fire line and the contours of the demilitarized zone. That task was completed on July 23. Four days later, at precisely 10:01 in the morning, Generals Harrison and Nam Il seated themselves at separate tables in the wooden armistice hall that the Communists had built for the occasion. It took the two men eleven minutes to sign all the sets of copies of the agreement in English, Chinese, and Korean for the principal military commands involved.[11] As soon as the signing was completed, Harrison and Nam Il left the hall without speaking a word to each other. Sets of copies of the armistice agreement were then rushed to the U.S./UN, North Korean, and Chinese Communist commanders for their signatures: General Clark, Kim Il-sung, and General Peng, respectively. At 10:00 that night — three years, one month, and two days after the North Koreans had launched their invasion of the south, and two years and seventeen days after the truce talks had begun — the armistice went into effect. Both at the front and at home the general feeling was more one of relief than of exhilaration. The Korean War was finally over.

Yet an end to the Cold War was nowhere in sight. World War II had brought about the eradication of Nazism and of Japanese militarism, but the Korean War yielded nothing like such a satisfying result to vindicate all the sacrifices. President Eisenhower sounded the dominant chord in his national broadcast to announce the signing of the armistice: "There is, in this moment of sober satisfaction, one thought that must discipline our emotions and steady our resolutions. It is this: we have won an armistice on a single battleground, not peace in the world."[12]

Epilogue

ALTHOUGH the armistice has remained in effect since July 1953, in the absence of a formal peace treaty a state of war technically continues to exist between North and South Korea. Glaring at each other across the demilitarized zone, the two regimes have as yet not even made any progress toward mutual recognition, let alone toward cooperation. They have no diplomatic or economic relations whatsoever, not even postal or telephone links. Thus, although some 10 million of South Korea's 42 million people have close relatives living in the north, they are unable to communicate with them except, in a very limited number of cases, by means of an occasional supervised visit of an hour or two along the border. Fears of a new Communist attack remain so intense that on the fifteenth of every month the wail of sirens sends the entire population of Seoul scurrying for shelter in a full-dress air-raid drill.

In October 1953 diplomatic representatives of the United States, North Korea, and the People's Republic of China met at Panmunjom to lay the groundwork for the full-scale political conference that the armistice called for, but these preliminaries quickly broke down when the Communists accused the United States of complicity in Syngman Rhee's June release of North Korean antirepatriates. Further negotiations led to the convening of a high-level conference in Geneva in April 1954, but there was never the slightest possibility that Secretary of State John Foster Dulles and Chou En-lai would be able to agree on a solution to the Korean problem. For lack of any alternative, the armistice was to remain in effect indefinitely. To this day, the Communist and anti-Communist delegates to the Military Armistice Commission still meet about once a month at Panmunjom, but the sessions of mutual reviling accomplish nothing. This is hardly surprising, given that there is as much hatred between the two Korean regimes as there is between Israel and the Palestine Liberation Organization.

The 140-mile-long demilitarized zone, stretching from coast to coast across the entire peninsula, is heavily fortified and guarded. The two-and-a-half-mile-wide DMZ is defined by two parallel complexes of barbed wire punctuated by searchlight-equipped watchtowers from which sentries peer day and night into no-man's-land and beyond, vigilant for any sign of hostile activity. In the virtual sanctuary of the demilitarized strip, largely deserted except for the armistice-commission buildings at Panmunjom, wildlife thrives, disturbed only by the competing loudspeakers that blare propaganda and patriotic music from each side toward the other.

On both sides of the DMZ huge forces are poised at a constant, hair-trigger state of readiness. North Korea, with a population of about 20 million, maintains an army, navy, and air force totaling more than 850,000 men — giving it the world's sixth-largest fighting force and the second-highest ratio (after Israel) of military personnel to civilians. This force has at its disposal a formidable arsenal of Soviet-made arms, none of them, however, nuclear. South Korea, with twice the population of the north, fields armed forces of 630,000. These, despite Jimmy Carter's ill-advised campaign promise to remove American troops from Korea, are still (at an annual cost of $2.4 billion) supplemented by 29,000 soldiers of the Eighth U.S. Army and 12,000 U.S. Air Force personnel, most of them stationed near Panmunjom. On April 8, 1987, the *New York Times* reported that "it is widely believed that Washington keeps as many as 1,000 tactical nuclear warheads on South Korean soil. All are under American control."

The American presence has served to restrain both the North and the South Koreans. The American commander of the Eighth Army heads the Korea-U.S. Combined Forces Command, which includes most of the South Korean forces, and the United States has been careful to give its ally only a defensive, and not an offensive, capability. (The north has twice as many tanks as does the south, though South Korea's new heavy industry is now beginning to reduce that imbalance.) The prevalent American view is that as long as U.S. troops are stationed in Korea, and as long as the Declaration of Sixteen remains in force, Kim Il-sung will never attempt another invasion. He must understand that any serious aggressive move by the north would almost automatically escalate into a major conflict; to prevent it from spreading and to preserve a Communist North Korea, the

Soviets and the Chinese would most probably take prompt steps to remove Kim in favor of a more tractable Communist leader. Nevertheless, Korea — with one of the world's densest concentrations of arms — remains one of the most sensitive of all points of confrontation between East and West.

The Korean War resolved nothing. It had arisen in the first place out of the extreme tension and frustrations of the Cold War, and it served mainly to intensify them. Before Korea, the United States and Communist China were adversaries; afterward they were mortal enemies locked in a blood feud. The most widely accepted estimate holds that about 4 million people were killed or wounded in Korea during the war, more than half of them civilians. Perhaps as many as 1 million civilians died. About 900,000 Chinese Communist and 520,000 North Korean soldiers were killed or wounded, as were approximately 400,000 UN Command troops, nearly two thirds of them ROKs. The South Korean army sustained 47,000 combat deaths (not counting POWs), Britain 686, Canada 294, and Australia 261. Altogether 54,246 American military personnel died in the Korean War. Of them, 25,801 died from wounds suffered in battle and 2,701 were officially listed as having died in captivity, though most of the additional 5,127 categorized as having died while missing were also victims of the Communist prison camps. Another 20,617 died from illness, exposure, and accidents. A total of 103,284 Americans sustained nonmortal wounds in combat. The Soviet Union suffered no casualties in the Korean War.

The war destroyed nearly half of Korea's industrial facilities, north and south, and one third of its homes. The economies of both halves of Korea were severely strained by the costs of reconstruction and by the need to provide for the millions whom the war had left homeless and/or jobless. Since the end of the war the United States has given South Korea approximately $5 billion in economic and military aid, some of it through the UN Korean Reconstruction Agency and UN Emergency Relief, to both of which the United States was the principal donor. The war itself cost America $20 billion. In return for this enormous investment, South Korea has proven itself to be a loyal ally, even going so far as to send 50,000 troops to aid the American cause in Vietnam.

*   *   *

In the aftermath of the Korean War, President Rhee became more autocratic than ever, and his venal government aggravated rather than ameliorated the economic chaos that was the war's legacy to the Korean people. In May 1960 widespread student riots following Rhee's fourth manipulated election to the presidency finally forced him to resign and go into exile, in Hawaii, where — bitter and heartbroken — he died in 1965 at the age of ninety.

A well-intentioned liberal government then proved unable to cope with the extreme instability caused by the dizzying factionalism that grew rampant in the political vacuum created by Rhee's departure. Kim's regime even began to hope that a majority of southerners might therefore come to demand peaceful unification under Communism simply to gain a measure of political stability and economic reform. This situation led in May 1961 to a military coup by the strongly anti-Communist major general Park Chung-hee, who proceeded to dissolve the National Assembly and to impose martial law. General Park was elected head of a civilian government in October 1963, but under his repressive regime neither democracy nor the standard of living made notable advances. In December 1971, threatened by political upheaval and economic disaster, Park declared a state of national emergency and soon thereafter reinstated martial law. After more than seven subsequent years of stifling absolutism, Park was assassinated in October 1979 by the director of the South Korean Central Intelligence Agency.

Late in 1980, after a brief liberalizing interlude that once again opened the doors to factional violence, Lieutenant General Chun Doo-hwan seized power, stating as he did so that he would serve no more than seven years as head of the government. Starting out with few supporters at any level of South Korean society, Chun was able to maintain his harsh rule largely because of two factors: the strong endorsement he received from the Reagan administration, and the ambitious policy of industrialization that his government undertook, bringing unprecedented prosperity not only to a rapidly growing middle class but also, gradually yet steadily, to Korean workers. Under Chun, South Korea expanded its foreign debt to $46 billion, the highest of any nation in Asia and the fourth highest of any developing nation in the world. But the money was invested well and is yielding dramatic returns.

Until the early 1980s South Korea's largest export industries were textiles and shoes. Under Chun the emphasis shifted decisively to such heavy industries as steel production, shipbuilding, and automobile manufacturing (South Korea has the world's largest steel mill and the largest dry dock) and to the assembly of electronic consumer goods. (The Koreans are only now beginning to manufacture the sophisticated electronic components that they have hitherto had to import from Japan.) The South Korean economy, which has grown at an average rate of 10 percent a year since 1980, is now the seventeenth largest in the non-Communist world, with a gross national product of $85 billion, and it stands twelfth in its volume of exports. Only six other nations in the world export more to the United States than does South Korea (its annual total is $25 billion), and such products as Hyundai cars, GoldStar television sets and videocassette recorders, Samsung microwave ovens, and Leading Edge personal computers are finding swiftly expanding American markets.

A turning point along the road to democratization came in June 1987, when Chun's protégé and successor-designate, Roh Tae-woo, confronted by massive and widespread riots in which not only radical students but also many middle-class citizens participated, announced his willingness to make a number of substantial reforms. (Among them were limitation of the presidency to a maximum of one five-year term and an end to the presidential power to suspend the constitution or to dissolve the National Assembly.) In the multiparty presidential elections held in December 1987, the freest in South Korea's history, Roh emerged victorious — not with a majority, but with a plurality of only 36 percent of the total vote. In the parliamentary elections held the following April, his party won just 34 percent of the seats, giving the opposition parties the possibility of great power if they can cooperate with each other. If South Korean politicians can finally overcome their traditional factionalism, the nation may at last be able to sustain a democracy.

In contrast, North Korea remains a poor and backward nation, as Stalinistic and xenophobic as Albania. It is still ruled by Kim Il-sung, who turned seventy-seven in April 1989 and is the object of a self-promoted personality cult as excessive as Stalin's ever was. His omnipresent image hangs in every home and office, and giant posters of his sinisterly benevolent face are plastered onto the walls of most public buildings. All wisdom and goodness are attributed to Kim, who is officially styled "the Great Leader." The nearly universal assumption is that after his death he will be succeeded by his eldest son, Kim Jong-il, now forty-eight, who holds several important government posts and whose title as heir apparent is "the Dear Leader."

Although North Korea possesses great potential wealth in the form of natural resources, the nation's gross national product is only about one-quarter that of South Korea's. This is so because North Korean society is one of the most regimented, collectivized, and antiindividualistic in the world (not even bicycles are privately owned) and because a ruinous 25 percent of the economy is devoted to the military. Kim rules over a nation of uniforms and group activities, a bleak and Spartan barracks in which individual initiative and enterprise are punished rather than rewarded.

One unexpected result of the Korean War was that it gave North Korea a high degree of independence within the Communist bloc. In the years following the war, Kim purged his government of both pro-Soviet and pro-Chinese zealots, and since then he has taken advantage of the Sino-Soviet antagonism to steer a remarkably autonomous and ultranationalistic course. Playing the Russians and the Chinese off against each other, he has won benefits and concessions from both. A virulent anti-Titoist who denounced the Yugoslavian leader mainly for his friendship and trade with the hated nations of the West, Kim has proven himself to be one of the most durable emulators of Tito's balancing of Communism and nationalism.

The Korean War led directly to the Sino-Soviet split. For one thing, China had overshadowed the Soviet Union as North Korea's principal protector and benefactor, and rivalry for continued influence was one factor in the rift. (Eighty thousand Communist Chinese troops remained in North Korea until October 1958.) For another, the war had transformed Communist China into Asia's foremost military power, with the potential to challenge the Soviets for leadership of Communist movements outside Europe. China owed Russia more than $1.2 billion for arms purchased during the Korean War, and Peking argued that since its intervention in Korea had been for the good of the entire Communist world, the Soviets should bear some of the expense. The Soviet refusal to wipe out any of China's mounting debt — which was being greatly increased throughout the 1950s by large Chinese imports of Soviet machinery and raw materials — was a major factor in the breakdown of relations between the two nations, for Peking quite rightly deduced that Moscow was trying to retard China's development.

As always, the Kremlin wanted a dependent, subservient, and exploitable China just strong enough to be a useful ally. Mao Tse-tung had rather more ambitious plans for China. Indeed, Communism was of interest to him only because he believed that it would enable China to become the world's greatest power. By the late 1950s he was not at all averse to the idea of a nuclear war between the Communist and anti-Communist blocs, not least because he speculated that such a war would hurt the United States and the Soviet Union far more than it would hurt China, which would then emerge supreme. Mao's truculence greatly embarrassed Soviet premier Nikita Khrushchev, who had come to favor a policy directed toward an economic and political victory over the West rather than a military confrontation. Like Mikhail Gorbachev today, Khrushchev wanted to reduce military commitments so that the Soviet Union could divert its resources to the development of industry and international trade.

Khrushchev and Mao were engaged in a personal struggle for leadership of the Communist world. Until 1962 Kim was careful to remain as neutral and noncommittal as he could vis-à-vis that struggle, since he didn't want to find himself on the losing side. In May 1961, for example, when Kim was gravely disturbed by the advent of the military regime in South Korea, he hastened to sign military and economic treaties with both the Soviets and the Chinese Communists.

The turning point was the Cuban missile crisis, in October 1962. Worried that Khrushchev's backing down to President John Kennedy signaled Soviet weakness — and fearing that if the Soviet leader really felt himself cornered by the West at some point he might sacrifice North Korea to the UN — Kim decided to align himself unequivocally with Peking. Consequently, from late 1962 until Khrushchev's overthrow, in October 1964, North Korea received no Soviet aid and was excommunicated by the Soviet bloc.

Once Khrushchev was out of the way, however, relations between Pyongyang and Moscow quickly improved, especially after the United

States began to bomb North Vietnam, in February 1965. In that time of heightened danger the Soviets and the North Koreans patched up their old alliance, and the Russians resumed military and economic aid. Nonetheless, for the next twenty years the Soviets would be reluctant to give sophisticated arms to the bellicose Kim, for fear that he might invade the south.

Dedicated to the unification of Korea under Communism but not daring to attempt another invasion, Pyongyang has mounted a war of subversion, assassination, and terrorism against the south. North Korean commandos made an unsuccessful attack on President Park's residence in 1968. (That same year Pyongyang's enduring hostility toward the United States manifested itself dramatically in the *Pueblo* incident. In January, North Korean patrol boats captured the American naval-intelligence vessel USS *Pueblo* offshore, and Kim's government denounced America for spying. "Confessions" were extracted from the crew members, and only after extended and acrimonious negotiations were the men released, in December.) In another assassination attempt on Park, in 1974, his wife was killed. In 1983 Communist assassins tried to kill President Chun during a state visit to Burma; they missed him, but four members of his cabinet and seventeen other people died in the attack. More recently, Communist terrorists have exploded bombs at Kimpo Airport and on a Korean Airlines passenger flight.

The time for such aggressive tactics is now passing, for one of Gorbachev's principal objectives in the Far East is to normalize relations between the two Koreas so that the Soviet Union can develop its incipient trade with Seoul. Ironically, Moscow has lately been supplying North Korea with some of its most advanced ground-attack planes, surface-to-air missiles, and an extremely sensitive early-warning radar system in an attempt to bribe Kim to adopt a less militant stand. (The Soviets have also been rewarded with overflight rights, and the burgeoning Soviet Pacific fleet has been calling at North Korean ports.) The growing rapprochement between the Soviets and the Chinese means that Kim will become less able to play the two Communist giants off against each other and will therefore have to show more willingness to come to terms with Seoul, since that is the wish of both of his powerful next-door neighbors. One of the most potent symbols of this change is the fact that both the Soviets and the Communist Chinese participated in the Seoul Olympics of 1988, despite Pyongyang's boycott.

Gorbachev wants the Soviet Union to be able to trade freely with all the Far Eastern nations of whose rapidly growing prosperity the Russians are profoundly envious. He hopes, for instance, to attract Japanese and South Korean investment for projects in Siberia, the economic development of which has until now been blocked by the area's role as an immense military preserve. The Soviets will feel safe in opening up Siberia and fully exploiting its staggering potential — as they cannot afford not to do — only if they are on friendly terms with China and Japan and if the Korean peninsula is defused as a possible detonator of a major war.

For the good of everyone, the United States, Japan, the Soviet Union, and the People's Republic of China must all give formal recognition to both of the Korean nations and acknowledge that (at least for the foreseeable future) the division of Korea is to be as permanent as the division of Germany. Furthermore, the two Koreas must eventually sign a peace treaty, establish full diplomatic and economic relations, and join the UN. The first tentative moves are now being made. South Korea and Hungary have recently exchanged ambassadors, and, as mentioned, Moscow is easing into what it hopes will be a lucrative trade partnership with Seoul. Although South Korean law forbids trade with Communist China, about $2 billion worth takes place each year through middlemen. And Pyongyang has just taken the tiny but extremely significant step of enlisting the aid of a Seoul businessman to develop a mountain resort a short distance north of the demilitarized zone. These are all developments dictated by reason. The tragedy of the Korean people is that today, no less than in the early years of the Cold War, the division of their peninsula into two sovereign states remains essential for world peace. And yet, in today's climate of rapid liberalization within the Communist world, who can say what the future holds for Korea?

A Note on Sources

NEARLY ALL QUOTATIONS from U.S. government documents — State and Defense Department memos and position papers, National Security Council minutes and policy papers, communications between General Douglas MacArthur and the Joint Chiefs of Staff, et cetera — are drawn from the series *Foreign Relations of the United States: Diplomatic Papers* (*FRUS*), edited under the auspices of the U.S. Department of State. This series is one of the marvels of democracy. Arranged chronologically within its volumes dealing with Korea are what were at the time of their writing the most secret and revealing papers, exchanges, and records of the highest American officials. These have now been declassified and published for the entire period of the Korean War. What historians wouldn't give for comparable volumes from Moscow and Beijing!

I have also relied heavily upon the *New York Times* and its annual index, the latter one of the most valuable tools at the disposal of scholars of twentieth-century history. The index provides, under its alphabetical main entries, encyclopedic day-by-day chronologies of many aspects of the Korean War. Reference to the appropriate issues of the newspaper itself enables the researcher to gain an unparalleled sense of overall context.

The definitive official history of the Korean War is the series *United States Army in the Korean War*, written under the aegis of the army's Office of the Chief of Military History. Three of its five projected volumes have been published so far: James F. Schnabel's *Policy and Direction: The First Year*; Roy E. Appleman's *South to the Naktong, North to the Yalu* (covering the period from June 25 to November 24, 1950); and Walter G. Hermes' *Truce Tent and Fighting Front* (covering the period from July 10, 1951, to July 27, 1953). As all historians of the Korean War must do, I have made extensive use of these volumes. Among other histories of the war that I have found to be most useful are those by Bevin Alexander, Clay Blair, Joseph C. Goulden, Max Hastings, David Rees, and I. F. Stone.

Memoirs by key American officials of the period — notably Presidents Harry S. Truman and Dwight D. Eisenhower, Secretary of State Dean Acheson, George F. Kennan, and Generals Omar N. Bradley, Matthew B. Ridgway, and Mark W. Clark — are naturally among the most important primary sources dealing with the war. But since the specifics of policy information that they provide have been to a great extent superseded by the publication of the relevant volumes of *FRUS*, these memoirs are now most valuable for their subjective insights — personal reactions to events, evaluations of other personalities — as well as for details that escaped the official record of meetings.

I wish to acknowledge my debt of gratitude to the authors of all the works cited in the Bibliography.

Preceding the numbered reference notes for each chapter is a selection of works suggested for those who wish to do further reading on the subjects listed. These lists of works are by no means intended to be comprehensive. For the titles of, and publication information for, these works, please refer to the Bibliography.

In general, sources are given only for direct quotations or for obscure or controversial material.

Notes

In these notes, works are generally cited by the author's name only; for full listings see the Bibliography. If the note is citing an author with more than one work in the Bibliography, a title for the work cited, sometimes abbreviated, is also given in the note. Other forms of citation are:

CQ   *Congressional Quarterly. China: U.S. Policy Since 1945*
FRUS   U.S. Department of State. *Foreign Relations of the United States: Diplomatic Papers*
NYT   *New York Times*

CHAPTER 1. Korea and Yalta

YALTA: Churchill; Clemens; Cumings, *Origins of the Korean War;* Dallek; Kennan, *Russia and the West;* U.S. Department of State, *China White Paper*. STALIN'S POSTWAR GOALS: Beloff; Deutscher; Gaddis; Mastny; Ulam. SOVIET DECLARATION OF WAR ON JAPAN: Toland; Ulam; Werth. TRUMAN'S DECISION TO USE THE ATOMIC BOMB: Churchill, vol. 6; Davidson and Lytle; Feis; Sherwin; Spector; Toland; Harry S. Truman, vol. 1; Werth.

1. U.S. Department of Defense, 38–41.
2. Ibid., 51–52.
3. Ibid., 38–41.
4. U.S. Department of State, *China White Paper*, 113–114.

CHAPTER 2. The Russo-Japanese Rivalry in Northeast Asia

GENERAL: Fairbank, Reischauer, and Craig; Griswold; Han; Reischauer; Seton-Watson; Shinn; Tupper. KWANTUNG ARMY AND MANCHURIA: Fairbank, Reischauer, and Craig; Jones; Reischauer; Sun; Toland. KOREA UNDER JAPANESE RULE: Cumings, *Origins of the Korean War;* Fairbank, Reischauer, and Craig; Han; Henderson; Jones; McCune. KOREAN COMMUNIST MOVEMENT: Han; Scalapino and Lee; Suh.

1. Griswold, 84.
2. Clubb, 136–137.
3. Griswold, 84.
4. Ibid., 96–97.
5. Ibid., 97.
6. Esthus, 101.
7. Griswold, 125–126.

8. Hopkirk.

9. Ulam, 177.

10. Hopkirk.

11. NYT, 4/29/88.

12. FRUS, 1946, vol. 8, 706–709; Harry S. Truman, vol. 2, 321.

CHAPTER 3. The Division of Korea

GENERAL: Cho; Cumings, *Origins of the Korean War;* FRUS, 1945, vol. 6; Han; Kolko and Kolko; McCune. (*Note:* McCune is the most objective of these historians; Cumings and the Kolkos have a decided anti-American bias.) SOVIET INVASION OF MANCHURIA: Jones; Nagai and Iriye; Harry S. Truman, vol. 1; Ulam; Werth. KIM IL-SUNG BACKGROUND: Baik; Cumings, *Origins of the Korean War;* Han; McCune. COMMUNIST REGIME IN NORTHERN KOREA: Cumings, *Origins of the Korean War;* McCune; Shinn.

1. Cumings, *Origins of the Korean War,* 108–109.

2. Ibid., 109.

3. FRUS, 1945, vol. 8, 967.

4. FRUS, 1945, vol. 6, 1039 (see also ibid., 658).

5. Cumings, *Origins of the Korean War,* 120.

6. FRUS, 1945, vol. 6, 659.

7. Ibid., 667–668.

8. Ibid., 670.

9. McCune, 52.

CHAPTER 4. The United States and the Establishment of South Korea

GENERAL: Cumings, *Origins of the Korean War;* Fairbank, Reischauer, and Craig; Han; Henderson; Rosalyn Higgins; Kolko and Kolko; McCune. SYNGMAN RHEE BACKGROUND: Cumings, *Origins of the Korean War;* Han; Oliver.

1. FRUS, 1945, vol. 6, 1046.

2. Ulam, 396.

3. Cumings, *Origins of the Korean War,* 385.

4. McCune, 24.

5. FRUS, 1945, vol. 6, 1050, 1135–1136.

6. Ibid., 1146.

7. McCune, 54–55.

8. FRUS, 1947, vol. 6, 817–818; Harry S. Truman, vol. 2, 325–326.

9. Ibid.

10. FRUS, 1947, vol. 6, 833–835.

11. Cho, 220; Rosalyn Higgins.

12. NYT, 8/15/48.

CHAPTER 5. The Korean War and the Cold War in Europe:
The Legacy of Appeasement

GENERAL: Acheson; Bullock; Gaddis; Halle; Isaacson and Thomas; Johnson; Kennan, *Memoirs, 1925–1950* and *Russia and the West*; LaFeber; Mastny; Pogue; Shulman; Sked and Cook; Thomas; Harry S. Truman, vols. 1 and 2; Ulam.

1. Baik, vol. 2, 275–276.
2. Ibid., 276.
3. Manchester, *Last Lion*, 512–563.
4. Churchill, vol. 2, 15.
5. Manchester, *Last Lion*, 542 (see also B. H. Liddell Hart, *A History of the World War, 1914–1918* [London: Faber & Faber, 1934]).
6. Morison, 1061.
7. Martin Gilbert, *Winston Churchill*. Companion to vol. 4. Pt. 1: Documents, January 1917–June 1919 (London: Heineman, 1977), 419. See also Gilbert, *Winston Churchill*, vol. 4, *The Stricken World, 1916–1922* (Boston: Houghton Mifflin, 1975), 225–228.
8. Churchill, vol. 6, 555.
9. Ibid., 573.
10. Harry S. Truman, vol. 1, 247.
11. For text of speech (abridged), see Bernstein and Matusow, 215–219.
12. Churchill, vol. 1, 199.
13. Ibid., 195.
14. Ibid., xxxiv.
15. Ibid., xxxiv–xxxv.
16. Ibid., 17–18.

CHAPTER 6. The Korean War and the Cold War in Europe:
To the Brink of War

GENERAL: See suggested reading for Chapter 5. SOVIET REACTION TO THE MARSHALL PLAN: Shulman; Ulam. NSC-68: Acheson; Bradley and Blair; Isaacson and Thomas; Kennan, *Memoirs, 1925–1950*; LaFeber. For the full text of NSC-68, see FRUS, 1950, vol. 1, 235–292.

1. Bullock, 534–535.
2. Harry S. Truman, vol. 2, 241.
3. Kennan, *Memoirs, 1925–1950*, 395, 498; *Memoirs, 1950–1963*, 39–46.
4. FRUS, 1948, vol. 1, pt. 2, 547.
5. Harry S. Truman, vol. 2, 242.
6. Acheson, 283.
7. Bradley and Blair, 488–490.
8. FRUS, 1950, vol. 1, 278.
9. Ibid., 240.
10. Paterson, Clifford, and Hagan, 457.

CHAPTER 7. Cold War Developments in Asia

GENERAL: In addition to suggested reading for Chapter 5 — Beloff; Dulles; Fairbank, Reischauer, and Craig; Koen; Nagai and Iriye; Stueck; Tsou. JAPANESE PEACE TREATY: Acheson; Bradley and Blair; Guhin; Kennan, *Memoirs, 1925–1950* and *Memoirs, 1950–1963;* Reischauer; Harry S. Truman, vol. 2. SINO-SOVIET TREATY: Clubb; Fairbank, Reischauer, and Craig; Schram; Tsou; Ulam; Whiting.

1. U.S. Department of State, *China White Paper*, xv–xvi.
2. Ibid., 763–764.
3. Ibid., 774.
4. Ibid., 770.
5. Ibid., 772.
6. Ibid., 767.
7. Ibid., 767.
8. Tsou, 460–461.
9. Kennan, *Memoirs, 1925–1950*, 368.
10. Ibid., 376.
11. Reischauer, 229.
12. Kennan, *Memoirs, 1925–1950*, 388.
13. Ibid., 389.
14. Ibid., 391.
15. Ibid., 375; Bradley and Blair, 525.
16. Kennan, *Memoirs, 1925–1950*, 385–386.
17. Bradley and Blair, 525.
18. FRUS, 1950, vol. 6, 451–452; Bernstein and Matusow, 443–444.
19. FRUS, 1950, vol. 6, 452; Bernstein and Matusow, 445.
20. NYT, 1/1/50.
21. Kennan, *Memoirs, 1950–1963*, 43.
22. U.S. Department of State, *China White Paper*, xvi.
23. CQ, 88; Tsou, 529.
24. CQ, 88; Tsou, 531.
25. CQ, 88.
26. The full text of Acheson's speech is printed in CQ, 304–310.
27. CQ, 308.
28. Whiting, 37.
29. McCune, 4.
30. CQ, 310.
31. CQ, 89.

CHAPTER 8. Setting the Stage

GENERAL: Acheson; Beloff; Bullock; Dulles; Fairbank, Reischauer, and Craig; Gaddis; Halle; Isaacson and Thomas; Johnson; Kennan, *Memoirs, 1925–1950* and *Russia and the West*; Koen; LaFeber; Mastny; Nagai and Iriye; Pogue; Shulman; Sked and Cook; Stueck; Thomas; Harry S. Truman, vols. 1 and 2; Tsou; Ulam. JAPANESE PEACE TREATY: See suggested reading for Chapter 7. SINO-SOVIET TREATY: See suggested reading for Chapter 7.

1. *Time*, 6/20/49; Cho, 235–236.
2. Rovere and Schlesinger, 113; Kolko and Kolko, 568.
3. *Time*, 6/5/50.
4. Schnabel, 63n.
5. Stueck, 158.
6. NYT, 5/7/49.
7. Goulden, 33.
8. NYT, 6/9/49.
9. Cho, 253.
10. Ibid., 254.
11. Tsou, 537.
12. *Time*, 1/30/50.
13. Tsou, 538.
14. *Time*, 2/20/50.
15. Whiting, 36–37; Reischauer, 268–269.
16. Khrushchev, 368.
17. Ibid., 370.
18. Ibid., 386.
19. Ibid., 367–368.
20. Paige, 124.

CHAPTER 9. The Real Thing?

GENERAL: Appleman; Bradley and Blair; Paige; Schnabel; Harry S. Truman, vol. 2.

1. Schnabel, 36; Bradley and Blair, 527.
2. John Merrill, "Internal Warfare in Korea, 1948–1950," in Cumings, *Child of Conflict*, 133–162.
3. Paige, 74–75.
4. Ibid., 73.
5. Schnabel, 63.
6. NYT, 2/8/50, 2/11/50.
7. Ibid., 3/12/50.
8. Ibid., 4/8/50.
9. *Time*, 6/5/50.
10. NYT, 5/30/50.
11. *Time*, 6/12/50; NYT, 6/1/50, 6/2/50.
12. Rovere and Schlesinger, 113.

13. Schnabel, 63.
14. Tuchman, 247; NYT, 5/9/50, 5/26/50, 5/31/50.
15. FRUS, 1950, vol. 7, 125–126; Harry S. Truman, vol. 2, 333–334; Paige, 91.
16. Rovere and Schlesinger, 115.
17. Bradley and Blair, 530.
18. Rovere and Schlesinger, 113.
19. Appleman, 12–17; Schnabel, 40; Kahn, 109.
20. FRUS, 1950, vol. 7, 93.
21. Ridgway, 15–17.
22. Appleman, 17.
23. Appleman, 8–12; Schnabel, 37–39.
24. Ridgway, 18–19.
25. NYT, 6/25/50.
26. Paige, 105.

CHAPTER 10. Washington's First Response

GENERAL: Acheson; Bradley and Blair; Paige; Schnabel; Harry S. Truman, vol. 2.
GERMANY: Acheson; Bradley and Blair; Bullock; Harry S. Truman, vol. 2; Vali. MAC-
ARTHUR BACKGROUND: Bradley; James; Manchester, *American Caesar;* Rovere and
Schlesinger; Spector; Toland.

1. Harry S. Truman, vol. 2, 332.
2. Ibid.
3. FRUS, 1950, vol. 7, 186–187.
4. Ibid., 197.
5. Paige, 117–118.
6. FRUS, 1950, vol. 7, 186–187.
7. Ibid., 187n; Bullock, 791.
8. Harry S. Truman, vol. 2, 332–333.
9. Bullock, 793.
10. LaFeber, 111.
11. FRUS, 1951, vol. 7, pt. 1, 77–79; Harry S. Truman, vol. 2, 435.
12. Harry S. Truman, vol. 2, 339.
13. FRUS, 1951, vol. 7, pt. 1, 77–79; Harry S. Truman, vol. 2, 435.
14. Harry S. Truman, vol. 2, 463.
15. Ibid., 334.
16. Ibid., 335.
17. Kolko and Kolko, 570–585, e.g. See also Stone.
18. Kennan, *Memoirs, 1925–1950,* 382.
19. Ferrell, 47.
20. William E. Leuchtenburg, *Franklin D. Roosevelt and the New Deal, 1932–1940.*
(New York: Harper, 1963), 96.

CHAPTER 11. The UN's First Response

GENERAL: Acheson; Goldman; Rosalyn Higgins; Paige; Harry S. Truman, vol. 2.
GREECE: Acheson; Clogg; Harry S. Truman, vol. 2; Woodhouse.

1. Ulam, 523; Rees, 33.
2. Kennan, *Memoirs, 1925–1950*, 490.
3. Acheson, 404.
4. Rosalyn Higgins, 175–178.
5. Paige, 148.
6. FRUS, 1950, vol. 7, 155–156.
7. Goldman, 148.
8. Rosalyn Higgins, 158–159; NYT, 8/27/49, 9/9/49.
9. NYT, 9/22/49, 9/30/49.
10. Ibid., 10/18/49.
11. CQ, 309; Acheson, 357.
12. Paige, 107.
13. Ibid., 117.
14. Rosalyn Higgins, 175–178; Bentwich and Martin, 93 ff.
15. NYT, 6/30/50. See also Rosalyn Higgins, 173–175.
16. Acheson, 450; Rosalyn Higgins, 164–165.

CHAPTER 12. The First Blair House Meeting

ACCOUNTS OF THE MEETING: Acheson, 405–407; Bradley and Blair, 533–536; FRUS,
1950, vol. 7, 157–161; Paige, 125–141; Schnabel, 68–69; Harry S. Truman, vol. 2,
333–336. BACKGROUND OF TRUMAN'S ADVISERS: *Current Biography;* Isaacson and
Thomas; *National Cyclopedia of American Biography.*

1. Acheson, 250.
2. Bradley and Blair, 502.
3. Ibid., 472.
4. Ibid., 513.
5. Ibid., 533.
6. Ibid., 534.
7. FRUS, 1950, vol. 7, 158.
8. Isaacson and Thomas, 507.
9. Acheson, 406; Kennan, *Memoirs, 1925–1950*, 486.
10. Paige, 149–150.

CHAPTER 13. The Decision to Intervene

GENERAL: Acheson; Bradley and Blair; Goldman; Paige; Schnabel; Harry S. Truman,
vol. 2. MINUTES OF THE SECOND BLAIR HOUSE MEETING: FRUS, 1950, vol. 7, 178–183.

1. Harry S. Truman, vol. 2, 337.

2. Goulden, 74.

3. Acheson, 407; Bradley and Blair, 536.

4. FRUS, 1950, vol. 7, 217.

5. Ibid., 202–203; Harry S. Truman, vol. 2, 338–339; Bernstein and Matusow, 437–438.

6. Ibid.

7. Paige, 196.

8. NYT, 6/28/50.

9. *Christian Science Monitor,* 6/29/50.

10. NYT, 6/28/50.

CHAPTER 14. The UN Goes to War

GENERAL: Acheson; Goldman; Rosalyn Higgins; Paige; Harry S. Truman, vol. 2.
COMPOSITION OF UN FORCES: Rosalyn Higgins, 199–201; Rees, 457.

1. Bernstein and Matusow, 439. See also Rosalyn Higgins and FRUS, 1950, vol. 7.

2. Harry S. Truman, vol. 2, 435.

3. Caridi, 56.

4. Ridgway, 221.

5. Harry S. Truman, vol. 2, 343.

CHAPTER 15. The Commitment of U.S. Ground Troops

GENERAL: Appleman; Bradley and Blair; Paige; Schnabel; Harry S. Truman, vol. 2.

1. Appleman, 33–34.

2. Schnabel, 71–72.

3. NYT, 6/30/50; Manchester, *American Caesar,* 553–555.

4. NYT, 6/30/50.

5. Ibid.

6. Gunther, 168–169.

7. Schnabel, 74.

8. Whitney, 327.

9. Manchester, *American Caesar,* 554–555.

10. NYT, 6/30/50.

11. For accounts of Truman's press conference, see NYT, 6/30/50; Paige, 242–244.

12. Paige, 219.

13. Schnabel, 76.

14. Ibid., 77n.

15. Paige, 244–252; Schnabel, 76–77.

16. For text of U.S. note and Soviet reply, see NYT, 6/30/50. See also FRUS, 1950, vol. 7, 229–230; Paige, 247.

17. Schnabel, 77.

18. Paige, 210, 248; CQ, 91.

19. FRUS, 1950, vol. 7, 248–250; Schnabel, 77–78.

20. For accounts of the MacArthur-Collins telecon, see FRUS, 1950, vol. 7, 250–253; Schnabel, 78–79; Paige, 253–256; Bradley and Blair, 539–540.

21. Margaret Truman, 570.

CHAPTER 16. The U.S. Army Begins to Fight

CONDITION OF THE U.S. ARMY IN JUNE 1950: Appleman; Bradley and Blair; Schnabel. EARLY PERFORMANCE OF U.S. TROOPS IN KOREA: Appleman; Bradley and Blair; Goldman; Marguerite Higgins; Knox, vol. 1; Manchester, *American Caesar*; Rees. INCREASE OF THE U.S. DEFENSE BUDGET AND ITS EFFECT ON THE AMERICAN ECONOMY: Bradley and Blair; Goldman; Manchester, *Glory and the Dream*; Harry S. Truman, vol. 2.

1. Paige, 257 ff.

2. FRUS, 1950, vol. 7, 263.

3. Harry S. Truman, vol. 2, 343.

4. Ridgway, 75–76, 244.

5. Veterans of Foreign Wars, 107.

6. Manchester, *American Caesar*, 538.

7. Marguerite Higgins, 83.

8. Ibid., 84.

9. Ibid., 84–85.

10. Schnabel, 83–85.

11. NYT, 9/2/50.

12. Ibid., 7/20/50.

13. Ibid., 7/25/50.

14. Blair, 168.

CHAPTER 17. Inchon

GENERAL: Appleman; Bradley and Blair; James, vol. 3; Manchester, *American Caesar*; Ridgway; Rovere and Schlesinger; Schnabel. MACARTHUR'S REPORT ON INCHON TO THE UN SECURITY COUNCIL: Excerpts in Rosalyn Higgins, 254–256; Veterans of Foreign Wars, 210–215.

1. Bradley and Blair, 544.

2. Ibid.

3. Rovere and Schlesinger, 119n; Manchester, *American Caesar*, 575.

4. Manchester, *American Caesar*, 579.

5. NYT, 10/6/50.

6. Isaacson and Thomas, 532.

CHAPTER 18. Toward a "Unified, Independent, and Democratic" Korea

GENERAL: Acheson; Bradley; Rosalyn Higgins; Schnabel; Spurr; Stueck; Harry S. Truman, vol. 2; Tsou; Whiting.

1. Veterans of Foreign Wars, 215.
2. Ibid., 250–251.
3. FRUS, 1950, vol. 7, 949; Rovere and Schlesinger, 275.
4. Ibid.
5. FRUS, 1950, vol. 7, 502.
6. Ibid., 582.
7. Ibid., 272.
8. Acheson, 445.
9. Bradley and Blair, 559.
10. FRUS, 1950, vol. 7, 386–387.
11. Ibid., 508–509.
12. Stueck, 250.

CHAPTER 19. Pushing China Toward War

GENERAL: See suggested reading for Chapter 18.

1. Schnabel, 107.
2. Kennan, *Memoirs, 1925–1950*, 486.
3. Ibid., 488–489.
4. Full text of the PPS paper: FRUS, 1950, vol. 7, 449 ff.
5. Ibid., 460–461.
6. Ibid., 514.
7. Whiting, 53, 57.
8. Bradley and Blair, 547–548.
9. Whiting, 64.
10. Bradley and Blair, 547.
11. FRUS, 1950, vol. 7, 180.
12. FRUS, 1950, vol. 6, 428; Harry S. Truman, vol. 2, 351–352.
13. Bradley and Blair, 549.
14. Appleman, 44–46; Manchester, *American Caesar*, 562–563.
15. NYT, 8/1/50.
16. NYT, 8/2/50.
17. FRUS, 1950, vol. 6, 427; Harry S. Truman, vol. 2, 351–352.
18. FRUS, 1950, vol. 6, 429; Harry S. Truman, vol. 2, 352.
19. FRUS, 1950, vol. 6, 439; Harry S. Truman, vol. 2, 354.
20. FRUS, 1950, vol. 7, 563.
21. NYT, 8/18/50; Whiting, 78–79.
22. Whiting, 79.
23. Ibid.
24. Ibid., 85.
25. NYT, 8/26/50; Harry S. Truman, vol. 2, 356–358.

26. Text of MacArthur's VFW message: FRUS, 1950, vol. 6, 451–453; Bernstein and Matusow, 443–446.
27. FRUS, 1950, vol. 7, 1456.
28. For full account of this episode, see FRUS, 1950, vol. 6, 453–460.
29. NYT, 8/26/50.
30. NYT, 9/1/50.
31. Ibid.
32. Ibid.
33. NYT, 9/2/50.
34. Ibid.
35. Ibid.

CHAPTER 20. Truman's Mistakes

GENERAL: See suggested reading for Chapter 18. JAPAN: Fairbank, Reischauer, and Craig; Manchester, *American Caesar;* Reischauer.

1. NYT, 9/15/50.
2. Full text of NSC-81/1: FRUS, 1950, vol. 7, 712–721.
3. Bradley and Blair, 559.
4. FRUS, 1950, vol. 7, 714.

CHAPTER 21. Crossing the 38th Parallel

GENERAL: See suggested reading for Chapter 18. WAKE ISLAND CONFERENCE: Bradley and Blair; James, vol. 3; Manchester, *American Caesar;* Rovere and Schlesinger; Harry S. Truman, vol. 2.

1. Gallup, vol. 2, 943.
2. FRUS, 1950, vol. 6, 428.
3. NYT, 9/19/50; Veterans of Foreign Wars, 145–146.
4. FRUS, 1950, vol. 7, 781; Bradley and Blair, 563.
5. FRUS, 1950, vol. 7, 781.
6. Bradley and Blair, 565.
7. NYT, 9/30/50.
8. FRUS, 1950, vol. 7, 826; Bradley and Blair, 566.
9. FRUS, 1950, vol. 7, 827; Rosalyn Higgins, 165–167, 256.
10. Whiting, 108.
11. FRUS, 1950, vol. 7, 796–797.
12. Ibid., 839; Whiting, 108.
13. Isaacson and Thomas, 533.
14. NYT, 10/2/50.
15. FRUS, 1950, vol. 7, 915.
16. Bradley and Blair, 567–568.

17. FRUS, 1950, vol. 7, 915–916.
18. Text of Truman's October 10 statement: NYT, 10/11/50.
19. Harry S. Truman, vol. 2, 364.
20. Transcript of Wake Island meeting: FRUS, 1950, vol. 7, 948–960; Rovere and Schlesinger, 275–285.
21. FRUS, 1950, vol. 7, 933–934.
22. Ibid., 935–938.
23. Rovere and Schlesinger, 47.

CHAPTER 22. Peking's Decision to Intervene

GENERAL: See suggested reading for Chapter 18.

1. Rosemary Foot, "How Far to Push the Americans," *New York Times Book Review*, 8/21/88.
2. FRUS, 1950, vol. 7, 1026.
3. Ibid., 532.
4. Ibid., 1026.
5. Ibid., 1074.
6. Ibid., 1183.

CHAPTER 23. China Enters the War

GENERAL: Acheson; Appleman; Bradley and Blair; James, vol. 3; Manchester, *American Caesar;* Schnabel; Spurr; Harry S. Truman, vol. 2; Whiting.

1. Rosalyn Higgins, 258; Veterans of Foreign Wars, 277–280.
2. Bradley and Blair, 578; Appleman, 670; Schnabel, 218.
3. FRUS, 1950, vol. 7, 1014.
4. Ibid., 1027 ff.
5. Ibid., 1023–1024.
6. Bradley and Blair, 583.
7. Harry S. Truman, vol. 2, 373.
8. FRUS, 1950, vol. 7, 1057.
9. Bradley and Blair, 585.
10. FRUS, 1950, vol. 7, 1058; Harry S. Truman, vol. 2, 375; Bradley and Blair, 585.
11. FRUS, 1950, vol. 7, 1075; Harry S. Truman, vol. 2, 376; Bradley and Blair, 586.
12. FRUS, 1950, vol. 7, 1097–1098.
13. Ibid., 1120–1121.
14. Ibid., 1107–1110.
15. Ibid., 1091–1092.
16. Caridi, 95.
17. NYT, 11/6/50.
18. Whiting, 137–138.

CHAPTER 24. "An Entirely New War"

GENERAL: See suggested reading for Chapter 23.

1. FRUS, 1950, vol. 7, 1175.
2. Ibid.
3. Ibid., 1149.
4. Ibid., 1161; NYT, 11/16/50, 11/17/50.
5. FRUS, 1950, vol. 7, 1126–1127.
6. Ibid., 1138–1140.
7. Ibid., 1205.
8. Ibid., 1222–1224.
9. Ibid., 1231–1233.
10. Ridgway, 60.
11. FRUS, 1950, vol. 7, 1237; Bradley and Blair, 597–598.

CHAPTER 25. World War III?

GENERAL: See suggested reading for Chapter 23.

1. Ferrell, 204.
2. FRUS, 1950, vol. 7, 1239 ff.
3. Harry S. Truman, vol. 2, 378.
4. Bradley and Blair, 640; Rovere and Schlesinger, 309.
5. Bradley and Blair, 611–614.
6. FRUS, 1950, vol. 7, 1276–1281, 1323–1334; Acheson, 475.
7. FRUS, 1951, vol. 7, pt. 1, 104–105.
8. FRUS, 1950, vol. 7, 1260.
9. Ibid., 1321; Kennan, *Memoirs, 1950–1963*, 26–33; Bradley and Blair, 603.
10. FRUS, 1950, vol. 7, 1469n; Bradley and Blair, 607.
11. FRUS, 1951, vol. 7, pt. 1, 71–72; Bradley and Blair, 621–622.
12. *U.S. News & World Report*, 12/1/50. Text also printed in NYT, 12/2/50.
13. Rovere and Schlesinger, 134.
14. NYT, 12/2/50; Manchester, *American Caesar*, 614; Acheson, 471–472; Bradley and Blair, 601–602.
15. Harry S. Truman, vol. 2, 383.

CHAPTER 26. Mr. Attlee Goes to Washington

ACCOUNTS OF THE TRUMAN-ATTLEE MEETINGS: Acheson, 478–485; Burridge; Harry S. Truman, vol. 2, 396–413. MINUTES OF THE MEETINGS DEALING WITH KOREA AND FORMOSA: FRUS, 1950, vol. 7, 1361–1374, 1392–1408, 1449–1465, 1468–1479.

1. NYT, 12/1/50; FRUS, 1950, vol. 7, 1261–1262.
2. Ibid.
3. FRUS, 1950, vol. 7, 1098 ff.

4. Ibid., 1300.

5. Ibid., 1396.

6. Ibid., 1366–1367.

7. Ibid., 1365, 1369, 1397–1399.

8. Ibid., 1406.

9. Ibid., 1402.

10. Ibid., 1397.

11. Ibid., 1407.

12. Ibid.

13. Ibid., 1144–1145; Bradley and Blair, 594.

14. FRUS, 1950, vol. 7, 1462.

15. Ibid., 1470.

CHAPTER 27. The Great Debate

GENERAL: Acheson; Bradley and Blair; Caridi; Isaacson and Thomas; Schnabel; Harry S. Truman, vol. 2.

1. Bradley and Blair, 609.

2. Ibid., 610.

3. NYT, 12/16/50; FRUS, 1950, vol. 7, 1548.

4. Acheson, 486–487.

5. Caridi, 133.

6. Acheson, 365–366; Harry S. Truman, vol. 2, 428–430; Isaacson and Thomas, 545.

7. FRUS, 1950, vol. 7, 1261.

CHAPTER 28. Enter General Ridgway

GENERAL: Bradley and Blair; Rees; Ridgway; Schnabel.

1. FRUS, 1950, vol. 7, 1631.

2. Ibid., 1630–1633.

3. Ridgway, 64–65, 79; Bradley and Blair, 543–544, 608.

4. Ridgway, 83.

5. Ibid., 95.

6. Ibid., 86–87, 97.

7. Ibid., 90, 108.

8. Ibid., 88–89, 111.

9. Bradley and Blair, 623.

10. Rees, 178; Ridgway, 108, 264.

11. FRUS, 1951, vol. 7, pt. 1, 77–79; Harry S. Truman, vol. 2, 435.

12. Blair, 742–743; Manchester, *American Caesar*, 633.

CHAPTER 29. MacArthur Goes Too Far

GENERAL: Acheson; Bradley and Blair; James, vol. 3; Manchester, *American Caesar;* Ridgway; Rovere and Schlesinger; Harry S. Truman, vol. 2.

1. Rosalyn Higgins, 167–168; CQ, 94.
2. FRUS, 1951, vol. 7, pt. 1, 263–264; Harry S. Truman, vol. 2, 439–440; Acheson, 518.
3. Harry S. Truman, vol. 2, 438–439; Acheson, 518; Bradley and Blair, 626; Rovere and Schlesinger, 168.
4. Acheson, 518.
5. Full text of MacArthur's statement: FRUS, 1951, vol. 7, pt. 1, 265–266; Harry S. Truman, vol. 2, 440–441; Rovere and Schlesinger, 168–170.
6. Manchester, *American Caesar,* 627.
7. Harry S. Truman, vol. 2, 416.
8. Rovere and Schlesinger, 297.
9. Ibid., 340.

CHAPTER 30. The Dismissal of MacArthur

GENERAL: Acheson; Bradley and Blair; Caridi; Donovan, vol. 2; James, vol. 3; Manchester, *American Caesar;* Rovere and Schlesinger; Harry S. Truman, vol. 2.

1. Harry S. Truman, vol. 2, 441–445, 448.
2. Acheson, 494–495; Caridi, 128–137.
3. Bradley and Blair, 628; Rovere and Schlesinger, 171; Caridi, 144; Manchester, *American Caesar,* 638.
4. Harry S. Truman, vol. 2, 445–446; Bradley and Blair, 629; Caridi, 145; Rovere and Schlesinger, 171–172; Manchester, *American Caesar,* 638–639.
5. Rovere and Schlesinger, 172.
6. Bradley and Blair, 629.
7. Harry S. Truman, vol. 2, 447.
8. Acheson, 521–522.
9. Blair, 742–743.
10. Ridgway, 121–122.
11. Bradley and Blair, 625; Ridgway, 116.
12. Rovere and Schlesinger, 289.
13. Bradley and Blair, 630.
14. FRUS, 1951, vol. 7, pt. 1, 309.
15. Bradley and Blair, 630–631.
16. Miller, 305.
17. Acheson, 523.
18. Rovere and Schlesinger, 290.
19. Caridi, 146.
20. Manchester, *American Caesar,* 649.

21. Caridi, 152; *Congressional Record*, 4/24/51, 4375.
22. Goldman, 202; CQ, 94.
23. Rovere and Schlesinger, 298–299.
24. Miller, 311.
25. Rovere and Schlesinger, 15–16.
26. Harry S. Truman, vol. 2, 451.

CHAPTER 31. Stalemate

GENERAL: Acheson; Bradley and Blair; Kennan, *Memoirs, 1950–1963;* Rees; Ridgway; Harry S. Truman, vol. 2. GLOUCESTERS ON THE IMJIN: Hastings; Kahn; Rees.

1. Blair, 742–743.
2. Rees, 250.
3. Ridgway, 174.
4. Sked and Cook, 92–93.
5. Acheson, 531; Rees, 262.
6. FRUS, 1951, vol. 7, pt. 1, 1671–1672.
7. Ibid., 1672.
8. Kennan, *Memoirs, 1950–1963*, 36–37; Acheson, 532–533; Harry S. Truman, vol. 2, 456.
9. FRUS, 1951, vol. 7, pt. 1, 560–561; Harry S. Truman, vol. 2, 457–458.
10. FRUS, 1951, vol. 7, pt. 1, 586–587; Harry S. Truman, vol. 2, 458.
11. Reischauer and Fairbank, 443.
12. Acheson, 529.
13. Blair, 743.
14. NYT, 11/28/51, 11/29/51.
15. NYT, 10/1/51.

CHAPTER 32. The War of Nerves

GENERAL: Acheson; Clark; Hermes; Joy; Rees; Ridgway; Harry S. Truman, vol. 2. BRITISH ELECTIONS: Burridge; Rees; Sked and Cook. POW RIOTS: Hermes; Rees; Ridgway. COMMUNIST ACCUSATIONS OF BACTERIOLOGICAL WARFARE: Hermes; Rees.

1. NYT, 7/25/51.
2. Rosalyn Higgins, 272; Rees, 292; Hermes, 38; Goulden, 569.
3. Hermes, 40–44, Ridgway, 199–200; Rosalyn Higgins, 273–274; Joy, 32–37.
4. Acheson, 540–541.
5. Ibid., 543.
6. Ridgway, 200–202; Rosalyn Higgins, 274–275.
7. FRUS, 1951, vol. 7, pt. 1, 618.
8. CQ, 97.
9. Goulden, xxv, 591.

10. NYT, 5/8/82; Harry S. Truman, vol. 2, 460–461.

11. Acheson, 656–657.

12. CQ, 98.

13. Ibid.

CHAPTER 33. Referendum on Korea

GENERAL: Ambrose, vol. 1; Bradley and Blair; Caridi; Donovan, vol. 2; Eisenhower; Goldman; Guhin; Manchester, *Glory and the Dream;* Patterson; Rees; Schlesinger and Israel; Harry S. Truman, vol. 2.

1. Harry S. Truman, vol. 2, 488.

2. Eisenhower, 19.

3. Goldman, 221.

4. NYT, 6/6/52.

5. Ibid., 10/5/52.

6. Ibid., 4/12/51. A copy of MacArthur's message of 1/6/51 recommending against arming more ROK divisions was included in the portfolio of supporting documents given to reporters when his dismissal was announced, for MacArthur had recently blamed Washington for failing to give more arms to South Korea. See Bradley and Blair, 632.

7. Ridgway, 176, 193–194, 218.

8. NYT, 9/26/52.

9. Caridi, 140.

10. Barton J. Bernstein, "The Election of 1952," in Schlesinger and Israel, vol. 4, 3246.

11. Caridi, 233.

12. Ibid., 232.

13. NYT, 10/25/52; Eisenhower, 72–73; Goldman, 232–233; Caridi, 233–235.

14. Ambrose, vol. 1, 569.

15. CQ, 98; Ambrose, vol. 1, 569.

CHAPTER 34. Eisenhower Takes Over

GENERAL: Ambrose, vol. 2; Clark; Eisenhower; Hermes.

1. Accounts of Eisenhower's trip to Korea: Eisenhower, 93–96; Ambrose, vol. 2, 30–31; Clark, 230–239.

2. Clark, 233; Bradley and Blair, 658.

3. CQ, 99.

4. Eisenhower, 95.

5. Ibid., 123; NYT, 2/3/53.

6. CQ, 100.

7. NYT, 2/11/53, 7/27/53.

8. Fairbank, Reischauer, and Craig, 872.

9. Ambrose, vol. 2, 91.

10. Clark, 242.

11. Ibid., 243.

12. Eisenhower, 145–147; Ambrose, vol. 2, 94–95.

13. FRUS, 1952–54, vol. 15, pt. 1, 1082–1086; Clark, 267.

14. FRUS, 1952–54, vol. 15, pt. 1, 1069.

15. Ibid., 1058–1059.

16. Ibid., 1056.

17. Clark, 267.

18. FRUS, 1952–54, vol. 15, pt. 1, 977.

19. Ibid., 1014.

20. Eisenhower, 179.

21. Ibid., 179–180.

22. FRUS, 1952–54, vol. 15, pt. 1, 1062–1063, 1067.

23. Ibid., 1066.

24. Ibid.

25. Ibid., 1068–1069.

26. Ibid., 1071.

CHAPTER 35. Final Crises

GENERAL: See suggested reading for Chapter 34.

1. FRUS, 1952–54, vol. 15, pt. 1, 935. Rhee had made the same threat, in slightly less urgent terms, in a letter to Eisenhower dated April 9, 1953. See FRUS, 1952–54, vol. 15, pt. 1, 902–903; Eisenhower, 181.

2. FRUS, 1952–54, vol. 15, pt. 1, 965–967.

3. Ibid., 1086–1090; Clark, 268–269.

4. Eisenhower, 183.

5. Clark, 279.

6. Eisenhower, 186–187.

7. Clark, 289.

8. FRUS, 1952–54, vol. 15, pt. 2, 1271.

9. Ibid., 1357–1359.

10. Goulden, 646.

11. NYT, 7/27/53. Full text of armistice agreement: Rosalyn Higgins, 290–308; Rees, 462–492.

12. NYT, 7/27/53.

EPILOGUE

GENERAL: *Handbook of Korea; Insight,* 10/12/87; Lockwood; NYT, 4/5–4/8/87 (series of four articles dealing with South Korea's political situation, its economy, the presence of U.S. troops, and relations with North Korea); *New York Times Magazine,* 12/14/86; Rees; Shinn; *Time,* 12/1/86, 6/29/87; Zagoria.

Bibliography

Acheson, Dean. *Present at the Creation: My Years in the State Department.* New York: W. W. Norton, 1969.

Alexander, Bevin. *Korea: The First War We Lost.* New York: Hippocrene, 1986.

Allen, Richard C. *Korea's Syngman Rhee: An Unauthorized Portrait.* Rutland, Vt.: Charles E. Tuttle, 1960.

Ambrose, Stephen E. *Eisenhower.* Vol. 1: *Soldier, General of the Army, President-Elect, 1890–1952.* Vol. 2: *President and Elder Statesman, 1952–1969.* New York: Simon & Schuster, 1983–84.

Appleman, Roy E. *South to the Naktong, North to the Yalu.* (U.S. Army, Office of the Chief of Military History. *United States Army in the Korean War,* vol. 2.) Washington, D.C.: U.S. Government Printing Office, 1961.

Baik, Bong. *Kim Il Sung: A Political Biography.* 3 vols. New York: Guardian Books, 1970.

Baldwin, Frank, ed. *Without Parallel: The American-Korean Relationship Since 1945.* New York: Pantheon, 1974.

Barnett, A. Doak. *China and the Major Powers in East Asia.* Washington: Brookings Institution, 1977.

Beloff, Max. *Soviet Policy in the Far East, 1944–1951.* London: Oxford University Press, 1953.

Bentwich, Norman, and Andrew Martin. *A Commentary on the Charter of the United Nations.* 2nd ed. London: Routledge & Kegan Paul, 1951. Reprint. New York: Kraus Reprint, 1969.

Bernstein, Barton J., and Allen J. Matusow, eds. *The Truman Administration: A Documentary History.* New York: Harper & Row, 1966.

Blair, Clay. *The Forgotten War: America in Korea, 1950–1953.* New York: Times Books, 1987.

Blumenson, Martin. *Mark Clark.* New York: Congdon & Weed, 1984.

Bradley, Omar N., and Clay Blair. *A General's Life: An Autobiography.* New York: Simon & Schuster, 1983.

Bullock, Alan. *Ernest Bevin: Foreign Secretary, 1945–1951.* New York: W. W. Norton, 1983.

Burridge, Trevor. *Clement Attlee: A Political Biography.* London: Jonathan Cape, 1985.

Caridi, Ronald J. *The Korean War and American Politics: The Republican Party as a Case Study.* Philadelphia: University of Pennsylvania Press, 1968.

Cho, Soon Sung. *Korea in World Politics, 1940–1950: An Evaluation of American Responsibility.* Berkeley and Los Angeles: University of California Press, 1967.

Churchill, Winston S. *The Second World War.* 6 vols. Boston: Houghton Mifflin, 1948–53.

Clark, Mark W. *From the Danube to the Yalu.* New York: Harper & Brothers, 1954.

Clemens, Diane Shaver. *Yalta.* New York: Oxford University Press, 1970.

Clogg, Richard. *A Short History of Modern Greece.* 2nd ed. Cambridge: Cambridge University Press, 1986.

Clubb, O. Edmund. *China & Russia: The "Great Game."* New York: Columbia University Press, 1971.

Cohen, Warren I. *Dean Rusk.* Totowa, N.J.: Cooper Square, 1980.

Collins, J. Lawton. *War in Peacetime: The History and Lessons of Korea.* Boston: Houghton Mifflin, 1969.

Congressional Quarterly. China: U.S. Policy Since 1945. Washington, D.C.: Congressional Quarterly Inc., 1980.

Cumings, Bruce. *The Origins of the Korean War: Liberation and the Emergence of Separate Regimes, 1945–1947.* Princeton, N.J.: Princeton University Press, 1981.

——, ed. *Child of Conflict: The Korean-American Relationship, 1943–1953.* Seattle: University of Washington Press, 1983.

Current Biography. Annual volumes for 1947–53. New York: H. W. Wilson.

Dallek, Robert. *Franklin D. Roosevelt and American Foreign Policy, 1932–1945.* New York: Oxford University Press, 1979.

Davidson, James West, and Mark Hamilton Lytle. *After the Fact: The Art of Historical Detection.* New York: Alfred A. Knopf, 1982.

Deutscher, Isaac. *Stalin: A Political Biography.* New York: Oxford University Press, 1949.

Donovan, Robert J. *The Presidency of Harry S. Truman.* Vol. 1: *Conflict and Crisis, 1945–1948.* Vol. 2: *Tumultuous Years, 1949–1953.* New York: W. W. Norton, 1977–82.

Dower, John W. *War Without Mercy: Race and Power in the Pacific War.* New York: Pantheon, 1986.

Dulles, Foster Rhea. *American Policy Toward Communist China: The Historical Record, 1949–1969.* New York: Thomas Y. Crowell, 1972.

Duncan, David Douglas. *This Is War!* New York: Harper & Brothers, 1951.

Eisenhower, Dwight D. *The White House Years.* Vol. 1: *Mandate for Change, 1953–1956.* Garden City, N.Y.: Doubleday, 1963.

Elson, Robert T. *The World of Time Inc.: The Intimate History of a Publishing Enterprise.* Vol. 2, *1941–1960.* New York: Atheneum, 1973.

Esthus, Raymond A. *Theodore Roosevelt and Japan.* Seattle: University of Washington Press, 1966.

Fairbank, John K. *The United States and China.* Cambridge: Harvard University Press, 1971.

Fairbank, John K., Edwin O. Reischauer, and Albert M. Craig. *East Asia: The Modern Transformation.* Boston: Houghton Mifflin, 1965.

Feis, Herbert. *The Atomic Bomb and the End of World War II.* Princeton, N.J.: Princeton University Press, 1966.

Ferrell, Robert H., ed. *Off the Record: The Private Papers of Harry S. Truman.* New York: Harper & Row, 1980.

Foot, Rosemary. *The Wrong War: American Policy and the Dimensions of the Korean Conflict, 1950–1953*. Ithaca, N.Y.: Cornell University Press, 1985.

Gaddis, John Lewis. *The United States and the Origins of the Cold War, 1941–1947*. New York: Columbia University Press, 1972.

Gallup, George H., ed. *The Gallup Poll: Public Opinion, 1935–1971*. Vol. 2: *1949–1958*. New York: Random House, 1972.

Goldman, Eric F. *The Crucial Decade: America, 1945–1955*. New York: Alfred A. Knopf, 1956.

Goulden, Joseph C. *Korea: The Untold Story of the War*. New York: Times Books, 1982.

Griswold, A. Whitney. *The Far Eastern Policy of the United States*. New York: Harcourt, Brace, 1938. Reprint. New Haven, Conn.: Yale University Press, 1962.

Guhin, Michael A. *John Foster Dulles: A Statesman and His Times*. New York: Columbia University Press, 1972.

Gunther, John. *The Riddle of MacArthur: Japan, Korea, and the Far East*. New York: Harper & Brothers, 1951.

Halle, Louis J. *The Cold War as History*. New York: Harper & Row, 1967.

Han, Woo-keun. *The History of Korea*. Translated by Kyung-shik Lee. Honolulu: University Press of Hawaii, 1974.

A Handbook of Korea. Seoul: Korean Overseas Information Service, Ministry of Culture and Information, 1979.

Hastings, Max. *The Korean War*. New York: Simon & Schuster, 1987.

Heller, Francis H., ed. *The Korean War: A 25-Year Perspective*. Lawrence, Kans.: Regents Press, 1977.

Henderson, Gregory. *Korea: The Politics of the Vortex*. Cambridge: Harvard University Press, 1968.

Hermes, Walter G. *Truce Tent and Fighting Front*. (U.S. Army, Office of the Chief of Military History. *United States Army in the Korean War*, vol. 4.) Washington, D.C.: U.S. Government Printing Office, 1966.

Higgins, Marguerite. *War in Korea*. Garden City, N.Y.: Doubleday, 1951.

Higgins, Rosalyn. *United Nations Peacekeeping, 1946–1967: Documents and Commentary*. Vol. 2: *Asia*. London: Oxford University Press, 1969.

Higgins, Trumbull. *Korea and the Fall of MacArthur: A Précis in Limited War*. New York: Oxford University Press, 1960.

Hopkirk, Peter. *Setting the East Ablaze: Lenin's Dream of an Empire in Asia*. New York: W. W. Norton, 1985.

Howard, Michael. *The Causes of Wars*. Cambridge: Harvard University Press, 1983.

Isaacson, Walter, and Evan Thomas. *The Wise Men*. New York: Simon & Schuster, 1986.

James, D. Clayton. *The Years of MacArthur*. Vol. 3, *Triumph and Disaster, 1945–1964*. Boston: Houghton Mifflin, 1985.

Johnson, Paul. *Modern Times: The World from the Twenties to the Eighties*. New York: Harper & Row, 1983.

Jones, Francis C. *Manchuria Since 1931*. New York: Oxford University Press, 1949.

Joy, C. Turner. *How Communists Negotiate*. New York: Macmillan, 1955.

Kahn, E. J., Jr. *The Peculiar War: Impressions of a Reporter in Korea*. New York: Random House, 1952.

Karnow, Stanley. *Vietnam: A History*. New York: Viking, 1983.

Kennan, George F. *American Diplomacy, 1900–1950*. Rev. ed. Chicago: University of Chicago Press, 1984.

———. *Memoirs, 1925–1950*. Boston: Atlantic Monthly Press/Little, Brown, 1967.

———. *Memoirs, 1950–1963*. Boston: Atlantic Monthly Press/Little, Brown, 1972. Reprint. New York: Pantheon, 1983.

———. *Russia and the West Under Lenin and Stalin*. Boston: Atlantic Monthly Press/ Little, Brown, 1961.

Khrushchev, Nikita S. *Khrushchev Remembers*. Translated by Strobe Talbott. Boston: Little, Brown, 1970.

Knox, Donald. *The Korean War: An Oral History*. Vol. 1: *Pusan to Chosin*. Vol. 2: *Uncertain Victory*. San Diego: Harcourt Brace Jovanovich, 1985–88.

Koen, Ross Y. *The China Lobby in American Politics*. New York: Macmillan, 1960. Reprint. New York: Octagon, 1974.

Kolko, Joyce, and Gabriel Kolko. *The Limits of Power: The World and United States Foreign Policy, 1945–1954*. New York: Harper & Row, 1972.

LaFeber, Walter. *America, Russia, and the Cold War, 1945–1980*. New York: John Wiley & Sons, 1980.

Lippmann, Walter. *The Cold War: A Study in U.S. Foreign Policy*. New York: Harper & Brothers, 1947.

Lockwood, Christopher. "Stand Tall: A Survey of South Korea." *The Economist*, May 21, 1988.

MacArthur, Douglas A. *Reminiscences*. New York: McGraw-Hill, 1964.

McCune, George M. *Korea Today*. Cambridge: Harvard University Press, 1950.

McLellan, David S. *Dean Acheson: The State Department Years*. New York: Dodd, Mead, 1976.

McNeill, William H. *America, Britain, and Russia: Their Cooperation and Conflict, 1941– 1946*. London: Oxford University Press, 1953. Reprint. New York: Johnson Reprint, 1970.

Manchester, William. *American Caesar: Douglas MacArthur, 1880–1964*. Boston: Little, Brown, 1978.

———. *The Glory and the Dream: A Narrative History of America, 1932–1972*. Boston: Little, Brown, 1974.

———. *The Last Lion: Winston Spencer Churchill*. Vol. 1, *Visions of Glory, 1874–1932*. Boston: Little, Brown, 1983.

Mastny, Vojtech. *Russia's Road to the Cold War*. New York: Columbia University Press, 1979.

Miller, Merle. *Plain Speaking: An Oral Biography of Harry S. Truman*. New York: Berkeley/G. P. Putnam's Sons, 1974.

Morison, Samuel Eliot. *The Oxford History of the American People*. New York: Oxford University Press, 1965.

Nagai, Yonosuke, and Akira Iriye, eds. *The Origins of the Cold War in Asia*. New York: Columbia University Press, 1977.

The National Cyclopedia of American Biography. Current Volume H: 1947–1952. New York: James T. White, 1952.

Neustadt, Richard E., and Ernest R. May. *Thinking in Time: The Uses of History for Decision-Makers*. New York: Free Press, 1986.

O'Ballance, Edgar. *Korea, 1950–1953*. London: Faber & Faber, 1969.

Oliver, Robert T. *Syngman Rhee: The Man Behind the Myth*. New York: Dodd, Mead, 1954.

Oshinsky, David M. *A Conspiracy So Immense: The World of Joe McCarthy*. New York: Free Press, 1983.

Paige, Glenn D. *The Korean Decision, June 24–30, 1950*. New York: Free Press, 1968.

Paterson, Thomas G., J. Garry Clifford, and Kenneth J. Hagan. *American Foreign Policy: A History, 1900 to Present*. Lexington, Mass.: D. C. Heath, 1988.

Patterson, James T. *Mr. Republican: A Biography of Robert A. Taft*. Boston: Houghton Mifflin, 1972.

Pogue, Forrest C. *George C. Marshall: Statesman, 1945–1959*. New York: Viking, 1987.

Rees, David. *Korea: The Limited War*. New York: St. Martin's, 1964.

Reischauer, Edwin O. *Japan: The Story of a Nation*. New York: Alfred A. Knopf, 1974.

Reischauer, Edwin O., and John K. Fairbank. *East Asia: The Great Tradition*. Boston: Houghton Mifflin, 1960.

Ridgway, Matthew B. *The Korean War*. Garden City, N.Y.: Doubleday, 1967. Reprint. New York: Da Capo, 1986.

Rovere, Richard H., and Arthur M. Schlesinger, Jr. *The MacArthur Controversy and American Foreign Policy*. New York: Farrar, Straus and Giroux, 1965. (Originally published in 1951 under the title *The General and the President*.)

Scalapino, Robert A., and Chong-sik Lee. *Communism in Korea*. 2 vols. Berkeley: University of California Press, 1972.

Schlesinger, Arthur M., Jr. *The Cycles of American History*. Boston: Houghton Mifflin, 1986.

Schlesinger, Arthur M., Jr., and Fred L. Israel, eds. *The History of American Presidential Elections, 1789–1968*. 4 vols. New York: Chelsea House, 1971.

Schnabel, James F. *Policy and Direction: The First Year*. (U.S. Army, Office of the Chief of Military History. *United States Army in the Korean War*, vol. 1.) Washington, D.C.: U.S. Government Printing Office, 1972.

Schram, Stuart. *Mao Tse-tung*. Harmondsworth, England: Penguin, 1967.

Seton-Watson, Hugh. *The Russian Empire, 1801–1917*. London: Oxford University Press, 1967.

Sherwin, Martin J. *A World Destroyed: The Atomic Bomb and the Grand Alliance*. New York: Alfred A. Knopf, 1975.

Shinn, Rinn-Sup, et al. *Area Handbook for North Korea*. Washington, D.C.: U.S. Government Printing Office, 1969.

Shulman, Marshall D. *Stalin's Foreign Policy Reappraised*. Cambridge: Harvard University Press, 1963.

Simmons, Robert R. *The Strained Alliance: Peking, Pyongyang, Moscow and the Politics of the Korean Civil War*. New York: Free Press, 1975.

Sked, Alan, and Chris Cook. *Post-War Britain: A Political History*. New York: Viking Penguin, 1984.

Spanier, John W. *The Truman-MacArthur Controversy and the Korean War*. New York: W. W. Norton, 1965.

Spector, Ronald H. *Eagle Against the Sun: The American War with Japan*. New York: Free Press, 1985.

Spurr, Russell. *Enter the Dragon: China's Undeclared War Against the U.S. in Korea, 1950–51*. New York: Newmarket Press, 1988.

Steel, Ronald. *Walter Lippmann and the American Century*. Boston: Atlantic Monthly Press/Little, Brown, 1980.

Stone, I. F. *The Hidden History of the Korean War*. New York: Monthly Review Press, 1952. Reprint. Boston: Little, Brown, 1988.

Stueck, William Whitney, Jr. *The Road to Confrontation: American Policy Toward China and Korea, 1947–1950*. Chapel Hill: University of North Carolina Press, 1981.

Suh, Dae-sook. *The Korean Communist Movement, 1918–1948*. Princeton, N.J.: Princeton University Press, 1967.

Sun, Kungtu C. *The Economic Development of Manchuria in the First Half of the Twentieth Century*. Cambridge: Harvard University Press, 1969.

Thiel, Erich. *The Soviet Far East: A Survey of Its Physical and Economic Geography*. London: Methuen, 1957. Reprint. Westport, Conn.: Greenwood Press, 1976.

Thomas, Hugh. *Armed Truce: The Beginnings of the Cold War, 1945–46*. New York: Atheneum, 1987.

Thompson, Reginald. *Cry Korea*. London: MacDonald, 1951. Reprint. London: White Lion, 1974.

Toland, John. *The Rising Sun: The Decline and Fall of the Japanese Empire, 1936–1945*. 2 vols. New York: Random House, 1970.

Truman, Harry S. *Memoirs*. Vol. 1: *Year of Decisions*. Vol. 2: *Years of Trial and Hope*. Garden City, N.Y.: Doubleday, 1955–56.

Truman, Margaret. *Harry S. Truman*. New York: William Morrow, 1973.

Tsou, Tang. *America's Failure in China, 1941–50*. Chicago: University of Chicago Press, 1963.

Tuchman, Barbara W. *The March of Folly: From Troy to Vietnam*. New York: Alfred A. Knopf, 1984.

Tucker, Nancy Bernkopf. *Patterns in the Dust: Chinese-American Relations and the Recognition Controversy, 1949–1950*. New York: Columbia University Press, 1983.

Tupper, Harmon. *To the Great Ocean: Siberia and the Trans-Siberian Railway*. Boston: Little, Brown, 1965.

Twentieth Century Fund. Task Force on the Military and the Media. *Battle Lines*.

Contains background paper by Peter Braestrup. New York: Priority Press, 1985.

Ulam, Adam B. *Expansion and Coexistence: The History of Soviet Foreign Policy, 1917–1967*. New York: Frederick A. Praeger, 1968.

U.S. Department of Defense. *The Entry of the Soviet Union into the War Against Japan: Military Plans, 1941–1945*. Washington, D.C.: Department of Defense (mimeograph), 1955.

U.S. Department of State. *The China White Paper, August 1949*. Stanford, Calif.: Stanford University Press, 1967. (Originally issued in 1949 under the title *United States Relations with China, with Special Reference to the Period 1944–1949*.)

———. *Foreign Relations of the United States: Diplomatic Papers. 1950*, vol. 7: *Korea* (published in 1976); *1951*, vol. 7: *Korea and China*, 2 pts. (published in 1983); *1952–54*, vol. 15: *Korea*, 2 pts. (published in 1984). Washington, D.C.: U.S. Government Printing Office. (For years before 1950 a section dealing with Korea is included in each year's volume on the Far East.)

U.S. Senate. Foreign Relations and Armed Services Committees. *Hearings: The Military Situation in the Far East. 82nd Congress, 1st Session, 1951*. Washington, D.C.: U.S. Government Printing Office, 1951. (Microfilm published by the Legislative and Diplomatic Branch of the National Archives reinstates all then-classified testimony and documents omitted from the 1951 edition.)

Vali, Ferenc A. *The Quest for a United Germany*. Baltimore: Johns Hopkins Press, 1967.

Veterans of Foreign Wars. *Pictorial History of the Korean War*. (Text: General MacArthur's reports to the UN Security Council.) N.p., Veterans' Historical Book Service, 1951.

Werth, Alexander. *Russia at War, 1941–1945*. New York: E. P. Dutton, 1964. Reprint. New York: Carroll & Graf, 1984.

Whiting, Allen S. *China Crosses the Yalu: The Decision to Enter the Korean War*. New York: Macmillan, 1960.

Whitney, Courtney. *MacArthur: His Rendezvous with History*. New York: Alfred A. Knopf, 1956.

Woodhouse, C. M. *The Struggle for Greece, 1941–1949*. Brooklyn, N.Y.: Beekman/Esanu, 1979.

Yearbook of the UN. New York: United Nations, 1950–53.

Zagoria, Donald S. "Soviet Policy in East Asia: A New Beginning?" *Foreign Affairs*, vol. 68, no. 1, 1989.

Index